Accountability of Armed Opposition Groups in International Law

Who is accountable under international law for the acts committed by armed opposition groups? In today's world the great majority of political conflicts involve non-state actors attempting to exert a political influence (such as overthrowing a government or bringing about secession). Notwithstanding their impact on the course of events, however, we tend to know little about these groups, and even less about how to treat their actions legally.

In this award-winning scholarship, Liesbeth Zegveld examines the need to identify legally the parties involved when internal conflicts arise, and the reality of their demands for rights. Her study draws upon international humanitarian law, human rights law and international criminal law to consider a fundamental question: who is accountable for the acts committed by non-state actors, or for the failure to prevent or repress these acts?

This study will be of interest to academics, postgraduate students and professionals involved with armed conflict and international relations.

LIESBETH ZEGVELD practises as an international and criminal lawyer. In 1998, she received a Fulbright Scholarship to do research at New York University and the Inter-American Commission on Human Rights in Washington, DC. For her dissertation on armed opposition groups she received the degree 'cum laude' and the Netherlands' Human Rights Award, 2000. She is the co-author, with Frits Kalshoven, of the third edition of *Constraints on the Waging of War: an Introduction to International Humanitarian Law* (ICRC 2001).

CAMBRIDGE STUDIES IN INTERNATIONAL AND COMPARATIVE LAW

This series (established in 1946 by Professors Gutteridge, Hersch Lauterpacht and McNair) is a forum of studies of high quality in the fields of public and private international law and comparative law. Although these are distinct legal subdisciplines, developments since 1946 confirm their interrelationship.

Comparative law is increasingly used as a tool in the making of law at national, regional and international levels. Private international law is increasingly affected by international conventions, and the issues faced by classical conflicts rules are increasingly dealt with by substantive harmonization of law under international auspices. Mixed international arbitration, especially those involving state economic activity, raise mixed questions of public and private international law. In many fields (such as the protection of human rights and democratic standards, investment guarantees and international criminal law) international and national systems interact. National constitutional arrangements relating to 'foreign affairs', and to the implementation of international norms, are a focus of attention.

Professor Sir Robert Jennings edited the series from 1981. Following his retirement as General Editor, an editorial board has been created and Cambridge University Press has recommitted itself to the series, affirming its broad scope.

The Board welcomes works of a theoretical or interdisciplinary character, and those focusing on new approaches to international or comparative law or conflicts of law. Studies of particular institutions or problems are equally welcome, as are translations of the best work published in other languages.

Cambridge Studies in International and Comparative Law (CSICL)

GENERAL EDITORS

Professor James Crawford SC FBA
Whewell Professor of International Law, Faculty of Law and Director, Lauterpacht Research Centre for International Law
University of Cambridge
Member of the International Law Commission

Professor John S. Bell FBA
Professor of Law
Faculty of Law
University of Cambridge

EDITORIAL BOARD
Professor Hilary Charlesworth, University of Adelaide
Professor Lori Damrosch, Columbia University Law School
Professor John Dugard, Universiteit Leiden
Professor Mary-Ann Glendon, Harvard Law School
Professor Christopher Greenwood, London School of Economics
Professor David Johnston, University of Edinburgh
Professor Hein Kötz, Max-Planck-Institut, Hamburg
Professor Donald McRae, University of Ottawa
Professor Onuma Yasuaki, University of Tokyo
Professor Reinhard Zimmermann, Universität Regensburg

ADVISORY COMMITTEE
Professor Sir D. W Bowett QC
Judge Rosalyn Higgins QC
Professor Sir Robert Jennings QC
Professor J. A. Jolowicz QC
Professor Sir Eli Lauterpacht QC
Professor Kurt Lipstein QC
Judge Stephen Schwebel

A list of the books in this series can be found at the end of this book

Accountability of Armed Opposition Groups in International Law

Liesbeth Zegveld

CAMBRIDGE UNIVERSITY PRESS

PUBLISHED BY THE PRESS SYNDICATE OF THE UNIVERSITY OF CAMBRIDGE
The Pitt Building, Trumpington Street, Cambridge, United Kingdom

CAMBRIDGE UNIVERSITY PRESS
The Edinburgh Building, Cambridge CB2 2RU, UK
40 West 20th Street, New York, NY 10011-4211, USA
477 Williamstown Road, Port Melbourne, VIC 3207, Australia
Ruiz de Alarcón 13, 28014 Madrid, Spain
Dock House, The Waterfront, Cape Town 8001, South Africa

http://www.cambridge.org

© Liesbeth Zegveld 2002

This book is in copyright. Subject to statutory exception
and to the provisions of relevant collective licensing agreements,
no reproduction of any part may take place without
the written permission of Cambridge University Press.

First published 2002

Printed in the United Kingdom at the University Press, Cambridge

Typeface Swift 10/13 pt.   *System* LATEX 2_ε [TB]

A catalogue record for this book is available from the British Library

ISBN 0 521 81130 9 hardback

Contents

Table of treaties and declarations	page ix
Table of cases	xiii
Table of other documents	xviii
List of abbreviations	xxvii
Introduction	1

PART 1   THE NORMATIVE GAP

1	**Legal restraints on armed opposition groups as such**	9
	Common Article 3 and Protocol II	9
	Other rules of humanitarian law	26
	Human rights law	38
	International criminal law	55
2	**Substantive obligations of armed opposition groups as such**	59
	Humane treatment of prisoners	59
	Protection of civilians	75
	Underdevelopment of the law	92

PART 2   THE ACCOUNTABILITY GAP

3	**Accountability of group leaders**	97
	Crimes	99
	Command responsibility of group leaders	111
	Criteria for accountability of group leaders	121
	Limited prospects for prosecution	131
4	**Accountability of armed opposition groups as such**	133
	Evidence for accountability of armed opposition groups	134

	Attributing acts to armed opposition groups	152
	Successful armed opposition groups	155
	Finding a suitable forum	157
5	**Accountability of the state for acts of armed opposition groups**	164
	Applicable law	166
	The obligation of the state to take action	180
	The pertinence of territorial control	207
6	**The quest for accountability**	220
	Group versus individual accountability	220
	Group versus state accountability	224
	Conclusion	229
	Bibliography	231
	Index	242

Table of treaties and declarations

1907 Hague Convention (IV) Respecting the Laws and Customs of War on Land, reprinted in Schindler and Toman, *Laws of Armed Conflicts* 57 103, 114

1945 Charter of the Nuremberg Tribunal, reprinted in Schindler and Toman, *Laws of Armed Conflicts* 826 (Agreement for the Prosecution and Punishment of the Major War Criminals of the European Axis) 55, 56, 98, 105, 106

1945 Charter of the United Nations, reprinted in Brownlie BDIL 1 2, 4, 88, 144

1945 Statute of the International Court of Justice, reprinted in Brownlie BDIL 438 4, 26

1946 Charter for the International Military Tribunal for the Far East, Special Proclamation of the Supreme Commander for the Allied Powers of 19 January 1946, reprinted in: Department of State Bulletin, Vol. XIV, No. 349 (10 March 1946) 98

1948 Convention on the Prevention and Punishment of the Crime of Genocide, reprinted in Brownlie BDHR 31 44, 108, 109, 178, 185, 186, 189, 197, 219, 221

1949 Convention for the Amelioration of the Condition of the Wounded and Sick in Armed Forces in the Field (Geneva Convention I) 75 UNTS 31 111

1949 Convention for the Amelioration of the Condition of the Wounded, Sick and Shipwrecked Members of Armed Forces at Sea (Geneva Convention II) 75 UNTS 85 111

1949 Geneva Convention Relative to the Treatment of Prisoners of War (Geneva Convention III) 75 UNTS 135 29, 38, 69, 70, 71, 111

1949 Geneva Convention Relative to the Protection of Civilian Persons in Time of War (Geneva Convention IV) 75 UNTS 287 29, 65, 66, 67, 71, 103, 104, 111, 200

1950 Convention for the Protection of Human Rights and Fundamental Freedoms, reprinted in Brownlie BDHR 326 39, 45, 161, 162, 166, 167, 168, 170, 171, 173, 180, 184, 186, 191, 198, 204, 209, 216

1951 Convention Relating to the Status of Refugees, reprinted in Brownlie BDHR 64 180

1954 Convention for the Protection of Cultural Property in the Event of Armed Conflict, reprinted in Schindler and Toman, *Laws of Armed Conflicts* 661 27, 28, 36, 81, 93, 146, 147, 148, 177, 185, 197

1961 European Social Charter, reprinted in Brownlie BDHR 363

1966 International Covenant on Economic, Social and Cultural Rights, reprinted in Brownlie BDHR 114 43, 44

1966 International Covenant on Civil and Political Rights, reprinted in Brownlie BDHR 125 38, 39, 43, 44, 45, 50, 64, 66, 70, 149, 161, 166, 168, 172, 173, 179, 180, 181, 183, 184, 185, 187, 198, 210–11, 216

1969 American Convention on Human Rights, reprinted in Brownlie BDHR 495 39, 40, 41, 45, 47, 50, 61, 159, 160, 161, 166, 167, 177, 180, 184, 198, 212, 216

1969 Vienna Convention on the Law of Treaties, reprinted in Brownlie BDIL 388 30, 45, 209, 212, 215, 216

1975 UN Declaration on the Protection of All Persons from being Subjected to Torture and Other Cruel, Inhuman or Degrading Treatment or Punishment, UN General Assembly Res. 3452 (XXX) 149

1977 Protocol Additional to the Geneva Conventions of 12 August 1949, and Relating to the Protection of Victims of International Armed Conflicts (Protocol I) 16 ILM 1391 (1977) 17, 18, 27, 29, 32, 33, 34, 35, 38, 65, 66, 73, 75, 76, 77, 78, 79, 80, 82, 102, 114, 115, 120, 122, 124, 128, 129, 130, 194

1977 Protocol Additional to the Geneva Conventions of 12 August 1949, and Relating to the Protection of Victims of Non-International Armed Conflicts (Protocol II) 6 ILM 1442 (1977) 9, 10, 11, 12, 13, 14, 15, 16, 17, 18, 19, 21, 22, 25, 26, 29, 30, 33, 34, 37, 42, 50, 51, 52, 53, 57, 59, 60, 61, 62, 63, 64, 65, 67, 69, 70, 71, 72, 73, 74, 75, 76, 77, 78, 79, 80, 83, 85, 86, 87, 89, 91, 92, 93, 99, 100, 101, 102, 103, 105, 112, 117, 136, 141, 142, 143, 144, 145, 146, 147, 148,

157, 158, 166, 174, 175, 176, 177, 178, 180, 184, 187, 189, 198, 199, 200, 206, 207, 218, 221, 225

1984 Convention against Torture and Other Cruel, Inhuman or Degrading Treatment or Punishment, reprinted in Brownlie BDHR 38 178, 179, 180

1989 Convention on the Rights of the Child, reprinted in Brownlie BDHR 182 63

1990 San José Agreement on Human Rights (El Salvador – *Frente Farabundo Marti para la Liberacion Nacional* (FMLN)), UN Doc. A/44/971, S/21541, Annex 49–50, 51, 186, 212

1992 Declaration on the Protection of all Persons from Enforced Disappearance, UN General Assembly Res. 47/133 198, 206

1993 Statute of the International Tribunal for the Prosecution of Persons Responsible for Serious Violations of International Humanitarian Law Committed in the Territory of the Former Yugoslavia Since 1991, reprinted in Brownlie BDIL 456 107, 109, 112, 113, 115, 116, 117, 118, 119, 120, 121, 124, 125, 128, 130, 131, 200, 222

1994 Statute of the International Tribunal for the Prosecution of Persons Responsible for Genocide and Other Serious Violations of International Humanitarian Law Committed in the Territory of Rwanda and Rwandan Citizens Responsible for Genocide and Other Such Violations Committed in the Territory of Neighbouring States Between 1 January 1994 and 31 December 1994, 33 ILM 1602 (1994) 100, 107, 109, 112, 114, 115, 116, 117, 118, 119, 120, 121, 124, 125, 128, 130, 131, 136, 200, 222

1996 Protocol on Prohibitions or Restrictions on the Use of Mines, Booby-Traps and Other Devices as Amended on 3 May 1996 (entry into force 3 December 1998), 35 ILM 1206 (1996) (Protocol II to the Convention on Prohibitions or Restrictions on the Use of Certain Conventional Weapons Which may be Deemed to be Excessively Injurious or to Have Indiscriminate Effects) 26, 36, 85, 86, 146, 147, 177, 184, 185, 187, 188, 197, 212, 218

1997 Convention on the Prohibition of the Use, Stockpiling, Production and Transfer of Anti-Personnel Mines and on their Destruction (entry into force 1 March 1999), 36 ILM 1507 (1997) 27, 177, 184, 185, 188, 197

1998 Statute of the International Criminal Court, 37 ILM 999 (1998) 55, 57, 58, 98, 101, 103, 104, 105, 106, 108, 109, 111, 113, 117, 119, 120, 124, 127, 128, 130, 141, 142, 200, 221, 222

1998 United Kingdom Human Rights Act 1998, 38 ILM 464 (1999)
1999 Second Protocol to the Hague Convention of 1954 for the Protection of Cultural Property in the Event of Armed Conflict, text available on www.icrc.org/ihl (visited, 1 January 2001) 27, 28, 82, 146, 147, 177, 185, 189, 197

Table of cases

International Court of Justice

Case Concerning the Application of the Convention on the Prevention and Punishment of the Crime of Genocide (Bosnia and Herzegovina *versus* Federal Republic of Yugoslavia) Application of 20 March 1993 178

Corfu Channel Case (UK *versus* Albania) (Judgment of 9 April 1949) (Merits) 1949 ICJ Rep. 4 209

Difference Relating to Immunity From Legal Process of a Special Rapporteur of the Commission on Human Rights (Advisory Opinion of 29 April 1999) 1999 ICJ Rep. 62 214

Gabcíkovo–Nagymaros Project (Hungary *versus* Slovakia) (Judgment of 25 September 1997) 37 ILM 162 (1998) 211, 212

Legal Consequences for States of the Continued Presence of South Africa in Namibia (Advisory Opinion of 21 June 1971) 1971 ICJ Rep. 16 209

Legality of the Threat or Use of Nuclear Weapons (Advisory Opinion of 8 July 1996) 35 ILM 809 (1996) 19, 26, 85, 227

Military and Paramilitary Activities In and Against Nicaragua (Nicaragua *versus* US) (Judgment of 27 June 1986) (Merits) 1986 ICJ Rep. 14 10, 13, 19, 20, 24, 174

Reservations to the Convention on Genocide (Advisory Opinion of 28 May 1951) 1951 ICJ Rep. 15 108

United States Diplomatic and Consular Staff in Teheran Case (US *versus* Iran) (Judgment of 24 May 1980), 1980 ICJ Rep. 3 182, 183

Vienna Convention on Consular Relations (Germany *versus* US) (Request for the Indication of Provisional Measures, 3 March 1999), 37 ILM 810 (1998) 214

European Court of Human Rights

Akkoc *versus* Turkey (Judgment of 10 October 2000) 193
Çakici *versus* Turkey (Judgment of 8 July 1999) (not yet published) 171
Ergi *versus* Turkey (Judgment of 28 July 1998) 81 Reports (1998-IV) at 1751 168, 190, 192, 194, 199, 204
HLR *versus* France (Judgment of 29 April 1997) 36 Reports (1997-III) at 745 167
Kaya *versus* Turkey (Judgment of 19 February 1998) 204
Kilic *versus* Turkey (Judgment of 28 March 2000) 193
Kurt *versus* Turkey (Judgment of 25 May 1998) 74 Reports (1998-III) at 1152 170, 204
Loizidou *versus* Turkey (Judgment of 23 March 1995) (Preliminary Objections) Ser. A 310 (1995) 209
Platform 'Ärzte Für Das Leben' (Judgment of 21 June 1988) Ser. A 139 (1988) 167, 182, 195
Yasa *versus* Turkey (Judgment of 2 September 1998) 88 Reports (1998-VI) at 2411 193, 198, 203
X and Y *versus* Netherlands (Judgment of 26 March 1985) Eur. Ct. HR Ser. A 91 (1985) 185

European Commission of Human Rights

W. *versus* United Kingdom, Appl. 9348/81, 32 DR 190 (1983) 191, 195, 199
X *versus* Ireland, Appl. 6040/73 (Decision of 20 July 1973) 16 YB ECHR 388 (1973) 185
Yasa *versus* Turkey, Appl. 22495/93, Report of the Commission (8 April 1997) 88 Reports (1998-VI) 193, 204

Inter-American Court of Human Rights

Las Palmeras (Judgment of 4 February 2000) 161
Velásquez Rodríguez *versus* Honduras, Ser. C 4 (1988) 167, 171, 182, 184, 196, 198

Inter-American Commission on Human Rights

Rep. No 26/97, Case No 11.142 (Colombia) (30 September 1997) 10
Tablada Case, Rep. No 55/97, Case No 11.137 (Argentina) (30 October 1997) 10, 41, 61, 136, 137, 138, 146, 160

International Criminal Tribunal for the Former Yugoslavia

Aleksovski Case, Prosecutor *versus* Aleksovski, Case No. IT-95-14/1-T (25 June 1999) 98–9, 106, 113, 116, 119, 120, 122, 123, 126, 127, 129, 130, 131, 142, 223

Aleksovski Case, Prosecutor *versus* Zlatko Aleksovski, Case No. IT-95-14/1-A (24 March 2000) (Appeal) 116

Blaškić Case, Prosecutor *versus* Tihomir Blaškić, Decision on the Defence Motion to Strike Portions of the Amended Indictment Alleging 'Failure to Punish Liability', Case No. IT-95-14-PT (4 April 1997) 129

Blaškić Case, Prosecutor *versus* Tihomir Blaškić, Case No. IT-95-14-T (3 March 2000) 104

Celebici Case, Prosecutor *versus* Zejnil Delalic, Zdravko Mucic, Hazim Delic, Esad Landzo, Case No. IT-96-21-T (16 November 1998) 24, 31, 100, 101, 103, 110, 111, 117, 118, 119, 121, 122, 125, 126, 127, 129

Furundžija Case, Prosecutor *versus* Anto Furundžija, Case No. IT-95-17/1-T (10 December 1998) 100, 112, 205

Furundžija Case, Prosecutor *versus* Anto Furundžija, Case No. IT-95-17/1-A (21 July 2000) (Appeal)

Karadzić Case, Prosecutor *versus* Radovan Karadzić and Ratko Mladic, Review of Indictment Pursuant to Rule 61 of the Rules of Procedure and Evidence, Case No. IT-95-5-R61 & No. IT-95-18-R61 (11 July 1996) 110, 117

Kordić Case, Prosecutor *versus* Dario Kordić, Mario Cerkez, Decision on the Joint Defence Motion to Dismiss the Amended Indictment for Lack of Jurisdiction Based on the Limited Jurisdictional Reach of Articles 2 and 3, Case No. IT-95-14/2-PT (2 March 1999) 20–1, 104, 129

Kupreskić Case, Prosecutor *versus* Kupreskić et al., Case No. IT-95-16-T (14 January 2000) 23, 60, 91

Martić Case, Prosecutor *versus* Milan Martić, Review of Indictment Pursuant to Rule 61 of the Rules of Procedure and Evidence, Case No. IT-95-11-R61 (8 March 1996) 90, 91

Milosović Case, Prosecutor *versus* Slobodan Milosovic, Milan Milutinovic, Nikola Sainovic, Dragoljub Ojdanic, Vlajko Stojilkovic, Decision on Review of Indictment and Application for Consequential Orders (24 May 1999) 117

Nikolić Case, Prosecutor *versus* Dragon Nikolić, Review of Indictment Pursuant to Rule 61 of the Rules of Procedure and Evidence, Case No. IT-94-2-R61 (20 October 1995) 107

Tadić Case, Decision on the Defence Motion for Interlocutory Appeal on Jurisdiction, Case No. IT-94-1-AR72 (2 October 1995) 19, 20, 21, 23, 25, 26, 27, 28, 29, 30, 31, 32, 34, 36, 61, 62, 77, 80, 81, 100, 101, 102, 104, 105, 107, 135, 144, 147, 148

Prosecutor *versus* Duško Tadić, Case No. IT-94-1-T (7 May 1997) (Merits) 60, 105, 107, 112

Prosecutor *versus* Duško Tadić, Case No. IT-94-1-A (15 July 1999) (Appeal on Merits) 35, 103, 112, 123

International Criminal Tribunal for Rwanda

Akayesu Case, Prosecutor *versus* Jean-Paul Akayesu, Case No. ICTR-96-4-T (2 September 1998) 11, 16, 19, 21, 100, 105, 108, 135, 136, 143, 145

Kayishema Case, Prosecutor *versus* Clément Kayishema and Obed Ruzindana, Case No. IT-95-14-PT & No. ICTR-95-1-T (21 May 1999) 16, 61, 75, 105, 110, 118, 121, 122, 123, 124, 128, 129

Musema Case, Prosecutor *versus* Musema, Case No. ICTR-96-13 (27 January 2000) 75, 105, 165

Rutaganda Case, Prosecutor *versus* Rutaganda, Case No. ICTR-96-3 (6 December 1999) 100

European Court of Justice

A. Racke GmbH & Co. *versus* Hauptzollamt Mainz, Case C-162/96 (Judgment of 16 June 1998), [1998-6] ECR, I-3655 215

Human Rights Committee

A. and H. Sanjuan Arevalo *versus* Colombia, Comm. No. 181/1984 (View adopted on 3 November 1989) Official Records of the Human Rights Committee 1989/90, Vol. II, at 392–4 171, 172

Committee against Torture

GRB *versus* Sweden, Comm. 83/1997, CAT/C/20/D/83/1997 (View adopted on 15 May 1998) 179

Mexican General Claims Commission

US *versus* Mexican General Claims Commission, Youmans Claim, US *versus* Mexico (1926), 4 RIAA 110 155

National Courts

USA *versus* Pohl 116

US *versus* Wilhelm von Leeb et al. (the High Command Case), Trials of War Criminals before the Nuremberg Military Tribunals under Control Council Law No. 10 1946-9, Vol. XI, at 543-4 (Washington DC, US Government Printing Office, 1950) 124

Yamashita Case, Trial of General Tomoyuki Yamashita (US Military Commission, Manila, 8 October – 7 December 1945), United Nations War Crimes Commission, 4 Law Reports of Trials of War Criminals, 1, 88 (1945) 98

Table of other documents

Human Rights Committee

General Comment 6/16 (27 July 1982) on Article 6 of the International Covenant, reproduced in A/37/40, Annex V 180, 181, 198

General Comment 20/44 (3 April 1992) on Article 7 of the Covenant, reproduced in A/47/40, Annex VI 185, 206

Decision of the Human Rights Committee on State Succession to the Obligations of the Former Yugoslavia under the International Covenant on Civil and Political Rights, reprinted in 15 EHRR, 233 (1992) 149

Concluding Observations on Sri Lanka, CCPR/C/79/Add.56 (3 October 1995) 199

Concluding Observations on Algeria, CCPR/C/79/Add.95 (4 August 1998) 169, 189, 199

Summary Records of the 19th Sess., CCPR/C/SR.442-444 (summer 1983) 211, 214

Summary Records of the 29th Sess., CCPR/C/SR.716 (8 April 1987) 201

Summary Records of the 42nd Sess., CCPR/C/SR.1067 (summer 1991) 185

Summary Records of the 54th Sess., CCPR/C/SR.1436 (28 June 1995) 196

Yearbook of the Human Rights Committee 1983-84, Vol. II., CCPR/4/Add.1 195, 199

Inter-American Commission on Human Rights

Report on the Situation of Human Rights in Nicaragua, OEA/Ser.L/V/II.45, Doc. 16 rev.1 (17 November 1978)

Report on the Situation of Human Rights in the Republic of Colombia, OEA/Ser.L/V/II.53, Doc. 22 (30 June 1981) 160

Report on the Situation of Human Rights in the Republic of Nicaragua, OEA/Ser.L/V/II.53, Doc. 25 (30 June 1981)

Report on the Situation of Human Rights in the Republic of Guatemala, OEA/Ser.L/V/II.61, Doc. 47, rev.1 (5 October 1983) 189

Second Report on the Situation of Human Rights in Colombia, OEA/Ser.L/V/II.84 (4 October 1993) 39, 62, 69, 158, 185, 192, 195

Report on the Situation of Human Rights in El Salvador, OEA/Ser.L/V/II.85, Doc. 28, rev. (11 February 1994) 205, 212

Third Report on the Situation of Human Rights in Colombia, OEA/Ser.L/V/II.102, Doc. 9, rev.1 (26 February 1999) 11–12, 16, 20, 21, 32, 36, 41, 54, 61, 65, 67, 75, 76, 79, 80, 81, 82, 84, 85, 145, 155, 158, 160, 196, 206

Annual Reports 1971–81, in Inter-American Commission on Human Rights, *Ten Years of Activities 1971–1981* (1982) 170, 180, 199

Annual Report 1992–3, OEA/Ser.L/V/II.83 Doc. 14, corr.1 (12 March 1993) 47, 159

Annual Report 1996, OEA/Ser.L/V/II.95, Doc. 7, rev. (14 March 1997) 47, 62, 64, 69, 90, 169

Committee against Torture

General Comment on the Implementation of Article 3 in the Context of Article 22 of the Convention Against Torture, A/53/44, Annex IX (1998)

UN Security Council

Res. 733 on Somalia (23 January 1992)[1] 88
Res. 788 on Liberia (19 November 1992) 32, 139
Res. 794 on Somalia (3 December 1992) 11, 32, 88, 113
Res. 808 on the Tribunal for the Former Yugoslavia (22 February 1993) 20, 111
Res. 812 on Rwanda (12 March 1993) 11
Res. 814 on Somalia (26 March 1993) 32, 138
Res. 993 on Georgia (12 May 1993) 31
Res. 837 on Somalia (6 June 1993) 113
Res. 851 on Angola (15 July 1993) 77, 88
Res. 955 on the Establishment of the Rwanda Tribunal (8 November 1994) 111
Res. 968 on Tajikistan (16 December 1994) 67

[1] The text of resolutions of the UN Security Council is available on www/un.org.

Res. 972 on Liberia (13 January 1995) 32
Res. 1001 on Liberia (30 June 1995) 32
Res. 1076 on Afghanistan (22 October 1996)
Res. 1193 on Afghanistan (28 August 1998) 11, 48, 104, 113, 150
Res. 1212 on Angola (3 December 1998) 48
Res. 1261 on Children in Armed Conflict (25 August 1999) 63
Res. 1265 on the Protection of Civilians in Armed Conflict (17 September 1999)
Res. 1315 on the Establishment of a Special Court for Sierra Leone (14 August 2000) 37
Res. 1325 on Women, Peace and Security (31 October 2000) 68
Final Report of the Commission of Experts for Yugoslavia Established Pursuant to Security Council Resolution 780 (1992) S/1994/674, Annex (27 May 1994) 100, 118
Final Report of the Commission of Experts for Rwanda Established Pursuant to Security Council Resolution 935, S/1994/1405, Annex (1994) 105, 107, 109

UN General Assembly

Final Declaration and Programme of Action of the 1993 World Conference on Human Rights, A/Conf.157/23, reprinted in 32 ILM 166 (1993)
Res. 174 (II) on the Establishment of the International Law Commission, A/519, at 105 *ff.* (1947)
Res. 2444 (XXIII) Respect for Human Rights in Armed Conflicts (19 December 1968), reprinted in Schindler and Toman, *Laws of Armed Conflicts* 199 31, 32, 76, 78
Res. 2675 (XXV) Basic Principles for the Protection of Civilian Populations in Armed Conflicts (9 December 1970), reprinted in Schindler and Toman, *Laws of Armed Conflicts* 203 31, 32, 76, 77, 78, 80, 87, 90, 91
Res. 40/32 Basic Principles on the Independence of the Judiciary (29 November 1985) 72
Res. 40/146 Basic Principles on the Independence of the Judiciary (13 December 1985) 72
Report of the Preparatory Committee, United Nations Diplomatic Conference of Plenipotentiaries on the Establishment of an International Criminal Court, A/CONF.183/2/Add.1 (14 April 1998) 56
Working Group on General Principles of Criminal Law, United Nations Diplomatic Conference of Plenipotentiaries on the Establishment of an International Criminal Court, A/Conf.183/C.1/WGGP/L.5/Rev.2 (3 July 1998) 57

UN Commission on Human Rights

Res. 1984/52, 'Situation of Human Rights in El Salvador' (14 March 1984)[2] 88

Res. 1986/39, 'Situation of Human Rights in El Salvador' (12 March 1986) 89

Res. 1988/65, 'Situation of Human Rights in El Salvador' (8 March 1988) 63

Res. 1989/67, 'Question of Human Rights and Fundamental Freedoms in Afghanistan' (8 March 1989) 67, 69, 88, 90

Res. 1989/68, 'Question of Human Rights and Fundamental Freedoms in El Salvador' (8 March 1989) 81, 145

Res. 1990/53, 'Situation of Human Rights in Afghanistan' (6 March 1990) 77

Res. 1990/75, 'Consequences of Acts of Violence Committed by Irregular Armed Groups and Drug Traffickers for the Enjoyment of Human Rights' (7 March 1990) 46

Res. 1990/77, 'Situation of Human Rights in El Salvador' (7 March 1990) 48

Res. 1991/29, 'Consequences on the Enjoyment of Human Rights of Acts of Violence Committed by Armed Groups that Spread Terror Among the Population and by Drug Traffickers' (5 March 1991) 43, 46

Res. 1991/75, 'Situation of Human Rights in El Salvador' (6 March 1991)

Res. 1992/42, 'Consequences on the Enjoyment of Human Rights of Acts of Violence Committed by Armed Groups that Spread Terror Among the Population and by Drug Traffickers' (28 February 1992) 46

Res. 1993/48, 'Consequences on the Enjoyment of Human Rights of Acts of Violence Committed by Armed Groups that Spread Terror Among the Population and by Drug Traffickers' (9 March 1993) 46

Res. 1993/60, 'Situation of Human Rights in Sudan' (10 March 1993) 46

Res. 1993/66, 'Situation of Human Rights in Afghanistan' (10 March 1993) 22, 65, 91

Res. 1993/71, 'Extrajudicial, Summary or Arbitrary Executions' (10 March 1993) 199

Res. 1993/83, 'Effects of Armed Conflicts on Children's Lives' (10 March 1993)

Res. 1994/39, 'Question of Enforced Disappearances' (4 March 1994)

Res. 1994/46, 'Human Rights and Terrorism' (4 March 1994) 48, 181

---

[2] The text of resolutions of the UN Commission on Human Rights is available on www/unhcr.ch.

Res. 1995/74, 'Situation of Human Rights in Afghanistan' (8 March 1995) 48, 66
Res. 1995/77, 'Situation of Human Rights in Sudan' (8 March 1995) 33, 65, 69
Res. 1996/47, 'Human Rights and Terrorism' (19 April 1996) 42
Res. 1996/73, 'Situation of Human Rights in Sudan' (23 April 1996) 88
Res. 1997/42, 'Human Rights and Terrorism' (11 April 1997) 48
Res. 1997/47, 'Assistance to Somalia in the Field of Human Rights' (11 April 1997) 150
Res. 1997/59, 'Situation of Human Rights in Sudan' (15 April 1997) 11, 88
Res. 1998/59, 'Assistance to Somalia in the Field of Human Rights' (17 April 1998) 139
Res. 1998/67, 'Situation of Human Rights in Sudan' (21 April 1998) 11, 22, 145
Res. 1998/70, 'The Question of Human Rights in Afghanistan' (21 April 1998) 150
Res. 1999/1, 'Situation of Human Rights in Sierra Leone (6 April 1999) 104, 139
Res. 1999/18, 'The Situation of Human Rights in the Federal Republic of Yugoslavia (Serbia and Montenegro), the Republic of Croatia and Bosnia and Herzegovina (23 April 1999) 11
Res. 1999/65, 'Fundamental Standards of Humanity' (28 April 1999) 46
Res. 2000/18, 'Situation of Human Rights in the Democratic Republic of the Congo' (18 April 2000) 37, 87
Res. 2000/69, 'Fundamental Standards of Humanity' (27 April 2000) 46
Summary Records of the 2nd Sess., E/CN.4/SR.431 (1947) and E/CN.4/AC.1/SR.34 (1948)
Report of the Working Group on Enforced or Involuntary Disappearances, E/CN.4/1435 (26 January 1981) 209
Final Report on the Situation of Human Rights in El Salvador of the Special Representative for El Salvador, J. A. Pastor Ridruejo, E/CN.4/1502 (18 January 1982) 202
Report by the Special Rapporteur on Extrajudicial, Summary or Arbitrary Executions, S. Amos Wako, E/CN.4/1983/16 (31 January 1983) 69
Final Report on the Situation of Human Rights in El Salvador of the Special Representative for El Salvador, J. A. Pastor Ridruejo, E/CN.4/1984/25 (19 January 1984) 11, 33, 202
Report on the Situation of Human Rights in El Salvador of the Special Representative, J. A. Pastor Ridruejo, E/CN.4/1985/18 (1 February 1985) 11, 13, 145

Report on the Situation of Human Rights in Afghanistan of the Special Rapporteur, F. Ermacora, E/CN.4/1985/21 (19 February 1985) 11, 13, 29, 48

Final Report on the Situation of Human Rights in El Salvador of the Special Representative, J. A. Pastor Ridruejo, E/CN.4/1987/21 (2 February 1987) 81

Report of the Special Rapporteur on Extrajudicial, Summary or Arbitrary Executions, S. Amos Wako, E/CN.4/1988/22 (19 January 1988) 64

Report of the Special Rapporteur on Extrajudicial, Summary or Arbitrary Executions, S. Amos Wako, E/CN.4/1989/25 (6 February 1989) 175

Report on the Situation in Afghanistan by the Special Rapporteur, F. Ermacora, E/CN.4/1989/24 (16 February 1989) 150, 211

Report on the Situation of Human Rights in Afghanistan by the Special Rapporteur, F. Ermacora, E/CN.4/1990/25 (31 January 1990) 79

Report of the Special Rapporteur on Extrajudicial, Summary or Arbitrary Executions, S. A. Wako, E/CN.4/1991/36 (3 February 1991) 42

Report of the Special Rapporteur on Torture, N. S. Rodley, E/CN.4/1992/17 (27 December 1991) 48

Report by the Special Rapporteur on Extrajudicial, Summary or Arbitrary Executions, Bacre Waly Ndiaye, E/CN.4/1994/7 (7 December 1993) 88, 181, 190, 201, 206

Report of the Special Rapporteur on Question of Torture, N. S. Rodley, E/CN.4/1994/31 (6 January 1994) 12, 42

Report of the Special Rapporteur for Sudan, Gáspár Bíró, E/CN.4/1994/48 (1 February 1994) 42

Final Report on the Situation of Human Rights in Afghanistan by F. Ermacora, E/CN.4/1994/53 (14 February 1994) 211

Report of Special Rapporteur on Extrajudicial, Summary or Arbitrary Executions, Bacre Waly Ndiaye, E/CN.4/1995/61 (14 December 1994) 175, 194

Joint Report of the Special Rapporteur on Question of Torture, N. S. Rodley, and the Special Rapporteur on Extrajudicial, Summary or Arbitrary Executions, Bacre Waly Ndiaye, E/CN.4/1995/111 (16 January 1995) 11, 145, 192, 202

Report of the Special Rapporteur for Sudan, Gáspár Bíró, E/CN.4/1995/58 (30 January 1995) 22

Report of the Special Rapporteur for Sudan, Gáspár Bíró, E/CN.4/1996/62 (20 February 1996) 68

Final Report on the Situation of Human Rights in Afghanistan of the Special Rapporteur, Choong-Hyun Paik, E/CN.4/1996/64 (27 February 1996) 214

xxiv TABLE OF OTHER DOCUMENTS

Statement of the Chairman on Chechnya, E/CN.4/1996/177 (24 April 1996) 67

Report of the Meeting of Special Rapporteurs/Representatives Experts and Chairpersons of Working Groups of the Special Procedures of the Commission on Human Rights and the Advisory Services Programme, E/CN.4/1997/3 (30 September 1996) 39, 42, 45

Report of the Special Rapporteur on Extrajudicial, Summary or Arbitrary Executions, Bacre Waly Ndiaye, E/CN.4/1997/60/Add.1 (23 December 1996) 48, 64, 77, 175, 200

Final Report on the Situation of Human Rights in Afghanistan of the Special Rapporteur, Choong-Hyun Paik, E/CN.4/1997/59 (20 February 1997) 154, 211

Guiding Principles on Internal Displacement, Report of the Representative of the Secretary-General, F. M. Deng, E/CN.4/1998/53/Add.2 (11 February 1998) 49, 52

Interim Report of the Special Representative on Children in Armed Conflict, O. A. Otunnu, E/CN.4/1998/119 (12 March 1998) 63

UN Sub-Commission on Prevention of Discrimination and Protection of Minorities

Res. 1994/26, 'Minimum Humanitarian Standards' (26 August 1994)[3] 49

Report of the Special Rapporteur of the Sub-Commission on Prevention of Discrimination and Protection of Minorities, L. Joinet, Study on Amnesty Laws and their Role in the Safeguard and Promotion of Human Rights, E/CN.4/Sub.2/1985/16 (21 June 1985) 206

UN High Commissioner for Human Rights

Report on the Situation of Human Rights in Kosovo, HC/Kosovo (7 September 1999)

UN Secretary-General

Report 'Respect for Human Rights in Armed Conflicts', A/7720 (20 November 1969) 15

Report 'Respect for Human Rights in Armed Conflicts', A/8052 (18 September 1970)

---

[3] Text available on www.unhcr.ch.

Report 'Respect for Human Rights in Armed Conflicts', A/83/70 (2 September 1971)
Report of the UN Secretary-General on the Situation in Somalia, Recommending the Establishment of UNOSOM, S/23829, and add. 1–2 (21 April 1992) 139
Report of the Secretary-General Pursuant to Paragraph 2 of Security Council Resolution 808 (1993), S/25704 (3 May 1993) 20, 55, 113
Report Pursuant to Paragraph 5 of Security Council Resolution 955 (1994), S/1995/134 (13 February 1995) 100
'Analytical Report on Minimum Humanitarian Standards', E/CN.4/1998/87 (5 January 1998) 12, 42–3, 45, 46, 52, 54, 109, 143, 144, 227
Report 'Fundamental Standards of Humanity', E/CN.4/1999/92 (18 December 1998) 46, 47, 200
Report on the Protection of Civilians in Armed Conflict, S/1999/957 (8 September 1999) 63
Report 'Fundamental Standards of Humanity', E/CN.4/2000/94 (27 December 1999) 46

Human Rights Division of the United Nations Observer Mission in El Salvador (ONUSAL)

First Report, A/45/1055, S/23037 (16 September 1991) 50, 145
Second Report, A/46/658, S/23222 (15 November 1991) 17, 51, 63, 69, 77, 78, 85, 153, 187
Third Report, A/46/876, S/23580 (19 February 1992) 70, 71, 72, 78, 82, 85, 86, 153, 186, 187

International Law Commission

Draft Code of Offences against Peace and Security of Mankind, A/2693 (1954), reprinted in *ILCYb* 1950, Vol. II, at 11 107, 175
Draft Articles on State Responsibility provisionally adopted by the Commission on first reading, A/51/10 (1996) 133
Draft Code of Crimes against the Peace and Security of Mankind, A/51/10, Supp. No. 10 (1996) 100, 106, 107, 109, 111, 118, 125, 200
Draft Articles on State Responsibility provisionally adopted by the Drafting Committee on second reading in 1998, A/CN.4/L.569 (4 August 1998) 133, 153, 154, 155, 156, 166, 181, 182, 212, 213, 215, 217, 226
First Report of the Special Rapporteur on State Responsibility, J. Crawford, A/CN.4/490/Add.5 (22 July 1998) 133, 156, 157, 182

ILCYb 1962, Vol. II (Law of Treaties) 30, 50
ILCYb 1975, Vol. II (Commentary to Draft Articles on State Responsibility) 157, 176
ILCYb 1979, Vol. II (Commentary to Draft Articles on State Responsibility) 217

General Assembly of the Organization of American States

Res. 'Consequences of Acts of Violence Perpetrated by Irregular Armed Groups on the Enjoyment of Human Rights', AG/RES.1043, (XX-0/90) (1990), reproduced in *Inter-American Yearbook on Human Rights 1990*, at 352-4 40

Res. 'Respect for International Humanitarian Law', AG/RES. 1335 (XXV-O/95) (9 June 1995), reproduced in: *Inter-American Yearbook on Human Rights 1995*, at 970-2

Other

1995 Turku Declaration on Minimum Humanitarian Standards (adopted at a meeting of experts convened in Turku/Åbo, Finland, 1990), revised version reprinted in (1995) 89 AJIL 218-23 48, 49, 55, 200

Abbreviations

AI	Amnesty International
AJIL	*American Journal of International Law*
Am. UJ Int'l L. & Pol'y	*American University Journal of International Law and Policy*
Ann. SDI	*Annuaire Suisse de Droit International*
Appl.	Application
Brownlie BDHR	I. Brownlie (ed.), *Basic Documents on Human Rights* (Clarendon Press, Oxford, 3rd edn, reprint 1994) (1992)
Brownlie BDIL	I. Brownlie (ed.), *Basic Documents in International Law* (Clarendon Press, Oxford, 4th edn. 1995)
BYIL	*British Yearbook of International Law*
Comm.	Communication
Denv. J. Int'l L. & Pol'y	*Denver Journal of International Law and Policy*
Doc.	Document
DR	*Decisions and Reports of the European Commission of Human Rights*
ECR	*European Court Reports. Reports of the Court of Justice of the European Communities*
EHRR	*European Human Rights Reports*
EJIL	*European Journal of International Law*
EPIL	*Encyclopedia of Public International Law*
Eur. Ct. HR	European Court of Human Rights
Ga. J. Int'l & Comp. L.	*Georgia Journal of International and Comparative Law*
GYIL	*German Yearbook of International Law*
HV	*Humanitäres Völkerrecht*

ICJ	International Court of Justice
ICJ Rep.	*International Court of Justice, Reports of Judgments, Advisory Opinions and Orders*
ICLQ	*International and Comparative Law Quarterly*
ICRC	International Committee of the Red Cross
ILC	International Law Commission
ILCYb	*Yearbook of the International Law Commission*
ILM	*International Legal Materials*
Inter-Am. Ct. HR	Inter-American Court of Human Rights
IRRC	*International Review of the Red Cross*
Israel YBHR	*Israel Yearbook on Human Rights*
Mich. J. Int'l L.	*Michigan Journal of International Law*
Mil. L. Rev.	*Military Law Review*
MLJ	*Manitoba Law Journal*
n.	note
NILR	*Netherlands International Law Review*
NJB	*Nederlands Juristenblad*
NQHR	*Netherlands Quarterly of Human Rights*
NWR	*Naval War Review*
NYIL	*Netherlands Yearbook of International Law*
NYUJ Int'l L & Pol.	*New York University Journal of International Law and Politics*
ONUSAL	United Nations Observer Mission in El Salvador
para.	paragraph
pr.	preamble
RBDI	*Revue Belge de Droit International*
Rep.	Report
Reports	*Reports of Judgments and Decisions.* Publication of the Case Law of the European Commission and Court of Human Rights (as from 1996).
Res.	Resolution
RIAA	Reports of International Arbitral Awards
Ser.	Series
UN	United Nations
US	United States
vol.	volume
Yale LJ.	*Yale Law Journal*
YB ECHR	*Yearbook of the European Convention of Human Rights*
YIHL	*Yearbook of International Humanitarian Law*
YB ILC	*Yearbook of the International Law Commission*

Introduction

This study examines the international accountability for acts committed by armed opposition groups during internal armed conflict. It aims to contribute to the improvement of the protection of civilian populations from abuses committed by these groups.

Armed opposition groups, as defined in this study, operate in internal armed conflict. These groups generally fight against the government in power, in an effort to overthrow the existing government, or alternatively to bring about a secession so as to set up a new state. The objectives of these groups may also include the achievement of greater autonomy within the state concerned. In other situations, where the existing government has collapsed or is unable to intervene, armed groups fight among themselves in pursuit of political power.

The degree of organization of armed opposition groups, their size, and the extent to which they exercise effective authority vary from one situation to the next. At one extreme, such groups resemble de facto governments, with control over territory and population. At the other extreme, they are militarily and politically inferior to the established government, exercising no direct control over territory and operating only sporadically. Some armed groups operate under clear lines of command and control; others are loosely organized and various units are not under effective central command.

Today, the majority of armed conflicts are internal, as opposed to international. In its 1998 Yearbook, the Stockholm International Peace Research Institute reported that of the twenty-five major armed conflicts that were waged in 1997 all but one were internal.[1] During mid-1997 to

---

[1] The Stockholm International Peace Research Institute (SIPRI), *SIPRI Yearbook 1998: Armaments, Disarmament and International Security*, (Oxford University Press, Oxford, 1998), cited in A. McDonald, 'The Year in Review' (1998) 1 *YIHL* 113, 121.

mid-1998 alone, there were fourteen internal conflicts, in each of which more than 1,000 people were killed, and which have, cumulatively, led to approximately 5 million deaths[2] since the conflicts first broke out, which, in some cases, was many years ago.

While in many cases the government is responsible for the greatest number of deaths, surveys of Amnesty International and Human Rights Watch show that armed opposition groups have also created many victims, primarily civilians. This is even clearer in conflicts where the government has collapsed, as occurred, for example, in Somalia in 1991, and in Afghanistan in 1992.

Neither the Charter of the United Nations, nor any other rule of international law, prohibits the use of force by armed opposition groups within a state. The mere fact of starting or engaging in an internal armed conflict does not entail the responsibility of the armed groups concerned. International law does, however, contain rules on the prevention, regulation, and punishment of violence committed by these groups against civilians. The applicable law is commonly divided into three specialized fields of international law: international humanitarian law, international criminal law and international human rights law.

Prior to 1949, in certain circumstances, customary *humanitarian* law applicable to international conflicts was also applied to large-scale internal conflicts. Armed opposition groups were then equated with governments. Such recognition of belligerent status has been very infrequent, however. The reason is that the criteria for applicability of the humanitarian rules were high. The armed opposition groups had to control and govern a substantial part of the state territory and engage in a widespread armed conflict. Even then, in practice, the consent of the government of the state against which they were fighting was required for the humanitarian rules to be applied. Also today, there are few situations to which these criteria apply. The adoption, in 1949, of Article 3 common to the four Geneva Conventions was meant to change the legal situation in internal conflicts. While recognition of belligerency was also concerned with the interests of third states (the wish to protect their property and economic relations in territory controlled by armed opposition groups) and their right to intervene in the armed conflict on behalf of one side or the other, the Geneva Conventions placed greater emphasis on the interests of humanity.

---

[2] So-called 'high intensity conflicts', conflict level 5 on the PIOOM scale, PIOOM (Interdisciplinary Research Program on Causes of Human Rights Violations) *World Conflict and Human Rights Map* (Leiden University, The Netherlands, 1998).

International law has a legitimate and increasing interest in armed opposition groups but is inadequate to this task. The aim of this study is to deal with a major question which arises in all internal armed conflicts and which has not been addressed before: Who is accountable under international law for the acts committed by armed opposition groups or for the failure to prevent or repress these acts?

The problem of accountability is that, in order to have effective enforcement of international law relevant to the acts of armed opposition groups, we should be able, so to speak, to climb up a chain of command, so as to reach to the top. It is easily seen how this is done on the government side, i.e. in traditional international law. Then there are three levels of accountability. At the first and lowest level, individuals who actually committed the crime can be held accountable. At the second level, superiors are potentially accountable on the basis of the principle of command responsibility. At the third level, the state itself may be accountable, in that it is responsible for acts committed by its agents. My concern is to discuss the extent to which there is – or can be – a parallel chain of accountability on the insurgent side which is a counterpart to the one just outlined, applicable to the government side. The first question then is whether members and leaders of armed opposition groups can be held criminally accountable for violations of international law. The second level of accountability would be the accountability of the armed opposition groups as such. A final possibility is to make the state accountable in certain cases for acts committed on its territory by armed opposition groups.

This study thus assumes the perspective of the *subjects* of the law relevant to the conduct of armed opposition groups in internal armed conflict. In doing so, it deviates from the common approach to internal conflicts focusing on the rights of victims. So far, the victim-oriented approach has not provided satisfactory answers to the problem of the protection of civilians from armed opposition groups. It has been established that civilians caught up in internal conflicts have fundamental rights and that these rights are apt to be abused by armed opposition groups. However, it remains unclear in relation to whom these rights apply, or, formulated differently, who is obliged to respect or ensure respect of these rights.

The term 'armed opposition groups' is preferred to other expressions such as 'rebels' or 'terrorists', as the former expression has the merit of being less emotive. The word 'group' points to a collectivity, being more than the sum of its members. While the word 'opposition' refers primarily to the conflict against the established government, it is proposed to use the same term even when the government does not participate in the hostilities, i.e. when armed opposition groups are fighting among themselves.

This study will evaluate the law relevant to armed opposition groups as applied and developed by *international bodies*. International bodies play an important role in the application and development of the law on armed groups. Various international bodies (international courts and tribunals and other bodies whose creation is related to specific treaties or the UN Charter) have been and are being confronted with abuses by armed opposition groups and, in response, have dynamically interpreted and developed the relevant law. In doing so, these bodies have exercised considerable influence on international treaty and customary law. Although Article 38 of the Statute of the International Court of Justice does not mention the practice of international bodies as a separate source of law, the practice of these bodies can provide decisive evidence of the law.

The focus on international bodies as important initiators of the development of the law relevant to armed groups implies that this study does not search for detailed rules relevant to the conduct of armed opposition groups. Such rules actually exist only to a limited extent. Applicable treaties contain only general norms rarely dealing in so many words with the acts of armed opposition groups. Relevant customary law is undeveloped and still in a state of development. A better approach is to identify trends in decision making in international law in the light of treaty and customary law which are relevant to the acts of these groups.

Fifteen internal armed conflicts serve as frame of reference throughout this study. The selection of these conflicts is based on the fact that they have been qualified as internal armed conflicts in terms of international humanitarian law, either by one or more international bodies, or by (specialized) non-governmental organizations, or authoritative commentators.

These conflicts are: the conflict in Afghanistan (1978–present); Algeria (1992–present); Cambodia (1980–present); Chechnya, Russian Federation (1994–96, and 1999–present); Colombia (1964–present); El Salvador (1981–92); Lebanon (1975–90); Nicaragua (1978–79 and 1981–90); Rwanda (1990–94); Somalia (1991–present); Sri Lanka (1983–present); Sudan (1983–present); Turkey (1983–present); Northern Ireland, United Kingdom (1969–present); and finally, the internal aspects of the conflict in the former Yugoslavia (1991–95), including the conflict in Kosovo, Federal Republic of Yugoslavia (1998–99).

The conflicts selected provide sufficient geographical coverage and diversity as regards their intensity and duration. In addition, together the chosen conflicts cover a wide period of time, namely from 1964 until the present. These conditions allow me to draw conclusions that are relevant for each of the conflicts or categories of conflicts examined, notwithstanding the fact that substantial differences exist between them, and between different periods within one conflict. It also allows me to comment on the law relevant to other internal conflicts not covered in detail by this study.

Accountability is an overarching term, which covers both the substantive obligations of the relevant actors and their responsibility for breaches of these obligations. The applicable substantive rules and the rules on responsibility operate as a coherent body of law. The standard for accountability of the leaders of armed opposition groups, armed opposition groups themselves, and the territorial state has thus to be found in the applicable substantive law and in the rules that render their responsibility operational. Accordingly this book is divided into two parts. Part 1 analyses the substantive law applicable to armed opposition groups as such. Part 2 addresses the problem of accountability. Successively, the accountability of leaders of armed opposition groups, armed opposition groups themselves, and the accountability of the territorial state will be addressed.

PART 1 · THE NORMATIVE GAP

1 Legal restraints on armed opposition groups as such

The first question is that of applicable law. It is only when the law to be applied has been settled that one can examine its content, which will be done in the next chapter.

Practice of international bodies convincingly demonstrates that international humanitarian law applicable to armed opposition groups extends well beyond Common Article 3 of the Geneva Conventions and Additional Protocol II to the Geneva Conventions. It remains the case, however, that the 'new' humanitarian law applicable to armed opposition groups concerns principles rather than detailed rules. It is unclear whether armed opposition groups are bound by human rights law. International criminal law as it currently stands does not apply to armed opposition groups as such, and probably rightly so.

Common Article 3 and Protocol II

Treaty law

International bodies have uniformly affirmed the applicability of Common Article 3 and Protocol II to armed opposition groups as a matter of treaty law.

Common Article 3 provides: 'In the case of armed conflict not of an international character occurring in the territory of one of the High Contracting Parties, each Party to the conflict shall be bound to apply as a minimum the following provisions.' Despite the clarity of this provision, both states and commentators have sometimes suggested that Common Article 3 does not bind armed opposition groups or that it applies only to the individual members of these groups, rather than to the group as a whole.[1] The proponents of this argument may support their view by pointing to Protocol II which does not refer to 'parties to the conflict', but only mentions the High Contracting Parties to the Protocol, which are states.[2]

Wide international practice confirms, however, that armed opposition groups are bound by Common Article 3 and Protocol II, and that they are so as a group. In *Military and Paramilitary Activities In and Against Nicaragua*, the International Court of Justice observed that the acts of the *Contras*, fighting against the Nicaraguan Government, were governed by the law applicable to armed conflict not of an international character, i.e. Common Article 3.[3] Similarly, in the so-called *Tablada* case, the Inter-American Commission considered:

Common Article 3's mandatory provisions expressly bind and apply equally to both parties to internal conflicts, i.e., government and dissident forces. Moreover, the obligation to apply Common Article 3 is absolute for both parties and independent of the obligation of the other. Therefore, both the MTP attackers [the armed opposition group fighting in the conflict under consideration] and the Argentine armed forces had the same duties under humanitarian law.[4]

[1] During the First Periodical Meeting on Humanitarian Law in 1998, several states re-emphasized their objections to the qualification of armed opposition groups as a party to the conflict within the meaning of international humanitarian law. In their view, the better way to deal with internal conflicts is through international criminal prosecution of individuals. The conclusions of the conference drawn up by the chairman avoid any reference to armed opposition groups as bearers of obligations under international humanitarian law, Chairman's Report of the First Periodical Meeting on International Humanitarian Law (Geneva, 19-23 January 1998) in ICRC, International Federation of Red Cross and Red Crescent Societies, Compendium of Documents, prepared for the 27th International Conference of the Red Cross and Red Crescent 31 October - 6 November 1999, Annex II (1999) (hereafter, Compendium of Documents); see also D. Plattner, 'The Penal Repression of Violations of International Humanitarian Law Applicable in Non-International Armed Conflicts' (1990) 30 *IRRC* 409, at 416 (hereafter, 'Penal Repression').

[2] See G.I.A.D. Draper, 'Humanitarian Law and Human Rights' (1979) *Acta Juridica* 199-206, reprinted in M. A. Meyer and H. McCoubrey (eds.) *Reflections on Law and Armed Conflicts*, (Kluwer Law International, The Hague, 1998) pp. 145-6 (hereafter, *Reflections on Law and Armed Conflicts*) ('The rules established in the Protocol [II] ... are not express obligations imposed upon the parties to the internal conflict, but are established as between the States which are parties to the Protocol, limited to the States Parties to the Geneva Convention of 1949') (hereafter, 'Humanitarian Law and Human Rights').

[3] *Nicaragua v. US* (Judgment of 27 June 1986) (Merits) 1986 ICJ Rep. 14, at 114, para. 119 (hereafter, *Nicaragua* Case).

[4] Report No 55/97, Case No 11.137 (Argentina), para. 174 (30 October 1997) (hereafter, *Tablada* case) (footnotes omitted); see also Report No 26/97 Case No 11.142 (Colombia), para. 131 (30 September 1997).

The UN Security Council and the UN Commission on Human Rights, in the context of various internal conflicts, have frequently called upon all parties to the hostilities, namely the government armed forces and armed opposition groups – to respect fully the applicable provisions of international humanitarian law, including Common Article 3.[5]

Similar practice can be found with regard to Protocol II. In *Prosecutor v. Akayesu*, the Rwanda Tribunal indicated that the Protocol states 'norms applicable to States and Parties to a conflict'.[6] Similarly, in resolution 1987/51, the UN Commission on Human Rights requested the armed opposition groups involved in the conflict in El Salvador to observe the Geneva Conventions and the Protocols, which includes Protocol II.[7] The Commission's Special Representative on the Situation of Human Rights in El Salvador observed:

The Republic of El Salvador is a party to the four Geneva Conventions of 1949 and the Additional Protocols of 1977 on the protection of victims of war. Since the current conflict in El Salvador is an 'armed conflict not of an international character' within the meaning of the Conventions and Protocols, the relevant rules apply, particularly those contained in Article 3 of each of the Conventions and in Protocol II, *and must be observed by each of the parties to the conflict – in other words, by the Salvadorian regular armed forces and the opposition guerrilla forces.*[8]

---

[5] UN Security Council, Res. 1193 (1998), para. 12 (28 August 1998) (on Afghanistan); UN Security Council, Res. 812 (1993), para. 8 (12 March 1993) (on Rwanda); UN Security Council, Res. 794 (1992), para. 4 (3 December 1992) (on Somalia); UN Commission on Human Rights, Res. 1999/18, para. 17 (23 April 1999) ('condemns abuses by elements of the Kosovo Liberation Army, in particular killings in violation of international humanitarian law'); UN Commission on Human Rights, Res. 1997/59, para. 7 (15 April 1997) (on Sudan); Commission on Human Rights, Res. 1998/67, para. 6 (21 April 1998) (on Sudan); see also UN Commission on Human Rights, E/CN.4/1985/21, at 43, para. 161 (Report of the Special Rapporteur, 19 February 1985) (hereafter, 1985 Report of the Special Rapporteur on Afghanistan).
[6] No. ICTR-96-4-T, at 248, para. 611 (2 September 1998) (hereafter, *Akayesu* case).
[7] Para. 3 (11 March 1987); see also UN Commission on Human Rights, Res. 1997/59, para. 7 (15 April 1997) (on Sudan).
[8] UN Commission on Human Rights, E/CN.4/1985/18, at 37 (Report of the Special Representative, 1 February 1985) (hereafter, 1985 Final Report of the Special Representative on El Salvador) (emphasis added); see also UN Commission on Human Rights, E/CN.4/1984/25, at 34 (Final Report on the Situation of Human Rights in El Salvador of J. A. Pastor Ridruejo, 19 January 1984); UN Commission on Human Rights, E/CN.4/1995/111, para. 129 (Joint Report of the Special Rapporteur on Question of Torture, N.S. Rodley, and the Special Rapporteur on Extrajudicial, Summary or Arbitrary Executions, Bacre Waly Ndiaye, 16 January 1995) (hereafter, 1995 Joint Report of the Special Rapporteur on Question of Torture, and the Special Rapporteur on Extrajudicial, Summary or Arbitrary Executions); Inter-American Commission on Human Rights, Third Report on the Situation of Human Rights in Colombia,

This practice, demonstrating that armed opposition groups are bound by Common Article 3 and Protocol II,[9] also shows that international bodies have assumed competence to determine the applicability of these norms in specific cases. Commentators have often raised the problem of the absence of an international machinery competent to characterize the conflict and therewith the applicability of the relevant law.[10] Were such machinery to exist, they suggest, the common state practice of denying the applicability of Common Article 3 and Protocol II to situations in which they clearly should be applied, might be reversed.

It is true that, in principle, states are free to interpret their rights and duties under international humanitarian law, as under general international law, without such interpretation having binding force upon other states.[11] Accordingly, during the drafting of Protocol II, several states emphasized that it is a matter solely for the state affected by a conflict to determine whether the conditions for applicability of the Protocol were fulfilled.[12] International bodies generally acknowledge the relevance of states' views, in particular the view of the territorial state, on the question whether the norms apply to a particular situation.[13]

OEA/Ser.L/V/II.102, Doc. 9, rev. 1, at 77–8, para. 20 and accompanying footnote 11, at 81–111, paras. 36–150 (26 February 1999) (hereafter, Third Report on Colombia) (applying Protocol II to the Colombian armed opposition groups).

[9] See also J. S. Pictet (ed.), *Commentary IV Geneva Convention Relative to the Protection of Civilian Persons in Time of War* (International Committee of the Red Cross, Geneva, reprint 1994) (1958) p. 37 (hereafter, *Commentary 4th Geneva Convention*); S-S. Junod, *Commentary on the Additional Protocols of 8 June 1977 to the Geneva Conventions of 12 August 1949*, eds. Y. Sandoz et al. (Martinus Nijhoff, Geneva, 1987), p. 1345 (hereafter, *Commentary Additional Protocols*).

[10] F. Kalshoven, *Constraints on the Waging of War* (International Committee of the Red Cross, Geneva, 2nd edn., 1991), p. 138 (hereafter, *Constraints*); T. Meron, *Human Rights in Internal Strife: their International Protection* (Grotius Publications Limited, Cambridge, 1987) p. 43–4 (hereafter, *Internal Strife*).

[11] P. Weil, 'Le droit international en quête de son identité' (1992) 237–VI *Recueil des Cours* at 222.

[12] F. Kalshoven, 'Reaffirmation and Development of International Humanitarian Law Applicable in Armed Conflicts: the Diplomatic Conference Geneva 1974–1977' (1997) 8 *NYIL* 107, at 112 (hereafter, 'Reaffirmation').

[13] Commission on Human Rights, E/CN.4/1998/87, para. 79 (Analytical Report of the Secretary General on Minimum Humanitarian Standards, 5 January 1998) (hereafter, UN Secretary-General 1998 Report on Minimum Humanitarian Standards; compare also Commission on Human Rights, E/CN.4/1994/31, para. 13 (Report of the Special Rapporteur on Question of Torture, N. S. Rodley, 6 January 1994) (asking whether, in determining whether an armed conflict exists and what entities may be appropriately considered as parties to the conflict, he should be guided by the view of the Government of the member state concerned) (hereafter, 1994 Report of the Special Rapporteur on Torture).

The freedom of states is, however, limited when courts and tribunals exist that are competent to interpret the law. There is no doubt that the International Court of Justice, the Yugoslavia and Rwanda Tribunals, and the future International Criminal Court, can make a legally binding declaration as to whether a conflict is an 'armed conflict not of an international character' and thereby as to the applicability of international humanitarian law to the parties involved in the conflict.[14] Moreover, the UN Security Council, when acting under Chapter VII, has claimed the authority to make a legally binding decision as to whether an armed conflict exists and whether the humanitarian rules apply to these situations. The effect of decisions of these bodies is to have a minimum legal standard apply, independently of the desire of the government, as soon as the violence and the armed opposition groups pass a certain threshold as to their organization and military power.

Other bodies, such as the Inter-American Commission, the UN Commission on Human Rights, and its rapporteurs, have also regularly qualified situations as internal armed conflicts within the meaning of international humanitarian law. Significantly, in some cases these bodies made such declarations contrary to the views of the governments concerned.[15] The views of these bodies are, however, not binding upon states.

Thus, while the determination of applicability of Common Article 3 and Protocol II is largely left to auto-interpretation, international bodies increasingly play a role in this determination. A different question,

[14] In the *Nicaragua* case, the International Court of Justice held that the conflict between the *Contras* and the Government of Nicaragua was an armed conflict not of an international character in terms of international humanitarian law; it made this decision in defiance of the position of the Government of Nicaragua, which refused to formally acknowledge the applicability of Common Article 3, Americas Watch Committee, *Violations of the Laws of War by Both Sides in Nicaragua 1981–1985* (New York, March 1985), p.16.

[15] Both the Governments of El Salvador and Afghanistan refused to acknowledge the applicability of Common Article 3 to the respective conflicts. Nonetheless, the UN Commission on Human Rights' Special Representative on the Situation of Human Rights in El Salvador, Pastor Ridruejo stated that the conflict in El Salvador was governed by Common Article 3 and Protocol II, 1985 Final Report of the Special Representative for El Salvador, see above, n. 8, at 37. Similarly, the UN Commission on Human Rights' Special Rapporteur on Afghanistan, Ermacora, considered that the conflict in Afghanistan 'must be considered as one of a non-international character within the meaning of Article 3 of the Geneva Conventions', 1985 Report of the Special Rapporteur on Afghanistan, above, n. 5, at 43; see also A/40/40 at 122 (1985), General Assembly of the United Nations (the Government of Afghanistan denying that the situation in that country constituted an armed conflict within the meaning of Common Article 3).

which will be addressed later, is whether third party monitoring can be improved by the creation of machinery specifically mandated to decide on the applicability of international humanitarian law in specific cases.

Origin of the obligations of armed groups under inter-state treaties

A difficult question remains, namely the origin of the obligations of armed opposition groups under multilateral treaties to which they are not a party. The Geneva Conventions and Protocol II are international agreements concluded between states. Armed opposition groups have not ratified or acceded to these treaties, nor are they able to become parties to the Geneva Conventions or Protocol II. The Geneva Conventions admit only states as 'High Contracting Parties'.[16] The same holds for Protocol II, since only the State Parties to the Geneva Conventions can become parties to the Protocol.[17] Furthermore, the applicability of Common Article 3 and Protocol II to armed opposition groups does not depend on their express declaration that they consider themselves bound by these rules.

Several armed opposition groups have tried to adhere to the 1949 Geneva Conventions. However, they have been challenged by their opponents and also by Switzerland, the depository of the Conventions.[18] Third states take the traditional view that when two authorities claim to

---

[16] Article 1 common to the Geneva Conventions stipulates that 'the High Contracting Parties undertake to respect and to ensure respect for the present Convention in all circumstances'; the notion 'High Contracting Parties' refers to the states for which the Conventions are in force, S-S. Junod, *Commentary Additional Protocols*, see above, n. 9, p. 1338; see also M. Takemoto, 'The 1977 Additional Protocols and the Law of Treaties', in C. Swinarski (ed.), *Studies and Essays on International Humanitarian Law and Red Cross Principles in Honour of Jean Pictet* (International Committee of the Red Cross, Martinus Nijhoff, Dordrecht, 1984) pp. 247–60 (hereafter, *Pictet*).

[17] Articles 20 and 22 of Protocol II.

[18] Both France and Switzerland challenged efforts by the Provisional Revolutionary Government of Algeria to adhere to the Conventions. Switzerland also challenged the attempted adherence by the Smith government in Rhodesia, D. P. Forsythe, 'Legal Management of Internal War: the 1977 Protocol on Non-International Armed Conflicts' (1978) 72 *AJIL* 272, 292, n. 93; also the Kosovo Liberation Army (KLA) has expressed its wish to sign the Geneva Conventions and other humanitarian instruments, 'Spokesman Explains Structure of Rebel Army', BBC Summary of World Broadcast, from Koha Ditore in Albania, 12 July 1998, and 'Koha Ditore Interview with Jakup Krasniqi, KLA Spokesman – Part II', Arta 12 July 1998, cited in: Human Rights Watch, 'Violations of the Rules of War by the Insurgent Forces', in *Federal Republic of Yugoslavia: Humanitarian Law Violations in Kosovo*, vol. X, No 9(D).

represent the government, only the authority that existed before the conflict, may bind the state to the Geneva Conventions and the Additional Protocols. When the established authority is challenged by another de facto authority, the latter will not be accepted as new accessor to the treaties.[19]

As armed opposition groups cannot become parties to the Geneva Conventions or Additional Protocols, and are not required to declare themselves bound by the relevant norms, they derive their rights and obligations contained in Common Article 3 and Protocol II through the state on whose territory they operate.[20] Once the territorial state has ratified the Geneva Conventions and Protocol II, armed opposition groups operating on its territory become automatically bound by the relevant norms laid down therein. The question arises as to the origin of the obligations of armed opposition groups under multilateral treaties. There is no international practice explicitly dealing with this question. However, in view of the fact that humanitarian law has great difficulty in regulating the behaviour of armed opposition groups, it is appropriate to give this question some consideration.

Two arguments, reflecting different conceptions of the international legal status of armed opposition groups, have been put forward to explain their obligations under interstate treaties. First, one may argue that they are bound as de facto authorities in a particular territory.[21] Armed opposition groups are then regarded as independent entities that exist side-by-side with the established authorities. This argument recognizes the reality of the internal conflict and the politically weakened position of the established authorities. It abandons the traditional conception of the state as an impermeable whole. This argument can, however, only apply to those groups which actually exercise de facto authority over persons or territory. It is unable to explain the obligations of groups lacking such authority, but which are, nonetheless bound by Common Article 3.[22]

---

[19] See S-S. Junod, *Commentary Additional Protocols*, above, n. 9, p. 1338.
[20] A/7720, para. 171 (Report of the Secretary General 'Respect for Human Rights in Armed Conflicts' 20 November 1969); see also S-S. Junod, *Commentary Additional Protocols*, see above n. 9, p. 1345.
[21] R. Baxter, 'Jus in Bello Interno: the Present and Future Law', in J. Moore (ed.), *Law and Civil War in the Modern World* (Johns Hopkins University Press, Baltimore, 1974), pp. 518, 527-8.
[22] Unlike Protocol II, Common Article 3 does not require armed opposition groups to exercise territorial control in order to be bound by the provisions set forth in this article, see below, Chapter 4, Section 1.

The obligations of this latter type of group can only be clarified by the second argument, namely that they are bound by humanitarian norms because they are inhabitants of the state that has ratified the relevant conventions.[23] This explanation views the relationship between the established government and armed opposition groups as hierarchical in nature. However, this is difficult to uphold. Armed opposition groups seek to exercise public authority, and in doing so they question the authority of the established government, including the government's laws. In this regard it must also be pointed out that armed groups must be distinguished from individuals. Like armed opposition groups, individuals cannot accede to international treaties, they derive their international rights and obligations through the state under which jurisdiction they live. However, the international rules applicable to individuals are limited to prohibitions on committing a limited number of international crimes. Common Article 3 and Protocol II do not merely require armed opposition groups not to commit the most serious crimes. In their position as a de facto authority, these groups are required to make a much greater effort to comply with international humanitarian law.[24]

There is some evidence that international bodies acknowledge the problem of the origin of the obligations of armed opposition groups under multilateral treaties. They have occasionally recognized the relevance of consent by armed opposition groups to the applicability of international norms to these groups. The Rwanda Tribunal, in its decision on the applicability of Protocol II to the conflict in Rwanda, took into account that the Rwandan Patriotic Front (RPF) had expressly declared that it considered itself bound by the rules of international humanitarian law.[25] The Human Rights Division of the United Nations Observer Mission in El Salvador (ONUSAL), in reviewing the legality of the acts of Frente Farabundo Martí para la Liberación Nacional (FMLN), generally referred to the San José Agreement on Human Rights, concluded

---

[23] Above, n. 21.

[24] For example, Protocol II prescribes various measures that armed opposition groups must take to ensure humane treatment of interned and detained persons, including separate accommodation of men and women and provision of medical examinations, Article 5(2)(a), and (d); see below, Chapter 2, discussing the substantive obligations of armed opposition groups.

[25] *Akayesu* case, above n. 6, at 248, para. 627; see also *Prosecutor v. Clément Kayishema and Obed Ruzindana*, No. ICTR-95-1-T, para. 156 (Judgment of 21 May 1999) (hereafter, *Kayishema* case); Inter-American Commission on Human Rights, Third Report on Colombia, above, n. 8, at 78, para. 20, n. 11 (noting that the ELN [Army of National Liberation] had specifically declared that it considered itself to be bound by the 1949 Geneva Conventions and Protocol II).

between the Salvadorian Government and FMLN, in which FMLN agreed to comply with Common Article 3 and Protocol II. ONUSAL thus preferred the Agreement to the Geneva Conventions and Protocol II, which were also binding upon FMLN. In the next section (Other rules of humanitarian law), I shall deal with special agreements concluded by armed opposition groups.

Special agreements and *ad hoc* declarations by armed opposition groups by which they expressly agree to comply with Common Article 3 and Protocol II do indeed remedy their failure to ratify these treaty rules.[26] Such agreements and declarations serve two purposes. First, they compel these groups to explicitly state their will and capacity to adhere to the relevant norms.[27] Secondly, they induce the state to accept the applicability of the relevant norms to the conflict in question.

However, the consent by armed opposition groups to rules imposed on them has played only a small role in international practice. International bodies have generally considered the ratification of the relevant norms by the territorial state to be a sufficient legal basis for the obligations of armed opposition groups. These bodies thereby establish the conception of international law as a law controlled by states, under which states can simply decide to confer rights and impose obligations on armed opposition groups.

It is noteworthy that a different construction applies to national liberation movements.[28] Like armed opposition groups, national liberation movements are not entities that are able to become a party to the

[26] M. Bothe *et al.*, *New Rules for Victims of Armed Conflicts* (Martinus Nijhoff, The Hague, 1982) p. 608 (hereafter, *New Rules*).

[27] The following example in the practice of the UN Mission in El Salvador, ONUSAL, shows the pertinence of this aspect. FMLN had detained an ambulance, while it knew that it was transporting a wounded man. The FMLN Political and Diplomatic Commission informed ONUSAL 'that no agreement existed between the parties for the evacuation of armed forces wounded and dead by road from war zones'. It added 'that a pledge is needed that armed forces and ambulances will not be used for military purposes and that the army will not obstruct the evacuation of FMLN wounded and disabled by the ICRC'. ONUSAL responded that, according to international humanitarian law, wounded persons, whether or not they have taken part in the armed conflict, must be respected and protected. It referred to Article 7, Protocol II. However, apparently, the FMLN did not consider itself bound by Protocol II, unless it had concluded an agreement to this effect, Second Report of ONUSAL, A/46/658, S/23222, paras. 64–5 (Human Rights Division, 15 November 1991) (hereafter, Second Report of ONUSAL), reprinted in United Nations, *The United Nations and El Salvador 1990–1995* (UN Blue Book Series, United Nations, New York, 1995) p. 179, vol. IV (hereafter, *UN and El Salvador*).

[28] These movements are covered by Article 1(4) of Additional Protocol I, which stipulates that the Protocol shall also apply to 'armed conflicts in which peoples are fighting

Geneva Conventions and the Protocols. However, unlike armed opposition groups, national liberation movements only become subject to Additional Protocol I on an equal footing with a High Contracting Party if they make a special declaration to this effect.[29] Apparently, it was thought that to give effect to the relevant rules, an explicit declaration by national liberation movements that they considered themselves bound was necessary.

The difference, at least formally, between national liberation movements and armed opposition groups is that the former are considered to fight in an *international* conflict. Armed groups on the other hand are a party to an *internal* conflict. Inclusion in Common Article 3 or Protocol II of a clause requiring armed opposition groups to make a declaration in which they agree to comply with the relevant norms would add to the internationalization of the conflict. The reason is that the applicability of these norms would then depend on the consent of an armed opposition group, which puts these groups on an equal footing with the state. This consequence has clearly been unacceptable for states and international bodies.

Customary law

Having demonstrated the applicability of Common Article 3 and Protocol II to armed opposition groups as treaty law, the question should be addressed as to the applicability of these norms as a matter of customary law. Until recently, there was only limited international precedent dealing with the customary law nature of international humanitarian law applicable in internal conflict.[30] However, since the

---

against colonial domination and alien occupation and against racist régimes in the exercise of their right of self-determination'.

[29] For that purpose, Article 96(3) provides: 'The authority representing a people engaged against a High Contracting Party in an armed conflict of the type referred to in Article 1, paragraph 4, may undertake to apply the Conventions and this Protocol in relation to that conflict by means of a unilateral declaration addressed to the depository. Such declaration shall, upon its receipt by the depository, have in relation to that conflict the following effects: (a) the Conventions and this Protocol are brought into force for the said authority as a Party to the conflict with immediate effect; (b) the said authority assumes the same rights and obligations as those which have been assumed by a High Contracting Party to the Conventions and this Protocol; and (c) the Conventions and this Protocol are equally binding upon all Parties to the conflict'.

[30] In fact, it was widely believed that no customary rules applied to internal conflicts. That is why the short version of the Martens Clause in Paragraph 4 of the Preamble of Protocol II, unlike the Martens Clause in Article 1(2) of Additional Protocol I, does not

establishment of the Yugoslavia and Rwanda Tribunals this situation has changed.[31]

There is ample evidence of international bodies having accepted the applicability of Common Article 3 and major parts of Protocol II to armed opposition groups as customary law. In the case of the *Military and Paramilitary Activities in and against Nicaragua*, the International Court of Justice pointed out that Common Article 3 reflects 'elementary considerations of humanity'.[32] The Court subsequently pointed out that the *Contras* were bound by Common Article 3.[33] In the *Advisory Opinion on the Legality of the Threat or Use of Nuclear Weapons*, the Court reinforced its view, stating that the fundamental rules of the Geneva Conventions, which undoubtedly include Common Article 3, are principles of customary law.[34] Similarly, in *Prosecutor v. Duško Tadić* (Appeal on Jurisdiction) the Yugoslavia Tribunal observed:

> The emergence of international rules governing internal strife has occurred at two different levels: at the level of customary law and at that of treaty law. Two bodies of rules have thus crystallised, which are by no means conflicting or inconsistent, but instead mutually support and supplement each other. Indeed, the interplay between these two sets of rules is such that some treaty rules have gradually become part of customary law. This holds true for Common Article 3 of the 1949 Geneva Conventions.[35]

In *Prosecutor v. Akayesu*, the Rwanda Tribunal affirmed the above observation of the Yugoslavia Tribunal, accepting the customary law status of Common Article 3.[36]

It is reasonable to assume that the Tribunals regarded the customary rules identified to be applicable to all parties to an internal conflict, including armed opposition groups. Although the criminal tribunals

---

refer to established custom. A commentary to the Protocol explains that 'this is justified by the fact that the attempt to establish rules for a non-international conflict only goes back to 1949 and that the application of Common Article 3 in the practice of States has not developed in such a way that one could speak of "established custom" regarding non-international conflicts', M. Bothe *et al.*, *New Rules*, above, n. 26, p. 620.

[31] Mention must be made here of the ICRC study being prepared on customary humanitarian law applicable in, *inter alia*, non-international armed conflicts. The study reflects on practice of states and international bodies. Publication is scheduled for 2002, Compendium of Documents, above, n. 1, Annex I, at 3.

[32] *Nicaragua Case*, n. 3, para. 218.   [33] *Ibid.*, para. 219.

[34] Opinion of 8 July 1996, 35 ILM 809, para. 79 (1996) (hereafter, Advisory Opinion on Nuclear Weapons).

[35] No. IT-94-1-AR72, para. 98 (Decision on the Defence Motion for Interlocutory Appeal on Jurisdiction, 2 October 1995), (hereafter, *Tadić Interlocutory Appeal*).

[36] *Akayesu* case, above, n. 6, para. 608.

are concerned with individual rather than group accountability, they have developed substantive humanitarian norms applicable to internal conflict. Since international humanitarian law applicable in internal conflict generally applies to all parties to the conflict, including armed opposition groups, it is reasonable to assume that the law as developed by the criminal tribunals also applies to armed opposition groups. The relevance of the jurisprudence of the Yugoslavia and Rwanda Tribunals is also evidenced by the fact that, in their analysis of the law applicable to internal conflict, these tribunals have often referred to agreements concluded by, and the conduct of, armed opposition groups.[37]

While the customary law status of Common Article 3 is generally of limited relevance because of the universal acceptance of the Geneva Conventions *qua* binding treaties,[38] this is different with regard to Protocol II. With 150 States Parties,[39] the customary law status of the rules contained in the Protocol is important with regard to armed opposition groups operating in the territory of states that have not ratified the Protocol.

There is ample evidence that various articles of Protocol II constitute customary law. Thus, in the *Tadić* appeal case, the Yugoslavia Tribunal considered: 'Many provisions of this Protocol can now be regarded as declaratory of existing rules or as having crystallised emerging rules of customary law or else as having been strongly instrumental in their evolution as general principles'.[40] The Tribunal did not specify which

---

[37] Also, the fact that other international bodies have taken the jurisprudence of these criminal tribunals as a guide for the international accountability of armed opposition groups indicates the relevance of this practice to the law applicable to armed opposition groups, Inter-American Commission on Human Rights, Third Report on the Situation of Human Rights in Colombia, above, n. 8, at 82, para. 39

[38] In the *Nicaragua* case the customary law status was relevant because the 'multilateral treaty reservation' of the United States might have precluded the International Court of Justice from considering the applicability of the 1949 Geneva Conventions, above, n. 3. For the Yugoslavia Tribunal the customary law status of Common Article 3 also has practical importance because the principle of *nullum crimen sine lege* requires that the tribunal only applies rules of international humanitarian law which are beyond any doubt part of customary law, *Tadić Interlocutory Appeal*, above, n. 35, para. 143, and Report of the UN Secretary-General Pursuant to Paragraph 2 of Security Council Resolution 808 (1993), S/25704, para. 34 (3 May 1993) (hereafter, 1993 Report of the UN Secretary-General); see further T. Meron, 'The Geneva Conventions as Customary Law' (1987) 81 *AJIL* 348, 361 (discussing the additional reasons for the relevance of the customary law status of the Geneva Conventions) (hereafter, 'Geneva Conventions as Customary Law').

[39] www.icrc.org (visited, 1 January 2001).

[40] *Tadić Interlocutory Appeal*, above, n. 35, para. 117; see also *ibid.*, para. 98; *Prosecutor v. Dario Kordić, Mario Cerkez*, Decision on the Joint Defence Motion to Dismiss the Amended Indictment for Lack of Jurisdiction Based on the Limited Jurisdictional

provisions of Protocol II it considered to be customary law. On closer analysis, it appears that the Tribunal particularly referred to the norms in the Protocol which overlap with Common Article 3, and which the Tribunal for that reason considered to be customary law.[41] These norms include Article 4(2) of Protocol II, providing fundamental guarantees to persons taking no active part in the hostilities. The Tribunal possibly also regarded Articles 5 and 6 of Protocol II as customary law, as these norms are also reflected in Common Article 3. These articles prescribe humane treatment of persons whose liberty has been restricted and provide rules on penal prosecution. In *Prosecutor v. Kordić and Others*, the Yugoslavia Tribunal extended the list of customary law provisions with Article 13(2) of Protocol II, concerning unlawful attacks on civilians.[42] The Inter-American Commission, in its Third Report on the Situation of Human Rights in Colombia, considered Articles 4(2) and 13 of Protocol II to reflect customary law.[43] In addition, the Commission identified as customary law the prohibition of recruitment of children under the age of fifteen or allowing them to take part in the hostilities, prohibition of starvation of civilians as a method of combat, attacks against cultural objects and places of worship and forced movement of civilians, rules which are laid down in Articles 4(3), 14, 16 and 17 of Protocol II, respectively.[44]

The Rwanda Tribunal took a more cautious position as to the customary law status of Protocol II. In *Prosecutor v. Jean-Paul Akayesu*, the Tribunal, following the UN Secretary-General, found that Article 4(2) of Protocol II reflects custom. However, it did not recognize the Protocol as a whole to be customary law:

As aforesaid, Protocol II as a whole was not deemed by the Secretary-General to have been universally recognized as part of customary international law ... Whilst the Chamber is very much of the same view as pertains to Protocol II as a whole, it should be recalled that the relevant Article in the context of the ICTR is Article 4(2) (Fundamental Guarantees) of Protocol II. All of the guarantees, as enumerated in Article 4 reaffirm and supplement Common Article 3 and, as discussed above, Common Article 3 being customary in nature, the Chamber is of the opinion that these guarantees did also at the time of the events alleged in the Indictment form part of existing international customary law.[45]

Reach of Articles 2 and 3, No. IT-95-14/2-PT, para. 30 (2 March 1999) ('while both Protocols [I and II] have not yet achieved the near universal participation enjoyed by the Geneva Conventions, it is not controversial that major parts of both Protocols reflect customary law') (hereafter, *Kordić* case).
[41] *Tadić Interlocutory Appeal*, above, n. 35, para. 117.   [42] Above, n. 40, para. 31.
[43] Above, n. 8, at 83, para. 42, and at 94–5, para. 82.   [44] *Ibid.*
[45] Above, n. 6, paras. 609–10 (footnotes omitted).

However, the viewpoint of the Rwanda Tribunal is isolated in international practice.

Attention should also be paid to the practice of the UN Commission on Human Rights. The Commission applied Protocol II to armed opposition groups operating in states that have not ratified the Protocol. For example, in resolution 1993/66, the Commission urged 'all the Afghan parties' 'to respect accepted humanitarian rules, as set out in the Geneva Conventions of 12 August 1949 and the Additional Protocols thereto of 1977'.[46] Afghanistan has not accepted Protocol II as binding upon it. The reference to the 'accepted humanitarian rules' may suggest that the Commission regards Protocol II in its entirety as reflecting customary law.[47] In any case, this and other resolutions of the Commission point towards a development of international humanitarian law, so that, in the course of time, international bodies may regard the entire Protocol II as having acquired the status of customary law.

Finally, a brief remark on how international bodies consider the customary law examined above to be made and changed is in order. Tribunals that have addressed the issue of customary humanitarian law have generally taken a rather liberal approach in this matter. More particularly, they have tended to avoid the difficult question of state practice, concentrating primarily on *opinio iuris*.[48] The Yugoslavia Tribunal affirms this trend:

Before pointing to some principles and rules of customary law that have emerged in the international community for the purpose of regulating civil strife, a word of caution on the law-making process in the law of armed conflict is necessary. When attempting to ascertain State practice with a view to establishing the existence of a customary rule or a general principle, it is difficult, if not impossible, to pinpoint the actual behaviour of the troops in the field for the purpose of establishing whether they in fact comply with, or disregard, certain standards of behaviour. This examination is rendered extremely difficult by the fact that not only is access to the theatre of military operations normally refused to independent observers (often even to the ICRC) but information on the actual conduct of hostilities is withheld by the parties to the conflict; what is worse,

---

[46] Para. 6 (10 March 1993).
[47] See also UN Commission on Human Rights, Res. 1998/67, para. 6 (21 April 1998) (on Sudan) (calling on all parties to the hostilities to respect Common Article 3 and the Additional Protocols). The Commission on Human Rights' Special Rapporteur for Sudan, Gáspár Bíró, recommended that the Government sign Protocol II, E/CN.4/1995/58, para. 63(c) (30 January 1995). The Commission referred to the '*applicable* provisions of international humanitarian law' (emphasis added), which included Protocol II.
[48] T. Meron, 'Geneva Conventions as Customary Law', above, n. 38, at 361.

often recourse is had to misinformation with a view to misleading the enemy as well as public opinion and foreign Governments. In appraising the formation of customary rules or general principles one should therefore be aware that, on account of the inherent nature of this subject-matter, reliance must primarily be placed on such elements as official pronouncements of States, military manuals and judicial decisions.[49]

In effect, the Tribunal considered not only official pronouncements of states, military manuals and judicial decisions relevant to the formation of customary law, but also resolutions of the UN General Assembly and the UN Security Council.

The Tribunal's assertion that, because of the 'inherent nature of the subject-matter', the formation of customary humanitarian law is different from the formation of customary law in other fields of international law, should be questioned. The peculiarity of international humanitarian law would lie, according to the Tribunal, in the fact that soldiers withhold information on the military conduct so that the Tribunal is unable to determine the actual behaviour of the troops in the field. In view of the numerous detailed reports on internal conflicts produced by non-governmental organizations such as Amnesty International and Human Rights Watch, as well as extensive media services, giving detailed accounts of the events in today's armed conflicts, this statement should be questioned. Rather the peculiarity of international humanitarian law seems to lie in the gap that exists between the actual behaviour on site and the behaviour prescribed by international legal standards. This discrepancy between the actual and the prescribed conduct forced Kalshoven to express his 'misgivings about the notion of customary law of armed conflict and about the frequency and occasional lightheartedness [with which] the phrase is currently used'.[50]

I do not intend to examine in detail all the problems relating to the making of customary humanitarian law. An extensive literature has already been devoted to these problems.[51] Suffice it to say that

---

[49] *Tadić Interlocutory Appeal*, above, n. 35, para. 99. See also Yugoslavia Tribunal *Prosecutor v. Kupreskić et al.*, Case No. IT-95-16-T, para. 527 (14 January 2000) (hereafter, *Kupreskić* case (2000)) ('Principles of international humanitarian law may emerge through a customary process under the pressure of the demands of humanity or the dictates of public conscience, even when State practice is scant or inconsistent').

[50] F. Kalshoven, 'Development of Customary Law of Armed Conflict' (Asser Colloquium, 27 November 1998) p. 1 (on file with author).

[51] T. Meron, 'Geneva Conventions as Customary Law', above, n. 38; T. Meron, 'Is International Law Moving Towards Criminalization?' (1998) 9 *EJIL* 18, 28-30 (hereafter, 'Criminalization').

the Tribunal's approach to identifying customary law, relying mainly on *opinio iuris* and largely disregarding actual practice, does not differ from that taken by other courts and tribunals. Further, the primary role international bodies play in articulating *opinio iuris* fits in with the current trend that the practice of international bodies is becoming increasingly important at the expense of the actual practice of states.[52]

Related to the question how customary law is made and changed is the question how international bodies disentangle customary law from treaty obligations. It is difficult, if not impossible, to distinguish Common Article 3 as customary from these norms as treaty law and to separately determine customary law as to its content. This is so because 188 states have ratified the Geneva Conventions. This may have been the problem Judge Sir Robert Jennings hinted at when he questioned, in his dissenting opinion on the *Nicaragua* case, the customary law status of Common Article 3.[53] The problem with identifying practice, which is not, or not only, based on treaties, is also prevalent in the practice of the Yugoslavia Tribunal. In the *Celebici* case, the Yugoslavia Tribunal recognized this problem:

The evidence of the existence of such customary law – State practice and *opinio juris* – may, in some situations, be extremely difficult to ascertain, particularly where there exists a prior multilateral treaty which has been adopted by the vast majority of States. The evidence of State practice outside of the treaty, providing evidence of separate customary norms or the passage of the conventional norms into the realms of custom, is rendered increasingly elusive, for it would appear that only the practice of non-parties to the treaty can be considered as relevant. Such is the position of the four Geneva Conventions, which have been ratified or acceded to by most States. Despite these difficulties, international tribunals do, on occasion, find that custom exists alongside conventional law, both having the same substantive content.[54]

---

[52] T. Meron, 'Criminalization', above, n. 51, at 28.

[53] Above, n. 3, at 537 (Jennings, J., dissenting) ('there must be at least very serious doubts whether those conventions [the 1949 Geneva Conventions] could be regarded as embodying customary law. Even the Court's view that the Common Article 3, laying down a 'minimum yardstick' (para. 218) for armed conflicts of a non-international character, is applicable as 'elementary considerations of humanity' is not a matter free from difficulty). It was also the problem of separating customary law from treaty law that compelled Meron to argue that 'it cannot be said that the Court has succeeded in clarifying the status of the Geneva Conventions as customary law', T. Meron, 'Geneva Conventions as Customary Law', above, n. 38, at 358.

[54] *Prosecutor v. Zejnil Delalic, Zdravko Mucic, Hazim Delic, Esad Landzo*, No. IT-96-21-T, paras. 302–3 (16 November 1998) (hereafter, *Celebici* case).

The Trial Chamber did thus not consider the difficulty of separate identification of customary law to be prohibitive for its finding of customary law. At the same time, it failed to indicate how it circumvents this difficulty. The problem of disentanglement raises pertinent questions as to the reality of customary law identified by international bodies. Consider the following example, which provided, according to the Yugoslavia Tribunal, evidence of the customary law status of Common Article 3 and Protocol II:

> A more recent instance of this tendency [of the formation of customary law for internal armed conflicts] can be found in the stand taken in 1988 by the rebels (the FMLN) in El Salvador, when it became clear that the Government was not ready to apply the Protocol II it had previously ratified. The FMLN undertook to respect both Common Article 3 and Protocol II: 'The FMLN shall ensure that its combat methods comply with the provisions of Common Article 3 of the Geneva Conventions and Protocol II, take into consideration the needs of the majority of the population, and defend their fundamental freedoms.'[55]

However, it can be questioned whether FMLN practice evidences customary law. Because this group was also bound by Common Article 3 and Protocol II *qua* treaty law, this practice could just as well involve the application of treaty law.[56] The fact that El Salvador refused to apply Protocol II does not affect the obligations of the FMLN under this Protocol, since the applicability of these norms does not depend on reciprocity.[57]

A similar problem exists with the suggestion of the Yugoslavia Tribunal that the conclusion of special agreements by parties to an internal conflict, bringing into force articles of the Geneva Conventions other than Common Article 3, would evidence the customary law status of these articles. Common Article 3 expressly provides for the possibility to extend the applicable law to other provisions of the four Geneva Conventions through the conclusion of agreements. In consequence, it is difficult to establish whether a particular agreement to apply the remainder of the Geneva Conventions evidences the customary law status of these articles or merely shows the application of treaty law.[58]

---

[55] *Tadić Interlocutory Appeal*, above, n. 35, para. 107 (FMLN, La legitimidad de nuestros metodos de lucha, ecretaria de promocion y proteccion de lo Derechos Humanos del FMLN, El Salvador, 10 October 1988, at 89) (unofficial translation).

[56] Several international bodies have indicated that the armed conflict between El Salvador and FMLN fulfilled the criteria for applicability of Protocol II.

[57] *Commentary 4th Geneva Convention*, above, n. 9, p. 37.

[58] *Tadić Interlocutory Appeal*, above, n. 35, para. 103.

Origin of the obligations of armed groups under customary law

The question of the origin of the obligations of armed opposition groups under customary law needs to be addressed. This is similar to the question posed earlier with regard to the obligations of armed opposition groups under inter-state treaties. Do armed opposition groups derive their obligations through the state on whose territory they are established or is their consent to these norms necessary in order for the norms to be binding upon them?

Article 38 of the Statute of the International Court of Justice states that the Court will apply 'evidence of a general practice accepted as law'. This article does not state that 'general practice' must concern state practice that is accepted by states as law. While there is no evidence of the International Court applying rules based on practice of armed opposition groups,[59] there is such evidence in the practice of the Yugoslavia Tribunal. In the *Tadić* appeal case, the Tribunal considered the behaviour of insurgents as 'instrumental in bringing about the formation of customary rules'.[60] Accordingly, in order to identify the customary norms applicable in internal conflict, it reviewed the practice of FMLN engaged in the conflict in El Salvador.[61] Similarly, the Tribunal considered agreements concluded by armed opposition groups to be evidence of customary law.[62] Thus, although the practice is still limited, there is some evidence that the consent of armed opposition groups is relevant for their obligations under international customary law.

Other rules of humanitarian law

Multilateral treaties

Three humanitarian treaties, other than the Geneva Conventions and Protocol II, apply to armed opposition groups: Amended Protocol II on Prohibitions or Restrictions on the Use of Mines, Booby-Traps and Other Devices to the Conventional Weapons Convention, of 3 May 1996;

---

[59] In its Advisory Opinion on Nuclear Weapons, the Court decided that the substance of customary law must be 'looked for primarily in the actual practice and *opinio iuris* of States', above, n. 34, para. 64; R. Jennings, A. Watts, *Oppenheim's International Law* (Longman, London, 9th edn., 1996) p. 26 (stating that 'the substance of this source of international law is to be found in the practice of states') (hereafter, *Oppenheim*).
[60] *Tadić Interlocutory Appeal*, above, n. 35, para. 108.   [61] *Ibid.*, para. 107.
[62] *Ibid.*, para. 103.

the 1954 Cultural Property Convention; and the Second Protocol to the Cultural Property Convention of 26 March 1999 (not yet in force).

Article 1 of Amended Protocol II to the Conventional Weapons Convention provides that the Protocol applies to situations referred to in Common Article 3 and that each party to the conflict is bound by it. It expands Protocol II to the 1980 Conventional Weapons Convention, which does not apply to armed opposition groups.[63] Amended Protocol II has not yet been applied by international bodies. The Protocol, however, codifies the long-standing view of international bodies, that armed opposition groups are prohibited from using landmines against civilians. Section 2 of the next chapter (on the substantive obligations of armed opposition groups) examines this prohibition in more detail.[64]

The Cultural Property Convention extends its core article to armed opposition groups. Article 19(1) requires armed opposition to implement the rules 'which relate to respect for cultural property'.[65] In the *Tadić*

---

[63] Article 1 of the 1980 Conventional Weapons Convention provides that the annexed Protocols shall apply to situations referred to in Article 2 common to the 1949 Geneva Conventions, including situations referred to in Article 1(4) of Additional Protocol I.

[64] Another recent treaty on the use of land mines, the Ottawa Convention on Prohibition of the Use of Anti-Personnel Mines of 18 September 1997, does not apply to armed opposition groups. This is noteworthy since this treaty is meant to apply specifically during internal armed conflicts. With the formulation that states shall 'never under any circumstances' use, develop, produce, acquire, stockpile or transfer anti-personnel mines, states secured the application of the Convention to internal conflicts, but circumvented its applicability to armed opposition groups. The treaty has been criticized for this, S. D. Goose, 'The Ottawa Process and the 1997 Mine Ban Treaty' (1998) 1 *YIHL* 269, 289; the International Campaign to Ban Landmines (ICBL) intends to press governments to improve the treaty on this point during the Annual Meetings of States Parties, the Review Conference and any Amendment Conference, *ibid*. An explanation for this omission may be that the Ottawa Convention has been negotiated by experts in the field of arms control rather than humanitarian law experts.

[65] While it is not entirely clear which rules are referred to, as a minimum it would seem that armed opposition groups are bound by Article 4 of the Convention, which provides: '1. The High Contracting Parties undertake to respect cultural property situated within their own territory as well as within the territory of other High Contracting Parties by refraining from any use of the property and its immediate surroundings or of the appliances in use for its protection for purposes which are likely to expose it to destruction or damage in the event of armed conflict; and by refraining from any act of hostility directed against such property. 2. The obligations mentioned in paragraph I of the present Article may be waived only in cases where military necessity imperatively requires such a waiver. 3. The High Contracting Parties further undertake to prohibit, prevent and, if necessary, put a stop to any form of theft, pillage or misappropriation of, and any acts of vandalism directed against, cultural property. They shall refrain from requisitioning movable cultural property situated in the territory of another High Contracting Party. 4. They shall refrain from any act directed by way of reprisals against cultural property. 5. No High Contracting

appeal case, the Yugoslavia Tribunal affirmed that this convention applies to internal armed conflicts.[66] However, otherwise, there is little practice applying the Cultural Property Convention to armed opposition groups.

The Second Protocol to the Cultural Property Convention, which aims to reinforce and supplement the Convention, applies in its entirety to armed opposition groups.[67] The Protocol refrained, however, from explicitly referring to armed opposition groups. While there is no doubt that armed opposition groups are bound by the rules in the Protocol, the absence of any reference to these groups reveals the trouble states had with the idea of armed opposition groups as bearers of international obligations. As said, this Protocol has not yet entered into force. It remains to be seen whether it will change the silence that has prevailed in international practice on the accountability of armed opposition groups for violations of norms relating to cultural property.

Special agreements

As explained earlier, special agreements concluded by armed opposition groups are another source of humanitarian obligations of these groups. These agreements are particularly important. Unlike multilateral treaties and customary law, the norms of which generally apply to armed opposition groups through the territorial state, the norms contained in special agreements have been explicitly consented to by them. This may contribute to greater willingness of armed opposition groups to comply with these norms. While by no means trying to provide a complete picture, I will touch upon some main points concerning international practice on special agreements.

Common Article 3 recognizes the legal capacity of armed opposition groups to conclude agreements, stipulating: 'The Parties to the conflict should further endeavour to bring into force, by means of special agreements, all or part of the other provisions of the present

---

Party may evade the obligations incumbent upon it under the present Article, in respect of another High Contracting Party, by reason of the fact that the latter has not applied the measures of safeguard referred to in Article 3', see below, Chapter 2, Section 2.

[66] *Tadić Interlocutory Appeal*, above, n. 35, para. 98; see also C. Greenwood, 'International Humanitarian Law' in F. Kalshoven (ed.), *The Centennial of the First International Peace Conference* (Kluwer Law International, Netherlands, 2000) pp. 161, 237, n. 138 (hereafter, 'International Humanitarian Law').

[67] Article 22.

Convention.'[68] This article does thus not contain a legal obligation to conclude agreements. It only encourages the parties to the conflict to conclude agreements supplementing this article.[69]

Common Article 3 does not state with whom armed opposition groups should conclude agreements. An obvious option would be with the territorial state or other armed opposition groups, possibly with the co-operation of third states or international organizations. Further, armed opposition groups may also commit themselves to the ICRC or international organizations.

As far as the substantive norms are concerned, there are two types of agreement. First, there are agreements that restate the norms of Common Article 3 and Protocol II, which are already applicable to armed opposition groups as treaty law. This category of agreement has been addressed in the previous section. As it does not raise specific legal problems, it will not be discussed here further. A second type of agreement, to which Common Article 3 refers and with which I am concerned here, extends the law applicable to armed opposition groups to humanitarian rules other than Common Article 3, which were originally applicable only to international conflicts. This type of agreement can bring into force rules of the Geneva Conventions and Additional Protocols I and II. An example is provided by the agreement concluded by the Afghan opposition groups, who agreed to apply the principles of the Third Geneva Convention relative to the Treatment of Prisoners of War.[70]

The Yugoslavia Tribunal affirmed that agreements constitute evidence of legal obligations of the parties to an armed conflict. In the *Tadić* appeal case, in the section entitled 'May The International Tribunal Also Apply International Agreements Binding Upon The Conflicting Parties?', the Tribunal considered that it was authorized to apply, in addition to customary international law, any treaty which: '(i) was unquestionably binding on the parties at the time of the alleged offence; and (ii) was not in conflict with or derogated from peremptory norms of international

---

[68] Para. 2, 3rd sentence.
[69] *Commentary 4th Geneva Convention*, above, n. 9, p. 42 ('legally ... the Parties to the conflict are bound to observe Article 3 and may ignore all the other Articles'). At the same time, the ICRC (International Committee of the Red Cross) commentary adds that the words 'should further endeavour' indicate that the conclusion of agreements is not merely a 'convenient possibility' but points out an obligation 'to try to bring about' the application of the remaining articles of the Geneva Conventions. Kalshoven points out that the conclusion of such agreements is more likely in conflicts resembling international armed conflicts, *Constraints*, above, n. 10, p. 60.
[70] 1985 Report of the Special Rapporteur on Afghanistan, above, n. 5, paras. 104, 163.

law'.[71] At the time the Appeals Chamber made this statement, it had not decided whether the conflict in the former Yugoslavia was international or internal in nature. It may be inferred that the Tribunal referred to agreements concluded by both states and armed opposition groups.

When evaluating whether an agreement is 'unquestionably binding' upon armed opposition groups, it should be noted that the Vienna Convention on the Law of Treaties is not applicable to agreements concluded by these groups. Article 1 of the Convention stipulates that it applies to treaties between states.[72] The Draft Articles on the Law of Treaties, which were adopted by the International Law Commission in 1962, employed a wider definition of a treaty, namely 'any international agreement... concluded between two or more States or other subjects of international law'.[73] This wording was intended to include *inter alia* the case of armed groups opposing the established authorities in an armed conflict, which may in some circumstances enter into treaties.[74] The phrase was, however, left out in the final version of the Convention.

International agreements outside the scope of the Vienna Convention may nevertheless be binding upon their parties, as the Convention expressly provides.[75] One therefore can legitimately conclude that special agreements concluded by armed opposition groups are binding upon them. This determination is supported by Common Article 3 and the practice of international bodies.

Customary law

The Yugoslavia Tribunal, the Inter-American Commission, and the UN Commission on Human Rights have taken the view that certain rules, other than Common Article 3 and Protocol II, apply, as a matter of customary law, to armed opposition groups in internal conflict. This practice is groundbreaking. Until recently, the general belief was that no customary law existed with regard to internal conflicts.[76] The relevant rules concern primarily the protection of civilians from the conduct of

---

[71] *Tadić Interlocutory Appeal*, above, n. 35, para. 143; compare P. H. Kooijmans, 'The Security Council and Non-State Entities as Parties to Conflicts', in K. Wellens (ed.), *International Law: Theory and Practice* (Kluwer Law International, The Netherlands, 1998) pp. 333, 338 ('insurrectionist movements who are parties to an internationalized peace-agreement or who have committed themselves in such an agreement have legal obligations under international law') (hereafter, 'Non-State Entities as Parties to Conflicts').
[72] Article 2(1)(a).   [73] *ILCYb* 1962, vol. II, p. 161.
[74] *Ibid.*, p. 162, para. 8; see also *ibid.*, p. 164.   [75] Article 3.   [76] Above, n. 30.

hostilities, rules which were traditionally considered to apply only to international conflicts.

In the *Tadić* appeal case, the Yugoslavia Tribunal determined that a corpus of general principles and norms applies to internal conflicts, which has a much greater scope than Common Article 3:

> It cannot be denied that customary rules have developed to govern internal strife. These rules... cover such areas as protection of civilians from hostilities, in particular from indiscriminate attacks, protection of civilian objects, in particular cultural property, protection of all those who do not (or no longer) take active part in hostilities, as well as prohibition of means of warfare proscribed in international armed conflicts and ban of certain methods of conducting hostilities.[77]

The Tribunal founded its statement, *inter alia*, on resolutions of the UN General Assembly and the UN Security Council. It referred to resolution 2444 (1968) on 'Respect for Human Rights in Armed Conflicts', in which the General Assembly determined that basic humanitarian principles on the conduct of hostilities apply 'in all armed conflicts', and must be observed 'by all governmental and other authorities responsible for action in armed conflicts'.[78] The Yugoslavia Tribunal further mentioned General Assembly resolution 2675 (1970), containing 'Basic Principles for the Protection of Civilian Populations in Armed Conflicts', which elaborated on General Assembly resolution 2444.[79] The Yugoslavia Tribunal found these two resolutions to be declaratory of customary law. It also considered that these resolutions stimulated the adoption of treaties progressively developing the humanitarian principles contained therein. Thus, in the view of the Tribunal, these resolutions, apart from reflecting existing law, play a separate role in the development of the law.[80]

In addition to resolutions of the General Assembly, the Tribunal also pointed to Security Council resolutions. It mentioned, *inter alia*, Security Council resolution 993 (1993), on Georgia, in which the Council reaffirmed 'the need for the parties to comply with international humanitarian law'.[81] Because the Security Council in this resolution, as in

---

[77] *Tadić Interlocutory Appeal*, above, n. 35, para. 127; the Yugoslavia Tribunal reaffirmed this decision in the *Celebici* case, above, n. 54, para. 301.

[78] Res. 2444 (XXIII) (19 December 1968), reprinted in D. Schindler, J. Toman, *The Laws of Armed Conflicts* (Sijthoff & Noordhoff, Alphen aan den Rijn, 1981) p. 199 (hereafter, Schindler and Toman, *Laws of Armed Conflicts*).

[79] Res. 2675 (XXV) (9 December 1970), reprinted in Schindler and Toman, *Laws of Armed Conflicts*, above, n. 78, p. 203.

[80] *Tadić Interlocutory Appeal*, above, n. 35, para. 112.   [81] Res. of 12 May 1993, pr.

other resolutions,[82] did not mention Common Article 3 of the Geneva Conventions, but adverted to 'international humanitarian law', the Tribunal found that the Council 'clearly articulat[ed] the view that there exists a *corpus* of general principles and norms on internal armed conflict embracing Common Article 3 but having a much greater scope'.[83] This is a notable interpretation of the term 'international humanitarian law'. The Security Council may not have intended to identify primary sources of the applicable law.[84] Nevertheless, this has not prevented the Yugoslavia Tribunal from interpreting the Council's resolutions as evidence of a broad set of legal norms applicable to armed opposition groups, which goes beyond Common Article 3. The Inter-American Commission embraced the conclusions of the Yugoslavia Tribunal laid out above concerning the state of customary law applicable in internal conflicts. In particular, it affirmed the Tribunal's decision that General Assembly resolutions 2444 (1968) and 2675 (1970) reflect customary law applicable to armed opposition groups in internal conflict.[85]

In addition, the Commission on Human Rights appears to have suggested that Additional Protocol I, which applies *qua* treaty law only to international armed conflicts, may be applied to armed opposition groups in internal conflicts. For instance, in resolution 1987/51 on the internal armed conflict in El Salvador, the Commission expressed its concern at the fact that:

serious and numerous violations of human rights continue to take place in El Salvador owing, *inter alia*, to the non-compliance with the humanitarian rules of war, and therefore requests the Government of El Salvador and *the insurgent forces*

---

[82] The Yugoslavia Tribunal referred also to UN Security Council Res. 788 (1992), para. 5 (19 November 1992) (Liberia); UN Security Council Res. 972 (1995) (13 January 1995) (Liberia); UN Security Council Res. 1001 (1995) (30 June 1995) (Liberia); UN Security Council Res. 794 (1992) (3 December 1992) (Somalia); UN Security Council Res. 814 (1993) (26 March 1993) (Somalia), *Tadić Interlocutory Appeal*, above, n. 35, para. 114.

[83] *Ibid.*, para. 116.

[84] T. C. van Boven, 'Reliance on Norms of Humanitarian Law by United Nations' Organs' in A. J. M. Delissen, G. J. Tanja (eds.), *Humanitarian Law of Armed Conflict – Challenges Ahead* (Martinus Nijhoff, The Hague, 1991) pp. 495, 502 (hereafter, *Challenges Ahead*).

[85] Third Report on the Situation of Human Rights in Colombia, above, n. 8 at 82, para. 39. See also International Institute of Humanitarian Law, 'Règles du droit international humanitaire relatives à la conduite des hostilités dans les conflits armés non internationaux' (XIVth mtg, San Remo, 14 September 1989), reprinted in (1990) 785 *IRRC* 415, 419 (affirming the customary law status of UN General Assembly Res. 2444 (1968) and Res. 2675(1970)). See also F. Kalshoven, *De Positie van de Niet-Bezette Burgerbevolking in een Gewapend Conflict, in het Bijzonder met het Oog op de Massaal Werkende Strijdmiddelen (NBC-Wapens)* (Mededelingen van de Nederlandse Vereniging voor Internationaal Recht No. 61, Kluwer, Deventer, February 1970) pp. 16, 17 (discussing the legal status of UN General Assembly Res. 2444 (1968)).

to adopt measures conducive to the humanization of the conflict by observing scrupulously the Geneva Conventions of 1949 and *the Additional Protocols thereto of 1977*.[86]

In this resolution the Commission refers to the Additional Protocols (in plural) namely Protocols I and II.[87] Maybe this resolution uses imprecise language, which may be a consequence of insufficiently precise knowledge of the Commission. It could also be interpreted as reflecting the Commission's view that the norms enshrined in Additional Protocol I apply as a matter of customary law to internal conflicts. Or, at the least, the resolution indicates the Commission's view that the law is developing in this direction.[88]

Diminishing relevance of the distinction between international and internal conflicts

At this point, some reflections regarding the consequences of the practice examined above for the traditional distinction between international and internal conflicts are in order.

Under existing conventional law the distinction between international and internal conflicts is important because the legal protection of civilians in international conflicts is considerably better than their protection in internal conflicts.[89] In the previous sections, I showed, however, that, according to international practice, treaty and customary norms that traditionally apply only to international conflicts now also govern internal conflicts and armed opposition groups active in such conflicts. With regard to conduct of hostilities, the use of land mines and protection of cultural property, armed opposition groups are under comparable basic constraints as national armed forces. Furthermore, as I will explain in the next chapter, it is common practice for international bodies to read the substantive norms of Protocol I and the Geneva

---

[86] Para. 3 (11 March 1987) (emphasis added); possibly, the Commission was encouraged to apply Additional Protocol I by the fact that FMLN suggested that Additional Protocol I applied to its acts, 1985 Final Report of the Special Representative on El Salvador, above, n. 8, at 34, para. 113.

[87] The Commission adopted similar resolutions on Sudan, see, for example, Res. 1995/77, para. 15 (8 March 1995). Sudan has not ratified Additional Protocol I.

[88] Chapter 4 will show that, apart from direct application, the importance of Additional Protocol I in international practice lies primarily in its indirect application as a standard of interpretation of Common Article 3 and Protocol II.

[89] R. Abi-Saab, 'Humanitarian law and internal conflicts: the evolution of a legal concern', in: A. J. M. Delissen and G. J. Tanja (eds.), *Humanitarian law of armed conflict – challenges ahead* (Martinus Nijhoff, The Hague, 1991) pp. 209, 212.

Conventions into Common Article 3 and Protocol II. Common Article 3 and Protocol II contain few and simple provisions, which are not always suited to the complex realities of internal conflicts. International bodies have therefore resorted to Protocol I and the Geneva Conventions, which serve as a standard of interpretation of Common Article 3 and Protocol II. International practice thus demonstrates a trend to diminish the relevance between the law applicable to international and internal armed conflicts.

The primary argument put forward by international bodies to ground this tendency is that from the perspective of protection of individuals, there is no reason to make a distinction between one and the other type of conflict. So the Yugoslavia Tribunal considered:

> It follows that in the area of armed conflict the distinction between interstate wars and civil wars is losing its value as far as human beings are concerned. Why protect civilians from belligerent violence, or ban rape, torture or the wanton destruction of hospitals, churches, museums or private property, as well as proscribe weapons causing unnecessary suffering when two sovereign States are engaged in war, and yet refrain from enacting the same bans or providing the same protection when armed violence has erupted 'only' within the territory of a sovereign State? If international law, while of course duly safeguarding the legitimate interests of States, must gradually turn to the protection of human beings, it is only natural that the aforementioned dichotomy should gradually lose its weight.[90]

Not only from the perspective of the protection of individuals, but also from the viewpoint of the subjects who must implement the law, is there no good reason for not further reducing the distinction between international and internal conflicts. An internal conflict distinguishes itself from an international conflict in that the parties involved are not exclusively states but also armed opposition groups. The involvement of armed opposition groups in internal conflict, in particular their capability to comply with humanitarian norms for international conflicts, means that there is no reason not to impose similar restraints on them as on national armies. I will explain this below.

First, the legal relevance of the capability of armed opposition groups to comply with such norms should not be overestimated. International bodies have rarely considered such capability to be a relevant factor when applying humanitarian law other than Common Article 3 and Protocol II. As I will explain in Chapter 4 (which deals with the

---

[90] *Tadić Interlocutory Appeal*, above, n. 35, para. 97.

criteria for accountability of armed opposition groups), international bodies have held armed opposition groups passing the threshold for applicability of Common Article 3 accountable under other humanitarian rules; no additional requirements were imposed. Moreover, the ability to comply with the law was not explicitly considered necessary for a national liberation movement to be able to apply the provisions of the Geneva Conventions and Protocol I. For example, national liberation movements are not required to exercise territorial control.[91]

Second, also as a matter of fact, the inability of armed opposition groups to comply with the humanitarian norms, which are traditionally only applicable in international conflicts does not hold true for all armed opposition groups operating in internal conflict. It is true that the organization of armed opposition groups is generally different from that of state armed forces: they are often primarily guerrilla armies with no rigid hierarchical structure, and with separate internal factions.[92] However, the fact that armed opposition groups are organized differently does not necessarily mean that they are not able to comply with the humanitarian standards. The point is that it is generally not known or understood how these entities function and, in consequence, they are easily qualified as chaotic and unorganized.[93] It is also important to distinguish between the possible reluctance by armed opposition groups to comply with the rules and their actual capability to do so. Furthermore, it should be noted that parties to an *international* armed conflict might not be as organized as one might think. As the Yugoslavia Tribunal observed with regard to present-day international conflicts: 'While previously wars were primarily between well-established States, in modern inter-ethnic armed conflicts such as that in the former Yugoslavia, new States are often created during the conflict.'[94]

While there is thus a clear trend in international practice to diminish the distinction between humanitarian law for international as opposed to for internal conflicts, the distinction between these conflicts has not been abolished. The Yugoslavia Tribunal considered:

---

[91] Articles 1(4) and 96(3) Additional Protocol I, although Article 43(1) of Additional Protocol I requires them to be organized, under responsible command and subject to discipline.

[92] For an excellent analysis of the structure, organization and functioning of armed opposition groups, see J-M. Balencie, A. de la Grange, *Mondes Rebelles* (Éditions Michalon, Paris, 1996) vol. II, pp 117–47 (hereafter, *Mondes Rebelles*).

[93] *Ibid.*, at II.

[94] *Prosecutor v. Duško Tadić*, IT-94-1-A, para. 166 (Appeals Chamber, 15 July 1999) (appeal on merits) (hereafter, *Tadić* case (1999, appeal on merits)).

The emergence of the... general rules on internal armed conflicts does not imply that internal strife is regulated by general international law in all its aspects. Two particular limitations may be noted: (i) only a number of rules and principles governing international armed conflicts have gradually been extended to apply to internal conflicts; and (ii) this extension has not taken place in the form of a full and mechanical transplant of those rules to internal conflicts; rather, the general essence of those rules, and not the detailed regulation they may contain, has become applicable to internal conflicts.[95]

There is uncertainty also exactly which rules apply to internal conflicts. Which rules can and should be transplanted to such conflicts is still to be examined.

The strongest argument against the abolition of the distinction seems to lie, however, in the premise underlying the Prisoners of War Convention, where it is maintained that members of armed forces fighting in an international conflict may not be subjected to punishment for the mere act of participating in hostilities.[96] States do not, and presumably will not in the future, accept the application of this principle to armed opposition groups.[97] Their position is reflected in the rule laid down in Common Article 3 stipulating that 'the application of the preceding provisions shall not affect the legal status of the Parties to the conflict'.[98] The aim of this provision is to preclude a claim by armed opposition groups to recognition as belligerents and the application of rules on prisoners of war to them.[99] Thus armed opposition groups cannot, on the basis of Common Article 3, claim immunity from prosecution and punishment when captured by the territorial state for their acts contrary to the laws of the territorial state.[100]

While the position of states is understandable, at the same time, it seriously compromises the effectiveness of international humanitarian law for internal conflicts. As Bond rightly points out, 'the rebel

---

[95] *Tadić Interlocutory Appeal*, above, n. 35, para. 126.
[96] C. Greenwood, 'International Humanitarian Law' above, n. 66, p. 234.
[97] Note, however, that not only armed opposition groups run the risk of being punished for having participated in the hostilities. The same treatment may fall to members of the national forces, during the conflict when they fall in to the hands of armed opposition groups, and after the conflict when the established authorities have lost the conflict and armed opposition groups have taken over power.
[98] Also Article 19(4) of the 1954 Cultural Property Convention; Article 1(6) Amended Protocol II on Prohibitions or Restrictions on the Use of Mines, Booby-Traps and Other Devices.
[99] *Commentary 4th Geneva Convention*, above, n. 9, p. 44.
[100] Inter-American Commission on Human Rights, Third Report on Colombia, above, n. 8, at 77, para. 18.

presently fights in a twilight zone between lawful combatancy and common criminality'.[101]

In this regard, it is noteworthy that international practice indicates that states do not in all cases have to make full use of their authority to punish rebels for mere participation in the conflict. This practice is in conformity with Article 6(5) of Protocol II which provides: 'At the end of the hostilities, the authorities in power shall endeavor to grant the broadest possible amnesty to persons who have participated in the armed conflict, or those deprived of their liberty for reasons related to the conflict, whether they are interned or detained'.[102] Accordingly, the UN Commission on Human Rights welcomed the general amnesty announced by President Kabila on 19 February 2000, under which 200 persons accused, convicted or detained for crimes against the internal or external security of the State of Congo have been released, as a 'timely and significant step towards reconciliation'.[103] Also the peace agreement signed by the warring sides in Sierra Leone's eight-year civil war, in July 1999, granted amnesty to the rebels.[104] The United Nations signed this agreement, entering a reservation to the effect that, for the United Nations, the amnesty could not cover crimes under international law.[105] The Secretary-General, in his report accompanying the Statute for the Sierra Leone Court, recognized that, although amnesty could not be granted in respect of international crimes, 'amnesty is an accepted legal concept and a gesture of peace and reconciliation at the end of a civil war or an internal armed conflict'.[106]

---

[101] J. E. Bond, 'Application of the Law of War to Internal Conflicts' (1973) 3 *Ga. J. Int'l & Comp. L.* 345, 367 (hereafter, 'Internal Conflicts').

[102] See on this article also Chapter 5, Section 2 (The obligation of the state to take action).

[103] Res. 2000/18, para 1f (18 April 2000); compare also, the Special Rapporteur on Afghanistan, in 1985, recommended that: 'Members of all forces engaged in the conflict, those of Governments as well as of the opposition, should be recognized as combatants within the framework of international humanitarian law', 1985 Report of the Special Rapporteur on Afghanistan, above, n. 5, at 50, para. 192.

[104] N. Onishi, 'Foes Agree on Ending Civil War in Sierra Leone' *International Herald Tribune* (8 July 1999) p. 1 (hereafter, 'Civil War in Sierra Leone').

[105] Security Council Res. 1315, pr. (14 August 2000) See below, Chapter 5, Section 2 (The obligation of the state to take action).

[106] UN Secretary-General, S/2000/915 (4 October 2000) (Report of the Secretary-General on the establishment of a Special Court for Sierra Leone) (hereafter, Statute Sierra Leone Court and SG Report on Sierra Leone Court). The Secretary-General referred here to Article 6 of Protocol II. (For the texts of the Statute of the Special Court and the Agreement between the UN and Sierra Leone, see Annex to the Report of the Secretary-General. See also UN Security Council Res. 1315 (14 August 2000)).

Even if members of armed opposition groups are granted some kind of immunity from prosecution for having participated in the conflict,[107] this does not mean that members of these groups need to be classified as prisoners of war.[108] Rather than using existing legal forms that are applicable to combatants fighting in international conflict with all the legal consequences such a status entails, it may be more fruitful to reflect upon whether members of armed opposition groups in internal conflict should be accorded equivalent treatment to some extent.

To summarize, international practice is clearly moving towards decreasing the distinction between the law applicable to parties to international as opposed to internal conflicts. In pursuing this course of action, international bodies should not aim at a full equation between the two types of conflicts. Rather those rules and principles should be adopted which are relevant to the specific context existing in internal conflicts and to the parties to such conflicts, in particular armed opposition groups.

Human rights law

According to their wording, multilateral human rights treaties impose obligations only on the state. Article 2 of the International Covenant on Civil and Political Rights stipulates: '*Each State Party* to the present Covenant undertakes to respect and to ensure to all individuals within its territory and subject to its jurisdiction the rights recognized in

---

[107] Support for the limitation of the state's right to prosecute and punish members of armed opposition groups can also be found in the literature. In view of the fact that the enforcement of international humanitarian law in internal conflicts presents great difficulties, Draper proposed to abolish the execution of death penalties on either side during the conflict, G.I.A.D. Draper, 'The Relationship Between the Human Regime and the Law of Armed Conflict (1971) 1 *Israel YBHR* 191–207, reprinted in *Reflections on Law and Armed Conflicts*, above, n. 2, pp. 125, 139. In the same vein, Plattner has questioned the wisdom of the authority of the state to prosecute and try the authors of violations of international humanitarian law when the conflict is still continuing. She suggested, following a proposal of the ICRC in 1949, authorizing the repression of violations only after the end of the hostilities, D. Plattner, 'Penal Repression', above, n. 1, at 415. She also noted that internal conflicts generally end with a national reconciliation, which includes an amnesty for members of armed opposition groups, *ibid.*, 416–17.

[108] Even if the Prisoners of War Convention were applicable, many members of armed opposition groups may not qualify as prisoners of war. Article 4(A)(2) of the Third Geneva Convention and Article 44(3) of Additional Protocol I list a number of requirements that must be fulfilled in order for a person to qualify as a prisoner of war. Members of armed opposition groups may frequently not qualify for prisoners-of-war status under these conditions.

the present Covenant'.[109] Hence, the Covenant, like the European and American Conventions on Human Rights, does not bind armed opposition groups. However, the impact of armed opposition groups on civilian suffering, both through their own acts and through the acts of the state being challenged by them to resort to ruthless counter-insurgency, as well as the substantive overlap between human rights and international humanitarian law have encouraged international bodies to examine the question whether armed opposition groups are capable of violating human rights standards. International bodies have affirmed that, in principle, human rights treaties do not bind armed opposition groups. Their practice is not entirely consistent, however. Occasionally, these bodies have asserted the applicability of human rights law to armed opposition groups. This section evaluates this practice. It closes with some reflections on the desirability of extending international human rights law to armed opposition groups.

The qualification of particular acts of armed opposition groups as human rights violations must be distinguished from the denunciation of these acts as 'abuses' of human rights. International bodies have often condemned acts of armed opposition groups as harming human rights without considering their acts to be breaches of human rights law. Thus, the Inter-American Commission stated that acts of armed opposition groups 'are detrimental to the exercise of the most important human rights'.[110] The special rapporteurs and chairpersons of working groups of the UN Commission on Human Rights spoke of 'the adverse effects their action [of armed opposition groups] might have on the enjoyment of human rights'.[111] Below, I shall examine the practice imposing a legal *obligation* on armed opposition groups to respect human rights and holding them responsible under human rights law.

Practice denying the applicability of human rights treaties to armed opposition groups

Various bodies, including the Inter-American Commission, the special rapporteurs and working groups of the UN Commission on Human

---

[109] Emphasis added.
[110] Second Report on the Situation of Human Rights in Colombia, OEA/Ser.L/V/II.84, at 213 (1993) (hereafter, Second Report on Colombia).
[111] UN Commission on Human Rights, E/CN.4/1997/3, para. 44 (Report of the Meeting of Special Rapporteurs/Representatives Experts and Chairpersons of Working Groups of the Special Procedures of the Commission on Human Rights and the Advisory Services Programme, 30 September 1996) (hereafter, 1996 Report of the Meeting of Special Rapporteurs).

Rights, and the UN Secretary-General have answered the question whether human rights treaties can be applied to armed opposition groups negatively. The principal reason is that human rights regulate the relationship between the government and the governed and aim to check the exercise of state power.

In 1990, pursuant to a resolution of the General Assembly of the Organization of American States,[112] the Inter-American Commission examined whether armed opposition groups can violate the rights laid down in the American Convention on Human Rights. To this end, the Commission looked back at the origin of the human rights concept and how it materialized in the American Convention. It considered:

The concept of human rights is often used to refer to acts that adversely affect the exercise of individual rights. In a very broad sense, the fundamental rights of a person, individual rights and human rights would seem to be synonymous: anything related to the attributes of the person is a right and, by extension, a human right. This idea is so sweeping, however, that the element of specificity is lost.[113]

The Commission did not agree with such a broad concept of human rights, including anything that benefited the human person. In particular, the Commission considered the state to be an essential element of the human rights concept. It is worth looking at the Commission's view in length:

In the case of the standards of international law that govern the international obligation of States in the matter of human rights, the type of juridical relationship that the respective rules formalize is a specific one. Here it should be noted that the individual rights or rights of the person are those recognized in the constitutions of the States as those attributes of the person that the State has the duty to protect by reaffirming them when they are in danger of being violated or by establishing some type of compensation when the violation has already been committed. This is the classic notion of the role of the State as an organ charged with protecting the individual vis-à-vis the actions of other individuals or groups. The situations that arose in Europe between the two world wars dramatically demonstrate the need to develop a system that contemplates those situations in which the State, whose function is to protect the individual, becomes his assailant. When it comes to the State, the individual is defenseless because he lacks the means to protect himself. This is where the rights of

---

[112] AG/RES.1043 (XX-0/90) para. 3, reprinted in *Inter-American Yearbook on Human Rights 1990*, at 354 (recommending the Inter-American Commission that 'in reporting on the status of human rights in the American states, it include reference to the action of irregular armed groups in such states').

[113] *Inter-American Yearbook on Human Rights 1990*, at 356.

the individual acquire an added dimension that puts them above the rights of States and makes the individual a subject under international law. Thus, his individual rights can be protected by the international community, organized and juridically regulated by means of treaties. This is the substance of the legal contract between the individual and the State that is formalized in the concept of human rights. This is the underlying principle of the international legal instruments on human rights. The American Convention concerns the duties of States vis-à-vis the rights and freedoms of persons, the full and free exercise of which they must not only respect but also guarantee. The entire system for protecting human rights is designed on the basis of the State's acknowledgment of itself as a party to a fundamental legal contract on the matter of human rights and it is against the State that complaints alleging violation of the rights upheld in the Convention are brought.[114]

The Commission thus put forward two arguments to support its view that the scope of the American Convention should be limited to states. First, the state has formally accepted human rights treaties as binding upon it and it has agreed that complaints can be brought against it. The second, more substantive, argument is that human rights treaties aim to regulate the relationship between the government and the governed. Both arguments exclude the application of human rights treaties to armed opposition groups. These groups have not ratified human rights treaties, nor are they able to do so. Furthermore, the relationship between armed opposition groups and the individuals to be protected can generally not be equated with a relationship between the government and governed, although there may be some analogous characteristics. The Inter-American Commission found that bringing acts of armed groups under the American Convention would mean expanding the concept of human rights, and found that it was the states' responsibility to decide whether such an expansion were desirable.[115] The Commission recently affirmed this viewpoint in its Third Report on Colombia, where it stated that the American Convention on Human Rights generally applies only to the state and that 'international humanitarian law provides the only legal standard for analysing the activities of armed dissident groups'.[116] Thus, in the Commission's view, a distinction must be made in this regard between human rights law and international humanitarian law.

In 1996, the special rapporteurs and working groups of the UN Commission on Human Rights, pursuant to a resolution of the

---

[114] Ibid., 356, 358.   [115] Ibid., 370.
[116] Third Report on the Situation of Human Rights in Colombia, above, n. 8, at 75-6, paras. 13-14; see also Inter-American Commission, *Tablada* case, above, n. 4, para 174.

Commission,[117] convened in a special meeting to discuss 'the problem of the relationship between terrorist activities and human rights in the context of participants' mandates'.[118] They disapproved of the application of human rights treaties to armed opposition groups:

> It was recognized that States were accountable for human rights violations because they had undertaken obligations to respect such rights and to guarantee their enjoyment and exercise to any person within their jurisdiction. It was also recognized that if ever a state of belligerency existed, namely a civil war, Protocol II additional to the Geneva Conventions, relating to the protection of victims of non-international armed conflicts should apply, as well as Common Article 3 of the Conventions. In such cases, international humanitarian law imposed obligations that to some extent were similar to those embodied in international human rights treaties. However, parties bound by international humanitarian law were not necessarily in a position to become parties of international human rights treaties.[119]

Thus, like the Inter-American Commission, the rapporteurs and working groups considered that armed opposition groups were not bound by human rights treaties, because they were not parties to these treaties, nor should they become so. Further, like the Inter-American Commission, the meeting noted that human rights law is distinct from international humanitarian law. The fact that armed opposition groups are bound by Common Article 3 and Protocol II does not imply that they can also be bound by human rights treaties.[120] Moreover, the meeting observed that, because they are bound by humanitarian standards, it may not be necessary to extend human rights treaties to them. In conformity with this standpoint, the special rapporteurs to the UN Commission have in their reports generally avoided characterizing armed opposition groups as human rights violators.[121]

Finally, the UN Secretary-General, in his 1998 report on Minimum Humanitarian Standards to the UN Commission on Human Rights,

---

[117] Res. 1996/47, para. 6 (19 April 1996) (urging 'all thematic special rapporteurs and working groups to address as appropriate the consequences of the acts, methods and practices of terrorist groups in their forthcoming reports to the Commission').
[118] 1996 Report of the Meeting of Special Rapporteurs, above, n. 111.
[119] Ibid., para. 46.   [120] Ibid., paras. 46–7.
[121] See, e.g., UN Commission on Human Rights, E/CN.4/1994/48, para. 121 (Special Rapporteur for Sudan, Gáspár Bíró, 1 February 1994) (concluding that the Government had committed human rights violations, while members of the SPLA factions had committed abuses); 1994 Report of the Special Rapporteur on Torture, above, n. 13, para. 13; UN Commission on Human Rights, E/CN.4/1991/36, para. 593 (Report of the Special Rapporteur on Extrajudicial, Summary or Arbitrary Executions, S. A. Wako, 3 February 1991).

analysed whether armed opposition groups were or should be bound by multilateral human rights treaties.[122] His final conclusion corresponds with the conclusion of the Inter-American Commission and the rapporteurs and working groups to the UN Commission on Human Rights, in that he considers human rights treaties to be restricted to states.[123] Nevertheless, unlike the Inter-American Commission and the rapporteurs and working groups, the Secretary-General does not categorically exclude extension of these treaties to armed opposition groups in the future. He proposed several arguments that he believed could support extension of the applicability of human rights to armed opposition groups:

This conception of human rights [applicable only to the state] (while dominant, and rightly so given the scale of violations of human rights by Governments) has never provided a fully adequate description of the scope of international human rights concern. The Universal Declaration of Human Rights, as well as the two International Covenants, in their preambular paragraphs recognize duties on individuals to promote respect for human rights. The two Covenants include this statement in their preambles: '*Realizing* that the individual, having duties to other individuals and to the community to which he belongs, is under a responsibility to strive for the promotion and observance of the rights recognized in the present Covenant.' Such references clearly indicate the responsibility of individuals to *promote* human rights, although it is not clear whether that includes legal obligations regarding human rights violations.[124]

While this argument is a useful starting-point when exploring possible human rights obligations of armed opposition groups, its strength should not be overestimated. It is doubtful, as the Secretary-General already suggested, whether preambular paragraph 5 common to both International Human Rights Covenants imposes on armed opposition groups the human rights norms stipulated in the Covenants.[125] It calls upon individuals to *strive* for the promotion and observance of human rights, rather than obliging them to do so.[126] Furthermore, it deals with

---

[122] UN Secretary-General 1998 Report on Minimum Humanitarian Standards, above, n. 13.
[123] *Ibid.*, paras. 59–61. [124] *Ibid.*, paras. 62–3.
[125] Article 29 of the Universal Declaration of Human Rights contains a provision comparable to preambular paragraph 5 of the two Covenants. In Res. 1991/29 pr. (5 March 1991) on 'Consequences on the Enjoyment of Human Rights of Acts of Violence Committed by Armed Groups that Spread Terror Among the Population and by Drug Traffickers' the UN Commission on Human Rights referred to this norm enshrined in the Covenants.
[126] N. S. Rodley, 'Can Armed Opposition Groups Violate Human Rights Standards?', in K. H. Mahoney, P. Mahoney, (eds.), *Human Rights in the Twenty-First Century* (Martinus Nijhoff, The Hague, 1993), p. 307 (hereafter, 'Armed Opposition Groups'). Rodley has

individuals rather than groups. The latter comment also applies to the Secretary-General's second argument:

> The very first United Nations-sponsored human rights treaty, the Convention on the Prevention and Punishment of the Crime of Genocide, clearly applied to 'constitutionally responsible rulers, public officials or *private individuals*'. More recently, resolutions adopted on 'Human rights and terrorism' in the Sub-Commission and Commission on Human Rights have expressed concern about the 'gross violations of human rights perpetrated by terrorist groups'. Also relevant is the fact that certain acts committed by individuals can attract international criminal responsibility regardless of whether the individual acts on behalf of a State or not. These include acts which violate human rights law. The crime of genocide, noted above, is an example, but it is just one of several crimes against humanity which can be committed by non-State agents.[127]

Crimes under international law create responsibility of *individuals* and not of armed opposition *groups*. As will be discussed in Chapter 3, the criminalization of acts committed by members and leaders of armed opposition groups is an appropriate way of regulating the behaviour of these groups. Nevertheless, armed opposition groups and their individual members are different subjects in international law.[128]

In spite of the fact that the UN Secretary-General regarded the International Covenants and international criminal law standards as providing some support for the extension of human rights treaties to armed opposition groups, he refrained from concluding that they in fact have obligations under human rights treaties. This cautious attitude was in part due to his fear that shifting the attention from state behaviour to the behaviour of the armed groups entailed the risk of undermining

---

examined several other articles of the Universal Declaration, the International Covenant on Civil and Political Rights, and the Convention on the Elimination of All Forms of Racial Discrimination on the question of obligations of armed opposition groups. In particular, he analysed Article 5 of the International Covenant, which virtually repeats Article 30 of the Universal Declaration, stating that 'Nothing in this Declaration may be interpreted as implying for any State, group or person any right to engage in any activity or to perform any act aimed at the destruction of any of the rights and freedoms set forth herein'; Article 20 of the International Covenant prohibiting war propaganda and Article 2(1)(d) and Article 4 of the Convention on the Elimination of Racial Discrimination. He concludes that these provisions do not contain obligations for armed opposition groups, *ibid.*, 305–9.

[127] Above, n. 124 (footnotes omitted, emphasis added).
[128] The same criticism applies to Rodley. In his analysis of possible accountability of armed opposition groups for human rights violations, he mixes group accountability with individual accountability, above, n. 126, at 302, 304.

the achievements of human rights law in protecting individuals from the state:

Clearly, given the divergent views on this issue, and its complexity, further study is needed. It seems beyond doubt that when an armed group kills civilians, arbitrarily expels people from their homes, or otherwise engages in acts of terror or indiscriminate violence, it raises an issue of potential international concern. This will be especially true in countries where the Government has lost the ability to apprehend and punish those who commit such acts. But very serious consequences could follow from a rushed effort to address such acts through the vehicle of existing international human rights law, not least that it might serve to legitimize actions taken against members of such groups in a manner that violates human rights. The development of international human rights law as a means of holding Governments accountable to a common standard has been one of the major achievements of the United Nations. The challenge is to sustain that achievement and at the same time ensure that our conception of human rights remains relevant to the world around us.[129]

The argument, which has also been made by other international bodies,[130] that the characterization of acts committed by armed opposition groups as human rights violations might legitimize human rights violations by the state must, however, be rejected. Unlawful acts by the adverse party do not justify failure on the part of the state to fulfil its obligations under human rights or humanitarian law treaties.[131]

---

[129] UN Secretary-General 1998 Report on Minimum Humanitarian Standards, above, n. 13, para. 64 (footnotes omitted).

[130] See, e.g., 1996 Report of the Meeting of Special Rapporteurs, above, n. 111, para. 44 ('giving terrorist groups the quality of violators of human rights would be dangerous and could amount to a sort of justification of human rights violations by Governments').

[131] No measure of suspension taken by way of reciprocity or of reprisal is admissible under the International Covenant and the European and American Convention. Furthermore, it is a clear rule of international humanitarian law that the prohibition of inhumane treatment or attacks against the civilian population remains valid, even if the adversary has committed breaches, Yugoslavia Tribunal *Kupreskić* case (2000) above, n. 49, paras 517–20; S-S. Junod, *Commentary Additional Protocols,* above, n. 9, p. 1452. *See* also Article 60(5) Vienna Convention on the Law of Treaties stipulating that the rules on termination or suspension of the operation of a treaty as a consequence of its breach do not apply 'to provisions relating to the protection of the human persons contained in treaties of a humanitarian character, in particular provisions prohibiting any form of reprisals against persons protected by such treaties'. Although some difficulties exist as to the scope of this article, it has been claimed to cover both international humanitarian law treaties and human rights treaties, P. Reuter, *Introduction to the Law of Treaties* (Kegan Paul International, London, 1995) pp. 200–1 (hereafter, *Law of Treaties*).

In taking a cautious approach, the Secretary-General has avoided distancing himself from the UN Commission on Human Rights. The Commission's position on the relationship between human rights and armed opposition groups has been ambiguous. Nevertheless, since 1990, when Peru, Colombia, and the Philippines brought the operations of armed opposition groups to its attention, the Commission has been unwilling to explicitly agree that armed opposition groups could directly violate human rights norms.[132] Similarly, when discussing the Secretary-General's aforementioned 1998 report, many states in the Commission objected to his suggestion that there may be the need to move 'beyond the duty of States to respect and ensure the observance of human rights and towards the creation of obligations applicable also to private individuals and other non-State actors including liberation movements and terrorist organizations'.[133] Hence, the Commission's resolution 1998/29 only asked that the Secretary-General, in coordination with the ICRC, continued to study the issues identified in the report and to submit a report to the fifty-fifth session in 1999.[134] In the report submitted pursuant to this request, the Secretary-General adopted a more cautious approach, confining himself to saying that 'some argue that non-State actors should also be held accountable under international human rights law, especially in situations where the State structures no longer exist or where States are unable or unwilling to mete out punishment for crimes committed by non-State actors'.[135]

---

[132] See, e.g., UN Commission on Human Rights, Res. 1990/75, para. 1 (7 March 1990) (referring to the 'adverse effects on the enjoyment of human rights' of acts committed by irregular armed groups); UN Commission on Human Rights, Res. 1991/29, para. 1 (5 March 1991); UN Commission on Human Rights, Res. 1992/42, para. 1 (28 February 1992); UN Commission on Human Rights, Res. 1993/48, para. 1 (9 March 1993); UN Commission on Human Rights, Res. 1993/60, para. 2 (10 March 1993) (urging 'the Government of Sudan to respect fully human rights and calls upon all parties to cooperate in order to ensure such respect').

[133] UN Secretary-General 1998 Report on Minimum Humanitarian Standards, above, n. 13, para. 65 (the Secretary-General cited here an earlier working paper by the Sub-Commission expert K. Koufa on 'Terrorism and Human Rights', E/CN.4/sub.2/1997/28 (26 June 1997)); see M. J. Dennis, 'The Fifty-Fourth Session of the UN Commission on Human Rights' (1999) 93 *AJIL* 246, 248 (reporting the discussion in the Commission).

[134] Para. 5 (17 April 1998), see also UN Commission on Human Rights Res. 1999/65 (28 April 1999) and Res. 2000/69 (27 April 2000). The subsequent report of the Secretary-General on this subject merely lists the different views of governments and non-governmental organizations E/CN.4/2000/94 (27 December 1999).

[135] UN Commission on Human Rights, E/CN.4/1999/92, para. 13 (Report of the Secretary-General on 'Fundamental Standards of Humanity', 18 December 1998)

Practice asserting the applicability of human rights treaties to armed opposition groups

According to the international practice analysed above, armed opposition groups are not parties to multilateral human rights treaties. Furthermore, the Inter-American Commission and the rapporteurs and working groups of the UN Commission on Human Rights found that an expansion of the applicability of human rights treaties to armed opposition groups is not desirable. There is, however, also a tendency in international practice, partly by the same bodies, to challenge this conclusion. Occasionally, the Inter-American Commission, the UN Commission on Human Rights, and the UN Security Council have applied human rights treaties to armed opposition groups.

In its Annual Report 1992–3, the Inter-American Commission observed: 'There has been increasing concern in international and regional human rights organizations with activities that constitute violations of internationally guaranteed human rights by armed groups that operate over a period of time and control, in varying degrees, the territory in which they operate'.[136] Similarly, in a press release of 3 June 1996, the Commission urged a Colombian armed group to respect the life and the personal safety of a person it was holding captive and which it threatened to execute, stating:

The American Convention on Human Rights expressly stipulates, with regard to states of emergency, that the right to life is absolute with no exception of any kind. This protection of the right to life is so important that violations of that right cannot be justified even in reprisal to violations of any kind committed by the other side in a conflict... Whatever the reasons given and regardless of any claims of justice or injustice that the group holding Juan Carlos Gaviria captive may use to explain its actions, kidnapping and taking the life of a defenseless person can never be justified under the rules and principles of international human rights law.[137]

Similarly, as from 1994, the UN Commission on Human Rights adopted various resolutions suggesting that armed opposition groups can violate human rights. The most notable illustrations are the Commission's

---

(hereafter, 1998 Report of the Secretary-General on Fundamental Standards of Humanity).

[136] OEA/Ser.L/V/II.83 Doc.14, corr.1, at 215–16 (12 March 1993) (hereafter, Annual Report 1992–3).

[137] Annual Report of the Inter-American Commission on Human Rights 1996, OEA/Ser.L/V/II.95, Doc. 7, rev., at 818–19 (14 March 1997) (hereafter, Annual Report 1996).

resolutions on 'Human rights and terrorism', where the Commission expressed concern about the 'gross violations of human rights perpetrated by terrorist groups'.[138] In the same vein, the rapporteurs of the UN Commission on Human Rights have occasionally suggested that armed opposition groups can violate human rights law. For example, with regard to the Liberation Tigers of Tamil Eelam (LTTE), the armed opposition group active in the conflict in Sri Lanka, the Special Rapporteur on Extrajudicial, Summary or Arbitrary Executions expressed his concern about:

> the alleged large number of violations of the right to life resulting from military activities in Sri Lanka, especially in the northern peninsula. While he recognizes the difficult circumstances arising from the situation of conflict between the Government and LTTE, he urgently calls upon the parties to the conflict to comply with international humanitarian and *human rights standards*. The Special Rapporteur wishes to reiterate that the right to life is absolute and must be respected even under exceptional circumstances.[139]

Finally, several UN Security Council resolutions show the same tendency. For example, in resolution 1193 (1998), the Council urged 'the Afghan factions' 'to put an end to the discrimination against girls and women and to other violations of human rights... and to adhere to the internationally accepted norms and standards in this sphere'.[140]

This trend in the practice of international bodies to apply human rights norms to armed opposition groups finds support in several unofficial texts not formally agreed to by states: most important has been the Turku Declaration on Minimum Humanitarian Standards.

---

[138] E.g., UN Commission on Human Rights, Res. 1997/42, pr (11 April 1997); UN Commission on Human Rights, Res. 1994/46, pr. (4 March 1994); see also UN Commission on Human Rights, Res. 1990/77, para. 7 (7 March 1990) (expressing its concern 'that the indiscriminate actions by *Frente Farabundo Martí para la Liberación Nacional* [FMLN] in towns and cities... represent serious and unpunished violations of human rights'); UN Commission on Human Rights, Res. 1995/74, para. 12 (8 March 1995) (urging 'all the Afghan parties to ensure respect for the human rights and fundamental freedoms of women in accordance with international human rights instruments').

[139] Special Rapporteur, Bacre Waly Ndiaye, made clear that the first conflict in the Republic of Chechnya was covered by international humanitarian law, UN Commission on Human Rights, E/CN.4/1997/60/Add.1, para. 450 (Report of the Special Rapporteur, 23 December 1996) (emphasis added) (hereafter, 1996 Report of the Special Rapporteur on Extrajudicial, Summary or Arbitrary Executions). See also UN Commission on Human Rights, E/CN.4/1992/17, para. 279 (Special Rapporteur on Torture, N. S. Rodley, 27 December 1991); 1985 Report of the Special Rapporteur on Afghanistan, above, n. 5, para. 184.

[140] Para. 14 (28 August 1998); see also UN Security Council, Res. 1212, para. 7 (3 December 1998) (calling on UNITA [in Angola] to respect international human rights law).

Since the beginning of the 1980s, experts have promoted the idea of developing a set of minimum humanitarian standards to provide a greater protection for human beings, *inter alia*, from armed opposition groups in internal armed conflict. The idea was first put forward by Meron, in 1983. In 1990, a group of experts embodied the idea in the Declaration of Minimum Humanitarian Standards in Turku/Åbo, Finland, also known as the Turku Declaration.[141] In 1994, the UN Sub-Commission on Prevention of Discrimination and Protection of Minorities to the UN Commission on Human Rights transmitted the Declaration for adoption to the UN Commission on Human Rights, which has not happened so far.[142] The Turku Declaration applies in all situations, including internal armed conflict, and applies to 'all persons, groups and authorities'.[143] It draws on both humanitarian and human rights norms. As suggested, one of the main reasons for developing the Declaration was the fact that armed opposition groups are not subjects of human rights treaties, which the drafters considered to be a major inadequacy of the law protecting human beings in internal armed conflict.[144]

Another relevant text is the Guiding Principles on Internal Displacement.[145] These Principles, also written by experts, apply to 'all authorities, groups and persons', in time of peace and war.[146] They include rules of international humanitarian law and human rights law.[147] Like the Turku Declaration, by regulating acts of armed opposition groups, the Guiding Principles intend to fill the gap in human rights law binding only states.[148]

Special agreements

Armed opposition groups may agree to apply human rights norms. An example, which has been mentioned before, is provided by the San José Agreement on Human Rights, concluded between FMLN and

---

[141] Turku Declaration on Minimum Humanitarian Standards (adopted at a meeting of experts convened in Turku/Åbo, Finland, 1990), revised version reprinted in (1995) 89 *AJIL* 218–23.

[142] UN Sub-Commission on Prevention of Discrimination and Protection of Minorities, Res. 1994/26, para. 1 (26 August 1994).

[143] Articles 1 and 2.

[144] A. Eide *et al.*, 'Combating Lawlessness in Gray Zone Conflicts Through Minimum Humanitarian Standards' (1995) 89 *AJIL* 215, 217.

[145] UN Commission on Human Rights, E/CN.4/1998/53/Add.2 (Report of the Representative of the Secretary-General, F. M. Deng, 11 February 1998).

[146] *Ibid.*, para. 2 of the Introduction to the Principles and Principle 2.

[147] *Ibid.*, para. 3 of the Introduction to the Principles.

[148] R.K. Goldman, 'Codification of International Rules on Internally Displaced Persons' (1998) 324 *IRRC* 463–6, text available on: www.icrc.org (visited, 1 January 2001).

the Salvadorian Government, in 1990.[149] The involvement of ONUSAL, charged with verification of this Agreement, indicates the international character of the Agreement; FMLN must be assumed to have committed itself not only to the Government, but also to the United Nations. The Agreement contained a number of human rights norms, which the Salvadorian Government and the FMLN accepted to respect. These norms were derived from international human rights treaties to which El Salvador was a party, including the International Covenant and the American Convention on Human Rights. Some of these rights were also enshrined in Common Article 3 and Protocol II and as such were applicable to FMLN, such as the right to life, integrity and security, and the freedom of the individual.[150] Through the Agreement, FMLN accepted to respect also various human rights to which it was not bound under international humanitarian law. These included the freedom of association, religion, expression, movement, and the effective enjoyment of labour rights.[151] It is particularly with regard to the latter category of human rights that the question arises whether FMLN was legally capable of agreeing to comply with these norms and thereby whether these norms were binding upon this group.

Armed opposition groups do not derive the capacity to conclude agreements in which they agree to be bound by human rights norms from a written rule of international law. The provision in Common Article 3 on special agreements only encourages these groups to agree to apply other norms of the Geneva Conventions. Yet, there appears to be no legal rule which would prevent the representatives of an armed opposition group, in the case of FMLN with the co-operation of international bodies, from making agreements with the established government that are valid on the international plane.[152] In this specific case, the

---

[149] Agreement of 26 July 1990, A/44/971, S/21541, Annex, also reprinted in *UN and El Salvador*, above, n. 27.

[150] Articles 1-4 of the San José Agreement on Human Rights, *ibid.*, see for the interpretation of these articles, First Report of ONUSAL, A/45/1055, S/23037 (16 September 1991) reprinted in *UN and El Salvador*, above n. 27, at 155-6, paras. 40-9 (hereafter, First Report of ONUSAL).

[151] Articles 5-9 of the San José Agreement on Human Rights, above, n. 149.

[152] Above, Section 2 and n. 74; see also *ILCYb* 1962, vol. II, p. 164 (Article 3 of the International Law Commission's Draft Articles on the Law of Treaties provides: 'Capacity to conclude treaties under international law is possessed by States and by other subjects of international law'. In its commentary to this article, the International Law Commission explains that the phrase 'other subjects of international law referred, *inter alia*, to insurgent communities to which a measure of recognition has been accorded).

Preamble of the San José Agreement expressly stipulated that FMLN was considered to have the legal capacity to conclude this agreement. It read: 'Bearing in mind that the FMLN has the capacity and the will and assumed the commitment to respect the inherent attributes of the human person'.[153] Furthermore, the Agreement had been concluded with the express consent of the parent state, and applied solely to the territory of El Salvador.[154] Thus, it seems that the Agreement created legal obligations for FMLN.

Nevertheless, ONUSAL made no attempt whatsoever to monitor FMLN's compliance with the human rights standards set forth in the Agreement. This body reviewed the acts of FMLN only under the Geneva Conventions and Protocol II.[155] By refraining from requiring FMLN's compliance with the Agreement, it implicitly questioned the instrument's binding force on this group. The Agreement between El Salvador and FMLN creating human rights obligations for both parties appeared rather to have a symbolic function, than intending to give equal rights and duties to each of them.[156]

Towards a reconceptualization of human rights?

The question has been addressed above whether international bodies are moving towards inclusion of armed opposition groups under the umbrella of human rights law, thereby going beyond the traditional dichotomy in human rights law of individual *versus* state. The practice discussed above reveals that international bodies are still far from achieving a consensus view – or even unified thinking – on this issue.

One reason for the practice extending human rights law to armed opposition groups may be that this law, as opposed to international

---

[153] Above, n. 152.

[154] The case may be different when the parent state has not consented to commitment of an armed opposition group to an international agreement, compare R. Jennings, A. Watts, *Oppenheim*, above, n. 59, p. 1218.

[155] Second Report of ONUSAL, above, n. 27, para. 147 ('FMLN, for its part, as indicated in the preamble to the Agreement, has declared that it has the capacity and the will and assumes the commitment to respect the inherent attributes of the human person. In particular, it must be understood that this declaration includes the rules of international humanitarian law contained in Article 3 of the four Geneva Conventions of 12 August 1949 and in the Protocol additional to those conventions, and relating to the protection of victims of non-international armed conflicts (Protocol II)').

[156] Interview with F. Vendrell, Director Department of Political Affairs of the United Nations (New York, 26 February 1998).

humanitarian law, has fairly extensive supervisory mechanisms. Because there is no body specifically mandated to supervise compliance by armed opposition groups with the humanitarian rules, human rights bodies have assumed this task. Their primary field of law is, however, human rights law, which encourages them to apply this law to armed opposition groups.

However, it would seem that the contrary practice is insufficient both in quantity and quality to challenge the principle that human rights law binds only the state in its relation with individuals living under its jurisdiction and not armed opposition groups involved in internal conflict. The examples of international bodies imposing human rights obligations on armed opposition groups are limited in number and not very authoritative. Besides, the Inter-American Commission, which in the past has applied human rights standards to armed opposition groups, has abandoned this practice in its most recent report on Colombia, of 1999. Furthermore, the practice asserting the applicability of human rights law to armed opposition groups is confined to unsupported statements. The practice disclaiming this applicability, on the other hand, is validated with detailed reasoning. These qualifications may suggest that the application of human rights treaties to armed opposition groups has been exceptional, not reflecting general practice of the relevant bodies.

With these points in mind, some pertinent questions nevertheless remain as to the need to extend human rights law to armed opposition groups. The first question is whether the asserted gap in substantive norms protecting individuals during internal conflict indeed exists. The drafters of the Minimum Humanitarian Standards and the Guiding Principles on Internal Displacement have argued the need for extension of human rights law to armed opposition groups, *inter alia*, because the scope of international humanitarian law would be too narrow to effectively protect persons in internal conflict. I do not believe such a gap to exist. Common Article 3 and Protocol II provide the most essential protections. The specific contribution of human rights standards to the content of these instruments is not significant, because the non-derogable norms are in essence reflected in international humanitarian law.

Related to this point is that the problems characteristic of internal conflict differ so markedly from the human rights context that the application of the same human rights principles will yield different rules, adjusted to the specific circumstances prevailing in conflict situations. This means that when applied in time of armed conflict, human rights norms will lose their specificity and come very close to or will even be identical to norms of international humanitarian law. If one accepts this argument, then there are strong reasons not to use the term human rights in connection with armed opposition groups, because it does not add anything.

Arguably, the relevance of human rights treaties is greater where states question the applicability of Common Article 3 or Protocol II to a concrete situation. In particular, one may argue that the threshold set by Protocol II is too high to be applied in most internal conflicts. Armed opposition groups would then at least remain bound by human rights law.[157] While I shall examine the threshold for the applicability of humanitarian norms to armed opposition groups in Chapter 4 (dealing with the accountability of armed opposition groups), here it suffices to say that, while this problem may exist, I doubt whether it provides an argument for extending human rights law to armed opposition groups. First, the difficulties of the threshold for applicability of Protocol II appear to have been overcome through identification of customary humanitarian law governing internal conflicts. As I will explain later, these norms apply when the lower threshold of Common Article 3 has been fulfilled. Second, I believe that rather than stretching human rights law to armed opposition groups, efforts should be directed towards promoting the application of Common Article 3 and Protocol II in all situations that arguably constitute internal armed conflicts within the meaning of these rules.[158] Finally, international bodies should aim at a progressive and flexible interpretation of the application clauses of Protocol II.

A second question that arises when considering the need to apply human rights law to armed opposition groups is of a conceptual nature. The main feature of human rights is that these are rights that people hold against the state only. Human rights law purports to govern the relations between the government representing the state and the governed by setting limits to the intrusion by the government upon those areas of human freedom thought to be essential to the proper functioning of the human being in society and for his development therein. These freedoms, as internationalized in human rights treaties, are neither intended, nor adequate, to govern an armed conflict between

---

[157] R. Abi-Saab, 'Humanitarian Law and Internal Conflicts: the Evolution of Legal Concern', in *Challenges Ahead*, above, n. 84, p. 222.

[158] See D. Petrasek, 'Moving Forward on the Development of Minimum Humanitarian Standards' (1998) 92 *AJIL* 557, 559.

the state and armed opposition group(s). The relationship between government and governed and the relationship between parties to the conflict and civilians are different in kind. Accordingly, the law that applies to these relationships has the same differences.[159] Human rights law and international humanitarian law do not represent alternative bodies of law for wartime. The common feature of the two regimes, which is the shared idea of humanity, is too vague to justify the application of human rights law to armed opposition groups by international bodies.

The above considerations leave room for application of human rights law to armed opposition groups that act as de facto governments or groups with a stable presence in part of the state territory. In those cases, the basic feature of human rights law namely the relationship between government and governed, is present. Chapter 4 examines whether practice of international bodies offers support for the argument that the exercise of government-like functions is indeed a ground for imposing human rights obligations on armed opposition groups. It should be remembered, however, that the number of armed opposition groups acting as de facto governments, or groups with a stable presence in a particular part of the territory, is small.

These propositions imply that the term 'human rights' should be reserved for the relationship between the established government and the governed and should not be applied to the relationship between parties to the conflict and persons not participating in the hostilities. This means, in turn, that the application of human rights law during internal conflict should be limited to cases not related to the conflict, in which the government still has sufficient control. Accordingly, the Inter-American Commission on Human Rights, in its Third Report on Colombia, considered that it would apply human rights norms 'alone in those cases involving alleged abuses by State agents which do not occur in the context of the hostilities'.[160] The Commission applied international humanitarian law, on the other hand, to all cases arising out of the context of the internal armed conflict.

It is difficult to predict the developments in the practice of international bodies in the future. The UN Commission on Human Rights' request for the report of the Secretary-General on Minimum Humanitarian Standards indicates that the proposal first made in the

---

[159] See G.I.A.D. Draper, 'Humanitarian Law and Human Rights', above, n. 2, p. 148.
[160] Third Report on the Situation of Human Rights in Colombia, above, n. 8 at 74, para. 11.

Turku Declaration of Humanitarian Minimum Standards to extend human rights standards to armed opposition groups is now receiving serious attention. The issue is on the Commission's agenda.

International criminal law

Currently international criminal law does not extend to armed opposition groups as such.[161] The Nuremberg Charter[162] and the draft texts of the Statute of the International Criminal Court suggest, however, that prosecuting armed opposition groups under international law may be conceivable. This section will briefly examine these texts.

Article 9 of the Nuremberg Charter provided: 'At the trial of any individual member of any group or organization the Tribunal may declare (in connection with any act of which the individual may be convicted) that the group or organization of which the individual was a member was a criminal organization.'[163] The purpose of this provision was threefold. First, it aimed to outlaw certain organizations the purpose of which was military government or occupation. A second aim was to punish membership of criminal organizations, in particular the SS (*SchutzStaffen*) Officers. Third, it intended to control the assets of such criminal organizations, partly with the purpose of making reparations or of paying damages for violations of international law.[164] On the basis of this article,

---

[161] See 1993 Report of the UN Secretary-General, above, n. 38, para. 51 ('the question arises... whether a juridical person, such as an association or organization, may be considered criminal as such and thus its members, for that reason alone, be made subject to the jurisdiction of the International [Yugoslavia] Tribunal. The Secretary-General believes that this concept should not be retained in regard to the International Tribunal. The criminal acts set out in this statute are carried out by natural persons; such persons would be subject to the jurisdiction of the International Tribunal irrespective of membership in groups'); see also V. Morris, M. P. Scharf, *The International Criminal Tribunal for Rwanda* (Transnational Publishers, Inc. New York, 1998) vol. I, pp. 268–9 (hereafter, *Rwanda Tribunal*); S. R. Ratner, J. S. Abrams, *Accountability for Human Rights Atrocities in International Law* (Clarendon Press, Oxford, 1997) p. 15 (stating that it is unclear whether international law generally imposes criminal responsibility on groups) (hereafter, *Accountability for Human Rights Atrocities*).

[162] Reprinted in Schindler and Toman, *Laws of Armed Conflicts*, above, n. 78, p. 826 (Agreement by the Government of the United Kingdom of Great Britain and Northern Ireland, the Government of the United States of America, the provisional Government of the French Republic and the Government of the Soviet Socialist Republics for the prosecution and Punishment of the Major War Criminals of the European Axis, signed at London, 8 August 1945).

[163] *Ibid.*

[164] J. J. Paust *et al.*, *International Criminal Law – Cases and Materials*, (Carolina Academic Press, Durham, 1996), pp. 73–4.

the International Military Tribunal declared several Nazi organizations to be criminal in character, notably the Leadership Corps of the Nazi Party and the SS.[165] Of course, these were all state-linked organizations.

While the Nuremberg Charter recognized for the first time the possibility of individual criminal responsibility under international law based on membership in a criminal group, it did not empower the International Military Tribunal to hold organizations as such criminally responsible. Indeed, the primary aim of this Tribunal was not to criminalize organizations, but to convict individuals against whom other evidence might be lacking.

The draft statute of the International Criminal Court[166] went further in this respect. Article 23 of the draft, as it was presented at the start of the Rome Conference, provided (between brackets) that the International Criminal Court had jurisdiction not only over natural persons, but also over legal persons:

23 [5. The Court shall have jurisdiction over legal persons, with the exception of States, when the crimes committed were committed on behalf of such legal persons or by their agencies or representatives.
6. The criminal responsibility of legal persons shall not exclude the criminal responsibility of natural persons who are perpetrators or accomplices of the same crime.][167]

Article 76 of the draft statute defined the penalties applicable to legal persons, which included fines, dissolution, prohibition of the exercise of certain activities, closure, forfeiture of proceeds, property and assets obtained by criminal conduct, and, finally, payment of reparation.[168]

The draft statute did not define the term 'legal person'. It may be interpreted as referring to organizations with legal status under national or international law or both.[169] Armed opposition groups will generally have no legal status under national law applicable in the territory where they are active, because domestic law is likely to have prohibited these groups. This means that under national law these groups are non-existent, legally speaking. Nevertheless, the absence of national

---

[165] Judgment of 1 October 1946, (1947) *AJIL* 172–333.
[166] United Nations Diplomatic Conference of Plenipotentiaries on the Establishment of an International Criminal Court, A/CONF.183/2/Add.1 (Report of the Preparatory Committee on the Establishment of an International Criminal Court, 14 April 1998).
[167] *Ibid.*
[168] *Ibid.* Article 99 of the draft statute regulated the enforcement of fines and forfeiture measures, stipulating that the relevant provisions of this article shall apply in a like manner to individuals and to legal persons.
[169] Some delegations found that the notion 'legal person' should be extended to organizations lacking any legal status, *ibid.*, footnote 3 to Article 23.

legal personality should not be a prohibitive obstacle in the criminal prosecution of armed opposition groups. These groups clearly exist in international law – they have limited legal personality, *inter alia*, under Common Article 3 and Protocol II.

During the Rome Conference, a new draft statute of the International Criminal Court was developed.[170] Unlike earlier draft texts, this text included a definition of a 'juridical person', which term replaced the term 'legal person' in older versions. The relevant part of draft Article 23 read as follows: 'For the purpose of this Statute, 'juridical person' means a corporation whose concrete, real or dominant objective is seeking private profit or benefit, and not a State or other public body in the exercise of State authority, a public international body or an organization registered, and acting under national law of a State as a non-profit organization.'[171]

According to this text 'juridical person' thus referred only to corporations. This means that armed opposition groups were excluded from the draft statute, because these groups generally exist primarily for political aims.[172] The restriction to corporations also implied that it must concern entities registered under national law. Thus, it appears that draft Article 23 would not have covered armed opposition groups.

In any case, draft Article 23 did not survive the discussions in Rome. In consequence, the Statute as finally adopted on 18 July 1998 does not include a reference to legal or juridical persons. In fact, there was a deep divergence of views as to the advisability of including criminal responsibility of legal persons in the Statute. Some states feared that it could be used against those struggling for self-determination.[173] This fear is not wholly unfounded. Indeed, criminalization of these groups may imply a de facto prohibition of rebellion against the state.[174] It may also imply

---

[170] United Nations Diplomatic Conference of Plenipotentiaries on the Establishment of an International Criminal Court, A/Conf.183/C.1/WGGP/L.5/Rev.2 (Working Group on General Principles of Criminal Law, 3 July 1998) reprinted in A. Clapham, 'The Question of Jurisdiction under International Criminal Law over Legal Persons: Lessons from the Rome Conference on an International Criminal Court', in M. T. Kamminga, S. Zia-Zarifi (eds.) *Liability of Multinational Corporations Under International Law* (Kluwer Law International, 2000) (hereafter, 'Legal Persons').

[171] *Ibid.*, Article 23 (5)(d) (footnotes omitted).

[172] A. Clapham, 'Legal Persons', above, n. 170.

[173] *Ibid.* Furthermore states perceived procedural problems to exist relating to who would represent the legal person in court and how assets could be obtained without affecting the rights of third persons, *id.*

[174] Compare H. Lauterpacht, *Development of International Law by the International Court of Justice* (Cambridge University Press, Cambridge, reprint 1996) (1958) p. 147 (noting that the institution of asylum as related to prosecution of revolutionary activities is a

that armed opposition groups aiming, for example, to overthrow a dictator, may be outlawed under international law for having committed war crimes, not an uncommon practice of these groups.

The merit of this approach is unclear, save that the effect of the Court's declaration is to stigmatize armed opposition groups with criminality. In addition there are doubts as to the legal validity of criminalizing armed opposition groups. For the purpose of enforcing international law, it would seem that civil responsibility of the armed opposition groups and criminal responsibility of their individual members and leaders would be adequate. Criminal responsibility of the groups as a whole is then unnecessary. Moreover, difficulties will arise as to the definition of armed groups' for the purposes of criminal prosecutions (see on this matter Chapter 4, Sections 1 and 2).[175]

In sum, while the Nuremberg trials criminalized certain organizations in order to hold the individual members of these organizations criminally responsible, the concern here is different. The question here is whether criminal responsibility by armed opposition groups in their own right can be established. While it was touched upon in the draft texts of the Rome Statute, the final Statute dropped any reference to criminal responsibility of collective entities as distinguished from criminal responsibility of natural persons.

> regional custom and that 'it may be a matter of dispute whether it is within the province of an international tribunal to discourage or to refuse full recognition to a typical regional custom for some such reason as that the institution of asylum results in protecting the actual leaders while exposing the mass of their supporters to all the risks and perils of the revolutionary struggle').
>
> [175] See for an excellent description of the difficulties that arose at the prosecution of the German groups and organizations indicted before the Nuremberg tribunal, T. Taylor, *The Anatomy of the Nuremberg Trials* (Bloomsbury, London, 1993).

2 Substantive obligations of armed opposition groups as such

Now that the question of applicable law has been settled, the contents of the law applicable to armed opposition groups can be examined in some detail. International practice has given ample application to the obligation of armed opposition groups to treat persons in their power humanely, including obligations relevant to detained persons and penal prosecution of persons. Furthermore, there is considerable practice on the protection of civilians from the conduct of hostilities, including the prohibition on the use of land mines and the prohibition of starvation of civilians. Finally, international bodies have accepted the prohibition on reprisals with regard to armed opposition groups. However, although international bodies have accepted the applicability of a wide range of international norms to armed opposition groups, they have rarely indicated which measures these groups must take to be in compliance with these norms.

In the previous chapter it has been shown, on the basis of international practice, that armed opposition groups may, under particular circumstances, incur accountability for violations of human rights law. However, and notably, to the extent armed opposition groups are bound by human rights law, there is little discussion in international practice of the specific contents of their obligations under this law. This might be taken to suggest that this law does not add much to international humanitarian law from the point of view of substance, a point which will be addressed below.

Humane treatment of prisoners

Common Article 3 and Articles 4 to 6 of Protocol II oblige armed opposition groups to treat humanely all persons outside combat who have fallen into their hands and to protect them from abuse of power. The general obligation to provide humane treatment consists of several specific obligations, three of which have been applied and developed by international bodies: the obligation to provide certain fundamental guarantees; obligations relating to detention and internment of persons; and obligations concerning penal prosecution. International bodies have applied the norms prescribing humane treatment both to acts committed outside and inside combat. Here I am, however, only concerned with the application of these norms to acts committed outside combat, against persons in the power of armed opposition groups. The next section will elaborate on the application of Common Article 3 to military operations.

I shall first address the personal, geographical and temporal scope of application of Common Article 3 and Articles 4 to 6 of Protocol II.

Which persons are entitled to humane treatment under Common Article 3 and Articles 4 to 6 of Protocol II? Common Article 3 stipulates that it protects 'Persons taking no active part in the hostilities, including members of the armed forces who have laid down their arms and those placed *hors de combat* by sickness, wounds, detention or any other cause'. Article 2 of Protocol II provides that it applies to 'all persons affected by an armed conflict as defined in Article 1'. According to these rules, armed opposition groups must guarantee humane treatment to *all* persons not involved in the hostilities and falling under their control. This conclusion is confirmed by the Yugoslavia Tribunal, which determined, in the *Tadić* case (1997, merits), that the test to be applied to establish if a person is protected under Common Article 3 is:

to ask whether, at the time of the alleged offence, the alleged victim of the proscribed acts was directly taking part in hostilities, being those hostilities in the context of which the alleged offences are said to have been committed. If the answer to that question is negative, the victim will enjoy the protection of the proscriptions contained in Common Article 3.[1]

The Inter-American Commission applied a similar test in the *Tablada* case. In this case, involving an attack by an armed opposition group on military barracks of the Argentine Armed Forces, the attackers claimed that, after the fighting had ceased, state agents participated in the summary executions of some of the captured members of the armed group. The Commission observed:

---

[1] *Prosecutor v. Duško Tadić*, Case No. IT-94-1-T, para. 615 (7 May 1997) (Merits) (hereafter, *Tadić* case (1997 Merits)); see also Yugoslavia Tribunal, *Kupreskić* case (2000) above, Chapter 1, n. 49, paras. 522–4.

The persons who participated in the attack on the military base were legitimate military targets only for such time as they actively participated in the fighting. Those who surrendered, were captured or wounded and ceased their hostile acts, fell effectively within the power of Argentine state agents, who could no longer lawfully attack or subject them to other acts of violence. Instead, they were absolutely entitled to the non-derogable guarantees of humane treatment set forth in both Common Article 3 of the Geneva Conventions and Article 5 of the American Convention. The intentional mistreatment, much less summary execution, of such wounded or captured persons would be a particularly serious violation of both instruments.[2]

The notion 'civilians' is therefore irrelevant for the question of protected persons under Common Article 3 and Articles 4 to 6 of Protocol II – although international bodies have sometimes used this term in the context of humane treatment. Neither Common Article 3 nor Articles 4 to 6 of Protocol II employ the term 'civilians'. This term is applicable in the context of hostilities, with regard to persons not in the power of armed opposition groups.

With regard to the geographical applicability of Common Article 3 and Articles 4 to 6 of Protocol II the Yugoslavia and Rwanda Tribunals determined that this extends beyond the scene of military operations.[3] In its Third Report on Colombia, the Inter-American Commission took a similar position:

The Commission also wishes to emphasize that, in internal armed conflicts, humanitarian law applies throughout the entirety of national territory, not just within the specific geographical area(s) where hostilities are underway. Thus, when humanitarian law prohibits the parties to the conflict from directing attacks against civilians or taking hostages in all circumstances, it prohibits these illicit acts everywhere. Thus, such acts of violence committed by the parties in areas devoid of hostilities are no less violative of international humanitarian law than if committed in the most conflictive zone of the country.[4]

Finally, as to the temporal applicability of Common Article 3 and Articles 4 to 6 of Protocol II, the Yugoslavia Tribunal determined that the temporal scope of internal conflicts extends beyond the exact time of hostilities. The relevant provisions therefore continue to apply after the hostilities have ended. It referred in this regard to Article 2(2) of Protocol II which specifies that:

---

[2] *Tablada* case, above, Chapter 1, n. 4, para. 189 (emphasis omitted).
[3] Yugoslavia Tribunal, *Tadić Interlocutory Appeal*, above, Chapter 1, n. 35, paras. 69–70; Rwanda Tribunal, *Kayishema* case, above, Chapter 1, n. 25, paras. 182–3.
[4] Above, Chapter 1, n. 8, at 95, para. 83.

At the end of the armed conflict, all the persons who have been deprived of their liberty or whose liberty has been restricted for reasons related to such conflict, as well as those deprived of their liberty or whose liberty is restricted after the conflict for the same reasons, shall enjoy the protection of Articles 5 and 6 until the end of such deprivation or restriction of liberty.

The Tribunal found that this provision clearly shows that the temporal scope of the applicable rules reaches beyond the actual hostilities.[5]

Having set the scope of application of Common Article 3 and Articles 4 to 6 of Protocol II, I shall now turn to the contents of the obligations of armed opposition groups as they emerge from international practice. Successively the obligation to provide certain fundamental guarantees, obligations relating to detention and internment of persons and obligations on penal prosecution shall be dealt with.

Fundamental guarantees

Common Article 3 prohibits, in addition to the general prohibition of inhumane treatment, a number of specific acts, including '(a) violence to life and person, in particular murder of all kinds, mutilation, cruel treatment and torture; (b) taking of hostages; (c) outrages upon personal dignity, in particular humiliating and degrading treatment'. Article 4(2) of Protocol II reiterates the essence of Common Article 3.[6] International bodies, such as the Inter-American Commission, the UN Commission on Human Rights and the UN Mission for El Salvador, have widely applied these norms, particularly the prohibition of violence to life and person. For example, in its 1996 Annual Report, the Inter-American Commission reported: 'The extremely difficult conditions caused by the various guerrilla movements in Colombia continued in 1996. These groups committed numerous violent acts, many of which constitute violations of humanitarian law applicable to the internal armed conflict in Colombia. These acts included killings outside of armed conflict, kidnapping for ransom.'[7]

[5] *Tadić Interlocutory Appeal*, above, Chapter 1, n. 35, paras. 67, 69–70.
[6] This article prohibits the following acts: '(a) violence to the life, health and physical or mental well-being of persons, in particular murder as well as cruel treatment such as torture, mutilation or any form of corporal punishment; (b) collective punishments; (c) taking of hostages; (d) acts of terrorism; (e) outrages upon personal dignity, in particular humiliating and degrading treatment, rape, enforced prostitution and any form of indecent assault; (f) slavery and the slave trade in all their forms; (g) pillage; (h) threats to commit any of the foregoing acts.'
[7] Annual Report 1996, above, Chapter 1, n. 137, at 662, para. 53; see also Inter-American Commission on Human Rights, Second Report on Colombia, above, Chapter 1, n. 110,

Alongside the prohibition of violence to life and person, international bodies urged armed opposition groups not to recruit children or allow them to take part in the hostilities. This rule is laid down in Article 4(3)(c) of Protocol II, which provides that 'children who have not attained the age of fifteen years shall neither be recruited in the armed forces or groups nor allowed to take part in hostilities'. The Human Rights Division of the United Nations Observer Mission in El Salvador (ONUSAL) gave a broad interpretation to this prohibition. According to ONUSAL, the prohibition did not only amount to an 'all-out ban on the voluntary enlistment of children under the age of 15' by FMLN; equally prohibited by Article 4(3) of Protocol II was 'the participation of minors in such military operations as gathering information, transmitting orders, transporting ammunition and foodstuffs and engaging in sabotage'.[8] According to this interpretation, armed opposition groups are thus not only prohibited to allow direct, but also indirect, participation of children in the hostilities, for example, through the transportation of food.[9]

While the internationally accepted minimum age for recruitment and participation in hostilities is currently fifteen years, the international effort is aimed at raising the minimum age to eighteen. Thus, the UN Secretary-General demanded that 'non-state actors involved in conflict not use children below the age of eighteen in hostilities, or face the imposition of targeted sanctions if they do not comply'.[10]

There is some evidence that the obligation to provide fundamental guarantees of protection to persons in the power of armed opposition groups exists not only under international humanitarian law but also under human rights law. For instance, in resolution 1988/65, the UN Commission on Human Rights requested that 'the Government of El Salvador ... and FMLN should take appropriate measures to put an end

---

at 219; UN Commission on Human Rights, Res. 1995/77, para. 15 (8 March 1995) (Sudan); Second Report of ONUSAL, above, Chapter 1, n. 27, at 25, para. 88.

[8] Second Report of ONUSAL, above, Chapter 1, n. 27, at p. 30, para. 116.

[9] See also S-S. Junod, *Commentary Additional Protocols*, above, Chapter 1, n. 9, p. 1380.

[10] UN Security Council, S/1999/957, paras. 40–2, recommendation 9 (Report of the Secretary-General on the Protection of Civilians in Armed Conflict, 8 September 1999). The UN Commission on Human Rights aims at the adoption of an optional protocol to the Convention on the Rights of the Child, which would prohibit the recruitment and participation of children below the age of eighteen in hostilities; however, as the Convention on the Rights of the Child does not apply to armed opposition groups, it would seem that the optional protocol would not apply to these groups either, see e.g. UN Commission on Human Rights, E/CN.4/1998/119, para. 26 (Interim Report of the Special Representative on Children in Armed Conflict, Olara A. Otunnu, 12 March 1998). See further UN Security Council, Res. 1261 (1999), paras. 2–3 (25 August 1999).

to attempts on the life and physical integrity of individuals, both in non-combat situation and in or as a result of combat, as well as to . . . all types of action constituting a violation of the *fundamental rights and freedoms* of the Salvadorian people'.[11]

By referring to 'fundamental rights and freedoms', the Commission suggested that it relied on human rights law. Another example is provided by the UN Commission's Special Rapporteur for Afghanistan, concerning executions by the Taliban movement:

> The Special Rapporteur . . . received distressing information indicating that in the areas under Taliban control, court-ordered executions of adulterers by stoning were reinstated . . . He calls on all warring factions in the country to respect *international human rights* and humanitarian law *standards* and, in particular, to protect at all times the right to life of civilians and other non-combatants.[12]

This practice demonstrates that there is a minimum standard of protection on the prohibition of violence to life and person in internal conflicts under humanitarian and human rights law, which is to some extent identical. This is not surprising since the norms protecting life and physical integrity in Article 4 of Protocol II are influenced by human rights law, in particular the International Covenant on Civil and Political Rights.[13] Consequently, there is a degree of homogeneity as to the substance between this fundamental rule in the Protocol and the Covenant.

At the same time, this practice also demonstrates that human rights law has little to add to international humanitarian law. The Special Rapporteur, in his report referred to above, like many other international bodies, mentioned human rights law together with international humanitarian law. They do not specify the relevant human rights standards, indicating that human rights law has little value in addition to international humanitarian law.

---

[11] Para. 5 (emphasis added).
[12] 1996 Report of the Special Rapporteur on Extrajudicial, Summary or Arbitrary Executions, above Chapter 1, n. 139, paras. 4, 7 (emphasis added); see also UN Commission on Human Rights, E/CN.4/1988/22, para. 182 (Report of the Special Rapporteur on Extrajudicial, Summary or Arbitrary Executions, S. Amos Wako, 19 January 1988) (Lebanon) (reporting the 'non-respect for the right to life by groups opposing the Government or not under its control') (hereafter, 1988 Report of the Special Rapporteur on Extrajudicial, Summary or Arbitrary Executions); Annual Report of the Inter-American Commission on Human Rights 1996, above, Chapter 1, n. 137, at 818–19.
[13] S-S. Junod, *Commentary Additional Protocols*, above, Chapter 1, n. 9, p. 1365.

Detention and internment

The first question to be addressed under this heading concerns the authority of armed opposition groups to detain or intern persons.

Under Common Article 3 and Protocol II, armed opposition groups are not prohibited from restricting the liberty of persons. These norms do not prescribe the reasons for which persons may be detained or interned, nor do they dictate the right to judicial control during detention or internment. International bodies have, however, prohibited detention or internment other than necessary for reasons related to the conflict. The Inter-American Commission stated, with regard to detentions carried out by the Colombian armed opposition groups, that 'international humanitarian law also prohibits the detention or internment of civilians except where necessary for imperative reasons of security'.[14] Similarly, the UN Commission on Human Rights appealed to armed opposition groups to refrain from 'arbitrary' detention of civilians.[15] These bodies appear to have derived this prohibition from conventional humanitarian law applicable to international conflicts. While Common Article 3 and Protocol II are silent on lawful reasons for detention, the Fourth Geneva Convention permits internment only when the party to the conflict considers a person dangerous to its security.[16]

The Fourth Geneva Convention must also have served as a guideline for the UN Commission on Human Rights when it stated that the Afghan armed opposition groups were prohibited from detaining persons unless these persons were tried within due time: '[The Commission] urges the unconditional release of all prisoners detained without trial on the Afghan territory by rival groups'.[17] Again, Common Article 3 and Protocol II do not contain such a norm. The Fourth Geneva Convention, on the other hand, prescribes the obligation to guarantee detained

---

[14] Third Report on Colombia, above, Chapter 1, n. 8, at 105, para. 122.
[15] Res. 1995/77, para. 15 (8 March 1995) (Sudan).
[16] Articles 42 and 43 of the Fourth Geneva Convention deal with the grounds and procedure for internment or assigned residence of aliens who are in the territory of a party to the conflict when hostilities break out; Articles 68 and 78 of the Convention deal with the position of persons deprived of their liberty in occupied territory; see also Article 75(3) of Protocol I, stipulating: 'Any person arrested, detained or interned for actions related to the armed conflict shall be informed promptly, in a language he understands, of the reasons why these measures have been taken. Except in cases of arrest or detention for penal offences, such persons shall be released with the minimum delay possible and in any event as soon as the circumstances justifying the arrest, detention or internment have ceased to exist.'
[17] Res. 1993/66, para. 8 (10 March 1993).

persons accused of penal offences a fair and regular trial, including the right to be brought to trial as soon as possible.[18]

Thus, the power of armed opposition groups to detain or intern persons has been limited by the procedures and rules laid down in the Fourth Geneva Convention.

In one case, the UN Commission on Human Rights absolutely denied the power of armed opposition groups to detain persons. In resolution 1995/74, the Commission called 'for the abolition of prisons run by political parties and armed groups' in Afghanistan.[19] This resolution departs from Common Article 3 and Protocol II. As these norms expressly regulate the treatment of detained persons, they acknowledge that armed opposition groups do detain persons. The Commission's resolution may be explained on the basis of human rights law, which is the primary field of activity of the Commission. Human rights treaties presume the state to be the only authority within the state territory, and under this law the state, represented by a government, is the only authority entitled to arrest and detain persons on such grounds and in accordance with the law.[20]

A question different from the authority of armed opposition groups to detain and intern persons, concerns the treatment of detained and interned persons. The obligation to provide humane treatment, as examined above, remains fully valid in relation to persons in prison or interned. Common Article 3 applies to all persons taking no active part in the hostilities, including those placed *hors de combat* by detention. Article 5 of Protocol II specifies a number of concrete measures armed opposition groups must take with regard to interned and detained persons, such as the provision of food and drinking water.[21] The UN

---

[18] Article 71 of the Fourth Geneva Convention (dealing with the penal procedure to be followed by the Occupying Power prosecuting accused persons).

[19] Para. 9 (8 March 1995).

[20] See, e.g., Article 9 of the International Covenant on Civil and Political Rights.

[21] Article 5(1) Protocol II further prescribes safeguards regarding health and hygiene, and protection against the climate and the dangers of the conflict; permission to receive individual or collective relief; permission to practise their religion; working conditions and safeguards equivalent to those of the local civilian population. In addition to these unconditional obligations; Article 5(2) of Protocol II prescribes obligations which take into account the resources available to armed opposition groups to provide, *inter alia*, separate quarters for men and women and to protect the physical and mental health and integrity of persons whose liberty has been restricted. This obligation of humane treatment, laid down in Common Article 3 and Protocol II, protects both detained persons, namely persons being penally prosecuted, and interned persons namely those deprived of their liberty for security reasons not being prosecuted under penal law, S-S. Junod, *Commentary Additional Protocols*, above, Chapter 1, n. 9, p. 1386.

Commission on Human Rights, like other international bodies, affirmed the humanitarian norms guaranteeing detained persons humane treatment. In resolution 1989/67, the Commission urged 'all parties to the conflict' in Afghanistan 'to treat all prisoners in their custody in accordance with the internationally recognized principles of humanitarian law and to protect them from all acts of reprisal and violence, including ill-treatment, torture and summary execution'.[22]

The UN Commission on Human Rights and the UN Security Council have stated that armed opposition groups must permit the International Committee of the Red Cross (ICRC) to go to places of internment and detention held by these groups. Thus, in 1994, the Security Council called for 'unhindered access to the ICRC... to all persons detained by all parties in relation to the armed conflict' in Tajikistan.[23] The Security Council appears to rely here on the law applicable to international conflicts. Neither Common Article 3 nor Protocol II expressly entitle the ICRC to carry out visits to places where protected persons are held. Under Common Article 3 such visits are considered as being merely one of the 'services' which the ICRC may offer to the parties to the conflict and which they are free to reject. The Fourth Geneva Convention, on the other hand, sets forth the right of civilians detained or interned to be visited by the ICRC.[24]

Prosecution

Common Article 3 and Protocol II do not expressly oblige armed opposition groups to prosecute violations of these norms by members of these groups or other persons under their control. Such an obligation may be deduced from Article 1 common to the Geneva Conventions, which obliges the States Parties to 'ensure respect' for the Conventions 'in all circumstances'. As will be demonstrated later on, this article also applies in internal armed conflicts. It may be inferred that it applies equally to armed opposition groups involved in these conflicts. International practice provides little support for the obligation of armed

---

[22] Para. 11 (8 March 1989); see also Inter-American Commission, Third Report on Colombia, above, Chapter 1, n. 8, at 106–7, paras. 129–30.

[23] Res. 968 (1994) para. 10 (16 December 1994); UN Commission on Human Rights, E/CN.4/1996/177, para. 371 (Statement of the Chairman, 24 April 1996) (calling for the ICRC to be permitted to have regular access to all persons detained by the parties to the conflict in Chechnya).

[24] Articles 76 and 143 Fourth Geneva Convention. See on access of the ICRC to persons under control of armed opposition groups, Section 2 (Protection of Civilians).

opposition groups to prosecute violators of humanitarian standards. The general feeling expressed by Plattner, that 'it is difficult to conceive of international humanitarian law giving insurgents the authority to prosecute and try authors of violations', thus finds wide recognition in international practice.[25]

An exception is provided by the UN Commission's Special Rapporteur for Sudan, indicating that armed opposition groups are not only obliged to respect the applicable norms, but that they also have to enforce compliance with the norms by those under their control. Pursuant to an incident in Ganyiel region, in Sudan, on 30 July 1995, where a large group of men attacked two villages, 210 people being reported killed, the Special Rapporteur concluded that the killings of civilians were committed by dissident commanders, mainly those who had split from the South Sudan Independence Army (SSIA) and by the Sudan People's Liberation Army (SPLA) both armed opposition groups involved in the conflict in Sudan. The Rapporteur stated that the SSIA and the SPLA must comply with the special agreement concluded by the leaders of the SSIA and the SPLA in which they expressed their support for the Convention on the Rights of the Child, the 1949 Geneva Conventions and the Additional Protocols of 1977. The Rapporteur observed that 'both the SPLA and the SSIA senior leadership should take the necessary measures without delay to prevent future violations by investigating the cases brought to their attention and holding the perpetrators responsible with special regard to the Ganyiel incident'.[26]

However, apart from this example, international bodies have not accepted an obligation by armed opposition groups to prosecute violations of international humanitarian law. Instead they have focused on the rules on a fair trial, which restrain prosecutions and punishments actually carried out by these groups. Common Article 3(d) prohibits 'the passing of sentences and the carrying out of executions without previous judgment pronounced by a regularly constituted court, affording all the judicial guarantees which are recognized as indispensable by civilized peoples'. In a great number of resolutions and reports, international

---

[25] D. Plattner, 'Penal Repression', above, Chapter 1, n. 1, at 415. See UN Security Council Res. 1325 paras. 10, 11 (31 October 2000) (calling on *'all parties to armed conflict'* 'to take special measures to protect women and girls from gender-based violence...', emphasizing 'the responsibility of all *States* to put an end to impunity and to prosecute those responsible for genocide, crimes against humanity and war crimes' (emphasis added)).

[26] UN Commission on Human Rights, E/CN.4/1996/62, at 24, paras. 73 and 87 (Report of the Special Rapporteur for Sudan, Gáspár Bíró, 20 February 1996).

bodies have applied this norm to armed opposition groups, denouncing in particular the practice of summary executions.[27]

Apart from the general prohibition on summary executions, the language of Common Article 3 does not make clear what specifically is expected from armed opposition groups. Phrases such as 'a regularly constituted court' and 'judicial guarantees which are recognized as indispensable by civilized peoples' are ambiguous. The Special Rapporteur on Extrajudicial, Summary or Arbitrary Executions has proposed that Protocol II and the Third Geneva Convention on Prisoners of War provide adequate points of reference in this regard.[28] Article 6 of Protocol II supplements and develops Common Article 3. It clarifies the notion of 'judicial guarantees' as prescribed in Common Article 3, providing a list of such essential guarantees.[29] The Protocol does not mention the notion 'regularly constituted court'; instead it prescribes a 'court offering the essential guarantees of independence and impartiality', which is reproduced from Article 84 of the Third Geneva Convention on Prisoners of War. In fact, during the drafting of the Protocol, some experts argued that it was unlikely that armed opposition groups could 'regularly constitute' a court under national law.[30] Article 84 of the Third Geneva Convention adds to Protocol II the rule that prisoners must be tried by military courts.[31] Article 105 of the same convention explicates 'the rights and means of defense' to which Protocol II refers. These include the right to defence by an advocate, who must have appropriate

---

[27] Annual Report of the Inter-American Commission on Human Rights 1996, above, Chapter 1, n. 137, at 662, para. 53; Second Report on Colombia, above, Chapter 1, n. 110, at 219; UN Commission on Human Rights, Res. 1995/77, para. 15 (8 March 1995) (Sudan); UN Commission on Human Rights, Res. 1989/67, para. 11 (8 March 1989) (Afghanistan); Second Report of ONUSAL, above, Chapter 1, n. 27, at 20, paras. 62–3.

[28] Commission on Human Rights, E/CN.4/1983/16, at 13, para. 56 (Report by the Special Rapporteur, S. Amos Wako, 31 January 1983).

[29] These include the right to information and defence; the principle of individual responsibility; the principle of non-retroactivity; the principle of presumption of innocence; the right of the accused to be present at his own trial; and the right not to be compelled to testify against oneself or to confess guilt. In addition, the Protocol prescribes the right to be informed of judicial remedies and of the time-limits in which they must be exercised and the prohibition on pronouncing the death sentence upon persons under eighteen years and on carrying out the death sentence on pregnant women and mothers of young children, Article 6(2), (3) and (4) of Protocol II.

[30] S-S. Junod, *Commentary Additional Protocols*, above, Chapter 1, n. 9, p. 1398.

[31] This article adds: 'Unless the existing laws of the Detaining Power expressly permit the civil courts to try a member of the Detaining Power in respect of the particular offence alleged to have been committed by a prisoner of war', Article 84 of the Third Geneva Convention.

time and facilities to conduct the defence.[32] The total of the norms in Protocol II and Article 84 of the Third Geneva Convention, provides the essential rights of an accused subjected to penal prosecution as recognized by international law.

The UN Mission for El Salvador, ONUSAL, has further clarified what is expected from armed opposition groups with regard to penal prosecution. ONUSAL reviewed the penal laws made by FMLN. In 1991, FMLN issued a document entitled 'Principles, Norms and Measures Ordered by FMLN in the Course of the War'.[33] In this document, the group established the fundamental norms applicable to its penal system.

At the outset it should be noted that ONUSAL did not make any objections to FMLN's laws as such. The fact that ONUSAL examined whether FMLN's penal document was in conformity with international humanitarian law implies that it accepted the group's competence to issue laws. This practice suggests that the requirement in Article 6 of Protocol II that penal prosecutions must be in accordance with the 'law', refers not only to the laws of the state, but also to laws that may have been adopted by armed opposition groups.[34] As the term 'law' has been copied from the International Covenant on Civil and Political Rights, one may think that it refers to the laws enacted by the existing government representing the state. This interpretation is, however, put in perspective by the practice of ONUSAL.

ONUSAL does not clarify the relationship between the laws of the Salvadorian State and the laws of FMLN. As will be explained in

---

[32] Furthermore, this article provides for the right to call witnesses and a competent interpreter.

[33] 'Principios, Normativos y Medidas Dispuestos por el FMLN en el Transcurso de la Guerra'. This document, from September 1991, consists of four parts. The first part is the introduction; the second part is entitled 'Norms ruling the conduct of military forces of the FMLN and the proceedings for the administration of justice in the controlled zones' ('Normativos reguladores de la conducta de la fuerza militar del FMLN y de los procedimientos para la administración de justicia en las zonas de control'); the third part is entitled 'Measures to protect the human rights of the civilian population in the context of war' (Medidas para proteger los derechos humanos de la población civil en el contexto de la guerra'); the fourth part concerns the 'Norms to promote a respectful conduct to prisoners of war and special provisions regarding the respect of spies serving the FAES' ('Normas para promover una conducta de respeto a los prisioneros de guerra y disposiciones especiales respecto a los espías al servicio de la FAES'), see Third Report of ONUSAL, A/46/876, S/23580, at 29, para. 113 and accompanying footnotes (Human Rights Division, 19 February 1992) (hereafter, Third Report of ONUSAL).

[34] See e.g., Article 6(2)(d) (stipulating that 'anyone charged with an offence is presumed innocent until proven guilty according to law').

Chapter 5, as a matter of principle, the laws of the established government continue to apply during internal armed conflict.[35] In dealing with the problem of the relationship between state laws and laws of armed opposition groups, international bodies will have to find a balance between the principle of continuity of the national legal system and the reality of a plurality of authorities. In this regard, the principles laid down in Article 64 of the Fourth Geneva Convention applicable to international conflicts, dealing with the relation between domestic legislation and the legislation of the occupying authorities, may be applied by analogy to internal conflicts. The basic rule would then be that armed opposition groups are to respect the domestic laws in force in the territory under their control. Only in exceptional situations, involving their own security, would these groups be permitted to adopt their own laws.

ONUSAL found that the 'Principles, Norms and Measures ordered by FMLN in the course of the War' were not in conformity with Article 6 of Protocol II. In its Third Report, ONUSAL stressed the lack of essential norms in this document, stating that it was 'far from being a compendium of the basic norms of a penal system'.[36]

ONUSAL expressed three criticisms. First, it found that FMLN's penal document did not establish the necessary rights and means of defence in the pre-trial and the trial phase, as required by Article 6(2)(a) of Protocol II. According to the commentary to this provision, the necessary rights and means include the right of the accused to be informed as soon as possible of the alleged offence; the right to be heard; the right to call witnesses for the defence; and the right to produce evidence. ONUSAL considered these procedural guarantees to be especially important in cases involving possible application of the death penalty.[37]

Secondly, ONUSAL criticized FMLN's penal document for the absence of a right to appeal.[38] Notably, Article 6 of Protocol II does not prescribe a right to appeal. This article merely provides that if judicial or other remedies exist, armed opposition groups must inform the person in question about them and the time-limits within which they must be exercised. In determining a right to appeal, ONUSAL presumably relied on Article 73 of the Fourth Geneva Convention and Article 106 of the Third Geneva Convention: these provisions guarantee civilians and prisoners of war, respectively, the right to appeal sentences pronounced upon them.

---

[35] Below, Chapter 5, Section 2 (The obligation of the state to take action – *Legislation*).
[36] Third Report of ONUSAL, above, n. 33, at 29, para. 113 and accompanying footnotes.
[37] *Ibid.*, para. 114. [38] *Ibid.*, para. 113.

Finally, ONUSAL denounced the lack of independence and impartiality of FMLN courts, in violation of Article 6(2) of Protocol II. In order to establish the exact meaning of the notions 'impartiality' and 'independence', ONUSAL referred to the Basic Principles on the Independence of the Judiciary, confirmed by the UN General Assembly in resolutions 40/32 (1985) and 40/146 (1985),[39] and which ONUSAL considered to be the 'most authoritative interpretative elements on the independence and impartiality of the courts'.[40] Significantly, according to their wording, the Principles do not apply to armed opposition groups, but only to states. On the basis of these 'Basic Principles', ONUSAL criticized the political composition of FMLN courts, in particular, judicial powers that were given to local commanders of FMLN, which enabled them to pronounce sentences, including the death penalty. Other deficiencies highlighted by ONUSAL were the lack of legal training of the persons who pronounced sentences.[41]

In view of this practice, it is legitimate to ask whether the requirements of Article 6 of Protocol II and the additional requirements imposed in international practice, such as the right to appeal, may in some cases exceed the capabilities of armed opposition groups. These groups may not always be able to set up a system of courts. Lack of stable territorial presence and lack of facilities in which to house prisoners may be one explanation for a policy by armed opposition groups of executing all captured persons. In any event, any proceedings instituted by armed groups will necessarily be ad hoc. ONUSAL acknowledged that it would be very difficult for the insurgent forces in an armed conflict to try accused persons before a court meeting the requirements of Protocol II. Nevertheless, ONUSAL observed that 'it has been considered that any

---

[39] Resolutions of 29 November and 13 December 1985, respectively, cited in Third Report of ONUSAL, above, n. 33, p. 29, para. 112.

[40] Third Report of ONUSAL, above, n. 33, at 29, para. 112. The Mission mentioned in particular the second principle of the Basic Principles, which provides: 'The judiciary shall decide matters before them impartially, on the basis of facts and in accordance with the law, without any restrictions, improper influences, inducements, pressures, threats or interferences, direct or indirect, from any quarter or for any reason', *ibid.*, p. 29, para. 112, footnote 34.

[41] *Ibid.*, FMLN made several attempts to adjust the fundamental principles of its criminal prosecutions. In the first months of 1991, the group presented to the ICRC a proposal for a system of internal judicial administration that aimed to resolve the deficiencies. Several norms included in Article 6 of Protocol II were envisaged in this document. The ICRC rejected FMLN's proposal, alleging that it did not observe the essential norms stipulated in Article 6 of the Protocol, T. F. Acuña, *The United Nations Mission in El Salvador – A Humanitarian Law Perspective* (Kluwer Law International, The Hague, 1995) p. 61, footnote 247 (hereafter, *UN Mission in El Salvador*).

responsible and organized entity can and must observe the principles established in Article 6 of Protocol II, which make up the right to an impartial trial'.[42] ONUSAL stated that these principles would continue to enjoy their validity and mandatory character, even if the dissident forces did not have a judicial administration similar to that of the state. When FMLN's penal system did not contain the norms required, ONUSAL observed, it should be modified. Moreover, if the group's penal system continued to be inadequate, ONUSAL suggested that it should apply the law of the Salvadorian Government in the zones under its control.[43] Furthermore, ONUSAL maintained that when the person charged with the offence was a member of the governmental armed forces, FMLN would be obliged to liberate the person and notify the governmental authorities about the violations committed.[44] The ICRC stated that even in response to serious violations of international humanitarian law, the rebels should have recourse to the national system of administration of justice.[45]

The above practice shows that to the extent armed opposition groups are unable to comply with the relevant norms, they must leave prosecutions to the governmental authorities.[46] ONUSAL preferred this approach to assisting FMLN in improving the group's penal procedure. Indeed, ONUSAL made no effort to instruct FMLN on the establishment of a

---

[42] *Ibid.*, p. 28, para. 111.

[43] Compare K. J. Partsch, 'Individual Penal Responsibility Provided by the Additional Protocols to the Geneva Conventions' (Second Round Table on Current Problems of International Humanitarian Law, San Remo, 3–6 September 1975) pp. 6–7 ('The insertion of "principles of penal law and of penal prosecutions" in Protocol II is based on the assumption that in an internal conflict also the adverse party is bound by the provisions of the Conventions and Protocols. If this basis is not accepted, Protocol II has no chance to be applied ... The question whether these forces shall be able in fact to respect the same judicial guarantees as the State, against whom they fight, is not put into doubt. It is left open, whether the material penal law remains in force or if it is substituted by new laws. It is also left open, whether the existing courts are continuing their activity or whether they shall be substituted by new courts').

[44] T. F. Acuña, *UN Mission in El Salvador*, above, n. 41, p. 61.   [45] *Ibid.*, footnote 247.

[46] Compare G. I. A. D. Draper, 'Wars of National Liberation and War Criminality', in *Restraints on War: Studies in the Limitation of Armed Conflict* (Oxford University Press, Oxford, 1979) pp. 135–162 reprinted in *Reflections on Law and Armed Conflicts*, above, Chapter 1, n. 2, 180, p. 190 (stating with regard to national liberation movements that 'It is clear that NLMs normally do not have the legislative and judicial apparatus required to meet the stringent requirements of the Conventions and of Protocol I as to the trial of a person accused of "grave breaches" of those instruments ... An NLM might, if it had prima facie evidence of commission, hand over a suspected offender to a neighbouring State which was a Party to the instruments for trial. Here the absence of an NLM legal system will not inhibit the rendition') (hereafter, 'Wars of National Liberation and War Criminality').

proper criminal procedure. Even in cases where armed opposition groups can implement the applicable standards, international practice suggests that they may be obliged to leave prosecution to the government. This practice joins with the absence in international practice, referred to earlier, of a recognition of the obligation of armed opposition groups to prosecute violations of international humanitarian law committed by persons under their control. It reveals the ambiguity of humanitarian law for internal conflicts. On the one hand, this law recognizes the factual situation of a civil war in which at least two authorities exist concurrently. Accordingly, it imposes equal obligations on all parties, both on the government and armed opposition groups, which may result in two separate systems of courts in the territory of a single state. On the other hand, humanitarian law for internal conflicts aims, albeit indirectly, at the re-establishment of the authority of the existing government and thus to elimination of the opposite party(ies), the armed opposition group(s).[47] This paradox may explain why ONUSAL, while accepting the reality of the existence of FMLN, refrained from assisting the movement in the setting up of a properly functioning penal system, and even denied its competence to prosecute. ONUSAL may well have feared that full application of international humanitarian law to FMLN would create a risk of institutionalization, at the cost of the restoration of peace.

ONUSAL's practice is not without problems. Its lack of attention to the special characteristics of FMLN or even denial of its authority to prosecute caused a situation of legal discrimination, favouring the legal institutions of the state to those of the armed opposition group.[48] Moreover, one may pose the question whether ONUSAL's policy resulted in the partial protection of the individuals living in areas controlled by FMLN, subjecting them to penal prosecutions by this group. The answer to this cannot be a categorical 'no'.

---

[47] See, e.g., Article 3(1) of Protocol II (stating that the state retains the right to restore law and order and to defend its territorial integrity). Also the state's competence to punish members of armed opposition groups for participating in the conflict supports the re-establishment of the state's authority.

[48] T. F. Acuña, *UN Mission in El Salvador*, above, n. 41, p. 62 (criticizing ONUSAL for having failed to guide the Salvadorian opposition group in their penal procedures. Acuña recommended that international organizations in charge of supervision of compliance with international humanitarian law should undertake coordinated efforts to improve the application of the law by armed opposition groups. These efforts should be oriented towards advising the insurgent force in the constitution of their own penal system, and in the practical application of the legal provisions required by due legal process).

Protection of civilians

The previous section examined the duty of armed opposition groups to provide humane treatment to all persons outside hostilities and under their control. Here the obligation of armed opposition groups to protect civilians who are not in their power in the course of military operations will be addressed. I will discuss successively the general obligation to protect civilians and civilian objects; the prohibition on using land mines; the prohibition on starvation of civilian populations; and finally, the prohibition on taking reprisals.

A preliminary question that arises is the definition of persons entitled to protection from military operations namely civilians and the civilian population. This question is of great importance since the distinction between civilians and those involved in the hostilities, and therefore not entitled to protection from hostilities, is often extremely difficult to draw in internal conflict. Members of armed opposition groups do not always wear uniforms; they may live or seek shelter in villages; and civilians may provide material support to armed opposition groups, voluntarily or by force, and as a consequence, become targeted.

Protocol II refers to civilians and the civilian population, but does not define these terms. Given the absence of a definition, the Rwanda Tribunal and the Inter-American Commission on Human Rights found that they had to look to the definitional standards in Article 50 of Protocol I for authoritative guidance.[49] Accordingly, these bodies defined civilians as anyone who is not a member of the parties to the conflict within the meaning of international humanitarian law.

In order to determine the scope of civilian immunity, the Inter-American Commission tried to clarify the dividing line between direct and indirect participation in the hostilities. The Commission affirmed Article 13(3) of Protocol II, stipulating that civilians will forfeit protection when and for such time as they take a direct part in military operations. The Commission emphasized that these persons nevertheless retain their status as civilians: once they cease their hostile acts, they can no longer be the object of an attack.[50] Remarkably, the Commission

---

[49] Rwanda Tribunal, *Kayishema* case, above, Chapter 1, n. 25, paras. 179–80; Rwanda Tribunal, *Prosecutor v. Musema*, case No. ICTR-96-13, para. 280 (27 January 2000) (hereafter, *Musema* case); Inter-American Commission, Third Report on Colombia, above, Chapter 1, n. 8, at 83–4, paras. 43–6. Article 50 of Protocol I defines the term 'civilian population' as comprising 'all persons who are civilians' and defines a 'civilian' negatively as anyone who is not a member of the armed forces or of an organized group of a party to the conflict.

[50] Third Report on Colombia, above, Chapter 1, n. 8, paras. 53–5.

suggested that civilians are even *obliged* to refrain from participating in the hostilities and that 'international humanitarian law is violated if this duty is not respected'.[51] However, apart from this example, international practice provides no support for such an obligation. Furthermore, such an obligation does not fit into the humanitarian law system. On the contrary, Article 13(3) of Protocol II providing that civilians shall enjoy protection 'unless and for such time as they take a direct part in hostilities', suggests that civilians are not prohibited from participation in the hostilities.[52]

The Commission also pointed out that indirect participation in hostilities, which supports the war effort of one of the parties to the conflict, does not affect civilian immunity. The Commission provided several examples of indirect participation: selling of goods to one or more of the parties to the conflict; expressing sympathy for the aim of one of the parties; and not preventing an attack by one of the parties.[53]

General protection of civilians and civilian objects

Part IV of Protocol II, entitled 'Civilian Population', contains general rules on the protection of civilians from hostilities. Article 13(1) prescribes that 'the civilian population and individual civilians shall enjoy general protection against the dangers arising from military operations'. Article 13(2) of Protocol II prohibits direct attacks against the civilian population: 'The civilian population as such, as well as individual civilians, shall not be the object of attack. Acts or threats of violence the primary purpose of which is to spread terror among the civilian population are prohibited.'

These general rules of protection are reflected in UN General Assembly resolutions 2444 (1968) and 2675 (1970) on the protection of the civilian population,[54] which, according to the Yugoslavia Tribunal, are declaratory of customary law.[55] Resolution 2444, applicable in all armed conflicts and to all authorities in armed conflicts, adds to Protocol II the principle of distinction: 'Distinction must be made at all times

---

[51] *Ibid.*, 87, para. 58.
[52] The argument of the Commission may go as follows: on the basis of the Hague Regulations and Protocol I, combatants have an exclusive right to take part in hostilities. Civilians do not have this right. Therefore, if they participate nonetheless, they do this without right, therefore, unlawfully.
[53] Third Report on Colombia, above, Chapter 1, n. 8, at 87, para. 56.
[54] Above, Chapter 1, nn. 78, 79.
[55] Above, Chapter 1, Section 2 (Other rules of humanitarian law).

between persons taking part in the hostilities and members of the civilian population to the effect that the latter be spared as much as possible.'[56] Resolution 2675 goes further than Protocol II by requiring precautionary measures in attack to prevent damage to the civilian population.[57]

These rules – the prohibition on making civilians the object of attack, the duty to distinguish between civilians and those taking part in the hostilities, and the duty to take precautions – have been affirmed and developed in international practice. The Security Council, in resolution 851 (1993) on Angola, strongly condemned the attack by UNITA forces, on 27 May 1993, against a train carrying civilians, reaffirming that 'such criminal attacks are clear violations of international humanitarian law'.[58] In the *Tadić* appeal case, the Yugoslavia Tribunal stated that civilians enjoy protection from hostilities, in particular from indiscriminate attacks.[59]

International bodies have further developed the norms of Protocol II and the General Assembly resolutions on protection of civilians from hostilities by applying, by analogy, norms of Protocol I. International bodies considered the application of Protocol I by analogy to be necessary in order to ensure the effectiveness of Common Article 3 and Protocol II. Part IV of Protocol II provides only the principles and not the rules of application. It does not make clear which measures armed opposition groups are obliged to take during the planning, decision, and action stages of an attack or when being attacked. By applying the more specific regulation of Protocol I, international bodies have sought to overcome the lacunae of Protocol II. The Protocols have been drafted simultaneously. In consequence, many terms and principles of Protocol I can also be found in Protocol II.[60] The analogical application by international bodies of certain provisions of Protocol I reinforces the conclusion drawn earlier, that the distinction between the law for

---

[56] Para. 1(c).
[57] Para. 3 (providing: 'In the conduct of military operations, every effort should be made to spare civilian populations from the ravages of war, and all necessary precautions should be taken to avoid injury, loss or damage to civilian populations').
[58] Para. 18 (15 July 1993); see also UN Commission on Human Rights, Res. 1990/53, para. 5 (6 March 1990) (urging all parties to the conflict in Afghanistan to halt the use of weapons against the civilian population); 1996 Report of the Special Rapporteur on Extrajudicial, Summary or Arbitrary Executions, above, Chapter 1, n. 139, paras. 4, 7, 450–1; Second Report of ONUSAL, above, Chapter 1, n. 27, at 18 para. 57.
[59] *Tadić Interlocutory Appeal*, above, Chapter 1, n. 35, para. 127.
[60] See S-S. Junod, *Commentary Additional Protocols*, above, Chapter 1, n. 9, p. 1450, footnote 9.

international armed conflicts and the law for internal conflicts is subject to erosion.[61]

An example of analogical application of Protocol I to armed opposition groups is provided by the UN Mission for El Salvador, ONUSAL. The Mission took this approach when considering FMLN's firing of heavy artillery at a populated area. According to ONUSAL, it was predictable that these attacks would cause casualties among the civilian population. It qualified the attacks as indiscriminate and appealed to FMLN to refrain from attacks 'which may strike military objectives and civilians... without distinction'.[62] In particular, it stressed the excessive character of these attacks in relation to the specific and direct military advantage that could be anticipated. To support its finding, ONUSAL not only referred to the norms laid down in Article 13(2) of Protocol II and General Assembly resolutions 2444 (1968) and 2675 (1970), but also applied, by analogy, Articles 51(4) and 51(5) of Protocol I, prohibiting indiscriminate attacks.[63]

In the same way, ONUSAL has stressed the obligation to take precautionary measures in attack, as laid down in UN General Assembly resolution 2675 (1970). It stated that for the determination of which precautionary measures FMLN should adopt, Article 57 of Protocol I contains information 'useful in its analogous application to internal armed conflicts'.[64] ONUSAL also applied, again by analogy, Article 58(b)

---

[61] See above, Chapter 1, Section 2 (Relevance of the distinction between internal and international conflicts).

[62] Second Report of ONUSAL, above, Chapter 1, n. 27, at 21, paras. 68–71.

[63] Ibid., para. 69, footnote 18; see also Third Report of ONUSAL, above, n. 33, at 34, para. 134. Article 51(4) of Protocol I provides: 'Indiscriminate attacks are prohibited. Indiscriminate attacks are: (a) those which are not directed at a specific military objective; (b) those which employ a method or means of combat which cannot be directed at a specific military objective; or (c) those which employ a method or means of combat the effects of which cannot be limited as required by this Protocol; and consequently, in each such case, are of a nature to strike military objectives and civilians or civilian objects without distinction.' Article 51(5) of Protocol I stipulates: 'Among others, the following types of attacks are to be considered as indiscriminate: (a) an attack by bombardment by any methods or means which treats as a single military objective a number of clearly separated and distinct military objectives located in a city, town, village or other area containing a similar concentration of civilians or civilian objects; and (b) an attack which may be expected to cause incidental loss of civilian life, injury to civilians, damage to civilian objects, or a combination thereof, which would be excessive in relation to the concrete and direct military advantage anticipated.'

[64] Third Report of ONUSAL, above, n. 33, at 33, para. 131. Article 57 of Protocol I provides: '1. In the conduct of military operations, constant care shall be taken to spare the civilian population, civilians and civilian objects. 2. With respect to attacks,

of Protocol I, which prohibits the location of military objectives within or near densely populated areas.[65] ONUSAL also invoked Article 51(7) of Protocol I, which prohibits the use of the civilian population as a shield.[66] The Inter-American Commission considered the prohibition against attacking, without the required precautions, to be a rule of customary law applicable to armed opposition groups.[67]

In addition to the obligation to protect civilian persons, armed opposition groups are obliged to protect civilian objects against the effects of hostilities. While Protocol II contains no rules expressly forbidding

the following precautions shall be taken: (a) those who plan or decide upon an attack shall: (i) do everything feasible to verify that the objectives to be attacked are neither civilians nor civilian objects and are not subject to special protection but are military objectives within the meaning of paragraph 2 of Article 52 and that it is not prohibited by the provisions of this Protocol to attack them; (ii) take all feasible precautions in the choice of means and methods of attack with a view to avoiding, and in any event to minimizing, incidental loss of civilian life, injury to civilians and damage to civilian objects; (iii) refrain from deciding to launch any attack which may be expected to cause incidental loss of civilian life, injury to civilians, damage to civilian objects, or a combination thereof, which would be excessive in relation to the concrete and direct military advantage anticipated; (b) an attack shall be cancelled or suspended if it becomes apparent that the objective is not a military one or is subject to special protection or that the attack may be expected to cause incidental loss of civilian life, injury to civilians, damage to civilian objects, or a combination thereof, which would be excessive in relation to the concrete and direct military advantage anticipated; (c) effective advance warning shall be given of attacks which may affect the civilian population, unless circumstances do not permit. 3. When a choice is possible between several military objectives for obtaining a similar military advantage, the objective to be selected shall be the attack which may be expected to cause the least danger to civilian lives and to civilian objects. 4. In the conduct of military operations at sea or in the air, each Party to the conflict shall, in conformity with its rights and duties under the rules of international law applicable in armed conflict, take all reasonable precautions to avoid losses of civilian lives and damage to civilian objects. 5. No provision of this Article may be construed as authorizing any attacks against the civilian population, civilians or civilian objects'.

[65] *Ibid.*, 34, para. 134, and accompanying footnote 42. Article 58(b) of Protocol I provides: 'The Parties to the conflict shall, to the maximum extent feasible: avoid locating military objectives within or near densely populated areas.'

[66] *Ibid.* Article 51(7) of Protocol I stipulates: 'The presence or movements of the civilian population or individual civilians shall not be used to render certain points or areas immune from military operations, in particular in attempts to shield military objectives from attacks or to shield, favour or impede military operations. The Parties to the conflict shall not direct the movement of the civilian population or individual civilians in order to attempt to shield military objectives from attacks or to shield military operations.' See also UN Commission on Human Rights, E/CN.4/1990/25, at 16, para. 10 (Report on the Situation of Human Rights in Afghanistan by the Special Rapporteur, F. Ermacora, 31 January 1990) (providing another example of analogous application of Protocol I to acts of armed opposition groups).

[67] Third Report on Colombia, above, Chapter 1, n. 8 at 82, para. 40.

armed opposition groups to attack civilian objects, UN General Assembly resolution 2675 (1970) provides: 'Dwellings and other installations that are used only by civilian populations should not be the object of military operations... Places or areas designated for the sole protection of civilians, such as hospital zones or similar refuges, should not be the object of military operations.'[68] According to the Yugoslavia Tribunal, customary law on the protection of civilian objects has developed to govern internal strife, although it did not elaborate on this statement.[69]

The Inter-American Commission has stated that Protocol I can function as a point of reference on the protection of civilian objects: 'Inasmuch as certain provisions of Protocol I codify for the first time customary law rules designed to protect... civilian objects from indiscriminate or disproportionate attacks, these provisions provide authoritative guidance for interpreting the extent of similar protection for these... objects during all internal conflicts.'[70] Accordingly, the Commission determined that the terms 'civilian objects' and 'military objects' in Article 52 of Protocol I should be given similar meanings for the purposes of Protocol II.[71] It is on the basis of these rules that the Commission subsequently reviewed attacks of the Colombian armed opposition groups:

Armed dissident groups frequently attack objects which would normally be considered civilian in nature, such as cars, buses, stores and residences. Although a civilian object may become a legitimate military target in certain cases, the information received by the Commission indicates that these groups generally attack these objects without having verified whether they were, at the time, making an effective contribution to military action, thereby losing their protection against attack. Armed dissident groups therefore act in a manner incompatible with the norms of international humanitarian law as a result of these attacks.[72]

---

[68] Paras. 5 and 6.   [69] *Tadić Interlocutory Appeal*, above, Chapter 1, n. 35, para. 127.
[70] Third Report on Colombia, above, Chapter 1, n. 8, at 92, para. 75.
[71] *Ibid.*, 89–90, paras. 67–8. Article 52 of Protocol I provides: '1. Civilian objects shall not be the object of attack or of reprisals. Civilian objects are all objects which are not military objectives as defined in paragraph 2. 2. Attacks shall be limited strictly to military objectives. In so far as objects are concerned, military objectives are limited to those objects which by their nature, location, purpose or use make an effective contribution to military action and whose total or partial destruction, capture or neutralization, in the circumstances ruling at the time, offers a definite military advantage. 3. In case of doubt whether an object which is normally dedicated to civilian purposes, such as a place of worship, a house or other dwelling or a school, is being used to make an effective contribution to military action, it shall be presumed not to be so used.'
[72] *Ibid.*, 108–9, para. 139.

The Commission paid particular attention to the attacks by the Colombian armed opposition groups on electric towers and oil and gas pipelines. It noted that these facilities have 'dual-uses' during hostilities, meaning that they may not always enjoy immunity from attack. It continued:

> However, in order to be lawfully attacked, the object in question must meet the test of a military objective in the circumstances ruling at the time of the attack. That is, the object must make an effective contribution to military action and its destruction must offer a 'definite military advantage'. Even in those cases where such objects may legitimately be attacked, international humanitarian law requires the attacker to take precautions to ensure that collateral damage to the civilian population is minimized and to cancel an attack if the collateral damage expected would be excessive in relation to the clear-cut advantage anticipated by the target's destruction or neutralization.[73]

The Commission concluded that some of the attacks on oil pipelines did not aim at obtaining a military advantage, but instead were intended to promote the ELN's ideology of opposition to foreign exploitation of Colombian resources. These attacks were held to constitute violations of international humanitarian law.[74]

In the view of the Yugoslavia Tribunal, civilian objects must be understood as including cultural property.[75] Article 19(1) of the Cultural Property Convention obliges armed opposition groups to apply as a minimum 'the provisions of the present Convention which relate to respect of cultural property'. The principal rule on respect for cultural property, as laid down in Article 4(1) of the Convention, obliges armed opposition groups to refrain 'from any use of the property and its immediate surroundings or of the appliances in use for its protection for purposes which are likely to expose it to destruction or damage in the event of armed conflict' and to refrain 'from any act of hostility directed against such property'.[76] In the *Tadić* appeal case, the Yugoslavia Tribunal found

---

[73] Third Report on Columbia, 109, para. 141.
[74] *Ibid.*, 109–10, para. 143; see also UN Commission on Human Rights, Res. 1989/68, para. 5 (8 March 1989) (requesting that the Government of El Salvador and FMLN: 'should take appropriate measures to put an end to... attacks on the economic infrastructure'); UN Commission on Human Rights, E/CN.4/1987/21, at 27 para. 133 (Final Report on the Situation of Human Rights in El Salvador by J. A. Pastor Ridruejo, 2 February 1987) (calling on the forces of FMLN to refrain from attacking El Salvador's economic infrastructure).
[75] *Tadić Interlocutory Appeal*, above, Chapter 1, n. 35, para. 127.
[76] Article 4(2) of the Cultural Property Convention adds that the obligations mentioned in the first paragraph of this article 'may be waived only in cases where military

that cultural property is protected in internal conflict as a matter of customary law.[77]

From the above practice, it is apparent that the obligation of armed opposition groups to protect civilians against the effects of hostilities is not absolute. Armed opposition groups, like parties to an international conflict, are subject to obligations of due diligence and non-discrimination.[78] They are obliged to balance military necessity with the protection of the civilian population and civilian objects. At a minimum, armed groups must distinguish between military and non-military targets, so that civilians and civilian objects are spared as much as possible. Furthermore, they must respect the principle of proportionality, and they must take precautions in attack. For the identification of these obligations, international bodies have relied extensively on rules of Protocol I.

Finally, a few words about the relevance of Common Article 3 for the conduct of hostilities are in order. International bodies have generally derived the norms on the protection of civilians and civilian objects from the 1977 Protocols. They have, however, occasionally based such obligations on Common Article 3 of the Geneva Conventions. For example, the Inter-American Commission stated that the immunity of the civilian population from direct attack is codified in Common Article 3, in particular in the prohibition, in all circumstances, against 'violence to life and person' to persons who 'do not or no longer actively participate in hostilities'.[79] Similarly, the UN Mission for El Salvador, ONUSAL, argued that the obligation to distinguish between civilians and participants in hostilities follows from Common Article 3(1)(a) prohibiting violence to life.[80]

Common Article 3 was never intended to have implications for the conduct of hostilities. The prohibition on violence to life was not

---

necessity imperatively requires such a waiver'. The Second Protocol to this convention supplements the Cultural Property Convention. In particular, the Protocol defines the notion 'military necessity' as used in Article 4(2) of the Convention (Article 6, Second Protocol); it prescribes precautions in attack (Article 7, Second Protocol); and it prescribes precautions against the effects of hostilities (Article 8, Second Protocol).

[77] Above, n. 75.
[78] See G. Abi-Saab, 'Non-International Armed Conflicts' in *International Dimensions of Humanitarian Law* (UNESCO, Martinus Nijhoff, Dordrecht, 1988) pp. 217, 235 (hereafter, 'Non-International Armed Conflicts').
[79] Third Report on Colombia, above, Chapter 1, n. 8, at 83, para. 41.
[80] Third Report of ONUSAL, above, n. 33, para 131.

intended to constitute a prohibition against attacking civilians.[81] This article intended to guarantee humane treatment of all persons who are in the power of one of the parties to the conflict. This follows from the notion of 'treatment' employed in Common Article 3 which presupposes a degree of control over the person in question.[82] The argument that provisions for humane treatment in Common Article 3 are not applicable to hostilities is supported by the fact that Protocol II deals with humane treatment and protection of the civilian population in separate parts.[83]

The only conventional rules on protection of civilians from hostilities are laid down in Protocol II. As will be described later, however, the accountability of armed opposition groups under the Protocol has been held to be very limited so that Common Article 3 is readily available as a source of a duty by armed opposition groups to provide general protection to civilians in their military operations.[84] It may be doubted whether such a use of Common Article 3 is really justified. For one thing, it would seem that the acceptance of international bodies of the customary status of rules governing the conduct of hostilities makes a resort to Common Article 3 for this purpose unnecessary.[85] Also, it is submitted that a distinction between the two categories of persons – detainees and civilian populations in general – is still relevant and useful.

A possible explanation for applying Common Article 3 to the conducting of hostilities may be that in internal conflicts the distinction between out-of-combat and combat situations is not always easily made.

---

[81] G. I. A. D. Draper, 'Wars of National Liberation and War Criminality', above, n. 46, p. 183. For this reason, the notions 'law of Geneva' and 'law of The Hague' are still useful as they indicate the distinction between obligations of humane treatment and conduct of hostilities, respectively. But see J. E. Bond, 'Internal Conflicts', above, Chapter 1, n. 101, at 348 ('to the extent that the Hague rules are intended to protect noncombatants, they are, as limited by reasonable interpretation, incorporated into Article 3).

[82] This also holds true for Article 4 of Protocol II.

[83] Compare G. Abi-Saab, 'Non-International Armed Conflicts', above, n. 78, p. 235 ('If Part II [of Protocol II] clearly follows a "human rights" approach, Part IV on "Civilian Population" is by contrast strongly influenced by a "law of war" approach. The difference is particularly clear when it comes to determining the protected persons. Part II prescribes "humane treatment" of all persons in their power by the parties to the conflict, without distinguishing between those who had taken part in hostilities and those who had not... Part IV on the other hand, necessarily distinguishes *civilians*, defined in Article 13 para. 3, as those who (and "for such time as they") do not "take a direct part in hostilities" and who are consequently entitled to "general protection against the dangers arising from military operations"').

[84] See below, Chapter 4, Section 1.   [85] See above, Chapter 1, Section 1.

Consider the following statement of the Inter-American Commission in its 1999 Report on Colombia, in a chapter entitled 'Protection for Civilians Against Direct Attacks':

The Commission is extremely concerned... that the deliberate targeting of civilians has become a routine, if not systematic, tactic employed by all the parties to the conflict in Colombia in varying degrees... The FARC, [Armed Revolutionary Forces of Colombia], the ELN [Army of National Liberation] and their allied groups have attacked, executed and abducted or taken hostage government officials, including local mayors and council members, and other civilians whom they believe are part of the State's 'repressive' apparatus or are otherwise dangerous to the security of their combatants and sympathizers. Thus, for example, the ELN has admitted that it carries out 'political detentions of persons who have been implicated in acts of administrative corruption or who have taken part in the dirty war as promoters of political groups referring to paramilitaries'. Given the practice of the ELN, it must be assumed that the organization applies an extremely broad definition to the term 'promoters of the paramilitaries', including all those individuals believed to have some connection to paramilitary groups, including family members of paramilitary group members. The ELN states that the persons it detains are subjected to 'popular revolutionary trials' where they are convicted or acquitted. In each of these cases, the responsible parties have erroneously equated the vocations and/or the non-hostile activities of their victims with actual participation in hostilities, thereby justifying attacks against them. Acceptance of such claims for attacking these and like civilians would not only obliterate any meaningful distinction between civilians and combatants, but could also lead to total unregulated warfare in Colombia. The Commission believes, therefore, that it is necessary to clarify the distinction between 'direct' or 'active' and 'indirect' participation by civilians in hostilities in order to identify those limited situations where it is not unlawful to attack civilians.[86]

This statement shows that it may be difficult to distinguish between in-combat and out-of-combat situations. The Commission was not able to indicate whether the above acts committed by the Colombian armed opposition group must be qualified as attacks or as inhumane treatment of persons in the power of the armed opposition group. The result is that it is unclear what protection the victims are entitled to. The protection provided by the Protocols sweeps more widely (i.e. covers the whole civilian population), but it is not absolute. The protection provided by Common Article 3 is absolute, but its sweep is narrower (i.e. it is confined to protecting persons in detention).

---

[86] Third Report on Colombia, above, Chapter 1, n. 8, at 84–6, paras. 47, 51–3 (footnotes omitted).

Land mines

Protocol II does not explicitly prohibit the use of land mines, or indeed any other weapon. Part IV of the Protocol, however, contains general rules on the protection of civilians from hostilities. As noted above, these rules, which also apply as a matter of customary law, oblige armed opposition groups to distinguish in their military operations between military and non-military targets and to take certain precautionary measures when attacking. According to international practice, the prohibition of the use of land mines against civilians is incorporated in the general rule of protection of civilians because these weapons necessarily violate the principle of distinction. Accordingly, the International Court of Justice, in its 1996 Advisory Opinion on *Legality of the Threat or Use of Nuclear Weapons*, stated that the principle of protection of the civilian population and the related principle of distinction between civilians and persons involved in the hostilities mean that states must never make civilians the object of attack and must consequently 'never use weapons that are incapable of distinguishing between civilian and military targets'.[87] Although this prohibition is addressed to states, the general principle of protection of civilians applies also to armed opposition groups in internal conflicts. It may therefore be inferred that the prohibition against indiscriminate weapons also applies to armed opposition groups. The Inter-American Commission, in its Third Report on Colombia, has made it clear that it considers the ban on land mines to be a general obligation applicable to any group conducting military operations.[88]

Apart from the general norm of protecting civilians from hostilities, a specific norm has recently been laid down by Amended Protocol II on Prohibitions or Restrictions on the Use of Mines, Booby-Traps and Other Devices.[89] This Protocol clearly applies to armed opposition groups as well as to states. Article 1 provides:

---

[87] Above, Chapter 1, n. 34, para. 78.

[88] Third Report on Colombia, above, Chapter 1, n. 8, at 100, para. 102–5. In addition, the International Court of Justice and ONUSAL have invoked the principle of humanity, as prescribed in the preambular para. 4 of Protocol II, which is inspired by the Martens Clause (providing: 'recalling that in cases not covered by the law in force, the human person remains under the protection of the principles of humanity and the dictates of the public conscience'), as a basis for the prohibition of the use of indiscriminate weapons, Advisory Opinion on Nuclear Weapons, above, Chapter 1, n. 34, para. 78; Second Report of ONUSAL, above, Chapter 1, n. 27, at 22, para. 74.

[89] Article 3(7) prohibits the directing of mines covered by the Protocol against the civilian population, individual civilians or civilian objects.

2. This Protocol shall apply, in addition to situations referred to in Article 1 of this Convention, to situations referred to in Article 3 common to the Geneva Conventions of 12 August 1949...
3. In case of an armed conflict not of an international character occurring in the territory of one of the High Contracting Parties, each party to the conflict shall be bound to apply the prohibitions and restrictions of this Protocol.

It may be noted that the UN Mission for El Salvador deemed the principles contained in the predecessor of Amended Protocol II to be customary international law applicable in non-international armed conflicts.[90]

Starvation

Armed opposition groups target civilians by, *inter alia*, restricting their access to food and other humanitarian relief, or, even purposely starving them. For example, in Somalia armed opposition groups impeded the delivery of vital food and medical supplies, because they felt it favoured the other parties to the conflict. They then kept the supplies for themselves. Such practices have given rise to a number of legal issues. One question is whether the consent of armed opposition groups is required when humanitarian bodies seek to operate in areas that they control.[91] Protocol II states that access of humanitarian relief organizations is dependent on the permission of the *state*. The commentary to the relevant article suggests that this requirement of governmental consent extends to the entire state territory, including areas under the control of armed opposition groups.[92] The commentary adds that, in rare cases, when it is unclear which entity must be qualified as the government, 'consent is to be presumed in view of the fact that assistance for the victims is of paramount importance and should not suffer any delay'.[93] In any case, it would seem that, under Protocol II, the consent of armed opposition groups even when they are in effective control of a part of the state territory, is not required for humanitarian relief to be provided to civilians in distress.[94]

---

[90] Third Report of ONUSAL, above, n. 33, at 36, para. 143. ONUSAL mentioned in particular Article 3 of Protocol II to the Convention on Conventional Weapons, prohibiting the indiscriminate use of mines, booby-traps and other weapons.
[91] *Commentary 4th Geneva Convention*, above, Chapter 1, n. 9, p. 41.
[92] The Protocol applies only to conflicts where armed opposition groups exercise territorial control, see below, Chapter 4, Section 1.
[93] S-S. Junod, *Commentary Additional Protocols*, above, Chapter 1, n. 9, p. 1479.
[94] Green has given another interpretation to this article, suggesting that 'since there is specific reference to the consent of only the High Contracting Party, it would appear

Another crucial legal question is whether armed opposition groups have a legal duty to allow humanitarian deliveries to areas under their control even if they have not themselves consented to those deliveries beforehand. In this regard, Article 14 of Protocol II, prohibiting starvation of civilians as a method of warfare, is pertinent: 'Starvation of civilians as a method of combat is prohibited. It is therefore prohibited to attack, destroy, remove or render useless, for that purpose, objects indispensable to the survival of the civilian population, such as foodstuffs, agricultural areas for the production of foodstuffs, crops, livestock, drinking water installations and supplies and irrigation works.'

This prohibition appears to apply to armed opposition groups as well as to states. It may be understood as imposing on armed opposition groups a positive duty to accept humanitarian relief and to facilitate distribution of relief.[95]

While there are few resolutions or statements from international bodies referring to the general prohibition of starvation,[96] the obligation of armed opposition groups to allow the delivery of relief has been affirmed by various international bodies. UN General Assembly resolution 2675 (1970), which, according to various international bodies, is declaratory of customary law,[97] sets forth such an obligation. It builds on the 'Declaration of Principles for International Humanitarian Relief of the Civilian Populations in Disaster Situations', adopted by the International Conference of the Red Cross in 1969.[98] The Declaration requests states 'to exercise their sovereign and other legal rights so as to facilitate the transit, admission and distribution of relief supplies provided by impartial international humanitarian organizations for the benefit of civilian populations in disaster areas when disaster situations imperil the life and welfare of such populations'.[99] While the Declaration applies to states and makes no specific reference to armed conflicts, resolution 2675 (1970) of the UN General Assembly stated that it extends

that those in the hands of revolutionaries are not entitled to similar assistance', L. C. Green, *The Contemporary Law of Armed Conflict* (Manchester University Press, Manchester, 1993) p. 133 (hereafter, *Armed Conflict*).

[95] See S-S. Junod, *Commentary Additional Protocols*, above, Chapter 1, n. 9, p. 1479; *Commentary 4th Geneva Convention*, above, Chapter 1, n. 9, p. 41.

[96] UN Commission on Human Rights, Res. 2000/18, para 8d (18 April 2000) indirectly refers to the prohibition of starvation of civilians (urging 'all Afghan parties' to refrain from the wanton destruction of food crops and civilian property').

[97] Above, Chapter 1, Section 2.

[98] Resolution XXVI, XXIst International Conference of the Red Cross (Istanbul, 1969) cited in: S-S. Junod, *Commentary Additional Protocols*, above, Chapter 1, n. 9, p. 1476.

[99] *Ibid.*, sub-para. 5.

88   THE NORMATIVE GAP

to situations of armed conflict, including internal armed conflicts, and to all parties to armed conflicts.[100]

The UN Security Council has invariably qualified the refusal of armed opposition groups to permit access to humanitarian organizations to territory under their control as a violation of international humanitarian law. In resolution 851 (1993), the Council appealed to 'both parties' to the conflict in Angola 'strictly to abide by applicable rules of international humanitarian law, including to guarantee unimpeded access for humanitarian assistance to the civilian population in need'.[101] Similarly, in resolution 1989/67, the UN Commission on Human Rights called upon 'all parties to the conflict' in Afghanistan, 'in order to alleviate the serious suffering of the Afghan people, strictly to respect human life and the principles and provisions of international humanitarian law and to co-operate fully and effectively... with international humanitarian organizations, in particular by granting them, and especially the International Committee of the Red Cross, unrestricted access to all parts of the country'.[102]

International bodies have stated that armed opposition groups should cooperate with humanitarian organizations, in particular by facilitating the rapid transit of relief consignments and by ensuring the safety of convoys. In resolution 794 (1992), the Security Council demanded that 'all parties, movements and factions in Somalia' desist from all breaches of humanitarian law, including 'the deliberate impeding of the delivery of food and medical supplies essential for the survival of the civilian population'.[103] In resolution 1984/52, the UN Commission on Human Rights appealed to 'all Salvadorian parties in

---

[100] Para. 8 ('The provision of international relief to civilian populations is in conformity with the humanitarian principles of the Charter of the United Nations, the Universal Declaration of Human Rights and other international instruments in the field of human rights. The Declaration of Principles for International Humanitarian Relief to the Civilian Population in Disaster Situations, as laid down in resolution XXVI adopted by the 21st International Conference of the Red Cross, shall apply in situations of armed conflict, and all parties to a conflict should make every effort to facilitate this application').

[101] Para. 19 (15 July 1993).

[102] Para. 4 (8 March 1989); see also UN Commission on Human Rights, Res. 1997/59, para. 18 (15 April 1997) (Sudan); UN Commission on Human Rights, Res. 1996/73, para. 17 (23 April 1996) (Sudan); UN Commission on Human Rights, E/CN.4/1994/7, paras. 707 (Report by the Special Rapporteur, Bacre Waly Ndiaye, 7 December 1993) (hereafter, 1993 Report of the Special Rapporteur on Extrajudicial, Summary or Arbitrary Executions).

[103] Para. 5 (3 December 1992); see also UN Security Council, Res. 733, para. 7 (23 January 1992) (Somalia).

the conflict' 'to co-operate fully and not to interfere with the activities of humanitarian organizations dedicated to alleviating the suffering of the civilian population..., wherever these organizations operate in the country'.[104]

The conclusion would appear to be that armed opposition groups are not to prohibit or interfere with deliveries of humanitarian relief. If this conclusion is correct then it must be concluded that Protocol II, making humanitarian relief dependent on the consent of the state, tells only part of the story. The state has the prerogative of consenting to the deliveries – and the armed opposition groups have a duty to allow distribution in areas that they control once consent has been given by the state.

Reprisals

In the context of internal conflicts, reprisals may be defined as acts of retaliation, normally illegal, in response to prior unlawful acts by the adverse party for the purpose of coercing the latter to comply with international humanitarian law.[105] Common Article 3 and Protocol II are both silent on the question of legality of reprisals taken by armed opposition groups against persons in their power. In fact, during the drafting of Protocol II, states contended that armed opposition groups are inherently incapable of committing reprisals. The rationale is that reprisals concern only relations between states which, as subjects of international law, possess the exclusive legal capacity to conduct war. Armed opposition groups might take analogous measures, but such acts could not be considered as means of enforcing international law.[106]

This reasoning is difficult to accept. Armed opposition groups are subjects of international law in that they have international rights and obligations. The obligations of armed opposition groups under Common Article 3 and Protocol II imply a corresponding right on their part to demand that their governmental adversaries comply with the same rules.[107] This in turn implies a right to enforce compliance with the

---

[104] Para. 5 (14 March 1984); see also UN Commission on Human Rights, Res. 1986/39, para. 6 (12 March 1986).
[105] L. C. Green, *Armed Conflict*, above, n. 94, p. 56, footnote 22.
[106] S-S. Junod, *Commentary Additional Protocols*, above, Chapter 1, n. 7, p. 1372, n. 18.
[107] See P. H. Kooijmans, 'Non-State Entities as Parties to Conflicts', above, Chapter 1, n. 71, p. 338.

relevant norms by the other party, including the possible resort to reprisals.[108] This argument is supported by UN General Assembly resolution 2675 (1970). This resolution uses the term 'reprisals' in relation to armed opposition groups, thereby implying that these groups are capable of committing these acts.[109]

While armed opposition groups are (it is submitted) able to commit reprisals, the trend in international practice is towards placing greater limits on the right of reprisal generally. There is, for example, a general rule against reprisals against detained persons (such as prisoners of war) and also against reprisals directed at civilian populations. These limitations apply equally to government and opposition forces. The UN Commission on Human Rights, in 1989, urged 'all parties to the conflict' in Afghanistan – clearly including armed opposition groups – 'to treat all prisoners in their custody in accordance with the internationally recognized principles of humanitarian law and to protect them from all acts of reprisal'.[110] Similarly, in a case involving hostage taking by a Colombian armed opposition group, accompanied by a threat to execute the hostage, the Inter-American Commission considered that 'violations of [the right to life] cannot be justified even in reprisal to violations of any kind committed by the other side in a conflict'.[111]

With regard to military attacks against civilians by way of reprisal, the General Assembly, in resolution 2675 (1970), affirmed as a basic principle for all armed conflicts that 'civilian populations or individual members thereof, should not be the object of reprisals'.[112] In the *Martić* case,[113] before the Yugoslavia Tribunal, the defendant was accused of knowingly and wilfully ordering the shelling of Zagreb in May 1995. The Yugoslavia Tribunal emphasized the absolute character of the rule: 'The prohibition against attacking the civilian population as such as well as individual civilians must be respected in all circumstances regardless of the behaviour of the other party... No circumstances would legitimise an

---

[108] See F. Kalshoven, *Belligerent Reprisals* (A. W. Sijthoff, Leiden, 1971) pp. 35, 266–7 (linking reprisals with acts committed by armed opposition groups in internal conflicts) (hereafter, *Reprisals*).
[109] Para. 7.   [110] Resolution 1989/67, para. 11 (8 March 1989).
[111] Annual Report of the Inter-American Commission on Human Rights 1996, above, Chapter 1, n. 137, at 818.
[112] *Ibid.*
[113] *Prosecutor v. Milan Martić*, Review of Indictment Pursuant to Rule 61 of the Rules of Procedure and Evidence, Case No. IT-95-11-R61 (8 March 1996) (hereafter, *Martić* case).

attack against civilians even if it were a response proportionate to a similar violation perpetrated by the other party.'[114]

The Tribunal derived this norm not only from General Assembly resolution 2675, but also from Article 4 of Protocol II. It found that such reprisals were contrary to the absolute and non-derogable prohibitions enumerated in that provision.[115]

Particular mention may be made of the prohibition against collective punishment, enshrined in Article 4(2)(b) of Protocol II. The Yugoslavia Tribunal found that this prohibition strengthened the prohibition of reprisals against civilians in internal conflicts.[116] Collective punishment may be defined as 'measures aimed against the collectivity of the population of a town, village or other locality and based on the collective responsibility of the population for a hostile act committed in or near the locality'.[117] Measures of collective punishment are distinguished from reprisals by the fact that they are intended to affect the conduct of the adverse party. They are in the nature of collective criminal law enforcement. However, because of the close connection between collective punishment and reprisals, Kalshoven has qualified the former as 'quasi-reprisals'.[118] The decision of the Yugoslavia Tribunal in the *Martić* case shows that the prohibition of reprisals should be understood to extend to the prohibition of collective punishments.[119]

---

[114] *Ibid.*, para. 15; see also Yugoslavia Tribunal, *Kupreskić* case (2000) above, Chapter 1, n. 49, paras. 526–7.

[115] *Ibid.*, paras. 10–18. Compare *Commentary 4th Geneva Convention*, above, Chapter 1, n. 9, pp. 39–40 ('the acts referred to under items (a) to (d) [of Common Article 3] are prohibited absolutely and permanently, no exception or excuse being tolerated. Consequently, any reprisal which entails one of these acts is prohibited, and so, speaking generally, is any reprisal incompatible with the "humane treatment" demanded unconditionally in the first clause of sub-paragraph (1)'); J. E. Bond, 'Internal Conflicts', above, Chapter 1, n. 101, at 359–60.

[116] *Martić* case, above, n. 113, para. 16.   [117] F. Kalshoven *Reprisals*, above, n. 108, p. 39.

[118] *Ibid.*, 38.

[119] See also S-S. Junod, *Commentary Additional Protocols*, above, Chapter 1, n. 9, p. 1374 ('to include the prohibition on collective punishments amongst the acts unconditionally prohibited by Article 4 is virtually equivalent to prohibiting "reprisals" against protected persons'). To support its argument that reprisals are prohibited in internal conflicts, the Yugoslavia Tribunal also referred to common Article 1 of the Geneva Conventions. According to the Tribunal, the obligation to 'respect and to ensure respect' for the Conventions 'in all circumstances' would apply even when the behaviour of the other party might be considered wrongful, *Martić* case, above, n. 113, para. 15. See for other examples of the prohibition of reprisals in the context of military operations, UN Commission on Human Rights, Res. 1993/66, para. 6 (10 March 1993) (Afghanistan).

Thus, although international humanitarian law on internal conflicts does not expressly either permit or prohibit reprisals, Common Article 3 and Protocol II implicitly permit reprisals equally by both sides – while simultaneously placing important limits on the circumstances in which either side can actually resort to them.

Underdevelopment of the law

From the practice of international bodies analysed in this chapter, it is apparent that the substantive obligations of armed opposition groups are limited to the duty to respect elementary norms of humanity. International practice leaves no doubt that armed opposition groups are prohibited from killing outside combat, torturing, summarily executing persons, or otherwise inflicting inhumane treatment. Also, there is uniform and consistent practice prohibiting armed opposition groups from attacking civilians or civilian objects, using land mines against civilians, starving the civilian population, prohibiting or impeding humanitarian relief, and taking reprisals against civilians or detained persons.

International bodies have formulated these norms applicable to armed opposition groups invariably in terms of 'prohibitions'. They have rarely indicated which *measures* armed opposition groups must take to be in compliance with their obligations. Or, in other words, international bodies have focused on what armed opposition groups must *not* do. Examples of practice according *rights* to armed opposition groups have been exceptional.

The obligations to respect and to ensure respect are, however, complementary. When penal prosecutions conducted by armed opposition groups must be in accordance with the law, it appears that these groups must adopt such law. Similarly, when a group must abstain from doing harm, it seems logical that it must take all necessary steps to make sure that all those over whom it has authority abstain from doing harm, including prosecution and punishment of these persons. Indeed, in many cases, the effectiveness of the law requires that armed opposition groups not merely respect the rules, but do everything in their power to make sure that humanitarian rules are complied with by the groups themselves and by everyone in their power.

Although Common Article 3 and Protocol II do not expressly oblige the parties to the conflict to ensure respect for the norms, conventional law does provide some support for such an obligation. For example, Article 1 common to the Geneva Conventions, applicable in internal armed conflict,[120] refers to the obligation to ensure respect for the norms in the Geneva Conventions. Furthermore, Article 5(2)(e) of Protocol II prescribes that armed opposition groups shall not endanger the health and integrity of detained or interned persons 'by any unjustified act or omission'. The reference to 'omission' indicates that, in particular circumstances, armed opposition groups must take measures to guarantee the objective of this article. Another example is contained in the Cultural Property Convention. Article 4(3) obliges armed opposition groups to 'undertake to prohibit, prevent and, if necessary, put a stop to any form of theft, pillage or misappropriation of, and any acts of vandalism directed against, cultural property'.

However, international practice provides little support for the obligation of armed opposition groups to ensure respect for the applicable law. It means that international bodies have done little to make the applicable law effective. It also means that international bodies do not regard armed opposition groups as responsible actors, exercising political and military authority over other persons. By limiting their duties to a duty to abstain, the position of armed opposition groups under international law has in fact become very similar to that of individuals, prohibited from committing international crimes.

[120] See Chapter 5, Section 3.

PART 2 · THE ACCOUNTABILITY GAP

3   Accountability of group leaders

Part 1 identified the substantive law applicable to armed opposition groups. It appeared that restraints indeed exist, although the relevant law is still primitive. The next question to be addressed is: who can be held accountable for violating these norms or for failure to prevent or redress such violations? This chapter will deal with the lowest level of accountability: leaders of armed opposition groups. The next two chapters will examine the accountability of armed opposition groups as such, and of the territorial state.

The first and lowest level of accountability for acts of armed opposition groups holds that the military and civilian leadership of these groups can be held accountable. The role of leaders is decisive in order to ensure observance of international norms by armed opposition groups. Whether the norms are concerned with the military operations, places of internment or detention, superiors of armed opposition groups must supervise their proper application in order to avoid a fatal gap between the obligations of the armed opposition group and the conduct of its individual members. If the leaders permit or condone violations of international humanitarian law, this law is unlikely to have any effectiveness.

Accountability of leaders of armed opposition groups manifests itself in the form of the individual criminal responsibility of these persons. The responsibility of leaders of armed opposition groups must be distinguished from the responsibility of ordinary members of armed opposition groups. As will be shown later, leaders of armed opposition groups can be held criminally responsible for acts committed by their subordinates. Ordinary members, on the other hand, can be held responsible only for their own acts.[1]

---

[1] B. V. A. Röling, 'Aspects of the Criminal Responsibility for Violations of the Laws of War', in A Cassese (ed.), *The New Humanitarian Law of Armed Conflict*, Editoriale

The principle of command responsibility for the leaders of armed forces is well established in traditional international law. One of the leading cases is the *Yamashita* case, decided ultimately by the United States Supreme Court.[2] But the question of the criminal responsibility of leaders of armed opposition groups has not come before international tribunals prior to the events of the 1990s. The international tribunals at Nuremberg and Tokyo only dealt with government or ruling party officials.[3] Furthermore, until recently, no international treaty existed imposing international criminal responsibility onto individuals not connected with the state.

The establishment of the Yugoslavia and Rwanda Tribunals has changed the legal situation. The Statutes and jurisprudence of these two tribunals envisage criminal responsibility for non-state leaders, whether in a purely military context or not. Moreover, these Statutes and case law show that the nature of the conflict – international or internal – , as well as the status of the superior – state agent or member of an armed opposition group – are irrelevant for the question of superior responsibility. The Rome Statute of the International Criminal Court of 1998 (not yet in force) reflects a similar tendency. Furthermore, present plans for a Special Court for Sierra Leone envisage the prosecution of the leadership of the Revolutionary United Front (RUF), the armed opposition group involved in the conflict in Sierra Leone since 1991.[4] International practice is still limited. So far, there has been only one judgment directly dealing with the responsibility of a superior of an armed opposition group, the *Aleksovski* judgment, passed by

---

Scientifica S.r.l., Napoli, 1979) pp. 199, 203 (distinguishing system criminality from individual criminality, considering the first type as the most important one).

[2] Trial of General Tomoyuki Yamashita (US Military Commission, Manila, 8 October – 7 December 1945), United Nations War Crimes Commission 4 *Law Reports of Trials of War Criminals*, 1, 88 (1945); see for the history of the doctrine of command responsibility, W. Parks, 'Command Responsibility for War Crimes' (1973) 62 *Mil. L. Rev.* 1–104 (hereafter, 'Command Responsibility'); L. C. Green, 'War Crimes, Crimes against Humanity, and Command Responsibility' (Spring 1997) NWR 26–68 (for an overview of recent application of the principle of command responsibility) (hereafter, 'Command Responsibility').

[3] Article 6 of the Nuremberg Charter, above, Chapter 1, n. 162 (which gave the international tribunal the authority to punish persons 'acting in the interests of the European Axis countries, whether as individuals or as members of organizations'); Article 5 of the Charter for the International Military Tribunal for the Far East, Special Proclamation of the Supreme Commander for the Allied Powers of 19 January 1946, reprinted in Department of State Bulletin, Vol. XIV, No. 349 (10 March 1946).

[4] Statute of the Sierra Leone Court of 4 October 2000, not yet in force, and SG Report on Sierra Leone Court, above, Chapter 1, n. 106.

the Yugoslavia Tribunal in 1999.[5] However, the legal principle has been established.

This chapter will first identify the substantive crimes for which leaders of armed opposition groups can be held responsible. There will then be an examination of international practice showing the applicability of the principle of command responsibility to these superiors, being a specific type of individual responsibility and hence a separate ground of attribution of criminal responsibility. Then the criteria for the responsibility of leaders of armed opposition groups will be discussed – specifically, the question of whether these criteria differ in any respect from the criteria for responsibility of superiors of state armies will be addressed. There will then be an evaluation of whether international practice provides sufficient basis for allocating accountability for acts committed by armed opposition groups to the leaders of these groups.

Crimes

Before appraising the applicability of the principle of command responsibility to group leaders, the crimes giving rise thereto warrant definition. Superior responsibility of leaders of armed opposition groups presumes that there are crimes the commission of which entails individual criminal responsibility of these leaders.

The crimes fall into three major areas: war crimes, crimes against humanity, and genocide. While these areas are still evolving, they provide for individual responsibility in internal conflicts, including responsibility of leaders of armed opposition groups. It will be seen that the traditional distinction between international and internal conflicts for the application of substantive international criminal law has been largely – though not fully – abolished.

War crimes

War crimes are offences against particular norms of international humanitarian law. Until recently, the common belief was that war crimes could not be committed in internal armed conflict by insurgents. Common Article 3 and Protocol II, which have been specifically written for application to armed opposition groups, do not expressly address

---

[5] *Prosecutor* v. *Aleksovski*, No. IT-95-14/1-T, paras. 58–65 (Judgment of 25 June 1999) (hereafter, *Aleksovski* case).

individuals; these provisions refer only to the parties to the conflict.[6] At present, however, although international practice has occasionally been inconsistent, it is safe to say that serious violations of Common Article 3 and part of Protocol II entail, both as a matter of treaty and customary law, individual criminal responsibility of leaders of armed opposition groups. For example, in the *Furundžija* case, the Yugoslavia Tribunal considered:

> The treaty and customary rules referred to above [inter alia Common Article 3 and Protocol II] impose obligations upon States and other entities in an armed conflict, but first and foremost address themselves to the acts of individuals, in particular to State officials or more generally, to officials of a party to the conflict or else to individuals acting at the instigation or with the consent or acquiescence of a party to the conflict. Both customary rules and treaty provisions applicable in time of armed conflict prohibit any act of torture. Those who engage in torture are personally accountable at the criminal level for such acts.[7]

Similar evidence can be found in the Statute and case law of the Rwanda Tribunal and in the work of the International Law Commission.[8]

---

[6] The commentaries to Common Article 3 and Protocol II do not make any reference to the criminal character of these provisions; see also D. Plattner, 'Penal Repression', above, Chapter 1, n. 1, at 414–17.

[7] *Furundzjia* case, No IT-95-17/1-T, para. 140 (10 December 1998) (hereafter, *Furundzjia* case); see also *Tadić Interlocutory Appeal*, above, Chapter 1, n. 35, para. 134; Yugoslavia Tribunal, *Celebici* case, above, Chapter 1, n. 54, para. 308.

[8] Article 4 of the Statute of the Rwanda Tribunal gives the Tribunal jurisdiction to prosecute violations of Common Article 3 and Protocol II; see also *Akayesu* case, above, Chapter 1, n. 6, para. 613–15; *Prosecutor v. Rutaganda*, No. ICTR-96-3, para. 88 (6 December 1999) (hereafter, *Rutaganda* case (1999)); International Law Commission's Draft Code of Crimes Against the Peace and Security of Mankind, A/51/10, Supp. No. 10, Article 20 (f) and Commentary (War crimes); (1996) (hereafter, ILC Draft Code of Crimes); see also T. Meron, 'International Criminalization of Internal Atrocities', (1995) 89 *AJIL* 561-2 (hereafter, 'Internal Atrocities'); S. R. Ratner, J. S. Abrams, *Accountability for Human Rights Atrocities*, above, Chapter 1, n. 161, pp. 94–9. Notwithstanding the practice of the two *ad hoc* tribunals and the International Law Commission, maintaining the applicability of the principle of individual criminal responsibility to persons violating Common Article 3 and Protocol II as a matter of treaty and customary law, there is also contrary evidence. The Commission of Experts for the Former Yugoslavia and the Secretary-General in his report on the Statute of the Rwanda Tribunal, adopted a restrictive approach as to the customary law applicable to internal armed conflicts. These bodies found that it was still necessary to distinguish between customary law applicable to international conflicts and to internal conflicts, and they considered the customary law for internal conflicts 'debatable' and not incorporating individual criminality, Final Report of the Commission of Experts S/1994/674, Annex, at 13, para. 42, and at 16, para. 52 (27 May 1994) (hereafter, 1994 Final Report of the Commission of Experts); Report of the UN Secretary-General, S/1995/134, para. 12 including footnote 8 (1995); see also D. Shraga, R. Zacklin, 'The International Criminal

The substantive norms of Common Article 3 and some norms of Protocol II have recently been incorporated into two criminal law treaties, the Rome Statute of the International Criminal Court and the Statute of the Sierra Leone Court. Article 3 of the Sierra Leone Statute criminalizes violations of Common Article 3 and Protocol II. Article 8(2)(c) of the Rome Statute classes serious violations of Common Article 3 as war crimes.

The question arises whether the Rome Statute is a source of substantive criminal law or only a treaty delimiting the jurisdiction of the International Criminal Court. The reference in Article 1 of the Statute that the Court 'shall have the power to exercise its jurisdiction over persons for the most serious crimes of international concern, as referred to in this Statute' may suggest that only the jurisdictional aspects of the crimes listed in the Statute are provided for. However, Article 22 of the Statute requires that persons can only be held criminally responsible under the Statute when the conduct concerned at the time it took place, constituted a crime within the jurisdiction of the Court. This *nullum crimen sine lege* rule indicates that the norms in the Statute are not only jurisdictional but also substantive in nature.[9] This argument is supported by the Yugoslavia Tribunal, which refers to the Statute as having a penal law content and not only as having a jurisdictional character.[10]

Tribunal for the Former Yugoslavia', (1994) 5 *EJIL* 360, at 366, footnote 22. However, notwithstanding this contrary practice, it would appear that the practice of the Yugoslavia Tribunal and Rwanda Tribunal, and the work of the International Law Commission can be considered to be the accurate reflection of the state of the law applicable to internal conflicts. The contrary evidence dates from before the decisions of the Yugoslavia Tribunal and Rwanda Tribunal determining criminal responsibility under Common Article 3 and Protocol II. Significantly, the International Law Commission has changed its position, denying the criminal character of these provisions under customary law, pursuant to the adoption of the Statute of the Rwanda Tribunal and the judgment of the Yugoslavia Tribunal in the *Tadić* case (1995 Interlocutory Appeal on Jurisdiction); compare B. Simma, A. L. Paulus, 'The Responsibility of Individuals for Human Rights Abuses in Internal Conflicts: a Positivist View', (1999) 93 *AJIL* 310–13 (discussing the criminal law status of violations of international humanitarian law in internal conflicts).

[9] H. Fischer, 'The International Criminal Court: a Critical Review of the Results of the Rome Conference' (Paper delivered at Symposium in Honour of Judge Antonio Cassese at the Occasion of the Award of an Honorary Doctorate by Erasmus University Rotterdam, Rotterdam, 5 November 1998) pp. 3–5 (on file with author).

[10] *Celebici* case, above, Chapter 1, n. 54, para. 309; see also *Aleksovski* case, above, n. 5, Dissenting Opinion of Judge Rodrigues, 17, paras 41, 43, 49 (arguing that Article 2 of the Statute of the Yugoslavia Tribunal has separate legal meaning); compare T. Meron, 'Crimes under the Jurisdiction of the International Criminal Court', in H. A. M. von Hebel *et al.*, eds., *Reflections on the International Criminal Court* (T. M. C. Asser Press, The

According to the practice of the Yugoslavia Tribunal, leaders of armed opposition groups in internal conflict can incur criminal responsibility not only for violations of Common Article 3 and Protocol II, but also for violations of other humanitarian norms. In the *Tadić* appeal case, the Appeals Chamber stated that 'customary international law imposes criminal responsibility for serious violations of Common Article 3, as supplemented by other general principles and rules on the protection of victims of internal armed conflict, and for breaching certain fundamental principles and rules regarding means and methods of combat in civil strife'.[11] The Tribunal did not identify the specific laws and customs of warfare that impose obligations on individuals in internal armed conflicts. Earlier in the *Tadić* judgment, the Tribunal stated that the laws and customs of war applicable in internal conflicts covered such areas as protection of civilians from hostilities, prohibition of means of warfare proscribed in international conflicts and the banning of certain methods of conducting hostilities. The Tribunal probably regarded these norms in these fields as also entailing individual criminal responsibility.[12]

The Rome Statute has given some clarity in this respect by thoroughly listing the laws and customs of war other than Common Article 3, giving rise to individual criminal responsibility in internal conflicts. Article 8(2)(e) exhaustively enumerates the crimes falling within this category of war crimes. In addition to Protocol II, this article draws from Protocol I,

---

Hague, 1999) pp. 47, 48 ('now part of treaty law, these Articles [6 to 8 of the Statute] not only constitute the principal offenses that the ICC will try, but will take a life of their own as an authoritative and largely customary statement of international humanitarian and criminal law') (hereafter, 'International Criminal Court'); but see A. Cassese, 'The Statute of the International Criminal Court: Some Preliminary Reflections' (1999) 10 *EJIL* 144, 151 (suggesting that the reference in Article 8(2)(e) of the Statute to 'the established framework of international law' may be interpreted as meaning that the war crimes laid down therein do not constitute a self-contained legal regime, but require the Court to determine the customary law status of each of the relevant crimes).

[11] *Tadić Interlocutory Appeal*, above, Chapter 1, n. 35, para. 134.

[12] The Tribunal's flexible approach when interpreting the scope of the notion 'laws and customs of war' of Article 3 of its Statute stands in sharp contrast to its rather conservative attitude towards the question of the applicability of grave breaches in internal conflicts, see main text below. Apparently, the boundaries of custom were less clear than those of treaty law; see *Tadić Interlocutory Appeal*, above, Chapter 1, n. 35, Separate Opinion of Judge Li, para. 13 (criticizing the paucity of the Tribunal's argumentation substantiating its conclusion on individual responsibility for violations of the laws and customs of war other than Common Article 3); T. Meron, 'The Continuing Role of Custom in the Formation of International Humanitarian Law' (1996) 90 *AJIL* 238, 242.

the Geneva Conventions and the Hague Conventions.[13] The Statute of the Sierra Leone Court also gives an exhaustive list of 'other serious violations of international humanitarian law', including attacks against the civilian population, attacks against humanitarian personnel and installations, and abduction and forced recruitment of children under the age of fifteen years into the armed forces.[14]

While there is at present little doubt that Common Article 3, the core of Protocol II, supplemented with some other humanitarian norms, is part of international criminal law, the grave breaches provisions present a more difficult case. The 1949 Geneva Conventions characterize as grave breaches a number of acts committed against persons or property protected by these Conventions, including wilful killing, torture, and wilful deprivation of the rights to a fair trial.[15] These norms overlap to a great extent with Common Article 3 and Protocol II. An important difference between grave breaches and serious violations of Common Article 3 and Protocol II, however, is that the grave breaches provisions confer universal criminal jurisdiction onto national courts – and even make the exercise of that jurisdiction mandatory. It was this difference which made the Yugoslavia Tribunal, following the UN Secretary-General, decide that the grave-breaches regime is not applicable to internal conflicts.[16] The position may change in the near future. The Yugoslavia Tribunal did not wholly exclude extension, at some point in the future, of the grave breaches provisions to internal conflict.[17] This standpoint of the Tribunal

---

[13] M. H. Arsanjani, 'The Rome Statute of the International Criminal Court', (1999) 93 *AJIL* 22, at 32–3 (hereafter, 'Rome Statute'); see also T. Meron, 'International Criminal Court', above, n. 10, p. 53.

[14] Art. 4 of the Statute. The Secretary-General, in his report accompanying the Statute of the Court, noted that while child recruitment, whether forced or voluntary, has reached by now the status of customary law, it is not clear whether it is customarily recognized as a war crime entailing individual criminal responsibility. This crime in the Sierra Leone Statute is therefore not the equivalent of Art. 8 (e) (vii) of the ICC Statute, which does criminalize the (voluntary or forced) conscription or enlistment of children under the age of fifteen years, SG Report on Sierra Leone Court, above, Chapter 1, n. 109, paras. 17, 18.

[15] See e.g., Article 147 of the Fourth Geneva Convention.

[16] *Tadić Interlocutory Appeal*, above, Chapter 1, n. 35, para. 80; 1993 Report of the Secretary-General, above, Chapter 1, n. 38, para. 37. The Tribunal reinforced its standpoint in several other cases, see e.g., *Tadić* case (1999, appeal on merits), above, Chapter 1, n. 97, para. 80; *Celebici* case, above, Chapter 1, n. 54, para. 317.

[17] *Tadić Interlocutory Appeal*, above, Chapter 1, n. 35, para. 83; see also *Aleksovski* case, above, n. 5, Dissenting Opinion of Judge Rodrigues, para. 44 ('I consider that the development of the rules of customary law since 1949 tends to advocate the extension of the grave breaches system to internal conflicts and, accordingly to reinforce the

may have induced the UN Commission on Human Rights to accept the applicability of the grave breaches provisions in internal armed conflict. In 1999, it adopted a resolution characterizing the acts of torture and wilful killing being committed in the conflict in Sierra Leone, as grave breaches of international humanitarian law, obliging all countries to prosecute such persons before their own courts regardless of their nationality.[18] A grave-breaches provision, however, was not included in

autonomy of Article 2 of the Statute in relation to the Geneva Conventions'); *Kordić* case, above, Chapter 1, n. 40, para. 15; see also UN Security Council res. 1193 (1998) para. 12 (28 August 1998) (reaffirming that 'all parties to the conflict [in Afghanistan] are bound to comply with their obligations under international humanitarian law and in particular the Geneva Conventions of 12 August 1949, and that persons who commit or order the commission of grave breaches of the Conventions are individually responsible in respect of such breaches'); *Tadić Interlocutory Appeal*, above, Chapter 1, n. 35, Separate Opinion of Judge Abi-Saab, at 5–6; T. Meron, 'Internal Atrocities', above, n. 8, at 569–70 (suggesting that we should take a new look at the question of universal jurisdiction in internal conflicts. In his view Article 1 of the Geneva Conventions obliging states to respect and ensure respect could be a proper legal basis); T. Meron, 'International Criminal Court', above, n. 10, p. 48 (arguing that Articles 6 to 8 of the Statute of the International Criminal Court 'may become a model for national laws to be enforced under the principle of universality of jurisdiction'). Since parties to an internal conflict are entitled, under Common Article 3 'to bring into force by means of special agreements, all or part of the other provisions of the present Convention', it would appear that, if the parties agree in concrete cases to try and punish those responsible for grave breaches, such an agreement provides an international legal basis for their individual accountability for such breaches, *Tadić Interlocutory Appeal*, above, Chapter 1, n. 35, paras. 89, 136; see also *Tadić Interlocutory Appeal*, above, Chapter 1, n. 35, Separate Opinion of Judge Abi-Saab, at 6; as explained above, Chapter 1, Section 2, the Yugoslavia Tribunal considered special agreements to constitute evidence of legal obligations of the parties to an armed conflict. A different way of enlarging the applicability of the grave breaches provisions is to diminish the distinction between international and internal conflicts. Accordingly, the Yugoslavia Tribunal put in perspective the concept of nationality of persons protected under Article 4 (1) of the Fourth Geneva Convention. In the *Blaškić* case, the Tribunal considered that in an inter-ethnic armed conflict, a person's ethnic background may be regarded as a decisive factor in determining his or her nationality for the purpose of defining his or her protected status. When it comes to determining the nationality of a group of people, its ethnicity rather than its citizenship plays the leading role. Clearly, this approach considerably lowers the threshold of applicability of the grave breaches provisions, *Prosecutor v. Tihomir Blaškić*, No. IT-95-14-T, paras. 125–33 (3 March 2000).

[18] Res. 1999/1, para. 2 (6 April 1999) (reminding 'all factions and forces in Sierra Leone that in any armed conflict, including an armed conflict not of an international character, the taking of hostages, wilful killing and torture or inhuman treatment of persons taking no active part in the hostilities constitute grave breaches of international humanitarian law, and that all countries are under the obligation to search for persons alleged to have committed, or ordered to be committed, such grave breaches and to bring such persons, regardless of their nationality, before their own courts').

the Statute of the Sierra Leone Court. At present, classification of the conflict as an internal one is still relevant to establish the applicable war crimes and universal jurisdiction.

One point needs to be emphasized. The Rwanda Tribunal determined that, in order to be convicted of war crimes, a person needs to have a demonstrable link with a party to the conflict namely state armed forces or an armed opposition group. According to this view, because violations of Common Article 3 and Protocol II can only be committed by the parties to the conflict, only members of organized groups can be held individually responsible for war crimes. In the words of the Tribunal, 'individuals of all ranks belonging to the armed forces under the military command of either of the belligerent Parties fall within the class of perpetrators. If individuals do not belong to the armed forces, they could bear the criminal responsibility only when there is a link between them and the armed forces'.[19] Accordingly, in the *Kayishema* case, the absence of a link between Kayishema and the armed forces meant that he could not be held responsible for war crimes.[20] The requirement of membership of an armed force does not apply, however, to crimes against humanity or genocide because these crimes can also be committed outside armed conflict – namely in situations where armed opposition groups, or other parties to the conflict, do not exist.[21]

---

[19] *Kayishema* case, above, Chapter 1, n. 25, para. 175.
[20] See also Rwanda Tribunal, *Musema* case, above, Chapter 2, n. 49, paras. 264–6. The Tribunal made clear that this does not mean that civilians cannot commit war crimes, provided that they have a link with a party to the conflict, *Musema* case, paras. 267–74.
[21] Although constrained by the language of the Yugoslavia Tribunal Statute (which explicitly requires a nexus to the armed conflict), the Yugoslavia Tribunal Appeals Chamber observed that the requirement of a nexus to the armed conflict was peculiar to the Nuremberg Charter and does not appear in subsequent instruments, *Tadić Interlocutory Appeal*, above, Chapter 1, n. 35, paras. 140–1. The Statute of the International Criminal Court makes no reference to a nexus to armed conflict.

Still, crimes against humanity cannot be the work of isolated individuals alone. These crimes require an organizational policy and an entity behind that policy, either a government, or in the words of the Yugoslavia Tribunal 'forces which although not those of the legitimate government, have de facto control over, or are able to move freely within, defined territory', *Tadić* case (1997 merits), above, Chapter 2, n. 1, para. 654, see also Rwanda Tribunal, *Akayesu* case, above, Chapter 1, n. 6, para. 580; Final Report of the Commission of Experts for Rwanda, S/1994/1405, Annex para. 135 (1994) reprinted in V. Morris, M. P. Scharf, *Rwanda Tribunal*, above, Chapter 1, n. 161, vol. II, p. 150 (hereafter, Final Report of the Commission of Experts for Rwanda). Similarly, the ILC Draft Code requires that, in order to constitute a crime against humanity, the enumerated acts must be 'instigated or directed by a Government or by any organization or group'. The commentary clarifies: 'This alternative is intended to exclude the situation in which an individual commits an inhumane act while acting

The Rwanda Tribunal differs from the Yugoslavia Tribunal on this point. While in the view of the latter body, war crimes must be committed in the context of an armed conflict, it required no direct connection between the superior and a party to the conflict.

The approach of the Yugoslavia Tribunal shows that the concept of parties to a conflict is of minor relevance for command responsibility and individual criminal responsibility in general. As Judge Rodrigues noted in his dissenting opinion to the *Aleksovski* case: 'International humanitarian law has, to a large extent, grown beyond its state-centered beginnings... The principle is to prosecute natural persons individually responsible for serious violations of international humanitarian law irrespective of their membership in groups.'[22]

Crimes against humanity

The predominant view of the past was that crimes against humanity require the involvement of the state.[23] However, recent international practice recognizes that members of armed opposition groups can incur individual criminal responsibility – and that, by extension, leaders can be held responsible on command responsibility grounds – for ordering these crimes or for failing to prevent or repress them. Leaders of

---

on his own initiative pursuant to his own criminal plan in the absence of any encouragement or direction from either a Government or a group or organization. This type of isolated criminal conduct on the part of a single individual would not constitute a crime against humanity... The instigation or direction of a Government or any organization or group, which may or may not be affiliated with a Government, gives the act its great dimension and makes it a crime against humanity imputable to private persons or agents of a State,' ILC Draft Code of Crimes, above, n. 8, at 94. The Statute of the International Criminal Court codifies this practice, requiring a link between the perpetrator of a crime and an entity. Article 7(2)(a) of the Statute stipulates that crimes against humanity must be committed 'pursuant to or in furtherance of a state or organizational policy to such an attack'. When committed in internal armed conflict, the 'organization' or 'group' engaged in crimes against humanity is likely to constitute at the same time a 'party to the conflict' within the meaning of international humanitarian law.

[22] *Aleksovski* case, above, n. 5, Dissenting Opinion of Judge Rodrigues, para. 31.

[23] The Nuremberg Charter, which marked the birth of the modern notion of crimes against humanity addressed crimes against humanity committed during international armed conflict. Further, the Nuremberg Charter required that the persons prosecuted and punished were connected with the state (policy). Article 6 of the Charter gave the international tribunal the authority to punish persons 'acting in the interests of the European Axis countries, whether as individuals or as members of organizations', above, Chapter 1, n. 165.

armed opposition groups may be held criminally responsible for, among others, murder, deportation, imprisonment, torture, rape, when these are acts of policy and are directed against a civilian population.

Crimes against humanity and war crimes overlap in so far as some war crimes target civilians. One distinction between the two is that war crimes may be isolated acts, while crimes against humanity result from an intentional systematic policy towards a civilian population. Thus, crimes against humanity are acts of policy, not sporadic acts by wayward individual soldiers.[24]

The Statutes of the Yugoslavia and Rwanda Tribunals give these tribunals subject-matter jurisdiction over crimes against humanity. Both tribunals have made clear that crimes against humanity as defined in their statutes can, as a matter of customary law, be committed in internal armed conflicts.[25] Further, while originally at the Nuremberg Trials these crimes were considered to be oppressive acts committed by a government against its own citizens, government involvement is no longer necessary to transform a simple crime into a crime against humanity.[26] Neither of the statutes of the *ad hoc* criminal tribunals makes reference to governmental action. In the *Nikolić* case, the Yugoslavia Tribunal stated that crimes against humanity need not be connected with a state.[27] It reiterated this view in the *Tadić* case (merits).[28]

---

[24] *Tadić* case (1997 merits), above, Chapter 2, n. 1, para. 653.
[25] *Tadić Interlocutory Appeal*, above, Chapter 1, n. 35, para. 141; Rwanda Tribunal, *Akayesu* case, above, Chapter 1, n. 6, para. 565.
[26] In its Final Report, the Commission of Experts for Rwanda suggested that the RPF was legally capable of committing crimes against humanity, above, n. 21, Annex para. 98; compare J. C. O'Brien, 'The International Tribunal for Violations of International Humanitarian Law in the Former Yugoslavia' (1993) 87 *AJIL* 639, 648–9.
[27] *Prosecutor v. Dragon Nikolić*, Review of Indictment Pursuant to Rule 61 of the Rules of Procedure and Evidence, No. IT-94-2-R61, para. 26 (20 October 1995).
[28] *Tadić* case (1997, merits), above, Chapter 2, n. 1, para. 654; but see *Kupreskić* case (2000) above, Chapter 1, n. 49 para. 555 (suggesting that crimes against humanity require a link to a governmental policy); the Rwanda Tribunal, in the *Kayishema* case, supports the interpretation of the Yugoslavia Tribunal in the *Tadić* case (merits). In this case, dealing with the command responsibility of the accused for failure to prevent or repress crimes against humanity, the Tribunal stated that its jurisdiction covered 'both state and non-state agents', *Kayishema* case, above, Chapter 1, n. 25; the ILC's 1954 Draft Code requires that crimes against humanity be committed by 'the authorities of a State or by private individuals acting at the instigation or with the toleration of such authorities', ILC's 1954 Draft Code of Offences Against Peace and Security of Mankind, A/2693 (1954), reprinted in *ILCYb* 1950, Vol. II, at p. 11 (Article 2 (11)). In the 1996 Draft Code, however, the ILC gives up this view and speaks of acts 'instigated or directed by a Government or *by any organization or group*' (emphasis added), ILC Draft Code of Crimes, above, n. 8, Article 18.

The Statute of the Sierra Leone Court also provides for jurisdiction over crimes against humanity.[29] As this court will be established for the express purpose of prosecuting the leadership of the RUF, there can be little doubt that non-state leaders can commit crimes against humanity.

With the adoption of the Rome Statute in 1998, crimes against humanity were for the first time set out in a treaty with a general scope. Article 7 of the Statute gives the International Criminal Court jurisdiction to prosecute crimes against humanity perpetrated during internal conflict. Unlike the Statutes of the Yugoslavia and Rwanda Tribunals, the Rome Statute expressly declares that members of non-state entities may commit this kind of crime. It defines crimes against humanity as attacks committed against any civilian population 'pursuant to or in furtherance of a state *or organizational policy* to commit such attack'.[30] 'Organizational policy' is intended to include armed opposition groups.[31]

Genocide

Genocide has been codified in a single, widely accepted international instrument, the Genocide Convention of 1948. The Convention defines genocide as consisting in various measures, including killing and causing serious physical or mental harm, committed with the intent to destroy a national, ethnical, racial, or religious group as such.[32] It expressly declares genocide to be a crime under international law carrying individual responsibility, which can be committed in times of peace and war.[33] Genocide was included by the Statute of the International Military Tribunal as part of the genus of crimes against humanity. Now they have been separated, although there continues to be some overlap between them.[34]

Article IV of the Genocide Convention indicates that the active backing or connivance of a government is not necessary in the commission of genocide: 'Persons committing genocide or any other acts enumerated in Article III shall be punished, whether they are constitutionally responsible rulers, public officials or *private individuals*'.[35] This text

---

[29] Art. 2. [30] Emphasis added.
[31] M. H. Arsanjani, 'Rome Statute', above, n. 13 at 31.
[32] Article II. [33] Article I.
[34] International Court of Justice, *Reservations to the Convention on Genocide* (Advisory Opinion of 28 May 1951), 1951 ICJ Rep. 15, at 23; Rwanda Tribunal, *Akayesu* case, above, Chapter 1, n. 6, para. 495; see also T. Meron, *Human Rights and Humanitarian Norms as Customary Law*, (Clarendon Press, Oxford, 1989), p. 11.
[35] Emphasis added.

suggests that leaders of armed opposition groups can incur criminal responsibility under this instrument.[36]

The UN Secretary-General, stating that the crime of genocide as laid down in this convention 'can be committed by non-State agents', supports this conclusion.[37] Furthermore, the Statutes of the Yugoslavia and Rwanda Tribunals provide these tribunals with the jurisdiction to prosecute persons committing genocide. The definition of genocide in Articles 4 and 2 respectively of these Statutes is a verbatim reproduction of the relevant provision of the Genocide Convention. The Rome Statute also includes genocide. Article 6 of the Statute repeats verbatim Article II of the Genocide Convention.[38] So these Statutes likewise leave open the possibility for prosecution of leaders of armed opposition groups for the commission of genocide.[39]

Article IV of the Genocide Convention incorporates the principle of command responsibility.[40] This article recognizes the criminal responsibility of constitutionally responsible rulers and public officials. Morris and Scharf suggested that the principle of superior responsibility would not necessarily apply to a commander who fails to act in relation to the crime of genocide committed by a subordinate, because it may be difficult to establish the specific intent required for the crime.[41] This

---

[36] This conclusion also follows from the drafting history of the Genocide Convention. Some representatives on the Sixth Committee found that Article IV of the Convention should make it clear that genocide is 'committed, encouraged, or tolerated by the rulers of a State'. This position must be seen in the light of the historical context in which the Convention was being drafted. The application of the crime of genocide in the context of the Nuremberg trials, the first legal recognition of this crime, concerned essentially the crimes committed by the state, and private individuals acting in collusion with the state, namely by Nazi Germany. Those who argued against this standpoint maintained that genocide could be committed without the active backing of a government – for example, by terrorist organizations or even private individuals – and that in some cases governments might be unable to prevent the commission of genocide. A formal proposal to include a provision in Article IV to the effect that government complicity is necessary in cases of genocide was overwhelmingly rejected, L. LeBlanc, *The United States and the Genocide Convention* (Duke University Press, Durham, 1991), pp. 29, 30.

[37] UN Secretary-General 1998 Report on Minimum Humanitarian Standards, above, Chapter 1, n. 13, paras. 62–3.

[38] Incitement to commit genocide is now dealt with in Article 25(3)(e) of the Statute.

[39] See also ILC Draft Code of Crimes, above, n. 8, Article 17 and Commentary (Crime of Genocide) (affirming that individuals not linked to a state can incur individual criminal responsibility for commission of the crime of genocide); Final Report of the Commission of Experts for Rwanda, above, n. 21, Annex, para. 98.

[40] Final Report of the Commission of Experts for Rwanda, above, n. 21, Annex, para. 174.

[41] V. Morris, M. P. Scharf, *Rwanda Tribunal*, above, Chapter 1, n. 161, vol. I, pp. 261–2 and accompanying footnote 958.

proposition is open to challenge following the *Kayishema* case in which the Rwanda Tribunal held Kayishema responsible as superior for genocide undertaken by his subordinates.[42]

To conclude, there is no serious doubt that leaders of armed opposition groups can incur individual criminal responsibility when committing this crime. While, so far, there have been no convictions of members of armed opposition groups for genocide,[43] and whereas probably factually, most armed opposition groups lack the capability to commit genocide,[44] the legal concept remains intact.

International practice as examined above reveals that the traditional distinction between international and internal conflicts for the application of substantive international criminal law has been blurred. This has, in turn, led to the division between state agents and members of armed opposition groups being abolished. In order for international norms to be meaningful in internal conflict, they must be applied to all persons involved in the conflict, including members of armed opposition groups. Thus, the Yugoslavia Tribunal noted in the *Celebici* case:

Traditionally, an act of torture must be committed by, or at the instigation of, or with the consent or acquiesence of, a public official or person acting in an official capacity. In the context of international humanitarian law, this requirement must be interpreted to include officials of non-State parties to a conflict, in order for the prohibition to retain significance in situations of internal armed conflicts or international conflicts involving some non-State entities.[45]

This trend is part of a greater move towards criminalization.

---

[42] *Kayishema* case, above, Chapter 1, n. 25, para. 555.

[43] The only trial before the Yugoslavia Tribunal containing such a charge was that of Kovacevic, which was aborted when he died in August 1998; in *Prosecutor* v. *Radovan Karadzić* and *Ratko Mladic*, Review of Indictment Pursuant to Rule 61 of the Rules of Procedure and Evidence, Nos. IT-95-5-R61 & No. IT-95-18-R61, paras. 92–5 (11 July 1996), the Yugoslavia Tribunal considered there to be reasonable grounds for believing that the accused committed genocide (hereafter, *Karadzić* and *Mladic* case). The Rwanda Tribunal convicted several persons of the crime of genocide. However, they all acted in collusion with the State Rwanda – and not as members of the RPF.

[44] In fact, most post-Second World War genocides (which allegedly occurred for instance in Rwanda, the former Yugoslavia and Cambodia, see S. R. Ratner, J. S. Abrams, *Accountability for Human Rights Atrocities*, above, Chapter 1, n. 161, p. 24) have been carried out within the territory of one state, but by the state and persons connected with the state, rather than by armed groups not linked to a state, see V. Morris, M. P. Scharf, *Rwanda Tribunal*, above, Chapter 1, n. 161, vol. I, pp. 168–9.

[45] *Celebici* case, above, Chapter 1, n. 54, para. 473; see also Rwanda Tribunal, *Kayishema* case, above, Chapter 1, n. 25, paras. 126, 554 (dealing with the command responsibility of the accused for the commission of genocide, and stating that its jurisdiction covers 'both State and non-State actors').

Command responsibility of group leaders

In traditional international law there are two different forms of superior responsibility.[46] The first concerns responsibility for ordering breaches of international law. Since this responsibility arises out of positive acts by the superior, it is also referred to as direct responsibility.[47] It is in the nature of complicity or incitement. The second form is command responsibility properly speaking: a superior's responsibility for a subordinate's unlawful conduct that was not directly based on a specific superior order. Command responsibility is therefore essentially based on omission. It consists of a failure in a duty to exercise due diligence in order to prevent a specific unlawful act or to repress unlawful conduct.[48] The focus here will be on both of these types of superior responsibility. Also the responsibility of the civilian, as distinguished from the military, leadership of armed opposition groups will be considered.

Ordering crimes

Until recently, no treaty expressly recognized criminal responsibility of leaders of armed opposition groups for ordering the commission of crimes. The 1949 Geneva Conventions require state parties to impose penal sanctions on persons ordering grave breaches of the Conventions to be committed, but these provisions apply to international armed conflicts only.[49]

The practice of international bodies, together with the adoption of the Statutes of the International Criminal Court and the Sierra Leone Court, has changed the legal situation. The Statutes[50] and the jurisprudence of the Yugoslavia and Rwanda Tribunals confirm that leaders of armed opposition groups can incur responsibility for having ordered the commission of crimes. Article 4 of the Statute of the

---

[46] Bing Bing Jia, 'The Doctrine of Command Responsibility in International Law – With Emphasis on Liability for Failure to Punish', (1998) XLV *NILR* 325, 327 (hereafter, 'Command Responsibility').

[47] Yugoslavia Tribunal, *Celebici* case, above, Chapter 1, n. 54, para. 333.

[48] *Ibid.*, paras. 333–4; ILC Draft Code of Crimes, above, n. 8, Article 6 and Commentary (Responsibility of the Superior).

[49] Article 49 of the First Geneva Convention; Article 50 of the Second Geneva Convention; Article 129 of the Third Geneva Convention; Article 146 of the Fourth Geneva Convention.

[50] Which have been adopted by resolutions of the UN Security Council (UN Security Council Res. 808 (22 February 1993) and UN Security Council Res. 955 (8 November 1994) concerning the Yugoslavia and Rwanda Tribunals respectively).

Rwanda Tribunal gives the Tribunal the power to prosecute persons who have ordered the commission of serious violations of Common Article 3 and Protocol II. In addition, Article 7(1) of the Statute of the Yugoslavia Tribunal and Article 6(1) of the Statute of the Rwanda Tribunal provide that a person who ordered the execution of a crime referred to in the Statutes shall be individually responsible for the crime. These latter provisions do not refer to the nature of the conflict, international or internal. Because, as has been shown earlier, the greater number of substantive crimes enshrined in the Statutes of the Yugoslavia and Rwanda Tribunals apply in both international and internal conflicts,[51] it is reasonable to assume that the provision regarding the responsibility for ordering crimes is equally relevant to both types of conflict. Furthermore, the general term 'person' suggests that these provisions apply not only to state agents but also to members of armed opposition groups.

This reading is supported by several judgments of the Yugoslavia and Rwanda Tribunals. Although no decision deals specifically with leaders of armed opposition groups having ordered the commission of crimes, general statements to this effect can be found in the case law of the Tribunals. The *Tadić* case (merits) provides relevant evidence. Tadić acted in pursuance of the policy of the authorities of *Republika Srpska*, an armed opposition group established inside Bosnia and Herzegovina.[52] At this stage of the proceedings, the Trial Chamber considered the conflict between the Bosnian Serbs and the Republic of Bosnia Herzegovina and Bosnian Croat forces to have been internal in nature at the relevant times.[53] It found that the various ways of participating in the crimes of the Statute as provided for in its Article 7, including the ordering of crimes, are prohibited in internal conflict. It found this rule to be part of customary international law.[54] Similar evidence can be found in the *Furundzjia* case. Furundzjia was a commander of the Jokers, a special unit of the HVO (Croatian Defence Council) military police. The HVO was established by the self-proclaimed para-state of the Bosnian Croats, inside the Republic of Bosnia and Herzegovina.[55] In this case the Yugoslavia Tribunal decided that a person who orders torture participates in the crime and for that reason is accountable.[56] The Tribunal

---

[51] *See* above, Section 2 of this chapter (dealing with the substantive crimes which can be committed by leaders of armed opposition groups in internal conflict).
[52] *Tadić* case (1997 merits), above, Chapter 2, n. 1, paras. 574–5.
[53] In the *Tadić* case (1999, appeal on merits), above, Chapter 1, n. 94, para. 166, the Tribunal revised its position, finding that the conflict in which the crimes were committed was international in nature.
[54] *Tadić* case (1997 merits), above, Chapter 2, n. 1, paras. 666–9.
[55] *Furundzjia* case, above, n. 7, paras. 51, 65.   [56] *Ibid.*, paras. 187, 253–4.

did not pronounce on the nature of the conflict in which the alleged offences were committed, nor did it examine the status of the accused. The implication, therefore, is that the ordering of the commission of crimes, whether by leaders of state armies or armed opposition groups, is prohibited in internal conflicts as well as international ones.[57]

This conclusion is in line with the resolutions of the UN Security Council. For example, in resolution 794 (1992) on Somalia, the Council condemned 'all violations of international humanitarian law occurring in Somalia, including in particular the deliberate impeding of the delivery of food and medical supplies essential for the survival of the civilian population, and affirms that those who commit or *order the commission of such acts will be held individually responsible in respect of such acts*'.[58]

This practice has also been affirmed in the Statute of the International Criminal Court. Article 25(3)(b) of the Statute determines that 'a person' is criminally responsible for a crime within the jurisdiction of the Court if that person 'orders...the commission of such a crime which in fact occurs or is attempted'. The term 'person' would appear to entail both state agents and members of armed opposition groups. Moreover, because, as has been shown earlier, certain crimes set out in this Statute are applicable to internal armed conflicts and can be committed by

---

[57] Support for the argument that a superior of an armed opposition group operating in internal conflict can incur responsibility for ordering the commission of crimes by subordinates can also be found in the *Aleksovski* judgment of the Yugoslavia Tribunal, above, n. 5, paras. 58–65.

[58] Para. 5 (3 December 1992) (emphasis added); see also UN Security Council Res. 1193 (1998), para. 12 (28 August 1998) (reaffirming that: 'all parties to the conflict [in Afghanistan] are bound to comply with their obligations under international humanitarian law and in particular the Geneva Conventions of 12 August 1949, and that persons who commit or order the commission of grave breaches of the Conventions are individually responsible in respect of such breaches'); UN Security Council Res. 837 (1993), para. 6 (6 June 1993) (Somalia). Support for the argument that the leadership of armed opposition groups can be held responsible for ordering the commission of crimes can also be found in the UN Secretary-General's report on the interpretation of the Statute of the Yugoslavia Tribunal, where he stated that 'a person in a position of superior authority should ... be held individually responsible for giving the unlawful order to commit a crime under the present statute', 1993 Report of the UN Secretary-General, above, Chapter 1, n. 38, para. 56. The Secretary-General left open the question whether the conflict in Yugoslavia should be qualified as internal or international, *ibid.*, e.g., para. 62 (stating that the clause of the Statute dealing with the temporal jurisdiction of the Yugoslavia Tribunal was 'clearly intended to convey the notion that no judgment as to the international or internal character of the conflict was being exercised'). Furthermore, he did not exclude the possibility of the responsibility of superiors of armed opposition groups for ordering the commission of crimes.

members of armed opposition groups,[59] and because Article 25 establishing individual criminal responsibility is of a general nature, applicable to all substantive crimes in the Statute, it is reasonable to read Article 25(3)(b) as applicable to leaders of armed opposition groups.

Finally, the Statute of the Sierra Leone Court contains a provision equivalent to that of the Statute of the Rwanda Tribunal. This Statute is specifically concerned with the non-state leaders involved in the Sierra Leonean conflict.

To summarize, the practice examined above in tandem with the Statutes of the International Criminal Court and the Sierra Leone Court indicates that leaders of armed opposition groups can incur individual criminal responsibility for ordering the commission of crimes by subordinates. Furthermore, international practice indicates that in the establishment of responsibility for ordering crimes, the nature of the conflict – internal or international – , and the status of the accused – state agent or member of an armed opposition group – is irrelevant.

Command responsibility proper

A separate issue is the responsibility of leaders of armed opposition groups for offences committed by persons under their authority but which the leaders did *not* order, on the ground that the leaders ought to have used their authority to prevent or repress these offences. Until recently, this type of responsibility was not regulated in any treaty applicable to leaders of armed opposition groups. The only treaty recognizing superior responsibility for acts of omission was Protocol I,[60] applicable to international conflicts only.

---

[59] See e.g., Article 8(c) contains violations of Common Article 3 which can clearly be committed by both state armies and armed opposition groups, see above, Section 2 of this chapter (dealing with the substantive crimes which can be committed by leaders of armed opposition groups in internal conflict).

[60] The 1907 Hague Convention (IV), applicable to international conflicts only, already recognized the principle that military commanders are responsible for the conduct of members of their forces, Article 1(1) Annex to the Convention, 'Regulations Respecting the Laws and Customs of War on Land', reprinted in Schindler and Toman, *Laws of Armed Conflicts*, above, Chapter 1, n. 81, p. 69; in 1993, the UN Secretary-General regarded the 1907 Convention as customary law, 1993 Report of the UN Secretary-General, above, Chapter 1, n. 38, paras. 41–4. The Geneva Conventions do not contain a provision on command responsibility for failure to prevent or repress crimes; these conventions rely solely on the responsibility of the parties to the conflict – in internal conflict the state and armed opposition groups – to prevent and punish violations of the relevant norms.

Protocol I, which codifies the principle of command responsibility as developed since the Second World War,[61] provides:

> The fact that a breach of the Conventions or of this Protocol was committed by a subordinate does not absolve his superiors from penal or disciplinary responsibility, as the case may be, if they knew, or had information which should have enabled them to conclude in the circumstances at the time, that he was committing or was going to commit such a breach and if they did not take all feasible measures within their power to prevent or repress the breach.

Command responsibility has been developed to apply primarily in the context of international conflicts, in which generally regular, clearly organized armed forces participate. The relationship between the superior and the subordinate in state armies normally involves direct subordination in a clearly and formally organized hierarchy. Hence, the ICRC commentary on Article 87 of Protocol I, dealing with the duty of commanders states:

> The first duty of a military commander, whatever his rank, is to exercise command. For this purpose the relationship between ranks and responsibilities are, as a general rule, exactly determined within the armed forces, and the authority of each of the different levels of the hierarchy is precisely defined. It is under these conditions that the armed forces can be submitted to a régime of internal discipline... This régime is inseparable from the status of armed forces... The disciplinary system must ensure, in particular, compliance with the rules of international law applicable in armed conflict.[62]

The condition of a superior–subordinate relationship may, however, be problematic when applied to leaders of armed opposition groups in internal conflicts, in particular when these groups are not organized as or functioning like regular armies. The authority of different levels and ranks in these groups may then not be precisely defined.

The provisions of the Statutes of the Yugoslavia and Rwanda Tribunals, unlike Protocol I, nevertheless apply to internal as well as external conflicts. Article 7(3) of the Statute of the Yugoslavia Tribunal provides:

> The fact that any of the acts referred to in articles 2 to 5 of the present Statute was committed by a subordinate does not relieve his superior of criminal responsibility if he knew or had reason to know that the subordinate was about to commit such acts or had done so and the superior failed to take the necessary

---

[61] See W. Parks, 'Command Responsibility', above, n. 2 ; L. C. Green, 'Command Responsibility', above, n. 2.
[62] J. de Preux, *Commentary Additional Protocols*, above, Chapter 1, n. 9, pp. 1017–18.

and reasonable measures to prevent such acts or to punish the perpetrators thereof.[63]

Further, the generic term 'superior' suggests that they may apply to both state actors and non-state actors engaged in internal conflict. This interpretation has been confirmed in the *Aleksovski* judgment of 1999, by the Yugoslavia Tribunal. This is the first and so far the only case dealing with the responsibility of a leader of what was arguably an armed opposition group operating in internal conflict. The case concerned the treatment of Bosnian Muslim detainees held by the Bosnian Croats in a prison in Bosnia-Herzegovina. The accused was a prison commander. According to the Yugoslavia Tribunal, the alleged crimes were committed in an internal conflict.[64] The Defence claimed that the principle of command responsibility did not apply to this case. In particular, it asserted that existing precedents on command responsibility did not apply because those precedents concerned commanders operating in an international conflict, whereas this conflict was internal.[65] The Tribunal, although considering the argument in detail, appeared to reject it. It found that 'any person acting de facto as a superior may be held responsible under art. 7(3)' of the Statute.[66] It based its finding on customary international law. Apparently, the Tribunal considered the nature of the conflict – internal or international – to be irrelevant to the question of superior responsibility for failure to prevent or repress crimes.[67] More significantly, the Tribunal paid no attention to the status of the accused, whether he was a state actor or a non-state actor. While Aleksovski appeared to belong to an armed opposition group (the Bosnian Croats operating in Bosnia-Herzegovina), the Tribunal refrained from making this explicit in the judgment. One may, therefore, conclude that, for superior responsibility

---

[63] The Rwanda Tribunal Statute contains a similar provision: Article 6(3) Statute of Rwanda Tribunal. The Statute is in accordance with earlier resolutions of UN Security Council, see, e.g., UN Security Council Res. 935 (1994), pr. (1 July 1994) (establishing the Commission of Experts on Rwanda, and recalling that 'all persons who commit or authorize the commission of serious violations of international humanitarian law are individually responsible for those violations and should be brought to justice').

[64] *Aleksovski* case, above, n. 5, para. 46. On appeal, the conflict was considered to be international. *Prosecutor v. Zlatko Aleksovski*, No. IT-95-14/1-A, paras. 120–52 (24 March 2000) (Appeal) (hereafter, *Aleksovski* case (2000, Appeal)).

[65] For example precedents set by cases such as *USA v. Pohl. Aleksovski* case, para. 74.

[66] *Ibid.*, para. 76.

[67] See also Bing Bing Jia, 'Command Responsibility', above, n. 46, at 345 (implying that command responsibility applicable in internal conflicts belongs to international customary law).

for omission it is irrelevant whether a person belongs to a state or is a member of an armed opposition group.[68]

This extension of the concept of superior responsibility for failure to prevent or repress crimes committed by subordinates to leaders of armed opposition groups is also reflected in the Statutes of the International Criminal Court and the Sierra Leone Court. The latter Statute contains a provision equivalent to the relevant provisions in the Statutes of the Yugoslavia and Rwanda Tribunals.[69] Article 28(1) of the Rome Statute recognizes the responsibility of 'a military commander or person effectively acting as a military commander' for failure to prevent or punish unlawful conduct by subordinates. If one does not want to call leaders of armed opposition groups commanders, reserving this term for leaders of state armies, these persons are in any case covered by the phrase 'person effectively acting as a military commander'. Furthermore, since the substantive crimes of the Statute also apply to internal conflicts, and the provisions on individual criminal responsibility are relevant to all the substantive crimes, it seems reasonable to conclude that a leader of an armed opposition group may be responsible for acts of omission under this rule.

Civilian leaders

Traditionally, the doctrine of command responsibility distinguishes between military and civilian superiors. In the context of international conflicts involving state armies, it is well established that the principle of superior responsibility for ordering the commission of crimes or for failure to prevent or repress crimes applies not only to military leaders, but also to the civilian leadership.[70] The question is whether civilian

---

[68] See further Halleck, *Elements of International Law and Laws of War*, (1866) p. 199, cited in J. J. Paust, 'Superior Orders and Command Responsibility', in M. C. Bassiouni (ed.), *International Criminal Law* (Transnational Publishers, Inc., New York, 1986) vol. III, pp. 73, 80 (reporting that 'rebel officers were responsible for the murder of our captured negro troops, whether or not by their orders'). One may also point to Protocol II, which recognizes in Article 1(1) the principle that groups engaged in a conflict should be placed under the authority of a responsible commander. The principle of command was thus viewed as a prerequisite for the application of the humanitarian rules in internal conflicts. This provision is the basis of the principle of command responsibility of superiors of armed opposition groups in internal conflict, see V. Morris, M. P. Scharf, *Rwanda Tribunal*, above, Chapter 1, n. 161, vol. I, p. 261.

[69] Art. 6(3).

[70] Examples are primarily provided by the Tokyo war crimes trials: see for an overview, *Celebici* case, above, Chapter 1, n. 54, paras. 357-63; see also *Karadzić* and *Mladic* case, above, n. 43; *Prosecutor v. Slobodan Milosovic, Milan Milutinovic, Nikola Sainovic, Dragoljub*

command responsibility is also relevant for leaders of armed opposition groups. There is not always a clear distinction between the two types of command. For example, although Sinn Fein (the armed opposition group involved in the conflict in Northern Ireland) split in 1969, since when its military arm has been the Irish Republican Army, in practice Sinn Fein and the IRA have the same command.[71] Some armed opposition groups may, however, have truly distinct military and political wings. This will be more likely in the case of de facto governments and other large armed opposition groups having a clear organizational structure.

The Statutes of the Yugoslavia and Rwanda Tribunals do not distinguish between military and non-military leaders. Articles 7(1) and 6(1) of the Statutes respectively refer to 'a person' who can be held responsible for ordering the commission of crimes. This term is broad enough to cover both military and civilian superiors. Similarly, the third paragraph of Articles 7(1) and 6(1) provides that all 'superiors' may be held criminally responsible for failure to prevent or punish crimes committed by their subordinates. In this way the Statutes clearly extend their application beyond military personnel.[72] These instruments thus apply equally to military and civilian leaders of armed opposition groups.

Ojdanic, Vlajko Stojilkovic, Decision on Review of Indictment and Application for Consequential Orders (24 May 1999); Rwanda Tribunal, *Musema* case (2000), above, Chapter 2, n. 49, paras 127–48 (applying the concept of superior responsibility in the context of an internal conflict to a civilian leader linked to the state); R. Dixon, 'Prosecuting the Leaders: the Application of the Doctrine of Superior Responsibility before the United Nations International Criminal Tribunals for the Former Yugoslavia and Rwanda', in A. L. W. Vogelaar *et al.* 'The Commander's Responsibility in Difficult Circumstances' *NL Arms Netherlands Annual Review of Military Studies 1998* (Gianotten BV, Tilburg, 1998) pp. 109, 119 (hereafter, 'Superior Responsibility').

[71] J. Laffin, 'The World in Conflict 1990' (1990) 4 *War Annual* at 141.

[72] It is true that Articles 7(2) and 6(2) of the Yugoslavia and Rwanda Tribunals' Statutes, which state that the official position of an accused does not relieve him or her of responsibility, refer only to Head of State or Government or a responsible Government official. However, this should not be read as excluding the responsibility of the civilian leadership of armed opposition groups. As the Yugoslavia Tribunal noted in the *Celebici* case, Article 7(2) clearly reflects the intention of the drafters to extend this provision of superior responsibility beyond military commanders, to 'encompass political leaders and other civilian superiors in positions of authority', *Celebici* case, above, Chapter 1, n. 54, para. 356; see also *Kayishema* case, above, Chapter 1, n. 25, para. 214. This interpretation corresponds to the position taken by the International Law Commission, ILC Draft Code of Crimes, above, n. 8, Article 6 and Commentary (Responsibility of the Superior) ('the reference to "superiors" is sufficiently broad to cover military commanders and other civilian authorities who are in a similar position of command and exercise a similar degree of control with respect to their subordinates'); see also 1994 Final Report of the Commission of Experts for the Former Yugoslavia, above, n. 8, para. 57.

The case law of the Yugoslavia and Rwanda Tribunals supports the above interpretation of the Statutes. In the *Aleksovski* case, concerning a superior of an armed opposition group operating in internal conflict, the Yugoslavia Tribunal found that the term 'superior' in Article 7(3) of its statute 'can be interpreted only to mean that superior responsibility is not limited to military commanders but may apply to the civilian authorities as well'.[73] The Tribunal considered the responsibility of civilian leaders to be a matter of customary law.[74] In this case the Prosecutor did not elucidate whether Aleksovski was regarded as a military or civilian leader, providing two reasons. First, it would be difficult to establish the formal status of the authorities in power in the former Yugoslavia at the time the alleged crimes were committed, because of the collapse of the existing control and command system. Moreover, the Prosecution argued that there was no need to ascertain the precise status of the accused. It only needed to determine that the accused exercised effective authority over the perpetrators of the unlawful acts.[75] The Tribunal appeared to accept this reasoning, concerning itself only with the accused's actual power:

The Trial Chamber considers that anyone, including a civilian, may be held responsible pursuant to Article 7(3) of the Statute if it is proved that the individual had effective authority over the perpetrators of the crimes. This authority can be inferred from the accused's ability to give orders and to punish them in the event of violations.[76]

It appears from this case that there is no legal distinction between military and civilian superiors of armed opposition groups.

Most recently, the Rome Statute for the International Criminal Court recognizes, in Article 25(3)(b) that 'a person' who orders the commission of a crime set out in the Statute is responsible. Reasonably, this term must be understood as including both military and civilian leaders. Article 28(2) of the Statute is more explicit on this matter. This article recognizes responsibility for all 'superior and subordinate relationships' not involving the failure of 'a military commander or person effectively acting as a military commander' to prevent or punish crimes committed by subordinates. There is no doubt that leaders of armed opposition groups, who do not serve a military function, are covered by this

---

[73] *Aleksovski* case, above, n. 5, para. 75.
[74] *Ibid.*; see also Yugoslavia Tribunal, *Celebici* case, above, Chapter 1, n. 54, paras. 357–63.
[75] *Aleksovski* case, above, n. 5, para. 90.   [76] *Ibid.*, para. 103.

provision.[77] At the same time, the Rome Statute upholds the distinction between military and non-military leaders. However, this distinction is formal rather than material: the standards applicable to military and civilian leaders set forth in the Statute are very similar.

Finally, as the Statute of the Sierra Leone Court has copied the provision on superior responsibility from the Statutes of the Yugoslavia and Rwanda Tribunals, it can reasonably be assumed that the Sierra Leone Court will similarly have jurisdiction over civilian non-state leaders.

This practice of holding military and civilian leaders of armed opposition groups equally responsible fits in with a trend in which the formal position of a superior, whether a state or non-state actor, military or civilian, has become increasingly unimportant. Instead, the emphasis is on the persons' actual power over subordinates. This practice has recently been embodied in the Statute of the International Criminal Court. Hence, the Statute is well equipped to meet the challenge of today's armed conflicts. Also the envisaged establishment of the Special Court for Sierra Leone, intended in particular for the prosecution of the leadership of an armed opposition group, evidences the trend towards criminalization of acts of non-state leaders.

In conclusion, international practice shows that for the doctrine of superior responsibility, distinctions between international and internal armed conflicts and between state and non-state actors are irrelevant. This trend toward criminalization of the acts or omissions of non-state leaders is of great importance. Until recently, it was generally recognized that these persons fell outside the reach of international criminal law. The norms laid down in the Geneva Conventions and Protocol I, originally only relevant to commanders of state armies in international conflicts, are now considered by international bodies to be part of customary law applicable to superiors of armed opposition groups. It is worth reiterating the observation of Judge Rodrigues in his dissenting opinion to the *Aleksovski* case: 'International humanitarian law has, to a large extent, grown beyond its state-centered beginnings... The principle is to prosecute natural persons individually responsible for serious violations of international humanitarian law irrespective of their membership in groups'.[78]

---

[77] R. Dixon, 'Superior Responsibility', above, n. 70, p. 117; see also M. H. Arsanjani, 'Rome Statute', above, n. 13, at 37; I. Bantekas, 'The Contemporary Law of Superior Responsibility' (1999) 93 *AJIL* 573, 575 (hereafter, 'Contemporary Law of Superior Responsibility').

[78] *Aleksovski* case, above, n. 5, Dissenting Opinion of Judge Rodrigues, para. 31.

Criteria for accountability of group leaders

A crucial question is whether the actual application of the command responsibility principle gives rise to any special legal obstacles when it is applied to opposition rather than government leaders. The answer, it is submitted, is that there is no fundamental distinction between internal and international conflicts or between state armies and armed opposition groups in this regard. The responsibility of superiors depends on their actual control and authority over the perpetrators of the crime, rather than on the type of conflict in which they are operating or their link with the state. Other criteria are the superior's knowledge of and ability to prevent and punish the unlawful acts.

Control and authority

As suggested earlier, the fundamental basis of the principle of superior responsibility is the hierarchical relationship between the superior and the subordinate. The justification for imposing criminal sanctions on superiors of armed opposition groups for crimes committed by their subordinates during internal conflict lies in the fact that these persons possess the power to control the acts of their subordinates.[79]

The Statutes and case law of the Yugoslavia and Rwanda Tribunals have adjusted the element of authority and control to the practical realities of armed opposition groups and their superiors. Article 7(3) of the Yugoslavia Tribunal Statute and Article 6(3) of the Rwanda Tribunal Statute refer in general terms to 'superiors'. While the terms of these Statutes offer little guidance as to the required relationship between superiors and subordinates, it would seem that these Statutes do not require the accused to occupy a formal commander position. The term 'superior' appears to be broad enough to embrace a position of authority based on the existence of de facto powers of control. The Rwanda Tribunal took this position in the *Kayishema* case, stating that the Tribunal is 'under a duty, pursuant to Article 6(3), to consider the responsibility of all individuals who exercised effective control, whether that control be *de jure* or *de facto*'.[80] In the *Celebici* case, the Yugoslavia

---

[79] See R. Dixon, 'Superior Responsibility', above, n. 70, p. 117.
[80] *Kayishema* case, above, Chapter 1, n. 25, para. 222. The Yugoslavia Tribunal has emphasized that while it is prepared to pierce veils of formalities, there must nonetheless always be a genuine link of control between the leader and the perpetrators. In the words of the Yugoslavia Tribunal: 'There is a threshold at which persons cease to possess the necessary powers of control over the actual perpetrators

Tribunal applied the standard of actual authority to structures of command that were not evident from formal authorizations:

> The requirement of the existence of a 'superior-subordinate' relationship which, in the words of the Commentary to Protocol I, should be seen 'in terms of a hierarchy encompassing the concept of control', is particularly problematic in situations such as that of the former Yugoslavia during the period relevant to the present case – situations where previously existing formal structures have broken down and where, during an interim period, the new, possibly improvised, control and command structures, may be ambiguous and ill-defined. It is the Trial Chamber's conclusion ... that persons effectively in command of such more informal structures, with power to prevent and punish the crimes of persons who are in fact under their control, may under certain circumstances be held responsible for their failure to do so. Thus, the Trial Chamber accepts the Prosecution's proposition that individuals in positions of authority, whether civilian or within military structures, may incur criminal responsibility under the doctrine of superior responsibility on the basis of their *de facto* as well as *de jure* positions as superiors. The mere absence of formal legal authority to control the actions of subordinates should therefore not be understood to preclude the imposition of such responsibility.[81]

While the *Kayishema* and the *Celebici* cases concerned state agents operating in internal and international conflict respectively, the emphasis on factual rather than formal authority also applies to leaders of armed opposition groups in internal conflict. In the *Aleksovski* case, which concerned a leader of an armed opposition group, the Yugoslavia Tribunal determined that superior responsibility is not limited to commanders officially authorized or ordered to command the subordinates in a well-defined military chain of command. In the words of the Tribunal: 'the decisive criterion in determining who is a superior according to customary

---

of offenses and, accordingly, cannot properly be considered their 'superiors' within the meaning of Article 7(3) of the Statute ... Great care must be taken lest an injustice be committed in holding individuals responsible for the acts of others in situations where the link of control is absent or too remote', *Celebici* case, above, Chapter 1, n. 54, para. 377.

[81] *Celebici* case, above, Chapter 1, n. 54, para. 354 (footnotes omitted), see also para. 371. This approach is in line with Article 87, Protocol I, stipulating that the duties of military commanders extend not only to 'members of the armed forces under their command' but also to 'other persons under their control'. The commentary to this article gives the following example: 'If the civilian population in its own territory is hostile to prisoners of war and threatens them with ill-treatment, the military commander who is responsible for these prisoners has an obligation to intervene and to take the necessary measures, even though this population is not officially under his authority', J. de Preux, *Commentary Additional Protocols*, above, Chapter 1, n. 9, p. 1020, footnote 9.

international law is not only the accused's formal legal status, but also his ability ... to exercise control'.[82]

Significantly, the Yugoslavia and Rwanda Tribunals make no principal distinction in this regard between international and internal conflicts, nor between state armies and armed opposition groups. In all these cases the decisive criterion is whether a superior exercises as a matter of fact power over his or her subordinates.

One explanation is that chaotic military situations may prevail not only in armed opposition groups but also in state armed forces. As the Yugoslavia Tribunal noted in the *Tadić* case (appeal on merits), parties to international conflicts are no longer well-established states. Instead, in many situations, the states have come into being during the armed conflict.[83] In consequence, in armed opposition groups and state armies alike, many of the structures and chains of command are not readily evident from formal authorizations or documentation. In consequence, in both situations, the *ad hoc* criminal tribunals must focus on the real power of superiors.[84]

As explained earlier, in addition to military leaders, political and other *civilian* leaders may also be held criminally responsible for ordering the commission of crimes or for failure to prevent or repress crimes committed by their subordinates. In fact, there are some indications that the distinction between military and civilian leaders is irrelevant for the question of superior responsibility. Since little international practice stating the responsibility of civilian leaders is available, the Yugoslavia Tribunal used the rules applicable to military commanders as a model to determine the degree of control and authority required of civilian leaders of armed opposition groups. This means that the decisive criterion for responsibility of leaders of armed opposition groups is de facto power rather than formal civilian or military status.[85] As noted by the Rwanda Tribunal in the *Kayishema* case, 'the crucial question in those

---

[82] *Aleksovski* case, above, n. 5, para. 76.
[83] *Tadić* case (1999, appeal on merits), above, Chapter 1, n. 94, para. 166.
[84] As Bantekas noted: 'When prosecuting persons for failure to act in both the ICTY [International Court for Yugoslavia] and ICTR [International Court for Rwanda], the Prosecution attempts to establish actual control of subordinate persons even if there exists overwhelming evidence of the accused's official appointment', I. Bantekas, 'Contemporary Law of Superior Responsibility', above, n. 77, at 584.
[85] Although the Tribunal considered the ability to impose sanctions not essential for civilian leaders, finding that the power to sanction is 'the indissociable corollary of the power to issue orders within the military hierarchy' and therefore 'does not apply to the civilian authorities', *Aleksovski* case, above, n. 5, para. 78.

cases was not the civilian status of the accused, but the degree of authority he exercised over his subordinates'.[86] The Tribunal makes no distinction in this regard between international and internal conflicts or between state armies and armed opposition groups.

As the provision on superior responsibility in the Statute of the Sierra Leone Court is worded similarly to the relevant provisions in the Statutes of the Yugoslavia and Rwanda Tribunals, it is reasonable to expect that the Sierra Leone Court will follow the jurisprudence of the Yugoslavia and Rwanda Tribunals, applying the standard of actual control and authority.

Finally, the Rome Statute has taken the same approach. Article 28(1) stipulates that a military commander or person effectively acting as such will be criminally responsible for acts 'committed by forces under his or her effective command and control or effective authority and control'. A similar standard applies to civilian leaders.[87]

In view of the practice examined above, one can reasonably assume that the same considerations apply to responsibility of leaders of armed opposition groups for having ordered the commission of crimes by their subordinates.

Knowledge

Criminal acts committed by subordinates cannot be charged to leaders of armed opposition groups merely on the basis of command relationship as such. There must be a personal dereliction on the part of the superior.[88] The standard to be applied in this regard is laid down in the Statutes of the Yugoslavia and Rwanda Tribunals, which standard is in turn drawn from Protocol I. Article 86(2) of Protocol I provides:

The fact that a breach of the Conventions or of this Protocol was committed by a subordinate does not absolve his superiors from penal or disciplinary responsibility, as the case may be, *if they knew, or had information which should have enabled them to conclude in the circumstances at the time*, that he was committing or was

---

[86] *Kayishema* case, above, Chapter 1, n. 25, para. 216. See also *Celebici* case, above, Chapter 1, n. 54, para. 378 ('the doctrine of superior responsibility extends to civilian superiors only to the extent that they exercise a degree of control over their subordinates which is similar to that of military commanders'); see also R. Dixon, 'Superior Responsibility', above, n. 70, p. 117.

[87] Article 28(2) and (2)(b).

[88] *US v. Wilhelm von Leeb et al.* (the *High Command* case), Trials of War Criminals before the Nuremberg Military Tribunals under Control Council Law No. 10 1946–9, Vol. XI, at 543–4 (Washington DC, US Government Printing Office, 1950).

going to commit such a breach and if they did not take all feasible measures within their power to prevent or repress the breach.[89]

The Statutes of the Yugoslavia and Rwanda Tribunals, although slightly differing from the corresponding language in Protocol I, must be understood to have the same meaning as Article 86(2) of the Protocol.[90] These statutes incorporate a general 'knew or had reason to know' standard. Article 7(3) of the Yugoslavia Tribunal Statute provides: 'The fact that any of the acts referred to in articles 2 to 5 of the present Statute was committed by a subordinate does not relieve his superior of criminal responsibility if he *knew* or *had reason to know* that the subordinate was about to commit such acts or had done so' [emphasis added].

In the *Celebici* case, concerning state armies involved in international conflict, the Yugoslavia Tribunal interpreted this standard as follows:

A superior may possess the *mens rea* required to incur criminal liability where: (1) he had actual knowledge, established through direct or circumstantial evidence, that his subordinates were committing or about to commit crimes referred to under Articles 2 to 5 of the Statute, or (2) where he had in his possession information of a nature, which at least, would put him on notice of the risk of such offences by indicating the need for additional investigation in order to ascertain whether such crimes were committed or were about to be committed by his subordinates.[91]

The standard of actual knowledge is straightforward. It means either that the leader knew, or that the totality of the circumstances may establish that the leader must have known that the subordinate was committing, was about to commit or had committed unlawful acts. In the *Celebici* case, the Yugoslavia Tribunal made clear that when explicit evidence of the superior's knowledge of the crimes committed by his subordinates is lacking, such knowledge cannot be presumed. On the other hand, the Trial Chamber recognized that the serious, widespread, massive, or continuing nature of the violations, may indicate whether a superior possessed the necessary knowledge.[92]

---

[89] Emphasis added.
[90] ILC Draft Code of Crimes, above, n. 8, Article 6 and Commentary (Responsibility of the Superior); *Celebici* case, above, Chapter 1, n. 54, para. 390.
[91] *Celebici* case, above, Chapter 1, n. 54, para. 383.
[92] *Ibid.*, para. 386. In determining whether a superior must have possessed the necessary knowledge, the Yugoslavia Tribunal considered a number of criteria relevant, listed by the Commission of Experts for the Former Yugoslavia in its 1994 Final Report, above, n. 8: (a) the number of illegal acts; (b) the type of illegal acts; (c) the scope of illegal acts; (d) the time during which the illegal acts occurred; (e) the number and type of troops involved; (f) the logistics involved, if any; (g) the geographical location of the acts; (h) the widespread occurrence of the acts; (i) the tactical tempo of operations;

The term 'had reason to know' raises more complex legal issues. The superior need then not have actual knowledge of the offences, but he must have sufficient relevant information that would enable him to conclude that unlawful conduct was about to take place or had taken place. As a starting point, the Yugoslavia Tribunal established that this expression imposes criminal responsibility for deliberately ignoring information within the leader's actual possession, which indicated that crimes were being committed or were about to be committed.[93]

It is more difficult when the leader lacks such information because of his omission to supervise his subordinates. With regard to these situations, the Tribunal held that leaders can be held responsible only if:

some specific information was in fact available to him which would provide notice of offences committed by his subordinates. This information need not be such that it by itself was sufficient to compel the conclusion of the existence of such crimes. It is sufficient that the superior was put on further inquiry by the information, or, in other words, that it indicated the need for additional investigation in order to ascertain whether offences were being committed or about to be committed by his subordinates.[94]

With this formulation, the Tribunal rejected the proposition that the mental standard should include the criminal responsibility of a superior for crimes by his subordinates in situations where he *should have had knowledge* concerning their activities, but where he lacks such information by virtue of his failure properly to supervise his subordinates.[95]

It was this standard that the Yugoslavia Tribunal, in the *Aleksovski* case, applied to a leader of an armed opposition group involved in internal conflict. Aleksovski was a prison commander in the Kaonik prison, which was used by Bosnian Croats to detain Muslims. The Tribunal considered the conflict between the Bosnian Croats and Bosnian Muslims to be internal in nature;[96] this determination allows the conclusion that the Bosnian Croats were at the time of the alleged offences an armed opposition group. In this case, the Tribunal restated its view expressed in the *Celebici* case that 'in the absence of direct evidence of the superior's

---

(j) the *modus operandi* of similar illegal acts; (k) the officers and staff involved; (l) the location of the commander at the time; see also, J. de Preux, *Commentary Additional Protocols*, above, Chapter 1, n. 9, pp. 1015–16 ('Ignorance does not absolve [superiors] from responsibility if it can be attributed to a fault on their part. The fact that the breaches have widespread public notoriety, are numerous and occur over a long period and in many places, should be taken into consideration in reaching a presumption that the persons responsible could not be ignorant of them').

[93] *Celebici* case, above, Chapter 1, n. 54, para. 387.
[94] *Ibid.*, para. 393.   [95] *Ibid.*, para. 391.
[96] *Aleksovski* case, above, n. 5, para. 46.

knowledge of the offences committed by subordinates, such knowledge cannot be presumed'.[97] The Tribunal rejected therefore any distinction in this regard between international and internal conflicts or between state-linked leaders and non-state leaders.

Furthermore, the Tribunal considered that the geographical and temporal circumstances are relevant factors in determining whether the superior had actual knowledge of the crimes committed by his subordinates.[98] This means that the physical distance between the crimes and the superior and repetition of the crimes, together with other factors, might preclude the responsibility of the leader. The Tribunal found that because Aleksovski lived for some time inside the Kaonik prison, he must have been aware of the repeated ill-treatment of the detainees.[99] Here also, the Tribunal made no principal distinction between state and non-state leaders.

The Statute of the Sierra Leone Court also employs the 'knew or had reason to know' standard. It may be anticipated that the Sierra Leone Court will interpret this standard along the lines developed by the Yugoslavia Tribunal, when holding the RUF leadership responsible for crimes committed by the subordinates.

Since the commission of the crimes at issue in the *Aleksovski* case, the Yugoslavia Tribunal has suggested that customary law on the *mens rea* requirement may have evolved so as to include a 'should have known' standard.[100] It referred in this regard to the Rome Statute. Article 28(1)(a) of the Statute provides that a superior of an armed opposition group can incur criminal responsibility for crimes committed by his subordinates where he 'knew or, owing to the circumstances at the time, should have known that the forces were committing or about to commit such crimes'. This provision imposes on leaders of armed opposition groups a duty to acquire knowledge of the activities of their members: the lack of knowledge will no longer be a defence.[101] This principle applies, however, only to military leaders or persons effectively acting as military leaders, not to civilian leaders, for whom the Rome Statute prescribes a different mental standard. Civilian leaders will be criminally responsible if they 'either knew, or consciously disregarded information which clearly indicated that the subordinates were committing or about to commit' crimes with the jurisdiction of the court.[102] Civilian leaders,

---

[97] Ibid., para. 80.   [98] Ibid.   [99] Ibid., case, para. 114.
[100] *Celebici* case, above, Chapter 1, n. 54, para. 393; see also I. Bantekas, 'Contemporary Law of Superior Responsibility', above, n. 77, at 590-1, 594.
[101] I. Bantekas, 'Contemporary Law of Superior Responsibility', above, n. 77, at 590.
[102] Article 28(2)(a).

under the Rome Statute, are thus not under an active duty to inform themselves of the activities of their subordinates.[103]

Ability to prevent or punish

Leaders of armed opposition groups, both military and civilian, incur criminal responsibility, when they have knowledge of crimes committed by their subordinates, and when they fail to take the necessary and reasonable measures to prevent such acts or to punish the perpetrators. This follows from the Statutes of the Yugoslavia and Rwanda Tribunals. Article 7(3) of the Statute of the Yugoslavia Tribunal and 6(3) of the Statute of the Rwanda Tribunal provide:

> The fact that any of the acts referred to in articles 2 to 5 of the present Statute was committed by a subordinate does not relieve his superior of criminal responsibility if he knew or had reason to know that the subordinate was about to commit such acts or had done so and *the superior failed to take the necessary and reasonable measures to prevent such acts or to punish the perpetrators thereof.*[104]

This provision presupposes a corresponding duty to ensure that the conduct of subordinates – whether ordered by the superior or not – is lawful. Article 87 of Protocol I, referring to international conflicts, is to the same effect.[105]

The context of an internal armed conflict and the features of armed opposition groups may, nonetheless, play a role in determining the content and scope of the duties of superiors of these groups. The Statutes of the Yugoslavia and Rwanda Tribunals stipulate that superiors are only

---

[103] *Kayishema* case, above, Chapter 1, n. 25, para. 227; I. Bantekas, 'Contemporary Law of Superior Responsibility', above, n. 77, at 590; N. Keijzer, 'Introductory Observations' to: *War Crimes Law and the Statute of Rome: Some Afterthoughts?* (Report of the International Society for Military Law and the Law of War, 1999) pp. 6, 7 (hereafter, 'Introductory Observations').

[104] Emphasis added.

[105] Article 87 of Protocol I provides: '1. The High Contracting Parties and the Parties to the conflict shall require military commanders, with respect to members of the armed forces under their command and other persons under their control, to prevent and, where necessary, to suppress and to report to competent authorities breaches of the Conventions and of this Protocol. 2. In order to prevent and suppress breaches, High Contracting Parties and Parties to the conflict shall require that, commensurate with their level of responsibility, commanders ensure that members of the armed forces under their command are aware of their obligations under the Conventions and this Protocol. 3. The High Contracting Parties and Parties to the conflict shall require any commander who is aware that subordinates or other persons under his control are going to commit or have committed a breach of the Conventions or of this Protocol, to initiate such steps as are necessary to prevent such violations of the Conventions or this Protocol, and, where appropriate, to initiate disciplinary or penal action against violators thereof'.

responsible if they fail to take the 'necessary and reasonable' measures to prevent or repress offences.[106] The Yugoslavia Tribunal specifies that 'a superior should be held responsible for failing to take such measures that are within his *material possibility*'.[107] The responsibility of leaders of armed opposition groups is thus not absolute. International law does not impose an obligation on them to perform the impossible. Hence, superiors of armed opposition groups may only be held criminally responsible if they exercise actual power over their subordinates, and only for failing to take such measures that are within their ability.

There is no international treaty imposing analogous duties onto leaders of armed opposition groups. However, in the *Aleksovski* case, the Yugoslavia Tribunal suggested that Article 87 of Protocol I may be equally relevant for armed opposition groups in internal conflicts.[108] Furthermore, in the same case the Tribunal relied on its reasoning in the *Celebici* case, dealing with necessary and reasonable measures, which concerned state armies in international conflict. This suggests that with regard to the superiors' duties, there is no important distinction between international and internal conflict, nor between state armies and armed opposition groups.

It can be envisaged that various steps might be required to be undertaken by leaders of armed opposition groups, including prosecution and punishment,[109] preventive action and investigations of alleged violations, providing clear orders and training, and establishing a proper

---

[106] Article 86(2) of Protocol I speaks of 'all feasible measures within their power'.
[107] *Aleksovski* case, above, n. 5, para. 81 (emphasis added); *Celebici* case, above, Chapter 1 n. 54, para. 395; see also Rwanda Tribunal, *Kayishema* case, above, Chapter 1, n. 25, paras. 229–31, 511; various commentators have expressed the same view, see W. H. Parks, 'Command Responsibility', above, n. 2, at 84; R. Dixon, 'Superior Responsibility', above, n. 70, p. 117.
[108] *Aleksovski* case, above, n. 5, para. 81 (relying on the commentary to Protocol I); see also V. Morris, M. P. Scharf, *Rwanda Tribunal*, above, Chapter 1, n. 161, vol. I, p. 261.
[109] In *Prosecutor v. Tihomir Blaškić*, No. IT-95-14-PT, Decision on the Defence Motion to Strike Portions of the Amended Indictment Alleging 'Failure to Punish Liability', para. 9 (4 April 1997), the defence claimed that the failure to punish subordinates guilty of crimes is not an offence in customary or conventional international humanitarian law and does not as such involve the criminal responsibility of the superior. However, the Yugoslavia Tribunal rejected the argument, finding 'that the case law and international conventions which enshrine the principle of the command responsibility of whoever fails to punish subordinates who have committed crimes are fully adequate; see also *Kordić* case, above, Chapter 1, n. 40, para. 15. In the *Aleksovski* case, the Tribunal determined, however, that civilian superior authorities are not required to have sanctioning powers similar to military superiors, *Aleksovski* case, above, n. 5, para. 78; see further on responsibility for failure to punish, Bing Bing Jia, 'Command Responsibility', above, n. 46, 345–7.

reporting system.[110] Since the action that leaders of armed opposition groups must take is closely related to the facts of their particular situation, it is not possible to identify the exact measures such leaders should undertake to prevent and punish. It should be recalled, however, that as was demonstrated in Chapter 2, international bodies have rarely formulated the measures actually to be taken by armed opposition groups. Instead, the focus has been on prohibitions.

The Statutes of the Sierra Leone Court and of the International Criminal Court reinforce the above conclusions. Article 6 of the former statute is a verbatim reproduction of the relevant provisions of the Statutes of the Yugoslavia and Rwanda Tribunals, imposing criminal responsibility on the leaders of the RUF for not having taken 'the necessary and reasonable measures to prevent such acts [referred to in Articles 2 to 4 in the Statute] or to punish the perpetrators thereof'. Under the Rome Statute, a military or civilian leader of armed opposition groups is criminally responsible when he or she fails to take 'all necessary and reasonable measures within his or her power to prevent or repress their commission'.[111] The Statute adds that, alternatively, superiors may be obliged 'to submit the matter to the competent authorities for investigation and prosecution'.[112] One commentator has raised the question whether 'it is fair that a commander or other superior, who knew of crimes being committed by his subordinates but has done nothing to stop them, should go free for the sole reason that he has submitted the matter to the competent authorities for investigation and prosecution'.[113] This may not, however, be a proper interpretation of the provision. The provision is probably better read as pertaining to cases in which the superior is unable to prevent or repress the crime, in which case he must report the matter to the appropriate authorities. On this interpretation, the obligation to report does not relieve him of the obligation to prevent or repress.[114]

[110] For example in the *Aleksovski* case, the Yugoslavia Tribunal considered that the accused could have transmitted reports to higher authorities. Although communications were cut off at the time of the offences in January 1993, the accused could at anytime have used the telephone, fax or military equipment, *Aleksovski* case, above, n. 5, para. 117. Article 87 of Protocol I requires leaders to prevent, suppress and report violations of the relevant norms to superiors. They must also make their subordinates aware of their obligations under the Geneva Conventions and Protocols, consistent with their level of responsibility. If necessary they must initiate penal or disciplinary actions against offenders.
[111] Article 28 (1)(b) and (2)(c).   [112] *Ibid.*
[113] N. Keijzer, 'Introductory Observations', above, n. 103, p. 3.
[114] I. Bantekas, 'Contemporary Law of Superior Responsibility', above, n. 77, at 592.

In conclusion, international bodies have eliminated the distinction between international and internal conflicts, and between state actors and non-state actors as regards the conditions for the responsibility of leaders of armed opposition groups.

The factual characteristics of armed opposition groups may, nonetheless, play a role in the application of the three above-mentioned conditions to their leaders. For example, the structure of armed opposition groups may be difficult to prove; the relationship between ranks and responsibilities in these groups may not be as easily determined as within national forces. The application of the doctrine of superior responsibility to persons will thus depend heavily on specific facts and may not be easy. Similarly, whether leaders of armed opposition groups failed to prevent or punish crimes committed by their subordinates depends on their material ability to take appropriate measures. This ability will depend on the features of the armed opposition groups of which they are a part.

All cases of criminal responsibility of leaders of armed opposition groups have to be examined separately, according to the circumstances involved. Nevertheless, the problems that may arise will be practical rather than involving issues of principle. Although international practice is still limited, the applicable rules have roughly been shaped by the Statutes and case law of the Yugoslavia and Rwanda Tribunals, and have been affirmed by the Statutes of the Sierra Leone Court and the International Criminal Court. They undoubtedly lie at the basis of the evolution of the rules applicable to leaders of armed opposition groups. It is only necessary, within this general framework, to refine the practicalities and consequences of the doctrine for leaders of armed opposition groups.

Limited prospects for prosecution

The main conclusion of this chapter, pointing out the accountability of leaders of armed opposition groups, is promising. However, this conclusion rests primarily on the Statutes and jurisprudence of the Yugoslavia and Rwanda Tribunals. These tribunals are *ad hoc* in nature, and concerned with only the two particular internal conflicts. Moreover, so far, there have been few trials charging leaders of armed opposition groups with international crimes. The focus of the Yugoslavia and Rwanda Tribunals has been on leaders linked to the state. In fact, until the present day, the *Aleksovski* case has been the only case in which the Yugoslavia Tribunal provided evidence of the actual application of the principle of command responsibility to leaders of armed opposition groups. The Rwanda Tribunal has focused on the genocide carried out by the Rwandan state and individuals connected with the state. One cannot escape the conclusion that these international criminal tribunals have been established for the purpose of prosecuting superiors linked to the state, rather than leaders of armed opposition groups.[115] The contribution of these tribunals to the further development of the law relevant to non-state leaders is therefore to be awaited. In this regard it is also interesting to note that the Prosecutor of the Yugoslavia Tribunal declared that she was considering prosecuting the political and military leadership of the Kosovo Liberation Army.[116] The envisaged establishment of the International Criminal Court and the Special Court for Sierra Leone are certainly important developments in this respect, enhancing the prospects for actual prosecution of leaders of armed opposition groups.

In any case, prosecution by international tribunals will be a rare event. It is therefore reasonable to ask whether there are other avenues for prosecuting leaders of armed opposition groups. Besides criminal legal action against the group as such, a second option would be prosecution of the individual wrongdoers by the armed opposition group itself. As noted earlier, however, international humanitarian law as it currently stands does not explicitly oblige armed opposition groups to prosecute violators of this law. Nor have international bodies accepted the authority of these groups to prosecute violators of international humanitarian law.

A third possibility may be prosecution of the actual wrongdoers by the territorial state. The duty of a government to prosecute members of armed opposition groups for violating humanitarian and human rights law is analysed in Chapter 5. As will be shown, international humanitarian law is slowly moving towards an obligation of the state to prosecute violations of international humanitarian law committed on its territory by members of armed opposition groups.

Another possibility is for third states to prosecute leaders of armed opposition groups for violations of international humanitarian law on the basis of universal jurisdiction. This would entail, in effect, expanding the grave breaches enforcement regime to cover internal conflicts.

---

[115] The Yugoslavia Tribunal, for example, makes considerable efforts in each case to demonstrate that the alleged crimes have been committed in an international armed conflict.

[116] Agence France Presse, 'ICTY on the Alert for Anti-Serb Ethnic Cleansing' (4 August 1999), available in LEXIS, News Library, Curnws File.

4 Accountability of armed opposition groups as such

In order to enforce international law applicable to armed opposition groups effectively, we should be able to involve the group itself as a collectivity. Indeed, the acts that are labelled as international crimes find their basis in the collectivity. These crimes are unlikely to be prevented nor will compliance with the relevant provisions of international law be significantly improved through punishment of one single individual. Therefore, the most challenging level of accountability is the accountability of armed opposition groups as such.

To make armed opposition groups themselves accountable under international law raises a host of problems. The principle that armed opposition groups may be held accountable for wrongful acts committed by them has been recognized.[1] But a number of difficulties remain to be resolved. For one thing, there is the important threshold question of defining armed groups, namely the threshold as to their level of organization

---

[1] Article 14(3) of the International Law Commission Draft Articles on State Responsibility, A/51/10 (1996) (Draft Articles provisionally adopted by the Commission on first reading), text available on www.law.cam.ac.uk/rcil/ILCSR/Statresp.htm (visited, 1 January 2001) (hereafter, ILC Draft Articles on State Responsibility 1996) provides: 'Similarly, paragraph 1 is without prejudice to the attribution of the conduct of the organ of the insurrectional movement to that movement in any case in which such attribution may be made under international law.' This paragraph has been deleted in the Draft Articles provisionally adopted on second reading by the Drafting Committee in 1998, UN Doc. A/CN.4/L.569 (4 August 1998) (hereafter, ILC Draft Articles on State Responsibility 1998). The reason is, according to the report of the Special Rapporteur, that this provision is concerned with movements, which are, 'ex hypothesi', not states. Therefore it falls outside the scope of the Draft Articles. The Rapporteur observed that, while the responsibility of insurrectional movements can be envisaged, for example, for violations of international humanitarian law, it can be dealt with in the commentary to the Draft Articles, First Report on State Responsibility by James Crawford, Special Rapporteur A/CN.4/490 (1998) (hereafter, 1998 First Report Special Rapporteur on State Responsibility).

and military power. In addition, international bodies have not yet defined the rules on attribution of the acts and omissions of individuals to armed opposition groups. In this regard, the question of attribution to successful armed groups, which have formed either a new government or a new state should also be considered. Another open question is: In what kind of forum could a claim be prosecuted? There is also the question of who has standing to bring a claim, and, who is entitled to represent armed opposition groups in a claim or at an arbitration? The following discussion will address these questions.

Evidence for accountability of armed opposition groups

Holding armed opposition groups as such accountable implies that they are to be regarded as international legal entities (subjects of international law). No clear definition exists, however, of armed opposition groups subjected to international law. The confusion surrounding the concept of armed opposition groups is illustrated by the multifarious terminology which international bodies use in denoting them. Apart from the phrase 'armed opposition groups', it includes 'insurgents', 'rebels', 'terrorists', 'subversive groups', 'guerrillas', 'criminals', 'non-governmental groups', 'movements', and 'clans'. The difficult question is whether groups should fulfil some set of minimum objective conditions, say as to their size and power, to qualify as international legal persons. On this issue, international bodies are pulled in different directions by different considerations. Reasons of humanity demand that international bodies put a low threshold on qualifications as a legal entity. States, however, are typically very resistant to grants of international status to insurgent groups, preferring to regard them as mere domestic-law criminals. While the question of definition is generally seen as an issue of international humanitarian law, it should be appreciated that general international human rights law is relevant as well.

Common Article 3 and Protocol II

Common Article 3 refers to, but does not define, the parties to the conflict that are bound by it. It requires 'each Party to the conflict' to adhere to the prescribed norms. The problem of the threshold for accountability under this article arose during the drafting Conference on the Geneva Conventions in 1949. States admitted that Common Article 3 could bind large insurgent bodies that could be acknowledged as de facto governments. There was disagreement, though, over the treatment of splinter entities.[2] For this reason, states proposed several conditions on which the accountability under Common Article 3 would depend. These included, *inter alia*, recognition of the insurgents a state-like organization of the insurgents and territorial control by the insurgents.[3] Although not incorporated in Common Article 3 and therefore not obligatory, the ICRC has regarded these conditions as a means of 'distinguishing genuine armed conflicts from a mere act of banditry or an unorganized and short-lived insurrection', the latter falling outside the scope of international humanitarian law.[4] However, these conditions have hardly played a role in the actual practice of international bodies.[5]

International practice provides no uniform answer to the question of what makes an armed group into a 'Party' to an 'armed conflict not of an international character'. The Yugoslavia and Rwanda Tribunals and the Inter-American Commission on Human Rights have set down minimum conditions which require armed opposition groups to be organized and to engage in military operations. The UN Security Council and the UN Commission on Human Rights, on the other hand, have applied Common Article 3 to a wide range of groups apparently lacking any real effectiveness.

In the *Tadić* appeal case, the Yugoslavia Tribunal defined the minimum conditions for accountability of armed groups under Common Article 3 as follows: 'an armed conflict exists whenever there is a resort to armed force between States or *protracted armed violence between governmental authorities and organized armed groups or between such groups within a State*'.[6] Two requirements follow from the Tribunal's statement. First, armed opposition groups must carry out protracted hostilities. Second, these groups must be organized. It would seem reasonable to expect that the group should be able to impose discipline upon its members in the name of the collectivity. The Rwanda Tribunal and the Inter-American Commission have formulated requirements largely similar to those set

---

[2] G. Best, *War & Law Since 1945* (Clarendon Press, Oxford, reprint 1996) p. 177 (hereafter, *War & Law*).
[3] *Commentary 4th Geneva Convention*, above, Chapter 1, n. 9, pp. 35-6.
[4] *Ibid.*
[5] The Rwanda Tribunal provides an exception. In the *Akayesu* judgment, the Tribunal reproduced these criteria for the applicability of Common Article 3. However, it did not apply them to the parties involved in the conflict in Rwanda in 1994, *Akayesu* case, above, Chapter 1, n. 6, paras. 619-21.
[6] *Tadić Interlocutory Appeal*, above, Chapter 1, n. 35, para. 70 (emphasis added).

down by the Yugoslavia Tribunal.[7] They have also identified some other important points.

First, according to these bodies, Common Article 3 does not require armed opposition groups to exercise territorial control.[8]

A second definitional issue dealt with by these bodies concerns the territorial sphere of validity of Common Article 3. The Article does not clearly define its territorial scope, providing that it applies to armed conflicts 'not of an international character occurring in the territory of one of the High Contracting Parties'. The term 'one' may be taken to refer to conflicts that take place within the territory of a single state. Conflicts crossing state borders would then be excluded. The term 'one', however, may simply mean 'a', signifying imprecise language. In fact, practice of the Yugoslavia and Rwanda Tribunals demonstrates that Common Article 3 applies to situations in which armed opposition groups operate across state lines. In particular, the Statute of the Rwanda Tribunal provides that the Tribunal's territorial jurisdiction extends to violations of Common Article 3 committed by Rwandan citizens 'in the territory of neighbouring states'.[9] Common Article 3 must therefore be understood as including violence of armed opposition groups spilling across the borders into neighbouring states, for instance crimes committed by armed opposition groups in refugee camps located across the border. The conclusion is that internal conflicts are distinguished from international conflicts by the parties involved rather than by the territorial scope of the conflict.

A third definitional problem involves distinguishing internal disturbances and tensions from internal armed conflicts such as civil wars.[10] Although Common Article 3, unlike Protocol II, does not expressly

---

[7] Rwanda Tribunal, *Akayesu* case, above, Chapter 1, n. 6, para. 620 ('the term "armed conflict" in itself suggests the existence of hostilities between armed forces organized to a greater or lesser extent'); Inter-American Commission on Human Rights, *Tablada* case, above, Chapter 1, n. 4, para. 152 ('Common Article 3 is generally understood to apply to low intensity and open armed confrontations between relatively organized armed forces or groups').

[8] *Tablada* case, above, Chapter 1, n. 4, para. 152.

[9] Articles 1 and 7 of the Statute for the Rwanda Tribunal. These articles refer to the territory of the states which are immediately adjacent to Rwanda, namely Uganda, United Republic of Tanzania, Burundi and Zaire, V. Morris, M. P. Scharf, *Rwanda Tribunal*, above, Chapter 1, n. 164, vol. I, pp. 292–3. Similarly, the Yugoslavia Tribunal has not accepted the criterion that armed opposition groups must act inside the borders of one state in order for Common Article 3 to be applicable.

[10] Rwanda Tribunal, *Akayesu* case, above, Chapter 1, n. 6, para. 620; Inter-American Commission on Human Rights, *Tablada* case, above, Chapter 1, n. 4, paras. 148–52.

exclude internal disturbances, the Rwanda Tribunal and the Inter-American Commission have both held the exclusion of mere disturbances to be a feature inherent in the notions 'armed conflict' and 'party to the conflict'. But the line separating an internal armed conflict from internal disturbances and tensions is not easily identified. Consider the following example of the Commission, characterizing the events at the Tablada military base:

Based on a careful appreciation of the facts, the Commission does not believe that the violent acts at the Tablada military base on January 23 and 24, 1989 can be properly characterized as a situation of internal disturbances. What happened there was not equivalent to large scale violent demonstrations, students throwing stones at the police, bandits holding persons hostage for ransom, or the assassination of government officials for political reasons – all forms of domestic violence not qualifying as armed conflicts. What differentiates the events at the Tablada base from these situations are the concerted nature of the hostile acts undertaken by the attackers, the direct involvement of governmental armed forces, and the nature and level of the violence attending the events in question. More particularly, the attackers involved carefully planned, coordinated and executed an armed attack, i.e., a military operation, against a quintessential military objective – a military base. The officer in charge of the Tablada base sought, as was his duty, to repulse the attackers, and President Alfonsin, exercising his constitutional authority as Commander-in-Chief of the armed forces, ordered that military action be taken to recapture the base and subdue the attackers. The Commission concludes therefore that, despite its brief duration, the violent clash between the attackers and members of the Argentine armed forces triggered application of the provisions of Common Article 3.[11]

Significantly, the Commission did not consider the duration of the conflict to be a relevant factor for the applicability of Common Article 3. This case concerned an armed confrontation between the Argentine Government and rebels, which lasted only thirty hours. Nonetheless, the Inter-American Commission decided that Common Article 3 was applicable. In the view of the Inter-American Commission, 'the direct involvement of governmental armed forces', together with other factors, compensated for the brief duration of the confrontation between the Argentine Government and the rebels. The ICRC agreed with the Inter-American Commission. It observed, in a document entitled *Armed Conflicts Linked to the Disintegration of State Structures* that 'the fact that a government is obliged to use its armed forces to combat an insurrection

---

[11] *Tablada* case, above, Chapter 1, n. 4, paras. 154–6.

is taken to mean that the rebels qualify as a party to the conflict and that Common Article 3 applies'.[12]

The reasoning of the Inter-American Commission and the ICRC is open to question. For one thing, much depends on the degree of involvement of the government armed forces. Of course, involvement of the entire body of the army is relevant in that it points to a degree of intensity of the fighting and a minimum level of organization of the armed opposition group. But the relevance of the engagement of the state army diminishes when the government employs only certain branches of its armed forces in the armed confrontation.

Further, involvement of the national army cannot be the only relevant factor, as the ICRC seems to suggest. The applicability of the law to a party to the conflict should not depend solely on the features of the other party to the conflict.[13]

Finally, the short duration of the confrontation between the Argentine Government and the armed groups is difficult to reconcile with the groups' supposed capability to engage in combat against the Government, a criterion applied by the Inter-American Commission in this case.[14] The fact that the rebels were defeated within two days suggests that this capability was extremely limited.

On the duration of the conflict, the Inter-American Commission differs from the Yugoslavia and Rwanda Tribunals, which required hostilities covered by Common Article 3 to be 'protracted'.

The practice of the Yugoslavia and Rwanda Tribunals also indicates that the requirements for applicability of Common Article 3 are equally pertinent when Common Article 3 applies as customary law.

In contrast to the above practice applying minimum conditions for the accountability of armed opposition groups under Common Article 3, there is also practice suggesting that there are actually no limitations to the reach of Common Article 3. The UN Commission on Human Rights and the UN Security Council have applied the provision to groups apparently not exercising effective power. The Security Council has taken the most liberal approach. It has applied humanitarian law to fragmented groups. For example, in resolution 814 (1993), the Council reiterates its demand that 'all Somali parties, including movements

---

[12] *Armed Conflicts Linked to the Disintegration of State Structures* (Preparatory Document For the First Periodical Meeting on International Humanitarian Law, Geneva, 19–23 January 1998) p. 9 (hereafter, *Disintegration of State Structures*).
[13] See S-S. Junod, *Commentary Additional Protocols*, above, Chapter 1, n. 9, pp. 1319–20.
[14] *Tablada* case, above, Chapter 1, n. 4, para. 152.

and factions, immediately cease and desist from all breaches of international humanitarian law'.[15] Clearly, here the Security Council posed no rigorous requirements as to the accountability of armed opposition groups under international humanitarian law, including Common Article 3. At the time of the adoption of this resolution, about thirty clans were involved in the conflict in Somalia. There were three relatively well-established organizations, plus numerous loosely organized factions and clans, lacking any real power.[16] The situation in Somalia induced the UN Secretary-General to characterize the conflict in Somalia as 'chaos'.[17]

Two interpretations of this and similar resolutions of the Security Council are possible. First, these resolutions may reflect the Council's view that Common Article 3 poses no requirements as to the organization or factual authority of the groups subjected to this article. It may take the view that, given a minimum level of violence, any band consisting of more than one person may be characterized as a 'Party to the conflict' in terms of this article. A possible alternative is that, in order to trigger the accountability under Common Article 3, the Council requires at least one of the groups involved to fulfil certain minimum requirements as to their organization and authority, which then qualifies as a party to the conflict. Once Common Article 3 applies to these relatively organized groups, all inhabitants of the territorial state, both individuals and groups, become bound by the relevant rules. The text of Common Article 3 supports only the first interpretation. It provides that parties to the conflict have to comply with the relevant rules. It makes

---

[15] Para. 13 (26 March 1993); UN Commission on Human Rights, Res. 1998/59, para. 3 (17 April 1998) (urging 'all parties in Somalia: to respect...international humanitarian law pertaining to internal armed conflict'); UN Commission on Human Rights, Res. 1999/1, para. 1 (6 April 1999) (appealing to 'all factions and forces in Sierra Leone to...abide by applicable international humanitarian law'), the civil war in the Republic of Sierra Leone, which started in 1991, resembles the conflict in Liberia in that multiple armed bands are involved in the fighting, which are uncontrolled and indisciplined, *Mondes Rebelles,* above Chapter 1, n. 92, vol. I, pp. 294–304.

[16] The relatively well-organized groups were the United Somali Congress (USC), the Somali National Movement (SNM) and the Somali National Front (SNF). All these armed opposition groups either created self-declared governments, or they claimed to exercise governmental authority.

[17] UN Security Council, S/23829, para. 57 (Report of the UN Secretary-General, 21 April 1992), and UN Security Council, S/23829/add. 2, para. 35 (Report of the UN Secretary-General, 21 April 1992), see also UN Security Council, S/23829/add. 1, para. 61 (Report of the UN Secretary-General, 21 April 1992). The UN Security Council adopted similar resolutions on Liberia, where a situation prevailed comparable to the one in Somalia, see, e.g., UN Security Council, Res. 788, para. 5 (19 November 1992).

no reference to other groups or to individuals being accountable under this article.

Yet, the Security Council practice needs a critical note. It is highly questionable whether the Somali factions lacking a minimum of organization and military power were able to comply with the humanitarian norms of Common Article 3 the Security Council imposed on them. While the prohibition against murder will not raise particular obstacles, the prohibition against passing sentences and carrying out executions without a fair trial are a different matter. Only if there is a minimum degree of organization can armed opposition groups reasonably be expected to apply the norms set forth in Common Article 3.

The position of the Security Council on Somalia can perhaps be explained by the fact that, if it had applied a higher standard, some Somali groups would have been bound by Common Article 3, while others would not. In other words, a higher threshold would have created mere outlaws instead of 'parties to the conflict'. This would have impeded the humanitarian objectives of the article. In 1998, the ICRC considered this consequence to be undesirable and therefore embraced the Security Council practice:

Given the humanitarian purpose of Common Article 3, its scope of application must be as wide as possible and should not be limited by unduly formal requirements. It is revealing in this respect that various recent UN Security Council resolutions have called upon 'all parties to the conflict' to respect international humanitarian law, and this also in the context of such 'anarchic conflicts' as those in Somalia and Liberia.[18]

In response to this position, it may be doubted whether the humanitarian cause is really served by a wide application of the norms to all involved in the conflict irrespective of their ability to implement them. It may be preferable, in view of the credibility of international humanitarian law, to restrict its application to those entities that can reasonably be expected to comply with it. Furthermore, if one accepts that only groups with a minimum of organization and control should be held accountable under international humanitarian law, this does not mean that the victims of anarchic conflicts such as in Somalia will lack protection. Even if the armed bands lack effectiveness and therefore fall outside the scope of Common Article 3, the individuals engaged in the conflict are bound in their personal capacities by international criminal law (by virtue of crimes against humanity and war crimes being

---

[18] *Disintegration of State Structures*, above, n. 12, p. 9.

prohibited).[19] Moreover, the victims of such conflicts remain 'under the protection of the principles of humanity and the dictates of the public conscience'.[20]

Another relevant factor one must take into account when trying to explain the Security Council practice, is that, at the time of the adoption of the Security Council resolutions referred to above, the State of Somalia itself lacked a government. As suggested earlier, states often consider the conferring of legal status on armed opposition groups as an encroachment on their sovereignty. The lack of a government meant that this problem did not exist in Somalia. The Security Council practice may mean, therefore, that the application of Common Article 3 may be wider when the territorial state lacks a government.

It is submitted that greater weight should be attached to the views of the Yugoslavia and Rwanda Tribunals than to the UN Security Council, since these Tribunals were established specifically to apply international humanitarian law. The Rome Statute, it may be noted, has adopted the definitions of internal armed conflicts and armed opposition groups developed by the ad hoc tribunals. Article 8(2)(f) of the Rome Statute defines an internal conflict as taking place 'in the territory of a State when there is protracted armed conflict between governmental authorities and organized armed groups or between such groups'. It is true that this article applies primarily to laws and customs of war other than Common Article 3. However, it is likely that this clause will also be relevant for the interpretation of the situations to which Common Article 3 applies. This argument is supported by the fact that the division in the Statute between Common Article 3 (set forth in Article 8(2)(c))[21] and 'other laws and customs of war' (enshrined in Article 8(2)(e)) is not

---

[19] In order to incur responsibility for crimes against humanity, an individual need not be a member of a party to the conflict; similarly, the Yugoslavia Tribunal held persons responsible for war crimes irrespective of their membership of a party to the conflict; the Rwanda Tribunal took a different approach to this matter, however, requiring a link between the perpetrator and a party to the conflict for war crimes to be committed. See above, Chapter 3, Section 2.

[20] Preamble to Protocol II, para. 4 (containing a short version of the Martens Clause: '*Recalling* that, in cases not covered by the law in force, the human person remains under the protection of the principles of humanity and the dictates of the public conscience').

[21] Article 8(2)(c) provides: 'In the case of an armed conflict not of an international character, serious violations of Article 3 common to the four Geneva Conventions of 12 August 1949, namely any of the following acts committed against persons taking no active part in the hostilities, including members of armed forces who have laid down their arms and those places hors de combat by sickness, wounds, detention or any other cause'; Article 8(2)(d) provides: 'Paragraph 2(c) applies to armed conflicts not

strict, in the sense that Common Article 3 standards are also covered by the latter provision. Article 8(2)(e)(vi) of the Statute of the International Criminal Court, for example, defines war crimes as 'rape, sexual slavery, enforced prostitution, forced pregnancy..., enforced sterilization, and any other form of sexual violence *also constituting a serious violation of article 3 common to the four Geneva Conventions*'.[22]

While the Rome Statute incorporates various substantive norms of Protocol II, it removes the requirement of territorial control for applicability of the Protocol.[23] Moreover, the Rome Statute abolishes the twofold standard of Common Article 3 and Protocol II, which currently applies to armed opposition groups in internal conflicts. While Article 8 of the Statute defines in two provisions a conflict not of an international character, these definitions are very much the same, and clearly closely related. This is a welcome addition to the law as it stands at present. Currently, Protocol II and Common Article 3 may apply simultaneously to different parties operating in what is, at least factually, one conflict.[24] This is highly undesirable from a practical point of view. It means that an armed opposition group may be obliged to apply two different legal regimes in its relations with other parties to the conflict.[25]

---

of an international character and thus does not apply to situations of internal disturbances and tensions, such as riots, isolated and sporadic acts of violence or other acts of a similar nature.'

[22] Emphasis added.

[23] Article 8(2)(f) containing the applicability clause for the Protocol II standards set forth in the Statute of the International Criminal Court, in Article 8(2)(e) provides that 'paragraph 2(e) applies to armed conflicts not of an international character and thus does not apply to situations of internal disturbances and tensions, such as riots, isolated and sporadic acts of violence or other acts of a similar nature. It applies to armed conflicts that take place in the territory of a State when there is protracted armed conflict between governmental authorities and organized armed groups or between such groups.'

[24] Similarly, it is possible that humanitarian rules for international conflicts apply simultaneously to humanitarian law for internal conflicts but in relation to different parties to the conflict. Accordingly, the Yugoslavia Tribunal determined in the *Celebici* case that 'should the conflict in Bosnia and Herzegovina be international, the relevant norms of international humanitarian law apply throughout its territory until the general cessation of hostilities, unless it can be shown that the conflicts in some areas were separate internal conflicts, unrelated to the larger international armed conflict, above, Chapter 1, n. 54, para. 209.

[25] Compare, *Aleksovski* case, above, Chapter 3, n. 5, Judge Rodrigues Dissenting, at 27 para. 27 (arguing that the conflict in the former Yugoslavia as a whole should be qualified as an international armed conflict, this approach being attractive 'because of its concern for clarity and consistency ... It precludes victims of similar acts from being protected in a given time and place but not in other times and places in the conflict as a whole').

The removal of the territorial control requirement in the Rome Statute for the applicability of Protocol II standards may be the result of the very limited application of this instrument. International bodies have applied Protocol II much less frequently than Common Article 3. One explanation appears to be the high threshold for accountability under the Protocol. Article 1 limits the application of the Protocol to non-international armed conflicts which 'take place in the territory of a High Contracting Party between its armed forces and dissident armed forces or other organized armed groups, which under responsible command, exercise such control over a part of its territory as to enable them to carry out sustained and concerted military operations and to implement this Protocol'.

Expressly excluded from the scope of the Protocol are 'situations of internal disturbances and tensions, such as riots, isolated and sporadic acts of violence and other acts of a similar nature, as not being armed conflicts'.

The rationale for these conditions was that only organized groups under a responsible command and in control of part of the territory were considered to be able to implement the Protocol.[26] Furthermore, the absence of a definition of an internal armed conflict in Common Article 3 proved to leave states too much freedom in their determination of the applicability of the law. The conditions stipulated in this Protocol were intended to limit this freedom.[27]

In accordance with the treaty texts, international bodies have interpreted the scope of accountability of Protocol II as being narrower than that of Common Article 3. In fact, they have considered the Protocol's threshold to be so high as to prevent the Protocol from applying to most cases. For example, the UN Secretary-General observed that the major difficulty with Protocol II is that its application is limited to 'situations at or near the level of a full-scale civil war'.[28] He found it revealing that

---

[26] S-S. Junod, *Commentary Additional Protocols*, above, Chapter 1, n. 9, p. 1353.
[27] *Ibid.*, p. 1348.
[28] UN Secretary-General 1998 Report on Minimum Humanitarian Standards, above, Chapter 1, n. 13, para. 79. See also Rwanda Tribunal, *Akayesu* case, above, Chapter 1, n. 6, para. 601 ('a clear distinction as to the thresholds of application has been made between...situations of non-international (internal) armed conflicts, where Common Article 3 and Protocol II are applicable and non-international armed conflicts where only Common Article 3 is applicable'); ICRC *Disintegration of State Structures*, above, n. 12, p. 10 (stating that the applicability clauses of Protocol II to armed opposition groups are 'hardly ever fulfilled by an armed faction party to an anarchic conflict'). It should be noted that groups which fall outside the scope of Protocol II may be bound by Common Article 3, which applies to all non-international armed conflicts, and

'there are occasions where the Security Council has determined that an internal situation amounts to a threat to international peace and security (so as to initiate action under the Charter), but where it is unclear as to whether Protocol II would apply'.[29] The Secretary-General was referring here to the situations in Somalia in 1992–3, and Liberia in 1993.

The high threshold for applicability has also prevented the Prosecutor of the Yugoslavia Tribunal from invoking Protocol II in the context of the conflict in the former Yugoslavia.[30] He found the criteria for applicability of the Protocol troublesome. Besides, the Prosecutor regarded the substantive norms of Common Article 3 to be adequate, enabling him to prosecute the cases brought before him.[31] In his view, Protocol II did not add much in these cases.

In those cases in which international bodies have applied Protocol II to armed opposition groups, they have strictly applied the criteria for accountability. They required armed opposition groups to control territory, to carry out sustained and concerted military operations and to be under responsible command. The Rwanda Tribunal applied these criteria to the RPF:

The Chamber, also taking judicial notice of a number of UN official documents dealing with the conflict in Rwanda in 1994, finds, in addition to the requirements of Common Article 3 being met, that the material conditions listed above relevant to Protocol II have been fulfilled. It has been shown that there was a conflict between, on the one hand, the RPF, under the command of General Kagame, and, on the other, the governmental forces, the FAR. The RPF increased its control over the Rwandan territory from that agreed in the Arusha Accords

which has retained its autonomous existence next to Protocol II, S-S. Junod, *Commentary Additional Protocols*, above, Chapter 1, n. 9, p. 1350.

[29] UN Secretary-General 1998 Report on Minimum Humanitarian Standards, above, Chapter 1, n. 13, para. 80.

[30] Protocol II falls within the material jurisdiction of the Yugoslavia Tribunal. In the *Tadić Interlocutory Appeal* case, above, Chapter 1, n. 35, the Tribunal decided that many provisions of Protocol II can now be regarded as 'declaratory of existing rules or as having crystallised emerging rules of customary law', above, Chapter 1, Section 1 and accompanying footnotes. As the Tribunal, in application of the principle of *nullum crimen sine lege*, applies only rules of international humanitarian law which are beyond any doubt part of customary law (1993 Report of the UN Secretary-General, above, Chapter 1, n. 38, para 34; *Tadić Interlocutory Appeal*, above, Chapter 1, n. 35, para. 143), Protocol II would appear to fall within its mandate.

[31] Interview with W. Fenrick, Office of the Prosecutor, Yugoslavia Tribunal (The Hague, 15 January 1998). An additional factor preventing the Yugoslavia Tribunal from applying Protocol II is likely to be the requirement of involvement of the state armed forces in the conflict.

to over half of the country by mid-May 1994, and carried out continuous and sustained military operations until the cease fire on 18 July 1994 which brought the war to an end. The RPF troops were disciplined and possessed a structured leadership which was answerable to authority.[32]

In other cases, international bodies also have stayed fairly close to the criteria for accountability laid down in Article 1 of Protocol II. The Protocol has only been applied to groups when there was little doubt that they met the threshold laid down in this article. The UN Commission on Human Rights, its Special Representative on the Situation of Human Rights in El Salvador, and the UN Mission for El Salvador have applied Protocol II to FMLN, in El Salvador.[33] The UN Commission on Human Rights has applied the Protocol to the SPLA in Sudan.[34] The Inter-American Commission has applied it to the armed opposition groups in Colombia.[35] There can be little doubt that these groups indeed met the requirements of Article 1 of Protocol II.[36]

As said, the restrictive approach taken by international bodies towards the applicability clauses of Protocol II stands in contrast to the practice on Common Article 3, which has been applied to a wide range of groups. One may wonder whether international bodies perhaps too easily assume the inapplicability of Protocol II. As the Inter-American Commission noted, the main distinction between Common Article 3

---

[32] *Akayesu* case, above, Chapter 1, n. 6, para. 627.
[33] UN Commission on Human Rights, Res.1989/68, pr. (8 March 1989); 1985 Final Report of the Special Representative on El Salvador, above, Chapter 1, n. 8, at 51, para. 122; First Report of ONUSAL, above, Chapter 1, n. 153, at 155, para. 39 and accompanying footnote 6, at 156, footnote 13.
[34] Res. 1998/67, para. 6 (21 April 1998).
[35] Third Report on Colombia, above, Chapter 1, n. 8, at 77, para. 20.
[36] First Report of ONUSAL, above, Chapter 1, n. 153, at 154, para. 38 (observing that 'FMLN has a relatively stable presence in conflict zones and has a decisive influence on the life of the population'); 1995 Joint Report of the Special Rapporteur on Question of Torture, and the Special Rapporteur on Extrajudicial, Summary or Arbitrary Executions, above, Chapter 1, n. 8, para. 35 (stating with regard to the armed opposition groups in Colombia: 'In certain areas, the guerilla groups are said to have replaced the State administration and exercise complete control'); G. Best, *War & Law*, above, n. 2, p. 347 (noting that FMLN in El Salvador by the mid-1980s seemed to meet the requirements of Protocol II); R. K. Goldman, 'International Humanitarian Law and the Armed Conflicts in El Salvador and Nicaragua', 2 *Am. U. J. Int'l L. & Pol'y* (1987) 539, 542 (arguing that in the case of El Salvador the warring parties are bound by Protocol II); Amnesty International, *Amnesty International Report 1999* (Amnesty International Publications, London, 1999) p. 314 (reporting that large parts of southern Sudan, Blue Nile state and parts of South Kordofan were under the control of SPLA, led by John Garang de Mabior).

and Protocol II lies in the requirement of territorial control.[37] While the assumption among international bodies seems to be that armed opposition groups generally lack territorial control,[38] in a number of conflicts this may appear to be false. Apart from armed opposition groups that are or were involved in the conflicts in Colombia, El Salvador, and Sudan, arguably also armed opposition groups in the conflicts in Angola, Congo, Sierra Leone, and Sri Lanka have for shorter or longer periods exercised territorial control.[39] It should be possible to hold these groups accountable under Protocol II. Admittedly, in specific cases, it may be difficult to establish that armed opposition groups actually control territory, the size of the territory and the period the territory was in their hands.

Other rules of humanitarian law

As explained in Part 1, armed opposition groups are bound by humanitarian standards other than those of Common Article 3 and Protocol II. These standards include rules on specific weapons, such as Amended Protocol II on Prohibitions or Restrictions on the Use of Mines, Booby-Traps and Other Devices, the Cultural Property Convention and the Second Protocol to this Convention. Furthermore, armed opposition groups will be bound by special agreements which they might conclude. Here, I am concerned with the conditions for the accountability of

---

[37] *Tablada* case, above, Chapter 1, n. 4, para. 152 and footnote 17 (pointing out that application of Common Article 3 does not require dissident armed groups to exercise control over parts of national territory; such large scale hostilities being regulated by Protocol II).

[38] See also C. Greenwood, 'International Humanitarian Law', above, Chapter 1, n. 66 p. 228–9; G. Best, *War & Law*, above, n. 2, p. 347 (noting that insurgent forces must already 'have progressed quite far in their struggles to satisfy such a stringent territorial-control requirement').

[39] *Amnesty International Report 1999*, above, n. 36, p. 314 (reporting that the armed opposition groups in Sierra Leone controlled parts of the country, effectively holding captive 10,000 civilians); L. van der Heide, 'Goma danst lingala op Congolese vulkaan' *NRC Handelsblad* 4 (Rotterdam, 30 September 1999) (reporting that the RCD (*Rassemblement Congolais pour la Démocratie*) controls Goma which in turn effectively functions as the capital of the non-recognized republic of East Congo); *Amnesty International Report 1999*, above, n. 36, p. 76 (reporting that UNITA, the armed opposition group engaged in the conflict in Angola, continued to hold territory); F. van Straaten, 'Tamil Tijgers zijn nog lang niet afgeschreven' *NRC Handelsblad* 6 (Rotterdam, 20 July 1996) (stating that the Tamil Tigers have controlled peninsula Jaffna for a number of years). Angola, Congo, and Sri Lanka have not ratified Protocol II; the armed opposition groups engaged in these conflicts are nonetheless bound by the provisions of the Protocol to the extent they reflect customary law.

armed opposition groups under these norms, and I intend to show that these conditions are the same as those relevant to Common Article 3.

Article 1(2) of Amended Protocol II to the Conventional Weapons Convention states that it applies to situations covered by Common Article 3. It adds that it shall not apply to situations of 'internal disturbances and tensions, such as riots, isolated and sporadic acts of violence and other acts of a similar nature, as not being armed conflicts'. Article 19(1) of the Cultural Property Convention and Article 22(1) of its Second Protocol, using the same terminology as Common Article 3, stipulate that they shall apply to the parties to an armed conflict not of an international character.[40] Like Common Article 3, none of these three instruments defines the parties to the conflict to which they apply. There is no practice of international bodies shedding further light on the conditions for accountability of armed opposition groups under these conventions. Nevertheless, in view of the fact that they are all based on or inspired by Common Article 3, it seems reasonable to assume that the conditions identified by international bodies for the accountability of armed opposition groups for breaches of Common Article 3 should apply equally to these conventions.

The position is much the same regarding the application of *customary* humanitarian law other than Common Article 3 and Protocol II to armed opposition groups. International bodies have only required the existence of an internal armed conflict within the meaning of Common Article 3. Therefore, here also Common Article 3 constitutes the minimum threshold for accountability.[41]

The extension of the law applicable to armed opposition groups beyond Common Article 3 and Protocol II has not been accompanied by an increase in the severity of the consequences for failing to comply with these norms. This is remarkable. The substantive norms of Amended Protocol II on Prohibitions or Restrictions on the Use of Mines, Booby-Traps and Other Devices, the Cultural Property Convention and other laws and customs of war, which norms are primarily designed to apply to states involved in international conflicts, require a higher standard

---

[40] Article 22(2) of the Second Protocol to the Cultural Property Convention adds that it shall not apply to situations of internal disturbances and tensions, such as riots, isolated and sporadic acts of violence and other acts of a similar nature.

[41] For example, in the *Tadić Interlocutory Appeal* case, once the Yugoslavia Tribunal had established that an internal armed conflict existed, it found that a variety of customary humanitarian law applied to the parties to the conflict other than Common Article 3 and Protocol II, see *Tadić Interlocutory Appeal*, above, Chapter 1, n. 35, para. 89.

of conduct than Common Article 3 and Protocol II.[42] Arguably, the conditions for accountability under these norms should also be higher. Alternatively, it may be argued that, as a minimum, the stricter requirements of Protocol II should apply.

The same holds true for special agreements concluded by armed opposition groups. As explained earlier, Common Article 3 and Article 19(2) of the Cultural Property Convention entitle armed opposition groups to conclude special agreements bringing into force other provisions of the treaties of which these articles are part. These provisions do not require groups to fulfil additional criteria in order to be held accountable for violation of other substantive norms agreed to. International practice affirms the principle that armed opposition groups that are bound by Common Article 3 may be held accountable under any other humanitarian rules.[43] Moreover, it could be maintained that agreements concluded by armed opposition groups with which they are by no means able to comply, cannot render them accountable.[44] However, the above-mentioned treaties and international practice do not support this argument.

Human rights treaties

Earlier I have contended that one cannot easily presume that international human rights law has invested armed opposition groups with obligations. Human rights treaties bind in principle only the state in its relation with individuals living under its jurisdiction. The purpose of these norms is to check abuse of state power. The justification for the accountability of armed opposition groups under human rights law may be found in the circumstances at issue and the factual characteristics of these groups. Indeed, it may be argued that, when armed opposition groups exercise *quasi*-governmental functions in part of the state territory, and in that sense resemble a government, human rights

---

[42] P. Herby, 'Third Session of the Review Conference of States Parties to the 1980 United Nations Convention on Certain Conventional Weapons (CCW)' (1996) 312 *IRRC* 361–8, text available on www.icrc.org (visited, 1 January 2001) (noting that parties to an internal armed conflict will have difficulty in implementing the norms of the Amended Protocol to the CCW since they may lack the resources or expertise).

[43] *Tadić Interlocutory Appeal*, above, Chapter 1, n. 35, para. 89.

[44] Compare K. Doehring, 'Effectiveness' (1995) 2 *EPIL* 46 (hereafter, 'Effectiveness') (stating that the lawful creation of rights presupposes in many cases the effectiveness of the exercise of these rights; the reason for this precondition is based on the fact that without its fulfilment neither the will of the creator of this right nor his capacity to perform the acquisition of the right can be proven).

treaty norms can be extended to them. In these cases, the reality of the human rights equation is present – namely the individual being dependent on a government or another power with effective power.[45] A relevant criterion to determine whether armed opposition groups can incur accountability under human rights law may therefore be the existence of an authority effectively controlling territory and persons. Armed opposition groups lacking effective power are unlikely to be able to comply with the human rights norms, since they lack the minimum infrastructure required for their implementation. The threshold for the applicability of human rights standards should therefore be higher than the threshold for applicability of international humanitarian law. If this high threshold is met, then the substantive duties of armed groups will go well beyond the bounds of international humanitarian law. Humanitarian rules merely require armed opposition groups to respect certain norms in their position as a party to the conflict, thus as a military authority. Human rights law, on the other hand, demands from armed opposition groups that they operate as a responsible political authority governing territory and population.

An example of international practice requiring effective authority as a precondition for accountability under human rights law is provided by the UN General Assembly. When this body adopted the UN Declaration on the Protection of All Persons from Being Subjected to Torture and Other Cruel, Inhuman or Degrading Treatment or Punishment, it stipulated that the Declaration was 'a guideline for all States and *other entities exercising effective power*'.[46] Similarly, Mullerson, a member of the Human Rights Committee, suggested in the context of the conflict in Bosnia–Herzegovina, that because the Bosnian Serbs were in control of territory, they were bound by the International Covenant on Civil and Political Rights:

> One problem... was that the Committee was not considering the situation in areas controlled by Bosnian Serbs, who were not successors to the treaties signed by the former Yugoslavia. Since they were belligerents, they were obliged under international law to observe the laws of war, some of which coincided with the Articles of the Covenant. Thus, they might be asked to explain how they complied with the Covenant, not as successor State, but *as an authority in control of a territory*.[47]

---

[45] N. S. Rodley, 'Armed Opposition Groups', above, Chapter 1, n. 126, p. 313.
[46] Declaration adopted by the UN General Assembly, Res. 3452 (XXX) (9 December 1975) (emphasis added).
[47] Human Rights Committee, Decision on State Succession to the Obligations of the Former Yugoslavia under the International Covenant on Civil and Political Rights, reprinted in (1992) 15 EHRR, 233, 236 (emphasis added).

In 1989, the Special Rapporteur on Afghanistan suggested that the Afghan opposition movements were obliged to respect human rights obligations. At that time, these groups administered part of Afghan territory, and tried to set up the necessary administrative infrastructure there. The Rapporteur observed: 'The territorial sovereignty of the Afghan Government is not fully effective since some provinces of Afghanistan are totally or partly in the hands of traditional forces. The responsibility for the respect of human rights is therefore divided'.[48]

In the above cases, the accountability of armed opposition groups under human rights law has been justified by the de facto authority of these groups over part of the state territory. There is, however, also practice suggesting that human rights standards can be invoked against groups, regardless of their effectiveness. Examples are provided by the UN Security Council and the UN Commission on Human Rights. In resolution 1193 (1998), the Security Council called upon 'the Afghan factions' 'to put an end to the discrimination against girls and women and to other violations of human rights... and to adhere to the internationally accepted norms and standards in this sphere'.[49] While arguably, in 1996, the Taliban movement exercised political authority over a substantial part of the Afghan territory, this certainly did not apply to all other Afghan armed opposition groups. Similarly, while the UN Commission on Human Rights held first and foremost the Taliban movement accountable for human rights violations, it imposed the same obligations on the other Afghan armed opposition groups.[50] A lack of concern over territorial control becomes even clearer in resolution 1997/47, where the UN Commission urged 'all parties in Somalia' 'to respect human rights and international humanitarian law pertaining to internal armed conflict'.[51] As explained earlier, many of the Somali groups lacked any control over territory or persons.

Finally, mention must be made of the Guiding Principles on Internal Displacement, which are designed by experts and drawn, *inter alia*, from

---

[48] UN Commission on Human Rights, E/CN.4/1989/24, para. 68 (Report on the Situation in Afghanistan by the Special Rapporteur, F. Ermacora, 16 February 1989) (hereafter, 1989 Report of the Special Rapporteur on Afghanistan).

[49] Para. 14 (28 August 1998).

[50] Res. 1998/70, paras. 2 and 5 (21 April 1998) (taking note of 'the continuing and substantiated reports of violations of the human rights of women and girls, including all forms of discrimination against them, particularly in areas under the control of the Taliban'; in the same resolution, the UN Commission urged 'all the Afghan parties... to bring to an end without delay all violations of human rights of women and girls').

[51] Para. 3 (11 April 1997).

human rights treaties.[52] Principle 2 provides that the Principles shall be observed by 'all authorities, groups and persons irrespective of their legal status'. Thus, armed opposition groups lacking any stable presence in the state territory or otherwise exercising effective authority could be held accountable for failure to observe human rights norms set forth in the Principles.

International practice is thus ambiguous on the question of conditions for accountability of armed opposition groups for violations of human rights law. There is some authority for the proposition that human rights instruments could govern armed opposition groups exercising governmental functions. However, this conclusion is mitigated by practice holding armed opposition groups apparently lacking any effectiveness accountable for human rights violations.

Conclusion

There is widespread international practice demonstrating that armed opposition groups can be held accountable for violations of international law. This practice further shows that armed opposition groups can be monitored according to standards in international treaties and customary law.

International practice demonstrates that international humanitarian law for internal armed conflicts and, to a lesser extent, human rights law, bind, in principle, all parties to the conflict namely the state and armed opposition group(s). These bodies therefore recognize the reality of a plurality of authorities in these situations. It follows that international bodies accept that, in particular circumstances, a group ceases to be just a group of private persons and becomes a subject of international law who is capable of being held accountable. This conclusion is not affected by the rules laid down in Common Article 3 stipulating that 'the application of the preceding provisions shall not affect the legal status of the Parties to the conflict'. This phrase emphasizes that armed opposition groups have no rights and duties *other* than those contained in Common Article 3. However, this leaves their obligations and responsibilities under Common Article 3, and other international rules for that matter, unaffected.[53] The legal personality of armed groups under these rules is objective in that it emanates from the Geneva Conventions, and other international instruments.

[52] Above, Chapter 1, n. 148.
[53] T. Meron, Internal Strife, above, Chapter 1, n. 10, p. 36.

There are good arguments to support this practice of international bodies. The legal personality of armed opposition groups is based on their position as parties to an internal armed conflict. It would be unrealistic and would have no functional purpose to deny such personality for the reason that armed opposition groups have no legal personality in the traditional sense. As Judge Kooijmans rightly pointed out, 'modern international law should be a *"ius inter potestates"* and therefore should encompass every political organization that acts as an effective factor in international relations'.[54]

At the same time, since the accountability of armed opposition groups is a direct consequence of their status as parties to the conflict, there should be a close link between their accountability and their status. This is also why international bodies are and should be very cautious about holding armed opposition groups accountable for violations of human rights norms. These norms presume the existence of a government, or at least, an entity exercising governmental functions. Armed opposition groups rarely function as de facto governments.

The limited nature of the legal personality of armed opposition groups also follows from their provisional nature. They exist only temporarily. They are either suppressed by the state and disappear, or they seize power and establish themselves as the new government, or they secede and join another state, or create a new state. It follows that these groups cannot possess rights based on the permanent nature of international actors. This means, for example, that armed opposition groups do not have sovereign rights over the territory in their power. They only exercise de facto authority.[55]

Attributing acts to armed opposition groups

Attribution is closely related to the problem of definition of armed opposition groups and it is a central aspect of their accountability. Armed opposition groups are abstractions. Like states, they act only through human beings. To hold a group accountable for the act of an individual, that act must be attributable to the group on some objective ground. The problem is illustrated by an example from the practice of the UN Mission for El Salvador, ONUSAL. ONUSAL received complaints from individuals saying that the FMLN threatened them for harvesting coffee

---

[54] P. H. Kooijmans, 'Non-State Entities as Parties to Conflicts', above, Chapter 1, n. 71, p. 339; see also R. Higgins, *Problems and Process: International Law and How We Use It* (Clarendon Press, Oxford, 1994), pp. 49–50.

[55] A. Cassese, *International Law in a Divided World* (Clarendon Press, Oxford, 1986), p. 84.

if they did not pay 'war tax'. ONUSAL transmitted the complaints to the FMLN local command, which categorically denied responsibility for any such threats. Significantly, the FMLN contended that these threats were probably being made by ordinary criminals who were using the name of FMLN as a cover.[56]

The International Law Commission has recognized that the concept of attribution is indeed relevant to armed opposition groups. Article 10 of the Draft Articles on State Responsibility refers to organs of an insurrectional movement, stating: 'Similarly, paragraph 1 is without prejudice to the attribution of the conduct of the organ of the insurrectional movement to that movement in any case in which such attribution may be made under international law'.[57]

The question which acts and omissions can be attributed to armed opposition groups has, however, not been answered in a coherent way by international bodies. While the Inter-American Commission on Human Rights, the UN Commission on Human Rights and its Rapporteurs, and the UN Security Council frequently qualify certain acts of armed opposition groups as contrary to their international obligations, they have rarely considered on the basis of which principles to attribute acts of individuals to these groups. Likewise they have not considered which persons or agencies are capable of giving rise to the responsibility of the group. The only rule on attribution that can be found in international practice is that members of armed opposition groups can engage the responsibility of such groups.[58]

A key initial question is: Who are members of these groups? As demonstrated in the previous section, 'armed opposition group' is not a fixed concept in international law. Large differences exist between these groups. Also, within an armed opposition group, a unified system may be lacking. Should persons have subscribed to the group in order to be a member of the group?; must they carry identity cards with them? Are only persons who actually participate in the hostilities members of armed opposition groups or can civilians also be counted to the membership? If civilians can qualify as members of armed opposition groups, what contribution must they make in order to qualify, and, in consequence, trigger the responsibility of the armed opposition group as a whole? International bodies have provided no criteria that can be applied to identify members of armed opposition groups.

---

[56] Third Report of ONUSAL, above, Chapter 2, n. 33, paras. 147–9.
[57] Above, n. 1.
[58] See e.g. Second Report of ONUSAL, above, Chapter 1, n. 27, para. 16.

In the absence of international practice and treaty rules on the subject of attribution of conduct to armed opposition groups, the question arises whether the International Law Commission's Draft Articles on State Responsibility may be applied by analogy to armed opposition groups. This question is legitimate in view of the fact that a degree of similarity exists between armed opposition groups and states, both being collective entities with a certain degree of organization. Further, armed opposition groups resemble states in that they pursue the exercise of political power and commonly aim to become the new government or form a new state. Does this imply that agencies of armed opposition groups can be equated with organs of the state for the purpose of the application of the Draft Articles on State Responsibility? If the answer to this question is affirmative, the questions still to be answered are: What are agencies of an armed opposition group, and do they resemble state organs? Do all armed opposition groups have such agencies?

Some groups can be said to have 'organs' as states do. An example is provided by the Taliban. A White House Executive Order of 4 July 1999, imposing sanctions on the Taliban for refusing to extradite Osama bin Laden, defines the Taliban as 'the political/military entity headquartered in Kandahar, Afghanistan that as of the date of this order exercises de facto control over the territory of Afghanistan..., its agencies and instrumentalities, and the Taliban leaders'.[59] While the order carefully avoids characterizing the Taliban agencies as organs, a term generally used for the state, the description of the Taliban makes clear that the movement has certain factual characteristics of a state. This view is supported by reports of the Special Rapporteur of the UN Commission on Human Rights for Afghanistan, referring to 'Deputy Minister for Foreign Affairs of the Taliban authorities', the judicial system of the Taliban and the Supreme Council in Kandahar being the Taliban authorities' central decision-making body.[60] It follows that draft Article 5 on State Responsibility may be applied by analogy to armed opposition groups exhibiting state-like features.

Difficulties will arise, however, when applying State Responsibility law to smaller armed opposition groups, lacking a clear organizational structure. These groups will generally lack territorial control.

---

[59] The White House Executive Order Blocking Property and Prohibiting Transactions with the Taliban, Executive Order 13129 of 4 July 1999, Federal Register, Vol. 64, No. 129, Section 4(c).

[60] UN Commission on Human Rights, E/CN.4/1997/59, paras. 6, 28 (Final Report on the Situation of Human Rights in Afghanistan by Choong-Hyun Paik, 20 February 1997) (hereafter, 1997 Final Report of the Special Rapporteur on Afghanistan).

International practice suggests that responsibility of these groups is based on their effective control over persons rather than on control of territory or on a predetermined concept of internal organization. For example, in its Third Report on Colombia, the Inter-American Commission on Human Rights established numerous violations of international humanitarian law by the Colombian armed opposition groups. It recommended that these groups should '*through their command and control structures*, respect, implement and enforce the rules governing hostilities set forth in international humanitarian law'.[61] This statement suggests that attribution of acts or omissions to smaller armed opposition groups is based on their actual control over individuals, rather than on the existence of a defined state-like structure.

Another important issue is whether acts of individuals belonging to armed opposition groups, who act outside their competence or contrary to instructions, can be attributed to the group. There is no international practice on this point. It is worth considering whether case-law applying to *states*, such as Youmans claim (1926), can be applied by analogy to armed groups.[62]

In sum, it is hardly discernible from international practice which conduct is capable of being attributed to armed opposition groups. While the Draft Articles on State Responsibility may be applied by analogy to de facto governments or other large, well-organized armed opposition groups and in that respect resemble a state, this may not be possible for small armed opposition groups lacking a clear organizational structure. In order to hold the latter category responsible for violations of international humanitarian law, it may be necessary to compose other rules, adapted to the special characteristics of these groups. Such rules could be based on effective control rather than presumptions of the internal organization of these groups.

Successful armed opposition groups

Erstwhile armed opposition groups that have formed a state or an established government can be held responsible for the acts committed in

---

[61] Above, Chapter 1, n. 8, at 158, recommendation 1 (emphasis added).
[62] US v. *Mexican General Claims Commission*, Youmans Claim, US v. Mexico (1926), 4 RIAA 110. The Commission decided that violent acts against Youmans committed by state officials, i.e. soldiers who were at the time on duty under immediate supervision and in the presence of a commanding officer could be imputed to the State (Mexico), regardless of whether the soldiers acted in contravention of instructions, para. 14.

their earlier careers as opposition groups. Article 15 of the International Law Commission's Draft Articles on State Responsibility provides:

(1) The act of an insurrectional movement which becomes the new government of a State shall be considered as an act of that State...
(2) The act of an insurrectional movement whose action results in the formation of a new State in part of the territory of a pre-existing State or in a territory under its administration shall be considered as an act of the new State[63]

Thus, conduct performed as an armed opposition group, which constitutes a breach of international obligations, and which is attributable to the armed opposition group, becomes an internationally wrongful act for which the state governed by the armed opposition group is responsible. Article 15 is based on the principle of organizational continuity of armed opposition groups that succeed in displacing the previous government or forming a new state.[64] Hence, the government of Congo under President Kabila, and the new states that resulted from the conflict in the former Yugoslavia, can be held responsible for all violations of international humanitarian law committed in their opposition period. The same will hold for the Taliban once it is recognized as the new government of Afghanistan. In these cases, the rules on state responsibility are applicable.

In such a situation, there is no gap in the accountability for acts committed by armed opposition groups. But the situation is not a common one, since most opposition groups do not become either governments or states. Opposition groups which fail to achieve their goals typically disintegrate and disappear after the conflict. Another obvious difficulty is one of timing: it is necessary to await the successful outcome before the state can be held responsible under international law for the acts of armed groups.

Further, there is the question of how to treat coalition governments formed following an agreement between the previous authorities and the leadership of the armed opposition group or with governments

---

[63] ILC Draft Articles on State Responsibility 1996 above, n. 1. The wording of this article, as adopted on its second reading, was slightly altered: '(1) The conduct of an insurrectional movement, which becomes the new government of a State shall be considered an act of that State under international law; (2) The conduct of a movement, insurrectional or other, which succeeds in establishing a new State in part of the territory of a pre-existing State or in a territory under its administration shall be considered an act of the new State under international law', ILC Draft Articles on State Responsibility 1998 above, n. 1.

[64] 1998 First Report Special Rapporteur on State Responsibility above, n. 1, Addendum 5 of 26 May 1998, at 38, para. 267.

which have been formed by more than one armed opposition group? As a general principle of international law, a state is an indivisible entity. This means that the state can be held responsible for acts committed by armed groups that have become members of the government. Once the perpetrators accede to government, the principle of state responsibility applies. The responsibility of the state for acts committed in the past by armed groups is also consistent with the rule that a state is responsible for acts committed by organs acting outside their authority or contrary to instructions that are attributed to the state.[65]

It is doubtful, however, whether this principle should be pressed too far in cases of governments of national reconciliation. A state should not be made responsible for the acts of a violent opposition group merely because, in the interests of an overall peace settlement, elements of the opposition are drawn into a reconstructed government.[66]

Finally, the question must be posed whether armed groups must fulfil certain characteristics during their opposition period in order later to be held responsible as a state. The International Law Commission found that the characteristics of a group in its opposition phase should not affect its responsibility once it has become the new government.[67] This is reasonable if the rationale for the rule of attribution in Article 15 is one of institutional continuity. However, it is arguable that, in order to be 'able' to violate norms of international law, armed opposition groups must be bound by those rules at the time that the violations occurred. On this view, later responsibility of the state should only be engaged if the armed groups had been bound by Common Article 3 or Protocol II at the time of the acts in question. It seems impossible to hold a government responsible for acts committed as a non-state entity, while this entity was – at that time – not bound by any international norms.[68]

Finding a suitable forum

Another problem to be dealt with when considering the accountability of armed opposition groups under international law is to find a forum in

---

[65] Art. 10 of the Draft Articles on State Responsibility; see commentary to Art. 15 of the Draft Articles, (1975) *II.CYb* 91–106.
[66] 1998 First Report Special Rapporteur on State Responsibility, above, n. 1, Addendum 5 of 26 May 1998, at 38, para. 267, footnote 172.
[67] *Ibid.*, at 40, para. 273.
[68] But see, D. Matas, 'Armed Opposition Groups' (1995) 24 *MLJ* 621, 630 (stating that if armed opposition groups succeed, they will be held responsible for the whole range of international human rights standards).

which to prosecute a claim against them and with jurisdiction to apply all relevant law. No international body is expressly mandated to monitor compliance by armed opposition groups with the applicable law.[69] States have been reluctant to supplement the relevant rules with any means of scrutinizing compliance. They feared that supervision might provide a basis for international interference.[70] Although not explicitly so mandated, several international bodies on their own initiative have extended their mandates to actions of armed opposition groups. These are the Inter-American Commission, the UN Security Council, and the UN Commission on Human Rights. However, the absence of international bodies formally competent to review armed opposition groups' compliance with international law, accounts, in part, for the primitive state of the accountability of these groups under international law.

The Inter-American Commission on Human Rights may be used as an example. The Commission has decided that it is competent, in the context of its function of receiving and reviewing reports by states, to monitor the behaviour of armed opposition groups on the basis of international humanitarian law.[71] For three reasons this competence is inherently limited.

First, the Inter-American Commission has made clear that it will not act upon petitions of individuals alleging to be victims of acts committed by armed opposition groups.[72] It will therefore not exercise its quasi-judicial functions with regard to acts of armed opposition groups. This

---

[69] The competence *ratione materiae* of international bodies to apply international humanitarian law does not affect their competence *ratione personae*. For example, while the Inter-American Commission on Human Rights considers itself competent to apply international humanitarian law in the individual complaints procedure, it found that evaluation of behaviour of armed opposition groups under international humanitarian law fell outside its mandate, Second Report on Colombia, above, Chapter 1, n. 110, at 3; Third Report on Colombia, above, Chapter 1, n. 8, at 72, para. 5.

[70] During the negotiations on Protocol II, it was argued that armed opposition groups might use provisions on supervision to call for assistance by an international body, even against the objection of the established authorities. This, states were afraid, would internationalize the conflict, A. Eide, 'The New Humanitarian Law in Non-International Armed Conflict', in A. Cassese (ed.), *The New Humanitarian Law of Armed Conflict* (Editoriale Scientifica S.r.l., Napoli, 1979), p. 297. Third-world states were even inclined to reduce the scope of Common Article 3 with regard to international supervision. The inclusion in Protocol II of the provision that 'nothing in this Protocol shall be invoked as a justification for intervening directly or indirectly, for any reason whatever' (Article 3(2) Protocol II), has clearly not removed these fears.

[71] Third Report on Colombia, above, Chapter 1, n. 8, at 72, para. 6.

[72] *Ibid.*, para. 5.

means that the Commission will not be able to solve difficult legal issues relating to armed opposition groups. The reporting procedure, being general in nature, is not suited for this purpose. Furthermore, limiting the Commission's activities with respect to armed opposition groups to its reporting function, implies that the Inter-American Court of Human Rights will not be able to adjudicate on the accountability of armed opposition groups, because the mandate of the Court is restricted to the consideration of individual petitions.[73]

Second, the scope of the Commission's activities with regard to armed groups is limited by the fact that the procedural framework within which it operates, has remained unchanged. This means that the procedural means necessary for the implementation of its findings on accountability of armed opposition groups for violations of international law are absent. For example, Article 62(a) of the Regulations of the Inter-American Commission states that, after a draft report has been approved by the Commission, it shall be transmitted to 'the government of the member state in question' for observations.[74] The purpose of this norm is that the state may have additional knowledge of the facts contained in the report. Also, consultation with the state will enhance its acceptance of the report and its willingness to comply with the Commission's recommendations. Similar norms for the execution of its competence relating to armed groups are absent.

Not surprisingly, the Commission has indicated that it encounters significant procedural problems in implementing its competence with regard to armed groups.[75] However, it is unlikely that it will adjust the relevant rules. The following observation of the Commission is illustrative in this respect:

If the Commission, in violation of its mandate, were to agree to process a denunciation involving some alleged acts of terrorism, in doing so it would implicitly place terrorist organizations on an equal footing with governments, as the Commission would have to transmit the denunciation to the subversive organization which allegedly is responsible for the act and request that it make such observations as it deems appropriate. Undoubtedly, such organizations would be

---

[73] Article 61 of the American Convention on Human Rights; the Court may be requested, however, to give an advisory opinion on legal issues related to armed opposition groups, Article 64 of the American Convention.
[74] Regulations of the Inter-American Commission, approved by the Commission at its 49th Sess., 8 April 1980, last modified at its 92nd Sess., 3 May 1996, reprinted in Basic Documents Pertaining to Human Rights in the Inter-American System, OEA/Ser. L.V/II.92, doc. 31 rev. 3, at 131 (3 May 1996).
[75] Annual Report 1992–3, above, Chapter 1, n. 136, at 219.

very pleased to be dealt with as if they were governments. But, what government in the hemisphere could tolerate an implicit recognition of quasi-governmental status for an organization of this kind?[76]

While this consideration concerned the individual complaints system, the same observation would seem to apply were the Commission to transmit its country reports to armed opposition groups for their observations.

Third, the Commission lacks an appropriate mandate to apply international humanitarian law.[77] In the so-called *Tablada* case of 30 October 1997, the Inter-American Commission developed an extensive argumentation to support its decision to extend its mandate to cover humanitarian law. Briefly, the Commission argued that, although an explicit legal basis was absent, several articles of the American Convention should be interpreted as mandating the Commission to apply international humanitarian law as such. To be clear, the Commission has directly applied humanitarian law, so it has not merely used humanitarian law as a means of or yardstick for interpretation of the American Convention.

However, the finding of the Inter-American Commission that it is competent to apply humanitarian law is not unproblematic. I will not deal in detail with the Commission's argumentation. It is submitted that closer analysis shows that it is highly questionable whether the American Convention offers the Commission a legal basis for applying humanitarian law.[78] It is therefore not surprising that one of the Member States of the Organization of American States has filed a complaint with the Inter-American Court of Human Rights against the Commission, challenging

---

[76] Report on the Situation of Human Rights in the Republic of Colombia, OEA/Ser.L/V/II.53, doc. 22, at 16 (30 June 1981); compare also Third Report on Colombia, above, Chapter 1, n. 8, at 72, para. 5. ('OAS member States opted deliberately not to give the Commission jurisdiction to investigate or hear individual complaints concerning illicit acts of private persons or groups for which the State is not internationally responsible. If it were to act on such complaints, the Commission would be in flagrant breach of its mandate, and, by according these persons or groups the same treatment and status that a State receives as party to a complaint, it would infringe the sovereign rights and prerogatives of the State concerned').

[77] Only the Security Council has an explicit mandate to include in its work the acts of armed opposition groups. As the Council is mandated to act whenever there is a threat to international peace and security, nothing in the Charter confines the Security Council to action with regard to states, see M. Akehurst, *A Modern Introduction to International Law* (HarperCollins, 6th edn, Chatham, 1987), p. 220.

[78] See L. Zegveld, 'The Inter-American Commission on Human Rights and International Humanitarian Law: a Comment on the *Tablada* Case', (1998) 324 *IRRC* 505–11.

its decision to apply humanitarian law. The Court has considered this complaint to be valid. In the *Las Palmeras* case, the Inter-American Court considered:

> Although the Inter-American Commission has broad faculties as an organ for the promotion and protection of human rights, it can clearly be inferred from the American Convention that the procedure initiated in contentious cases before the Commission, which culminates in an application before the Court, should refer specifically to rights protected by that Convention (*cf.* Articles 33, 44, 48.1 and 48). Cases in which another Convention, ratified by the State, confers competence on the Inter-American Court or Commission to hear violations of the rights protected by that Convention are excepted from this rule; these include, for example, the Inter-American Convention on Forced Disappearance of Persons.[79]

On the same grounds, the Court rejected the Commission's claim that it would have competence to apply humanitarian law.

The Inter-American Commission's reasoning could be relevant to the International Covenant on Civil and Political Rights and the European Convention on Human Rights, as these treaties are structured the same way and contain articles similar to those in the American Convention. However, in view of the problems mentioned, it appears highly unlikely that the Human Rights Committee and the European Court of Human Rights will follow the example of the Inter-American Commission.

An alternative is for the Inter-American Commission and other human rights bodies to use humanitarian law indirectly – i.e., as a source of authoritative guidance when applying the human rights treaties in time of armed conflict. Christopher Greenwood has suggested this approach, by posing that: 'the monitoring mechanisms of human rights conventions could be used in an *indirect* way to assist in ensuring compliance with the law applicable in internal conflicts'.[80] However, this does not go far enough. What is needed is improvement of supervision of compliance by armed opposition groups with humanitarian law. The aim is not to improve application of human rights law. Using humanitarian law as a means of interpretation of human rights law is only an indirect way to reach our aim.

In summary, the Inter-American Commission has found that it has the implied power to consider acts of armed opposition groups on the basis

---

[79] Judgment of 4 February 2000, para. 34. The Court ruled on five preliminary objections raised by Colombia, the second and third preliminary objections contending that the Commission and Court 'lacked the competence to apply international humanitarian law and other international treaties.'

[80] Emphasis added.

of international humanitarian law. However, the scope of this power is limited. The Commission can apply international legal humanitarian norms to these groups only in an indirect way. Furthermore, to the extent it establishes the accountability of these groups for violating these norms, it cannot implement this accountability. Clearly, from the point of view of individuals, the Inter-American Commission does not provide them with an effective remedy against violations of their rights.[81]

A gap currently exists therefore in the enforcement of international humanitarian law. There are no judicial or quasi-judicial mechanisms specifically competent to examine claims against armed opposition groups. What may be needed is a forum to which individuals can submit complaints of breaches of international humanitarian law, which can be examined by experts independent of states and whose findings governments cannot dispute. Members of such a forum must be independent and impartial. The ICRC is not suited to this role. It operates mainly through confidential discussions with governments rather than through public processes like human rights bodies.

One might, however, consider setting up an 'international humanitarian law committee' competent to receive and examine communications from individuals claiming to be victims of violations of international humanitarian law. Such a committee, equipped with an individual complaints procedure, might be a suitable forum in which to file a claim against armed opposition groups. The individual complaints procedure under human rights treaties could serve as an example.

To be sure, many obstacles, both legal and political, will then have to be overcome. One problem is that international bodies, in dealing with armed opposition groups, are governed by two, contradictory, interests. On the one hand, the number of internal conflicts and the impact of armed groups on civilians means that international bodies cannot afford to ignore them. The consequence, leaving civilians unprotected, is clearly undesirable. At the same time, the application of the law to armed opposition groups is hampered by states' unfavourable attitudes towards according any international status to armed opposition groups.

[81] Similar problems are likely to arise when other human rights bodies become more actively involved in the implementation of international humanitarian law, see, for example, Parlementary Assembly of the Council of Europe, Recommendation 1427 (1999) and Order No. 556 (1999) of 23 September 1999 (recommending that the Committee of Ministers study the possibility of helping the victims of violations of international humanitarian law through the mechanisms of the European Convention on Human Rights).

States do not wish to attribute government-like qualities to these groups. Conferring international legal personality upon armed groups would involve recognizing the existence of another authority within the state territory, at the expense of the existing government. One commentator has formulated the problem as follows:

> [Common Article 3] placed these obligations upon 'each Party to the conflict', terminology guaranteed to cause the Government of any State facing a rebellion to hesitate to accept the applicability of Article 3 to its rebellion. What government would want to acknowledge that its rebels constituted a 'Party' to an armed conflict entitled to rights and duties with respect to it under international law? The final provision of Article 3, which states that the application of the Article 'shall not affect the legal status of the Parties to the conflict' seems more likely to underline the problem caused by the chosen terminology than to cure it.[82]

This observation shows that holding armed opposition groups accountable for humanitarian law violations is considered to be incompatible with the fundamental right of the state to preserve its existence and to remain the only authority. These considerations make the prospects of further development of the international accountability of armed opposition groups very small indeed.

---

[82] G. H. Aldrich, 'The Law Applicable in Non-International Armed Conflicts: Problems and Prospects' (speech delivered at the Symposium 'Law and Conflicts in Our Times – The Meaning of International Humanitarian Law in Internal Armed Conflicts' (The Hague, 13 November 1997)) (on file with author); G. Best, *War & Law*, above, n. 2, pp. 171–2.

5 Accountability of the state for acts of armed opposition groups

In its current form, international law is unable to make armed opposition groups themselves fully accountable for their abuses against the civilian population. It is, therefore, legitimate to question whether the traditional roads of international law can fill the accountability gap. Indeed, the conclusions drawn in the previous chapter validate the quest for the accountability of the territorial state for failure to prevent or repress acts of armed opposition groups. Its supreme authority over all persons and things within its territory and its ensuing status as the primary subject of international law justify the decision to extend the quest for accountability to the state.[1] This choice is also warranted by the fact that international bodies consider primarily the conduct of the state.

A survey of international practice shows that the state's accountability may arise when armed opposition groups are fighting each other, with the established government making no effort to shield the civilian population from the effects of the hostilities. Moreover, state accountability may exist when the government armed forces fight armed opposition groups with the sole aim of defeating them militarily, at the cost of putting civilians at risk, whether from the government or from the armed opposition groups. Attacks on civilians by opposition groups may even further the government's aim of defeating these groups by bringing them into disrepute with the civilian population, in the hope that the population will then side with the government. Finally, state accountability may apply when the state, after the conflict has ended, adopts a general amnesty law, granting immunity to members of armed opposition groups for abuses committed by them.

---

[1] See R. Jennings, A. Watts, *Oppenheim*, above, Chapter 1, n. 59, pp. 122, 382.

It should not be assumed, however, that the state's accountability for failure to protect civilians is easily determined in concrete cases. In establishing such accountability, international bodies are guided by different principles that are sometimes difficult to apply or combine. Most importantly, they have to balance the principle of protection of civilians against the principle of military necessity and the state's right to defend its territorial integrity. Indeed, forceful reaction on the part of the state against the acts of armed opposition groups can be squared with international law standards. Furthermore, the state is liable on a command responsibility basis (namely the duty to prevent); it is not liable for the actual acts of armed groups. This means that the principle of control plays a dominant role in international practice. Only when the established government exercises control over territory, over acts of armed opposition groups or over civilians in need of protection, can it be obliged actually to provide such protection. The concept of control is difficult to define and needs flexible interpretation when applied in practice. This chapter will analyse how these different principles interplay in the practice of international bodies. The key question in every case will be: How much scope do international bodies grant the state to repress armed opposition groups at the expense of the civilian population?

Throughout this chapter distinction must be made between 'state' and 'government'. The term 'state' refers to the international subject, consisting of a territory, a people and a government. A state cannot exist for long unless it has a government. The government, consisting of legislative, administrative (including the armed forces), and judicial bodies, acts for the state. Although there is a trend in international practice to address governments instead of states, the state must not be identified with its government.[2] For example, the state's rights and obligations are not affected by lack of territorial control by the government or even by the temporary absence of the government. The concern here is with the international accountability of the state. The term 'government' refers to the political unit governing the state, not possessing legal personality in international law.

---

[2] For example, the Rwanda Tribunal held that 'a non-international conflict is distinct from an international armed conflict because of the legal status of the entities opposing each other: the parties to the conflict are not sovereign States, but the government of a single State in conflict with one or more armed factions within its territory, *Musema* case (2000) above, Chapter 2, n. 49, para. 247. I take the view that – legally speaking – the state is in fact involved in the conflict, and can be held accountable for acts committed by the existing government. The government as such lacks international legal status.

Finally, it should be noted that, while the government is often called the de jure government, this study uses, apart from 'government', the more neutral term 'established authorities' or 'established government'. The words 'de jure' are misleading, because they suggest that international law supports the established authorities, which is partly but not wholly true.

First, the sources of the state's obligations requiring the state to take, in particular situations, positive action will be examined. Then, the scope and contents of the state's obligations will be determined. Finally, the criteria for the state's accountability will be discussed.

Applicable law

A precondition for accountability of the territorial state for acts committed by armed opposition groups is the clarification of the obligations applicable to the state. Below, the state's duties under human rights treaties, under Common Article 3 and Protocol II, under other international humanitarian law treaties, and, finally, under international criminal law treaties will be discussed.

Human rights treaties

The International Covenant on Civil and Political Rights and the European and American Conventions on Human Rights require the state to 'secure' or to 'ensure' the rights recognized in these treaties. In its ordinary sense, 'to ensure' means 'to make it certain that something will happen'.[3] A state's obligation to guarantee the rights and freedoms in the human rights treaties thus amounts to an obligation to make certain that these rights and freedoms are respected.[4] Next to this typology, another typology exists, which has been used in particular by the International Law Commission in the Draft Articles on State Responsibility, in particular in Articles 20, 21 and 23. This is the distinction between 'obligations of result' and 'obligations of conduct'. However, the latter classification is not helpful as the difference between

---

[3] *Longman Dictionary of Contemporary English* (Longman National Dictionaries, Essex, 3rd edn., 1995).

[4] The obligation 'to ensure' or 'to secure' respect, sometimes also called the obligation 'to protect', is also referred to as an 'affirmative' or 'positive' obligation, requiring the state to take some form of action. These obligations are distinguished from the obligation 'to respect' or 'negative obligations', obliging the state to refrain from action.

'obligations of result' and 'obligations of conduct' is not significant. In cases of obligations of conduct there is often an objective towards which that conduct is aimed. Similarly, obligations of result will invariably require a specific course of action. The classification of a particular obligation within one category or the other will rest primarily upon the amount of emphasis or specificity given to either the requisite conduct or result.[5]

In several decisions, human rights bodies have held that the state has a duty to safeguard human rights from infringements not only by the government but also by private individuals. In Platform 'Ärzte Für Das Leben', the European Court of Human Rights held that the European Convention's right of freedom of assembly obliges a state to take reasonable and appropriate measures to protect demonstrators from physical violence by opposing groups.[6] In the Velásquez Rodríguez case, the Inter-American Court of Human Rights established that agents acting under cover of state authority carried out the disappearance of Manfredo Velásquez. But, 'even had that fact not been proven', the Court found that 'the failure of the State apparatus to act, which was clearly proven, is a failure on the part of Honduras to fulfill the duties it assumed under Article 1(1) of the American Convention, which obligated it to ensure Manfredo Velásquez the free and full exercise of his human rights'.[7]

These examples show that states sometimes have positive obligations to protect individuals from other individuals.[8] However, the cases so far

---

[5] See C. Tomuschat, 'What is a "Breach" of the European Convention on Human Rights?' in R. Lawson, M. de Blois (eds.), *The Dynamics of the Protection of Human Rights in Europe* (Kluwer Academic Publishers, Dordrecht, 1994) pp. 315, 323–4 (hereafter, 'What is a Breach').

[6] Judgment of 21 June 1988, Ser. A 139, para. 32 (1988) (hereafter, Platform 'Ärzte Für Das Leben' Case). The same court decided in HLR v. France (Judgment of 29 April 1997) 36 Reports (1997 III) at 745, para. 40, that 'owing to the absolute character of the right guaranteed, the Court does not rule out the possibility that Article 3 of the Convention may also apply where the danger emanates from persons or groups of persons who are not public officials. However, it must be shown that the risk is real and that the authorities of the receiving State are not able to obviate the risk by providing appropriate protection'.

[7] Velásquez Rodríguez v. Honduras, Ser. C 4, para. 182 (1988) (hereafter, Velásquez Rodríguez case).

[8] The state's positive obligation to control and regulate the conduct of private individuals is also widely recognized in the literature, see D. J. Harris et al., *Law of The European Convention on Human Rights* (Butterworths, London, 1995), pp. 19–22; A. Clapham, *Human Rights in the Private Sphere* (Clarendon Press, Oxford, reprint 1998) (1996), chapter 7; D. Shelton, 'State Responsibility for Covert and Indirect Forms of Violence' in K. E. Mahoney, P. Mahoney (eds.), *Human Rights in the Twenty-First Century* (Martinus Nijhoff, The Hague, 1993), pp. 265–76; P. van Dijk, '"Positive Obligations"

have concerned private individuals acting in time of normality. The question is whether such a positive obligation of the state also exists in time of conflict when the 'other individuals' are an armed opposition group.

International practice shows that, to the extent that human rights treaties apply to internal armed conflicts,[9] they indeed oblige the state to prevent and repress acts of armed opposition groups. In *Ergi v. Turkey*[10] the European Court concluded that Turkey had a positive obligation to take precautions against the effects of attacks by the Workers' Party of Kurdistan (PKK) in southeast Turkey. That case concerned an ambush operation carried out by the Turkish security forces in the night of 29 September 1993, in the vicinity of a village, intended to capture members of the PKK. The operation led to the death of the applicant's sister. The Court found that there was insufficient evidence to establish that the Turkish security forces killed the applicant's sister. It considered, however, that Turkey was obliged to conduct its military operations with the requisite care to protect the civilian population from the PKK:

Under Article 2 of the Convention, read in conjunction with Article 1, the State may be required to take certain measures in order to 'secure' an effective enjoyment of the right to life. In the light of the above considerations, the Court agrees with the Commission that the responsibility of the State is not confined to circumstances when there is significant evidence that misdirected fire from agents of the State has killed a civilian. It may also be engaged where they fail to take all feasible precautions in the choice of means and methods of a security operation mounted against an opposing group with a view to avoiding and, in any event, to minimizing, incidental loss of civilian life. Thus, even though it has not been established beyond reasonable doubt that the bullet which killed Havva Ergi had been fired by the security forces, the Court must consider whether the security force's operation had been planned and conducted in such a way as *to avoid or minimize, to the greatest extent possible, any risk to the lives of the villagers, including from the fire-power of the PKK members caught in the ambush.*[11]

Other treaty-based bodies reached similar conclusions. The Human Rights Committee established under the International Covenant on Civil and Political Rights, in its concluding observations on the situation in

---

Implied in the European Convention on Human Rights: Are the States Still Masters of the Convention?' in M. Castermans, F. van Hoof (eds.), *The Role of the Nation State in the 21st Century* (Kluwer Law International, The Netherlands, 1998), pp. 17–33.

[9] In internal armed conflicts the state is allowed to derogate from a number – though not all – of the rights and freedoms contained in the human rights conventions.
[10] Judgment of 28 July 1998, 81 Reports (1998-IV) at 1751.
[11] *Ibid.*, para. 79 (emphasis added).

Algeria in 1998, formulated the positive obligations of Algeria as follows:

> The Committee is also concerned at the lack of timely or preventive measures of protection to the victims from police or military officials in the vicinity... The Committee urges the State party to adopt effective measures: a) to prevent those attacks and, if they nevertheless occur, to come promptly to the defense of the population; b) to ensure that proper investigations are conducted by an independent body to determine who the offenders are and to bring them to justice.[12]

Although the Committee abstained from clarifying who was factually responsible for the attacks on the victims, it appears from the context that it referred to attacks by the Islamic groups, including the Islamic Salvation Army (FIS) and the Armed Islamic Group (GIA).

The Inter-American Commission found with regard to the conflict in Colombia that, in particular circumstances, the state may not remain passive in the face of the injurious conduct of the Armed Revolutionary Forces of Colombia (FARC), the Army of National Liberation (ELN), and other armed opposition groups active in Colombia. In its 1996 Annual Report, the Commission considered:

> The Commission fully comprehends that Colombia faces extremely difficult circumstances at this time and the State of Colombia is not directly responsible for all the harm caused to its citizens. However, the State of Colombia is responsible for... acts committed by private persons, which are tolerated or acquiesced in by the State. The Commission also notes that the State may also incur international responsibility for the illicit acts of private individuals or groups when the State fails to adopt the necessary measures to prevent the acts and/or where it fails to properly investigate and sanction those responsible for committing the acts and to provide adequate compensation to the victims.[13]

According to the Inter-American Commission, positive obligations of the state also apply when the fighting is between two or more armed opposition groups, the state armed forces not being involved:

> One source of concern to the Commission is the concept that the government will be responsible only for violations attributable to their officials or agents and could sit back and do nothing in the face of the threats to these rights that result from the armed conflict *between enemy groups*. The duty of the state is to guarantee the safety of its inhabitants, and it can fail in its duty both by action

---

[12] CCPR/C/79/Add.95, para. 6 (Concluding Observations on Algeria, 4 August 1998) (hereafter, Concluding Observations on Algeria 1998).
[13] Annual Report 1996, above, Chapter 1, n. 137, at 668–9, para. 80.

and by omission. The state cannot disqualify itself on so fundamental a matter and should do everything possible to effectively protect these rights.[14]

Notwithstanding this practice providing evidence of the state's obligation to preserve the safety of its inhabitants against armed opposition groups, there is conflicting practice, which questions such obligations as a matter of principle. An example is provided by the European Court of Human Rights' decision in *Kurt v. Turkeyi*,[15] concerning the detention of the applicant's son, Üzeyir Kurt, by soldiers and village guards in 1993. After the incident, four and a half years passed without the applicant receiving any information as to his subsequent fate. She maintained that, even though no specific evidence existed that her son had died at the hands of the Turkish authorities, his disappearance occurred in a context which was life-threatening. The state would therefore be in breach of its positive obligation under Article 2 to protect her son's life. Turkey, for its part, submitted that there were strong grounds for believing that Kurt had in fact joined or been kidnapped by the PKK.[16] The Court, following the Commission, disagreed with the applicant's argument:

The Court must carefully scrutinize whether there does in fact exist concrete evidence which would lead it to conclude that her son was, beyond reasonable doubt, killed *by the authorities* either while in detention in the village or at some subsequent stage. It also notes in this respect that in those cases where it has found that a Contracting State had a positive obligation under Article 2 to conduct an effective investigation into the circumstances surrounding an alleged unlawful killing by the agents of that State, there existed concrete evidence of a fatal shooting which could bring that obligation into play.[17]

The Court thus limited its examination to the question of whether it could be established beyond doubt that *the state authorities* killed the applicant's son. The Court did not refrain from considering positive obligations on the part of Turkey, because, for example, it found that the State lacked control over the PKK, or that the acts or omissions of Turkey were necessary in the context of the armed conflict. Rather the Court ignored the question of whether Article 2 of the European Convention may under particular circumstances also imply a duty to investigate a

---
[14] Annual Report of the Inter-American Commission 1975, at 22, in Inter-American Commission on Human Rights, *Ten Years of Activities 1971–1981*, at 333 (1982) (emphasis added).
[15] Judgment of 25 May 1998, 74 Reports (1998-III) at 1152 (hereafter, Kurt case).
[16] *Ibid.*, paras. 101, 106.
[17] *Ibid.*, para. 107 (emphasis added); see also paras. 99 and 106.

disappearance carried out by *others than the state* namely the PKK.[18] In the case of *Çakici v. Turkey* of 8 July 1999, the Court confirmed this approach.[19]

It is noteworthy that, in the *Kurt* case, the European Court ignored the Inter-American Court of Human Rights' decision in the *Velásquez Rodríguez* case, in spite of the applicant's explicit reference to this decision.[20] In the latter case, the Inter-American Court found that, even when it had not been established that Honduras was involved in the disappearance under consideration, it was nonetheless obliged to ensure respect for the life of Manfredo Velásquez. The explanation of the difference between these decisions may be that while the *Velásquez Rodríguez* case concerned protection from other *private individuals*, in *Kurt v. Turkey*, the European Court had to consider the possibility that an *armed opposition group* carried out the disappearance. The difference between these decisions might be taken to suggest that the state's obligation to protect individuals against 'other individuals' is not applicable if the 'individuals' belong to armed opposition groups.

Another case raising doubts as to the applicability of the state's positive obligations to acts of armed opposition groups during internal conflict comes from the Human Rights Committee, in its view in *A. and H. Sanjuan Arevalo v. Colombia*.[21] This case concerned the disappearance of

---

[18] This interpretation is supported by the Court's reasoning in the same case on a violation of Article 5 of the European Convention: 'The Court considers that having regard to the applicant's insistence that her son was detained in the village, the public prosecutor should have been alert to the need to investigate more thoroughly her claim... The public prosecutor was unwilling to go beyond the gendarmerie's assertion that the custody records showed that Üzeyir Kurt had neither been held in the village nor in detention. He accepted without question the explanation that Üzeyir Kurt had probably been kidnapped by the PKK during the military operation and this explanation shaped his future attitude to his enquiries and laid the basis of his subsequent non-jurisdiction decision,' *Ibid.*, para. 126. This reasoning indicates that, had it been beyond reasonable doubt that the PKK had kidnapped the applicant's son, the public prosecutor would not have been obliged to investigate the applicant's claim, or at least not in a similar manner to when the state had been involved. In that case, the Court might not have established a violation of Article 5.

[19] Para. 85, case available on www.dhcour.coe.fr (visited, 1 January 2001) (stating that 'it may be concluded beyond reasonable doubt that Ahmet Çakici died following his apprehension and detention by security forces. This case is therefore to be distinguished from the *Kurt* case... in which the Court examined the applicant's complaints about the disappearance of her son under Article 5. In the *Kurt* case, although the applicant's son had been taken into detention, no other elements of evidence existed as regarded his treatment or fate subsequent to that').

[20] *Kurt* case, above, n. 15, para. 101.

[21] Communication No. 181/1984, Official Records of the Human Rights Committee 1989/90, Vol. II, at 392–4.

the author's two sons in 1982. It was not clear who was responsible for the disappearance. At the time of the Committee's examination, the investigations by the Colombian police were still ongoing. After the Committee found that it had sufficient evidence of the direct involvement of state agents in the disappearance, it concluded that Colombia had violated the International Covenant on Civil and Political Rights (the Covenant). The Committee considered:

> The Committee notes that the parents of the Sanjuán brothers received indications that their sons had been arrested by *agents of the 'F2'* [a section of the Colombian police forces]. The Committee further notes that in none of the investigations ordered by the Government has it been suggested that the disappearance of the Sanjuán brothers was caused by persons *other than government officials*. In all these circumstances, *therefore*, the Committee ... finds that the right to life enshrined in article 6 of the Covenant and the right to liberty and security of the person laid down in article 9 of the Covenant have not been effectively protected by the State of Colombia.[22] [Emphasis added.]

This statement may be understood as restricting the state's positive obligation to protect to disappearances in which government officials are directly involved. This point was more explicitly elaborated by Nisuke Ando, a member of the Human Rights Committee. In an individual opinion on the communication, he made a reservation to the Committee's final view that Colombia had violated the Covenant. In his opinion, as long as the investigations of the case were not terminated, it was still possible that private persons were involved in the disappearance. He thereby suggested that, if the Committee had found that Colombian armed opposition groups had carried out the disappearance, the Committee would not have established violation of the Covenant by Colombia.[23]

Nevertheless, careful consideration of the above two examples leads to the conclusion that they do not affect the finding that human rights treaties in principle oblige the state to afford protection against armed opposition groups. In the first place, it should be noted that neither the European Court of Human Rights nor the Human Rights Committee has ever held that a duty to prevent and repress acts of armed opposition groups *never* arises. They only decided that the duty arises only in cases in which the state was directly involved. It is only by a reasoning *a contrario* that one might conclude that these obligations do not apply to acts carried out by the armed opposition.

Second, there are only two decisions that may raise doubts as to the positive obligations of the state to control acts of armed opposition

---

[22] *Ibid.*, 393, para. 11. [23] *Ibid.*, Appendix, 393–4.

groups, as opposed to numerous decisions of the treaty bodies indicating the opposite.

In conclusion, international practice demonstrates that the general obligation resting on the state under human rights treaties to 'ensure' or 'secure' the relevant rights and freedoms entails the obligation to protect individuals from armed opposition groups on its territory. This allows the conclusion that no distinction exists between unorganized private individuals and armed opposition groups – in both cases the state being obliged to prevent or suppress their abuses. An internal conflict in itself, therefore, does not remove the state's positive obligations under human rights treaties to regulate and control the conduct of actors under its jurisdiction. If international bodies reject positive obligations of states with regard to armed opposition groups, the effect would be that these treaties would provide no protection to civilians against violence committed by armed opposition groups. This may be unacceptable for international bodies whose aim is to safeguard the rights of victims in all situations, including internal conflict.

Common Article 3 and Protocol II

Article 1 common to the 1949 Geneva Conventions stipulates that contracting states must ensure respect for these conventions at all times. Commentators have suggested that this obligation is equivalent to the obligation 'to ensure respect' contained in human rights treaties, such as the International Covenant on Civil and Political Rights and the European Convention on Human Rights.[24] This may lead one to argue that, like the human rights treaties, the Geneva Conventions and Additional Protocols oblige the state to protect civilians from all other individuals under its jurisdiction, including from armed opposition groups. This thesis finds some support in international practice.

---

[24] K. Obradovic, 'Que faire face aux violations du droit humanitaire? – quelques réflexions sur le rôle possible du CICR', in Pictet, above, Chapter 1, n. 16, pp. 483, 487; ('L'interprétation donnée aux mots 'faire respecter' devient d'autant plus convaincante aujourd' hui qu'il y a trente-cinq ans, vu justement l'état actuel de développement des droits de l'homme, la place qu'ils occupent dans la hiérarchie des normes du droit international moderne et finalement le fait que le droit humanitaire s'intègre dans le complexe des droits de l'homme. L'obligation analysée ainsi doit, d'après notre opinion, être comprise de nos jours en corrélation avec les obligations générales qu'ont les sujets de droit international pour le respect des droits de l'homme'); compare also N. Levrat, 'Les conséquences de l'engagement pris par les Hautes Parties Contractantes de "faire respecter" les conventions humanitaires' in F. Kalshoven, Y. Sandoz, (eds.), Implementation of International Humanitarian Law (Martinus Nijhoff, Dordrecht, 1989), pp. 263, 276–7.

In *Military and Paramilitary Activities In and Against Nicaragua*,[25] the International Court of Justice determined that the obligation to ensure respect of Common Article 1 of the Geneva Conventions also extends to the norms set forth in Common Article 3 applicable in internal armed conflicts:

> The Court considers that there is an obligation on the United States Government, in the terms of Article 1 of the Geneva Conventions, to 'respect' the Conventions and even 'to ensure respect' for them 'in all circumstances', since such an obligation does not derive only from the Conventions themselves, but from the general principles of humanitarian law to which the Conventions merely give specific expression. The United States is under an obligation not to encourage persons or groups engaged in the conflict in Nicaragua to act in violation of the provisions of Article 3 common to the four 1949 Geneva Conventions.[26]

The drafting history of Article 1 also supports the argument that the obligation under Article 1 common to the Geneva Conventions extends to activities which occur in the context of internal armed conflict. The main concern of the drafters was the implementation of the humanitarian principles in a civil war by the entire population, including a future insurgent party.[27] Furthermore, the interpretation of the International Court of Justice in the *Nicaragua* case of Article 1 common to the Geneva Conventions is in accordance with the terms of this article. This article obliges the state to ensure respect for the Conventions 'in all circumstances'. This means that it is relevant whenever international humanitarian law is applicable, that is, pursuant to common Article 2 and 3 of the Geneva Conventions, both in international and internal conflicts. The obligation 'to ensure respect' applies not only to Common Article 3, to which the International Court of Justice referred in the *Nicaragua* case, but also to Protocol II. Being additional to Common Article 3 of the Geneva Conventions, the Protocol is subject to the general provisions of the Geneva Conventions.[28]

The *Nicaragua* case concerned the obligations of a third state (the United States), acting in close cooperation with an armed opposition group (the *Contras*). The question therefore remains whether Article 1

---

[25] Above, Chapter 1, n. 3.   [26] *Ibid.*, at 114, para. 220.
[27] See F. Kalshoven, 'The Undertaking to Respect and Ensure Respect in All Circumstances: From Tiny Seed to Ripening Fruit', in (1999) 2 *YIHL* 22–3, 27 (hereafter, 'Ensure Respect'); see also T. Meron, 'Internal Atrocities', above, Chapter 3, n. 8, at 569–70; D. Plattner, 'Penal Repression', above, Chapter 1, n. 1, at 419.
[28] But see *Commentary 4th Geneva Convention*, above, Chapter 1, n. 9, p. 16; but, the ICRC reviewed its position later, arguing that common Article 1 does apply in internal conflicts, see ICRC, *Disintegration of State Structures*, above, Chapter 4, n. 12, p. 16.

common to the Geneva Conventions also obliges the territorial state (Nicaragua, in this instance) that is fighting against an armed group, to ensure respect for Common Article 3 by this group. International practice indeed provides some evidence for such an obligation. International bodies have accepted one duty in particular – the obligation to prosecute and punish harmful acts by armed opposition groups. In 1997, the UN Special Rapporteur on Extrajudicial, Summary or Arbitrary Executions expressed his concern with regard to the conflict in Sudan about:

> Violations of the right to life of civilians committed by government and opposition forces, in particular in the south of the Sudan, and calls on all combatants to respect international humanitarian law and human rights standards. He also urges the Government to investigate the allegations and to take the necessary measures to prevent the recurrence of violations of the right to life.[29]

The Rapporteur made a similar statement with regard to the conflict in Chechnya (Russian Federation).[30] This practice is supported by the International Law Commission's Draft Code of Crimes Against the Peace and Security of Mankind, which obliges states to prosecute or extradite those alleged to have committed violations of international humanitarian law applicable in internal conflicts, in particular of Common Article 3 and Article 4 of Protocol II.[31]

No international bodies, however, have accepted such positive obligations of the state under this law with regard to acts of armed opposition groups. Moreover, the obligation that emerges from the available practice is limited to the specific obligation of penal repression. International bodies are silent on any other obligations of the state to prevent and repress acts by armed opposition groups acting on its territory under Common Article 3 and Protocol II.

How is this silence to be interpreted? How can the difference between international practice on international humanitarian law and human rights law be explained? The explanation may be that Common Article 3

---

[29] 1996 Report of the Special Rapporteur on Extrajudicial, Summary or Arbitrary Executions, above, Chapter 1, n. 139, para. 460.
[30] Ibid., para. 418; see also UN Commission on Human Rights, E/CN.4/1995/61, para. 49 (Report of Special Rapporteur, 14 December 1994) (Algeria) (hereafter, 1994 Report of the Special Rapporteur on Extrajudicial, Summary or Arbitrary Executions); 1988 Report of the Special Rapporteur on Extrajudicial, Summary or Arbitrary Executions, above, Chapter 2, n. 12, paras 122–3; UN Commission on Human Rights, E/CN.4/1989/25, paras. 95, 97 (Report of the Special Rapporteur, S. Amos Wako, 6 February 1989) (El Salvador); Ibid., paras. 189–90 (Nicaragua); Ibid., paras. 250–3 (Sri Lanka).
[31] Above, Chapter 3, n. 8, Article 9.

and Protocol II do not specify the state's obligation to ensure respect for the norms. Instead, they impose the duties directly onto the contending forces themselves. This may lead international bodies to consider it unnecessary to address the state with regard to acts committed by armed opposition groups, because these groups can be held accountable in their own right. This interpretation is supported by the International Law Commission. The Commission suggested that the responsibility of the state with regard to acts of armed opposition groups is modified by the armed opposition groups' *own* responsibility under international law:

> The injurious conduct of organs of an insurrectional movement is to be distinguished from that of individuals or groups of individuals during a riot or demonstrations by a rebellious mob. This is because, in the case of a genuine insurrectional movement in the sense in which that term is understood in international law, there is a possibility of holding the movement itself responsible for the wrongful acts of its organs.[32]

Also, the lack of practice under international humanitarian law may be explained by the nature of the relationship between the state and armed opposition groups underlying these norms. Under international humanitarian law, the relationship between the state and armed opposition groups is not a 'human rights relationship', i.e., is not a hierarchical relationship between a government and the governed. Rather, under this law the state's government and the armed opposition groups are equal parties fighting each other. The effect is that these groups are seen as being, by definition, outside the control of the territorial state – and consequently outside the accountability of the state as well.[33]

The limited practice on positive obligations of the state under Common Article 3 and Protocol II, in contrast to the extensive practice under human rights treaties, indicates that the content and scope of the obligation 'to ensure respect' in both categories of treaties is not identical. This obligation has no autonomous or universal meaning, but must be read together with the substantive obligations laid down in the human rights and humanitarian law treaties. The state must 'ensure respect' *for the*

---

[32] ILC Commentary to Draft Articles on State Responsibility, *ILCYb* 1975, Vol. II, p. 98, para. 28.

[33] See G. I. A. D. Draper, 'Human Rights and the Law of Armed Conflicts: General Principles of Implementation', *Résumé des cours: cinquième session d'enseignement* (International Institute of Human Rights at Strasbourg, July 1–26, 1974), reprinted in *Reflections on Law and Armed Conflicts*, above, Chapter 1, n. 2, pp. 141, 142–4.

treaty in which this rule is set out.[34] Thus, the substance of the obligation 'to ensure respect' in human rights treaties and humanitarian treaties depends on the material norms and the object of the respective treaties.

Other international humanitarian law treaties

A number of humanitarian law treaties, other than the Geneva Conventions and Protocol II, are relevant to the state's accountability for failure to prevent or repress acts by armed opposition groups in internal conflict. Among these are Amended Protocol II on Prohibitions or Restrictions on the Use of Mines, Booby-Traps and Other Devices of 3 May 1996; the Ottawa Convention on Anti-Personnel Mines of 18 September 1998; the Cultural Property Convention of 1954; and the Second Protocol on Cultural Property of 26 March 1999 (not yet in force). These treaties oblige the state to take measures of national implementation and precautionary measures. The Land Mines and Cultural Property Conventions impose a duty to adopt penal sanctions to repress them or take precautions or both.

The above-mentioned treaties bind all parties to the conflict, including armed opposition groups to observe the norms set forth, except for the Ottawa Convention on Anti-Personnel Mines, which applies only to the state.[35] The obligation to prosecute violators of those norms is reserved to the state. The obligation to take precautionary measures to protect civilians from the indiscriminate use of land mines and to prevent the extensive destruction of cultural property, however, rests on all parties to

---

[34] Article 1 common to the 1949 Geneva Conventions provides: 'The High Contracting Parties undertake to respect and to ensure respect *for the present Convention* in all circumstances' (emphasis added); similarly, in the *Velásquez Rodríguez* case, the Inter-American Court stated with regard to Article 1 of the American Convention: 'This article specifies the obligation assumed by the States Parties *in relation to each of the rights protected*. Each claim alleging that one of those rights has been infringed necessarily implies that Article 1(1) of the Convention has also been violated' (emphasis added), above, n. 7, para. 162.

[35] Amended Protocol II to the Conventional Weapons Convention applies to all parties to a conflict within the meaning of Common Article 3, see Article 1(2) and (3) of the Protocol. According to Article 19(1) of the Cultural Property Convention of 1954, this convention applies to internal armed conflicts and binds all parties to such conflicts, both the state and armed opposition groups. Article 22 of the Second Protocol on Cultural Property stipulates that the Protocol shall apply to internal armed conflicts. The Ottawa Convention on Anti-Personnel Mines prescribes that states shall 'never under any circumstances' develop, produce, stockpile, transfer or use anti-personnel mines. While this treaty thus applies in internal armed conflict, it applies only to one party to the conflict, that is the state.

the conflict, including armed opposition groups. These treaties therefore modify the conclusion drawn in the previous section, namely that the limited international practice on positive obligations of the state under Common Article 3 and Protocol II may be partly clarified by armed opposition groups' own obligations under these instruments. They show that positive obligations of the state to protect civilians from armed opposition groups are not wholly inconceivable under humanitarian law treaties binding also armed opposition groups.

Because these treaties have not (yet) given rise to practice of international bodies on the state's positive obligations with regard to armed opposition groups, they will not be considered further.

International criminal law treaties

Finally, the state's positive obligations to prevent and repress acts of armed opposition groups on its territory will be considered in relation to two criminal law treaties: the Genocide Convention of 1954, and the 1984 Convention Against Torture. The Genocide Convention obliges the state to prevent and to punish the crime of genocide at all times, whether committed in external or internal conflicts or in 'peacetime'.[36] The obligation to punish genocide applies equally when private persons have committed the genocide, which includes members of armed opposition groups.[37] There is no international practice applying this obligation. This practice might emerge, however, from current International Court of Justice (ICJ) cases.[38]

The definition of torture employed by the Convention against Torture appears to exclude the application of this treaty to the state when the actual acts of torture are committed by armed opposition groups. Article 1 of the Convention defines torture as 'any act by which severe pain or suffering, whether physical or mental, is intentionally inflicted on a person ... when such pain or suffering is inflicted by or at the instigation of or with the consent or acquiescence of *a public official or other person acting in an official capacity*'.[39] In 1998, the Committee against

---

[36] Article I.   [37] Article IV, see discussion above, Chapter 3, Section 1.
[38] For example, in the Case Concerning the Application of the Convention on the Prevention and Punishment of the Crime of Genocide (*Bosnia and Herzegovina* v. *Federal Republic of Yugoslavia*) Bosnia and Herzegovina requested the ICJ to declare that the Federal Republic of Yugoslavia had violated the Genocide Convention by virtue of having failed to prevent and to punish acts of genocide (see, for example, the Application filed to the Court by Bosnia and Herzegovina of 20 March 1993, para. 128).
[39] Emphasis added.

Torture established under the Torture Convention, confirmed that the Convention does not impose positive obligations on the state to prevent torture committed by entities other than the state: 'The Committee considers that the issue whether the State party has an obligation to refrain from expelling a person who might risk pain or suffering inflicted by a non-governmental entity, without the consent or acquiescence of the Government, falls outside the scope of Article 3 of the Convention'.[40] The Committee restated its view in a general comment.[41] While this concerned a case of expulsion by a third state, there is no reason to assume that there is a difference under the Torture Convention between the obligations of an expelling state vis-à-vis torture committed by armed opposition groups in another state, and the obligations of a state with regard to torture committed by armed opposition groups on its own territory.

The position of the Committee should be criticized, however. It would seem that the interpretation of the Committee of the notion 'public official or other person acting in an official capacity' as referring exclusively to *state* agents, is too narrow. There is no good reason not to include 'officials' of armed opposition groups that operate as de facto governments and of other large armed groups exercising territorial authority. In fact, this approach would be in line with current practice of other human rights bodies, such as the Human Rights Committee and the UN Commission on Human Rights. Furthermore, the Human Rights Committee interpreted torture as prohibited under Article 7 of the International Covenant on Civil and Political Rights (the International Covenant) as also governing torture by armed opposition groups.[42] Also, according to the Yugoslavia Tribunal, armed opposition groups are capable of committing torture within the meaning of Article 1

---

[40] *GRB* v. *Sweden*, Comm. 83/1997, CAT/C/20/D/83/1997 (View adopted on 15 May 1998). Article 3 of the Torture Convention stipulates: '1. No State Party shall expel, return ("*refouler*") or extradite a person to another State where there are substantial grounds for believing that he would be in danger of being subjected to torture. 2. For the purpose of determining whether there are such grounds, the competent authorities shall take into account all relevant considerations including, where applicable, the existence in the State concerned of a consistent pattern of gross, flagrant or mass violations of human rights'.

[41] General Comment on the Implementation of Article 3 in the Context of Article 22 of the Convention Against Torture, A/53/44, Annex IX (1998) ('Article 3 is confined in its application to cases where there are substantial grounds for believing that the author would be in danger of being subjected to torture as defined in article 1 of the Convention').

[42] Below, Section 2.

of the Convention against Torture.[43] Finally, it should be noted that it is accepted that persons who are persecuted by private actors, including armed opposition groups, are refugees within the meaning of the 1951 Convention Relating to the Status of Refugees.[44]

The obligation of the state to take action

It has been demonstrated that, according to international practice, human rights treaties and to a lesser extent international humanitarian and criminal law treaties, in certain circumstances, oblige the state to prevent and repress acts of armed opposition groups operating on its territory. This section examines the scope and contents of the state's positive obligations in those parts of the territory where it exercises a degree of control. Practice of international bodies shows that these obligations consist primarily of basic requirements to implement the right to life in the domestic legal order. International bodies have distinguished the following three specific obligations: the obligation to protect civilians from armed opposition groups through legislation; the obligation to physically protect civilians from armed opposition groups; and the obligation to prosecute acts of armed opposition groups prohibited under the applicable treaties.

Two preliminary remarks are in order. First, the practice of international bodies is mostly restricted to protection of civilian *life* from attacks by armed opposition groups.[45] There are good reasons to pay ample attention to the right to life, or in terms of international humanitarian law, the prohibition of violence to life. It is obvious that during internal conflict this right is exposed to serious risks. Moreover, without its protection all other rights are devoid of meaning. In the words of the Inter-American Commission on Human Rights: 'Respect for the right to life warrants special consideration, for it unquestionably is the basis and support of all other rights.'[46]

---

[43] Above, Chapter 3, Section 1.
[44] G.S. Goodwin-Gill, *The Refugee in International Law* (Clarendon Press, Oxford, 2nd edn., 1996), pp. 69-70.
[45] Article 6(1) of the International Covenant provides: 'Every human being has the inherent right to life'; Articles 2(1) of the European Convention and 4(1) of the American Convention contain similar provisions. Common Article 3 and Article 4 of Protocol II prohibit violence to life of those not directly participating in the hostilities.
[46] Annual Report of the Inter-American Commission on Human Rights 1971, at 33, in Inter-American Commission on Human Rights, *Ten Years of Activities 1971-1981*, above n. 14, at 331; see also Human Rights Committee, General Comment 6/16, para. 1

Nevertheless, the focus of international bodies on the right to life entails a significant limitation of their contribution to the application and development of the state's accountability for failure to restrain acts of armed opposition groups.[47] Human rights, humanitarian, and criminal law treaties contain obligations other than the right to life, which would seem to be of direct relevance for the regulation of the conduct of armed opposition groups. Deprivation of liberty and ill treatment of detainees in prisons by armed groups are obvious areas to which the state's accountability could extend.

The second remark concerns the nature of the state's obligations. The state is not responsible for injurious acts of armed opposition groups in internal armed conflict. In each case, responsibility can only be based upon the state's *own* failure to act, the act of armed opposition groups merely constituting the objective condition which gives rise to a breach of the relevant treaty provisions on the part of the state. This is in accordance with the International Law Commission's Draft Articles on State Responsibility stating that the conduct of an insurrectional movement can never, by itself, justify holding the state responsible. Article 10 of the Draft Articles provides:

(1) The conduct of an organ of an insurrectional movement which is established in the territory of a State or in any other territory under its administration shall not be considered as an act of that State under international law.
(2) Paragraph 1 is without prejudice to the attribution to a State of any other conduct which is related to that of the organ of the insurrectional movement

---

(27 July 1982) on Article 6 of the International Covenant, reproduced in A/37/40, Annex V (stating that the right to life is 'the supreme right'); UN Commission on Human Rights, Res. 1994/ 46, pr. (4 March 1994) ('bearing in mind that the most essential and basic human right is the right to life'); see also Y. Dinstein, 'The Right to Life, Physical Integrity, and Liberty' in L. Henkin (ed.), *The International Bill of Rights* (1981) p. 114 ('The right to life is incontestably the most important of all human rights') (hereafter, 'The Right to Life'). The fundamental nature of the right to life is reflected in human rights treaties, placing this right at the forefront of the rights. It is one of the non-derogable rights which may not be suspended in the case of an emergency including internal armed conflicts. In the International Covenant the special significance of the right to life is also underlined by the adjective 'inherent', which is only used in the article on the right to life and which attests its primacy.

[47] The focus on the right to life by the Special Rapporteur on Extrajudicial, Summary or Arbitrary Executions is inherent in his mandate, however. The Rapporteur has defined his mandate as covering 'all acts and omissions of state representatives that constitute a violation of the general recognition of the right to life embodied in [various international human rights and humanitarian law instruments]', 1993 Report by the Special Rapporteur on Extrajudicial, Summary or Arbitrary Executions, above, Chapter 2, n. 102, paras. 9–10.

and which is to be considered as an act of that State by virtue of articles 5 to 10.[48]

The state is thus only responsible for its own acts or omissions. What, then, does a state have to do with regard to the acts of armed opposition groups?

The fact that an armed opposition group acts within the state's territory, where the state exercises certain control, does not mean that the state must prevent and repress its conduct at all costs.[49] International practice demonstrates that the state is only responsible for harm caused by armed opposition groups when it has failed to exercise *due diligence*.[50] This means that the state must undertake appropriate measures to prevent and repress the injurious acts of armed opposition groups. Appropriate measures are those measures, which the state can reasonably be required to take in view of its own capabilities and the situation.[51]

The limitation of the state's positive obligations to due diligence is realistic. Since the state is not an all-powerful entity, it cannot give an absolute guarantee at the international level that no harmful actions will be committed in its territory by armed opposition groups. Supreme legal authority is a necessary but not sufficient condition for protection, nor is the existence of a government exercising a degree of territorial control. Whenever the state must make an effort in order to achieve a particular material result, international bodies must take account of the

---

[48] 1996 ILC Draft Articles on State Responsibility, above, Chapter 4, n. 1. In the Draft Articles provisionally adopted on second reading by the Drafting Committee in 1998, above, Chapter 4, n. 1, paragraph 1 of Draft Article 14 has been deleted. The Special Rapporteur on State Responsibility explained that this basic principle is well established and need not be stated specifically in this article, 1998 First Report Special Rapporteur on State Responsibility, Addendum 5 of 26 May 1998, para. 276. See also United States Diplomatic and Consular Staff in Teheran case (*US v. Iran*) (Judgment of 24 May 1980), 1980 ICJ Rep. 3 (the International Court of Justice considered it necessary, in order for the acts of the rioters and other militants to be regarded as acts of State, that it be 'established that, in fact, on the occasion in question the militants acted on behalf of the State, having been charged by some competent organ of the Iranian State to carry out a specific operation') (hereafter, *US Staff in Teheran* case).

[49] See *Platform 'Ärzte Für Das Leben'* case, above, n. 6, para. 34 ('while it is the duty of Contracting States to take reasonable and appropriate measures to enable lawful demonstrations to proceed peacefully, they cannot guarantee this absolutely').

[50] See generally I. Brownlie, *System of the Law of Nations – State Responsibility* (Clarendon Press, Oxford, reprint 1986) (1983) vol. I, p. 172 (hereafter, *State Responsibility*); R. Jennings, A. Watts, *Oppenheim*, above, Chapter 1, n. 59, p. 549.

[51] See *Velásquez Rodríguez* case, above n. 7, paras. 174–5; see also C. Tomuschat, 'What is a Breach', above, n. 5, p. 330.

fact that a degree of factual capability, which can be employed to that effect, is required. Moreover, it should be kept in mind that the state is entitled under international law to defend its territorial integrity against armed attacks by armed opposition groups. International bodies must balance this entitlement against the state's obligation to protect civilians from armed groups.

While the due diligence principle follows from the obligations laid down in human rights, humanitarian and criminal law treaties,[52] these treaties do not establish the detailed content of the principle. According to international bodies, the degree of diligence that a state must observe depends on the substantive obligation in question and on a number of general factors, such as the availability of means, the foreseeability of the harm caused by armed opposition groups, and the particular circumstances of the case.[53] The state is entitled to suppress an insurrection against it and to use the force necessary to that end. Accordingly, the application of the duty to protect civilian life from armed opposition groups is also mitigated by the military necessity prevailing in the conflict.

A state's obligation to prevent and repress acts committed by armed opposition groups can be discharged by several means: through legislation, through physical protection, and, finally, through prosecution. Each of these will be discussed briefly.

Legislation

International practice demonstrates that the state is obliged to have in place a legal framework for the prevention and repression of attacks by armed opposition groups on civilian life. This obligation to legislate is set forth in human rights treaties. Article 6(1) of the International Covenant on Civil and Political Rights provides: 'Every human being

---

[52] See R. Pisillo-Mazzeschi, 'Forms of International Responsibility for Environmental Harm' in F. Francioni, T. Scovazzi, (eds.), *International Responsibility for Environmental Harm*, (Graham & Trotman, London 1991), pp. 15–16; G. A. Christenson, 'Attributing Acts of Omission to the State' (1991) 12 *Mich. J. Int'l L.* 312, 329.

[53] Compare *US Staff in Teheran* case, above, n. 48, para. 68 (where the International Court of Justice held Iran to be in breach of its international obligations to take steps to protect United States diplomatic and consular premises in Iran from the attack and, generally, to restore the *status quo*. Among the reasons underlying the Court's decision were: (a) the Iranian authorities were fully aware, as a result of the appeals for help made by the US Embassy, of the urgent need for action on their part; (b) the Iranian authorities had the means at their disposal to perform their obligations; (c) the Iranian authorities completely failed to comply with these obligations).

has the inherent right to life. This right shall be protected by law'.[54] The European Convention and the American Convention contain similar provisions.[55]

The obligation to adopt legislation to prevent and repress violations of Common Article 3 and Protocol II by armed opposition groups is not explicitly contained in these instruments. Certain provisions in Protocol II, however, presuppose the existence of domestic legislation by expressly referring to it. For instance, Article 6(2)(c) of Protocol II states: 'no one shall be held guilty of any criminal offence on account of any act or omission which did not constitute a criminal offence, *under the law*, at the time when it was committed; nor shall a heavier penalty be imposed than that which was applicable at the time when the criminal offence was committed'.[56] Furthermore, the obligation to implement the humanitarian standards through domestic legislation can be inferred from the state's obligation to prosecute violations thereof by armed opposition groups. International bodies have accepted that the state's obligation to prosecute extends not only to grave breaches but also to violations of Common Article 3 and Protocol II. This obligation can only be implemented through some kind of criminal law statute.[57]

Other humanitarian law treaties, such as the Ottawa Convention on Land Mines, Amended Protocol II on Prohibitions or Restrictions on the Use of Mines, Booby-Traps and Other Devices, and the Second Protocol on Cultural Property explicitly oblige the state to adopt appropriate

---

[54] In addition to this provision, the general obligation to ensure respect for the rights stipulated in the Covenant (Article 2(2) of the International Covenant) requires states to give effect to the rights recognized in the conventions by legislative and other measures. The formulation 'legislative or other measures' demonstrates the priority of legislative measures, M. Nowak, *UN Covenant on Civil and Political Rights – Commentary* (N. P. Engel, Kehl, 1993), p. 55.

[55] Article 2(1) of the European Convention; Article 4(1) of the American Convention. In the *Velásquez Rodríguez* case, the Inter-American Court of Human Rights affirmed that the existence of a legal system is one of the means for a state to comply with its obligation to ensure the right to life, above, n. 7, para. 167; see generally on the duty to protect by law, K. Vasak, 'Human Rights: As a Legal Reality', in K. Vasak, (ed.), *The International Dimensions of Human Rights* (Greenwood Press, Westport, 1982), pp. 3, 7.

[56] Emphasis added. Other examples are Articles 6(2) (d) and 10(3) and (4) of Protocol II.

[57] As Meron argued: 'As regards the national state of the perpetrators of nongrave breaches, its obligations go further. Given the purposes and objects of the Geneva Conventions and the normative content of their provisions, *any state that does not have the necessary laws in place*, or is otherwise unwilling to prosecute and punish violators of clauses other than the grave breaches provisions that are significant and have a clear penal character, calls into serious question its good faith compliance with its treaty obligations' (emphasis added), T. Meron, 'Internal Atrocities', above, Chapter 3, n. 8, at 570.

legislation.[58] The Genocide Convention also obliges the state to enact the legislation necessary to give effect to the Convention, in particular to provide appropriate penalties for persons guilty of genocide.[59]

Human rights treaties also entail an obligation of the state to have appropriate legislation as contained in human rights treaties. In X v. Ireland, the European Commission on Human Rights affirmed that the state is obliged to render illegal the taking of life by armed opposition groups under its domestic laws. The case concerned an applicant on whose life the IRA made an attempt in the Irish Republic in 1969. The applicant complained that the police authorities refused to protect his life. The Commission observed: 'Art. 2 provides that everyone's right to life shall be protected by law. However, the applicant has not even suggested that there are no laws in Ireland protecting the right to life'.[60]

The Human Rights Committee pointed out in its general comment on Article 7 of the International Covenant that the state party is obliged to protect persons from torture or cruel, inhuman or degrading treatment or punishment also when committed by persons 'acting in a private capacity'. The Committee stated that it is the state's duty in this regard to take the necessary legislative measures.[61]

The obligation to adopt laws so as to prevent and repress acts of armed opposition groups injuring civilians already exists before an internal conflict has broken out and irrespective of whether any injurious acts have actually been committed. Its fulfilment is therefore in principle not dependent on external uncertain factors and can be implemented by every state.

It seems that arbitrary killings by armed opposition groups require *criminal* law. Human rights treaties do not specify the kind of law, criminal or civil. Under these instruments, the choice of measures suited to ensure the relevant rights, is free.[62] The existence of criminal liability must be inferred from the state's obligation to prosecute

---

[58] Article 9 of the Ottawa Convention on Anti-Personnel Mines; Article 14 of the Amended Protocol II to the Conventional Weapons Convention; Articles 15(2), 16(1) of the Second Protocol on Cultural Property; a similar provision is absent in the 1954 Cultural Property Convention.

[59] Article IV.

[60] Appl. 6040/73 (Decision of 20 July 1973) 16 YB ECHR 388 (1973); see also Human Rights Committee, CCPR/C/SR.1067, 42nd Sess. para. 55 (El Shafei, 1991) (Sudan); Inter-American Commission on Human Rights, Second Report on the Situation of Human Rights in Colombia, above, Chapter 1, n. 110, at 5.

[61] General Comment 20/44, para. 2 (3 April 1992) reproduced in A/47/40, Annex VI.

[62] See X and Y v. Netherlands (Judgment of 26 March 1985) Eur. Ct. HR Ser. A 91, para. 24 (1985).

abuses by armed opposition groups, which will be examined below.[63] This is because international human rights treaties are not in themselves capable of being the basis of criminal judgments – they need to be supplemented by some kind of criminal statute.[64] There is no practice developing this point.

The question arises as to the *territorial scope* of this duty to legislate. International practice shows that state laws, which, pursuant to an international obligation, have been adopted for the entire territory, remain in force in the entire state territory, including in those parts where the state temporarily exercises no control. This is illustrated by the Human Rights Division of the United Nations Observer Mission in El Salvador (ONUSAL). ONUSAL was, during the internal conflict in El Salvador, charged with the verification of compliance with the San José Agreement on Human Rights concluded between the Salvadorian State and FMLN.[65] Of interest are ONUSAL's considerations on the right to freedom of movement. During the conflict, this right was particularly impeded by the problem posed by undocumented persons. In response to this, Article 8 of the San José Agreement provided: 'All persons shall be guaranteed freedom of movement in the areas involved in the conflict, and the necessary steps shall be taken to provide the inhabitants of such areas with the identity documents required by law.'[66] Although both the Salvadorian Government and FMLN signed the Agreement, and both parties were therefore bound to implement this provision, ONUSAL interpreted 'required by law' as referring only to the state's law. In the Mission's view, providing documents was a task of the Salvadorian

---

[63] See J. E. S. Fawcett, *The Application of the European Convention on Human Rights* (Clarendon Press, Oxford, 2nd edn., 1987) p. 37 (interpreting Article 2(1) of the European Convention: 'it could ... reasonably be implied that the State must make the deliberate taking of life by individuals a punishable offence').

[64] C. K. O'Boyle, 'The Concept of Arbitrary Deprivation of Life', in B. G. Ramcharan (ed.), *The Right to Life in International Law* (Martinus Nijhoff, Dordrecht, 1985) p. 234; the Genocide Convention (Article V) obliges the state to adopt criminal legislation to implement the relevant rules.

[65] Above, Chapter 1, n. 149; on the Human Rights Division see Articles 10–19.

[66] *Ibid.*, (emphasis added); in addition, Article 7 of the San José Agreement provided: 'Displaced persons and returnees shall be provided with the identity documents required by law and shall be guaranteed freedom of movement'. Freedom of movement in El Salvador was furthermore guaranteed by Article 12 of the International Covenant. The UN Mission noted that, under Article 4 of the International Covenant, freedom of movement may be suspended in time of a public emergency; however, El Salvador had not made use of this right; according to the UN Mission, the right to freedom of movement was therefore fully in effect in El Salvador, Third Report of ONUSAL, above, Chapter 2, n. 33, para. 99.

Government. Moreover, ONUSAL held the opinion that this domestic law applied to the entire territory of El Salvador including the 'conflict zones', which were areas controlled by FMLN.[67] ONUSAL noted that it was precisely in these zones that the greatest restrictions were imposed on the right of freedom of movement, because FMLN used to cut off tracks and main roads.[68] Apparently, it considered the absence of state control there to be irrelevant for the applicability of the law of El Salvador.

Problems are likely to arise when armed opposition groups have adopted their own laws for areas that they control. As has been shown in Chapter 2, armed opposition groups, as temporary holders of authority, do actually enact laws. In the conflict in El Salvador, FMLN enacted its own legislation applicable to the territory under its control.[69] ONUSAL refrained, however, from discussing the question of the relationship and compatibility between the laws of El Salvador and FMLN.

Nor does humanitarian law offer a solution to this problem. Common Article 3 and Protocol II, like human rights norms, presuppose the continued applicability of national legislation. For example, Protocol II prescribes penal prosecutions to be in accordance with 'the law'. This term appears to have been copied from the International Covenant on Rights Civil and Political and must therefore be understood as referring to state law.[70] Amended Protocol II to the Conventional Weapons Convention is more explicit on this matter. While binding on all parties to an internal conflict, it obliges only States Parties to take legislative measures to ensure compliance with the rules. It would follow that this state legislation binds all parties to the conflict, including armed opposition groups.[71] The drafters of these instruments failed to examine problems that may arise from the concurrent existence of laws of armed opposition groups. Nonetheless, the notion of state law as being problematic was acknowledged – but not resolved – in the commentary on Protocol II: 'The possible co-existence of two sorts of national legislation,

---

[67] Second Report of ONUSAL, above, Chapter 1, n. 27, paras 163–4; Third Report of ONUSAL, above, Chapter 2, n. 33, paras. 92, 103.
[68] Third Report of ONUSAL, above, Chapter 2, n. 33, para. 96.
[69] America's Watch Committee, *Violations of Fair Trial Guarantees by the FMLN's Ad Hoc Courts*, (May 1990), p. 512.
[70] S-S. Junod, *Commentary Additional Protocols*, above, Chapter 1, n. 9, pp. 1399–1400; Ibid., p. 1344; but see Third Report of ONUSAL, above, Chapter 2, n. 33, at 102, para. 113 (interpreting 'law' in Article 6(2)(c) Protocol II as referring also to the laws of the FMLN).
[71] Article 14(1).

namely, that of the State and that of the insurgents, makes the concept of national law rather complicated in this context.'[72]

As for the content of the obligation to legislate, it appears that the state has a broad discretion in fulfilling this duty. Violation of this obligation has only been established when the legislation was manifestly inadequate. International practice demonstrates that this may be the case when a state adopts amnesty laws granting immunity to members of armed opposition groups for alleged injurious acts. (This issue will be discussed in more detail later.)

Precautions against attacks by armed groups

The humanitarian law treaties, including Amended Protocol II to the Conventional Weapons Convention, the Ottawa Convention on Anti-Personnel Mines, and the Second Protocol on Cultural Property impose on the state a duty to take precautionary measures against the effects of attacks of armed opposition groups in internal conflict. Article 5(4) of Amended Protocol II prohibits the use of anti-personnel mines other than remotely-delivered mines, unless the effective exclusion of civilians from the area where the mines are placed is ensured and such weapons are cleared before the area is abandoned. This article subsequently provides: 'If the forces of a party to a conflict gain control of an area in which weapons to which this Article applies have been laid, such forces shall, to the maximum extent feasible, maintain and, if, necessary, establish the protections required by this Article until such weapons have been cleared.'[73]

Thus, if the state gains control of an area previously controlled and mined by an armed opposition group, it must provide protection from such mines. Article 5(1) of the Ottawa Convention requires each State Party to destroy mines that have already been laid 'in mined areas under the jurisdiction or control' of a State Party. This means that the obligation extends to parts of the state territory that were previously under

---

[72] S-S. Junod, *Commentary Additional Protocols*, above, Chapter 1, n. 9, p. 1399. Similar observations on the relationship and compatibility of state laws and laws of armed opposition groups apply to the Guiding Principles on Internal Displacement, above, Chapter 1, n. 145. The Principles are addressed to 'all authorities, groups and persons' (Principle 2) and provide that 'every human being has the inherent right to life which shall be protected *by law*' (Principle 10) [emphasis added].

[73] See also Article 3 (prescribing precautionary measures to protect civilians from the effects of mines, booby-traps and other devices).

control of armed opposition groups.[74] Finally, Article 8 of the Second Protocol on Cultural Property prescribes that precautionary measures be taken against attacks by other parties to the conflict, including armed opposition groups, which may destroy cultural property. These measures include the removal of cultural property from the vicinity of military objectives and preventing the location of military objectives near cultural property.

Neither Common Article 3 nor Protocol II expressly prescribe intervention with or precautions against acts of armed opposition groups. The Genocide Convention also does not expressly oblige the state to physically protect civilians from attacks by armed opposition groups in internal conflict. Nor do human rights treaties impose such a duty.

Nevertheless, international bodies have accepted that a duty to take action against armed opposition groups may, under particular circumstances, arise from the general obligation to ensure respect for the relevant rights. For example, the Inter-American Commission considered that the state might be obliged to take forcible action against armed opposition groups attacking civilians:

> The violence, springing from terrorist groups on both the right and the left, leads the Commission to once again emphasize its well-known doctrine on this matter. The Commission has repeatedly stressed the obligation the governments have of maintaining public order and the personal safety of the country's inhabitants. For that purpose, the governments must prevent and suppress acts of violence, *even forcefully*, whether committed by public officials or private individuals whether their motives are political or otherwise.[75]

Similarly, the Human Rights Committee observed that Algerian security forces and police, who were in the vicinity of victims attacked by the Islamic groups, were obliged to prevent such attacks, and if they nonetheless took place to come immediately to the defence of the victims.[76] The Rapporteur on Extrajudicial, Summary or Arbitrary Executions suggested that the state might also be obliged to intervene in an effort to stop the violence between armed groups, the government not being directly involved:

---

[74] S. Maslen, P. Herby, 'An International Ban on Anti-Personnel Mines – History and Negotiation of the "Ottawa Treaty"' (1998) 325 *IRRC* 693–713, text available on www.icrc.org (visited, 1 January 2001) (hereafter, 'Ottawa Treaty').
[75] Report on the Situation of Human Rights in the Republic of Guatemala, OEA/Ser.L/V/II.61, Doc.47, rev.1, para. 10 (5 October 1983) (emphasis added).
[76] Concluding Observations on Algeria 1998, above, n. 12, para. 6.

The Special Rapporteur would once again like to draw the attention of the international community to the problem of communal violence, understood as acts of violence committed by groups of citizens of a country against other groups. In Burundi, Nigeria, Rwanda and Zaire, where violent confrontations were reported between different ethnic groups, government forces allegedly... did not intervene to stop the violence... The Special Rapporteur... strongly appeals to all governments to refrain from supporting groups, on ethnic or other grounds, either actively or by simply tolerating acts of violence committed by them.[77]

In *Ergi v. Turkey*, the European Court of Human Rights held that Turkey must plan and conduct military operations so as to prevent or decrease risk to civilian life from such operations, which included protection from firing by the PKK:

There was no information to indicate that any steps or precautions had been taken to protect the villagers from being caught up in the conflict. Accordingly, in the absence of evidence from gendarmes involved in the planning and conduct of the operation, the Commission was not satisfied that the ambush operation carried out close to Kesentas village had been implemented with the requisite care for the lives of the civilian population. The Court, having regard to the Commission's findings... and to its own assessment, considers that it was probable that the bullet which killed Havva Ergi had been fired from the south or south-east, that the security forces had been present in the south and that there had been a real risk to the lives of the civilian population through being exposed to cross fire between the security forces and the PKK. In the light of the failure of the authorities of the respondent State to adduce direct evidence on the planning and conduct of the ambush operation, the Court, in agreement with the Commission, finds that it can reasonably be inferred that insufficient precautions had been taken to protect the lives of the civilian population.[78]

This practice shows that under particular circumstances human rights treaties oblige the state to take action against attacks by armed opposition groups. There is no doubt, however, that this obligation is conditional on the due diligence rule. The state must have a degree of factual capability to prevent and repress violent attacks by armed opposition groups. Further, the general proposition made earlier that internal conflict, due to its scale and the consequences for state authority, has its impact on the due diligence requirement, is fully applicable here. The state is permitted to put down armed opposition groups fighting against it and to use the force necessary to that end. Hence, the application of the

[77] 1993 Report of the Special Rapporteur on Extrajudicial, Summary or Arbitrary Executions, above, Chapter 2, n. 102, para. 709.
[78] Above, n. 10, paras. 80 and 81; The Court explicitly extended Turkey's obligations to the risks to civilian lives from the firepower of the PKK, *ibid.*, para. 79.

duty to take action against armed opposition groups must be balanced against military necessity.

The application of the due diligence rule means that the state will not actually have to act against attacks by armed opposition groups in each and every case; nor will the state have to be successful in its attempts to stop or decrease the injurious effects of attacks of armed opposition groups. Accordingly, in *Mrs W. v. United Kingdom*, the European Commission considered that, while Article 2 of the European Convention may give rise to positive obligations 'that, however, does not mean that a positive obligation to exclude any possible violence could be deduced from this Article'.[79] The relevant part of the application concerned a complaint about the lack of protection offered to the applicant's brother, who was murdered in Northern Ireland by the IRA, and her family's future protection. With regard to the question of what effort the United Kingdom had to make to act in compliance with its positive obligations under Article 2 of the European Convention, the Commission considered:

It cannot find that the United Kingdom was required under the Convention to protect the applicant's brother by measures going beyond those actually taken by the authorities in order to shield life and limb of the inhabitants of Northern Ireland against attacks from terrorists. Nor can it find that the applicant can under Art. 2 require such further measures as regards her own protection. In this connection the Commission notes... that, while the peace-time army strength in Northern Ireland was 4,000 men, it currently stands at about 10,500 and that, between August 1969 and December 1981, several hundred members of the armed and security forces lost their lives there combating terrorism.[80]

Thus, the increase of armed forces and the number of deaths among these forces added to the Commission's decision that the United Kingdom had not violated its positive duties to protect the applicant's right to life.[81]

While this case shows that the degree of diligence that the state must observe depends largely on the particular circumstances of each specific situation, two general factors relevant to the due diligence requirement emerge from the practice of international bodies. Those are the *availability of means* and the *foreseeability of harm*.

---

[79] Appl. 9348/81, 32 DR 190, para. 12 (1983).   [80] *Ibid.*, paras. 15–16.

[81] According to J. A. Frowein, *The Legal Aspects of International Terrorism* (Martinus Nijhoff, Dordrecht, 1988), p. 87, this decision 'seems to assume a certain right to be protected against terrorism can indeed be seen as forming part of the Convention guarantees. This is not astonishing since Article 2(1) states expressly: "everyone's right to life shall be protected by law."'

The administrative means or resources that are at the state's disposal determine the due diligence obligation of the state to take action against armed opposition groups. The possession of adequate resources is a matter of fact not regulated by human rights treaties. Accordingly, in their Joint Report on Colombia of 1995, the Special Rapporteur on Extrajudicial, Summary or Arbitrary Executions and the Special Rapporteur on Torture took note of the deficiencies of the Colombian State apparatus; however, they refrained from formulating any obligation in this respect.[82]

The second factor relevant to the required degree of diligence is the *foreseeability* of harm as a result of attacks by armed opposition groups. The Inter-American Commission referred to this factor in its Second Report on the Situation of Human Rights in Colombia:

> Apart from the responsibility that the State bears for actions committed directly by its agents, there is also the State's international responsibility for the actions of irregular armed groups, although there is no single criterion to establish the type and degree of that State responsibility. Here again it is objective responsibility vis-à-vis the terrorist phenomenon. This responsibility is in respect of all its inhabitants, whether national or foreign, under the laws and jurisprudence governing aggravating circumstances such as improvidence, negligence, criminal complicity, impunity, etc., and by the mitigating circumstances of "necessary diligence", *unforeseeability, the surprise factor*, a lack of proportion that could not have been anticipated.[83]

This statement is somewhat ambiguous. For example, it is unclear what 'objective responsibility' of the state regarding terrorism means. What is important for present purposes, however, is that the Commission has indicated that the duty of the state to respond to acts of armed opposition groups may be mitigated by the unforeseeability of these acts or by what the Commission termed 'the surprise factor'. Similarly, in *Ergi* v. *Turkey*, the European Court, considering whether Turkey had taken adequate precautionary measures to avoid or decrease any risk to the lives of the villagers, including from the fire-power of the PKK, took into account the extent to which cross-firing was predictable:

---

[82] 1995 Joint Report of the Special Rapporteur on Question of Torture, and the Special Rapporteur on Extrajudicial, Summary or Arbitrary Executions, above, Chapter 1, n. 8, para. 51. The situation of internal conflict may differ on this point from that of a time of normality. In the latter situation the state may be obliged to have a functioning administrative state apparatus, see R. Pisillo-Mazzeschi, 'The Due Diligence Rule and the Nature of International Responsibility of States' (1992) 35 *GYIL* 9, 26–7.

[83] Second Report on Colombia, above, Chapter 1, n. 110, at 217 (emphasis added).

The gendarme officers' testimonies to the Commission had suggested that the ambush was organized in the north-west of the village without the distance between the village and the ambush being known. It was to be *anticipated* that PKK terrorists could have approached the village either following the path from the north or proceeding down the river bed to the north-east and in the latter event, they would have been able to penetrate to the edge of the village without being seen by the security forces to the north-west. The Commission found on the evidence that security forces had been present in the south... In these circumstances, the villagers had been placed at *considerable risk* of being caught in cross-fire between security forces and any PKK terrorists who had approached from the north or north-east. Even if it might be assumed that the security forces would have responded with due care for the civilian population in returning fire against terrorists caught in the approaches to the village, *it could not be assumed that the terrorists would have responded with such restraint.*[84]

In *Yasa v. Turkey*, the European Commission of Human Rights suggested that if the applicant had made a specific request to the state authorities for protection or brought to their attention his fear of attack, Turkey would have been obliged to go beyond the general measures of deployment of security forces. In that case the Turkish Government would have been aware of the threats against the life of the applicant and his uncle, and therefore under a specific duty to protect them. In *Kilic v. Turkey*,[85] the European Court developed a more specific standard to determine the enforcement measures the state must take to prevent certain risks from materializing. The Court found that:

for a positive obligation to arise, it must be established that the authorities *knew or ought to have known* at the time of the existence of a real and immediate risk to the life of an identified individual or individuals from the criminal acts of a third party and that they failed to take measures within the scope of their powers which, judged reasonably, might have been expected to avoid that risk.[86]

Although this standard could equally be applied to risks created by armed groups, in this case the third party was believed to be contra-guerrilla groups or terrorist groups acting with the acquiescence and

---

[84] Above, n. 10, para. 80 (emphasis added); see also *Yasa v. Turkey*, Application 22495/93, Report of the Commission, para. 98 (8 April 1997), 88 Reports (1998–VI). In the latter case the applicant alleged that he was seriously injured and that his uncle was killed in attacks by state agents as part of a campaign against persons involved in the distribution of certain newspapers. The Turkish government refuted the applicant's claim, stating that an armed conflict was taking place between armed organizations or internal conflicts within organizations in Southern-Eastern Anatolia, thereby indirectly blaming the PKK for the attacks.
[85] Judgment of 28 March 2000.
[86] Para. 63 (emphasis added). See also *Akkoc v. Turkey*, Judgment of 10 October 2000, para. 78.

possible assistance of members of the Turkish security forces. For this reason, I will not consider this standard further.

The frequency of the attacks by armed opposition groups is closely related to foreseeability, and is therefore also relevant in determining whether in a particular case the state was obliged to act. Although, in principle, a single attack could result in liability for failure to protect civilians,[87] this is different when the state could possibly not have foreseen the act concerned. If, however, the state systematically and pervasively fails to make reasonable efforts to prevent or respond to a pattern of abuses by armed opposition groups, it will demonstrate a lack of due diligence to protect civilians.[88]

This practice points out that human rights law is reasonably capable of solving questions arising specifically out of the context of internal conflicts. For example, this law, as applied by international bodies, has given, through the concept of due diligence, effect to the principle of military necessity, which is a humanitarian law principle. Another example of the suitability of human rights law to the special circumstances of an internal armed conflict is the European Court's decision in *Ergi v. Turkey*, which shows that, although human rights treaties do not explicitly provide rules on the conduct of military operations, they may have an impact on such conduct.[89]

International bodies have rarely specified what kind of action is actually expected from the national police or armed forces. Instead, they

---

[87] 1994 Report of the Special Rapporteur on Extrajudicial, Summary or Arbitrary Executions, above, n. 30, para. 399 (stating with regard to the state's obligation to prevent human rights violations, in particular those affecting the physical integrity of the victim, 'a single act is sufficient for a State party to be obliged to undertake these measures').

[88] Amnesty International, 'Draft Note on the Standards of Complicity, Acquiescence and Lack of Due Diligence' (unpublished, on file with author).

[89] In this case, the European Court interpreted the obligation to ensure respect for the right to life as requiring the state to take precautions in the planning and conducting of military operations to reduce the effects of the attacks by the armed opposition group. A comparable rule has been laid down in international humanitarian law, e.g. Article 58 of Additional Protocol I (providing: 'The Parties to the conflict shall, to the maximum extent feasible: (a)... endeavor to remove the civilian population, individual civilians and civilian objects under their control from the vicinity of military objectives; (b) avoid locating military objectives within or near densely populated areas; (c) take the other necessary precautions to protect the civilian population, individual civilians and civilian objects under their control against the dangers resulting from military operations'). See F. Hampson, referred to in L. Zegveld, H. van Sambeek, 'Law and Conflicts in Our Times – The Meaning of International Humanitarian Law in Internal Armed Conflicts' (1998) 1 *HV* 70–1.

leave the state a wide margin of appreciation in the choice of measures and means adopted to fulfil its obligation.[90] In *Mrs W. v. United Kingdom*, the European Commission pointed out that 'the Commission does not find that it can be its task, in its examination of the present applicant's complaint under Article 2, to consider in detail ... *the appropriateness and efficiency of the measures* taken by the United Kingdom to combat terrorism in Northern Ireland'.[91] In the same way, in its Second Report on Colombia of 1993, the Inter-American Commission, pursuant to death threats being made by Colombian armed opposition groups against the president of the National Committee of Victims of the Guerrilla War, requested Colombia to take measures to protect the life and safety of the president; however, it left open which measures the state had to take.[92]

An exception is provided by the Human Rights Committee, which pointed out the specific actions the Lebanese armed forces were required to take in response to armed opposition groups active in the Lebanese civil war:

> The task before the Committee was to assess what the Lebanese Government had done effectively to establish a national police force and army, to disarm private groups whose rivalry had led to bloodshed and to ensure human rights for all those residing under its authority... Information was also requested as to whether the police force was able effectively to prevent arrests of people by private groups; whether there were 'private' detention camps, how many people were held there and whether there had been any progress in that respect.[93]

The Committee thus specifically indicated the tasks that were to be carried out by the Lebanese police and armed forces, namely disarmament of armed opposition groups and prevention of arrests of persons by these groups. Nevertheless, this exception cannot affect the conclusion that generally the state is left a large margin of appreciation in its choice of actions it undertakes to physically protect civilians from armed opposition groups.

Of course, the margin of appreciation is limited by the requirement that, in discharging its duty to provide physical protection from armed opposition groups, the state's choice of means and methods not be

---

[90] See *Platform 'Ärzte Für Das Leben'* case, above, n. 6, para. 34 ('While it is the duty of Contracting States to take reasonable and appropriate measures to enable lawful demonstrations to proceed peacefully,... they have a wide discretion in the choice of the means to be used'); see also C. Tomuschat, 'What is a Breach', above, n. 5, p. 323.
[91] Above, n. 79, para. 14 (emphasis added).   [92] Above, Chapter 1, n. 110, at 223.
[93] *Yearbook of the Human Rights Committee* 1983-84, Vol. II, CCPR/4/Add.1, at 468, para. 339, and at 470, para. 348 (remarks by Tomuschat).

contrary to international law.[94] A difficult case in this regard concerns the state's right to arm civilians to enable them to protect themselves against armed opposition groups. Such a case occurred in Sri Lanka. In response to the massacres committed by the LTTE against the Singalese Muslim community in the north and east of the country, the government of Sri Lanka authorized civilians to carry weapons. Sri Lanka argued that this measure was justified by the government's inability to guarantee the civilians' safety. During the examination of the third periodic report of Sri Lanka, Bhagwati, a member of the Human Rights Committee, disapproved of the measures taken by Sri Lanka, expressing his fear that it may promote more violence.[95] Similar armed civilian defence groups exist in Colombia, known as CONVIVIR. The Inter-American Commission has expressed its concern about these groups. First, because they have acted contrary to human rights and international humanitarian law. Second, because, while formally CONVIVIR was created for the purpose of self-defence, it actually cooperates with the Colombian military forces; the Commission noted that members of CONVIVIR must therefore be considered to be state agents. Third, because the groups blur the distinction between those involved in combat and civilians, and thereby impair the protection of the latter.[96] There is, however, no practice stating a general prohibition of armed civilian groups.

In sum, under particular circumstances, the state is obliged to take action against attacks by armed opposition groups, including precautionary measures. The obligation to take action is, however, one of due diligence, the content being determined by the specific circumstances of the case. Furthermore, international bodies have rarely indicated which measures the state is required to take to be in compliance with its duty to physically protect civilians from armed opposition groups; the state is left a large margin of appreciation in this respect.

Prosecution

Some commentators have asserted that states commonly prosecute members of armed opposition groups who have perpetrated human rights, humanitarian law, or criminal law abuses, unless the governments are

---

[94] See *Velásquez Rodríguez* case, above, n. 7, para. 154.
[95] Human Rights Committee, CCPR/C/SR. 1436, 54th Sess. (28 June 1995); ibid., para. 36 (Lallah).
[96] Third Report on Colombia, above, Chapter 1, n. 8, at 150–5, paras. 316–39.

implicated.[97] This statement is too general to be valid. Different factors appear to hamper prosecution. For example, the state may choose to prosecute members of armed groups for treason against the state, rather than for violations of humanitarian or human rights laws. In addition, there have been examples in which the state, after the conflict, granted members of armed opposition groups immunity from prosecution through an amnesty law. Also factual circumstances may contribute to impunity. Often states torn by internal armed conflict have questionable judicial structures. For instance, in the Rwandan conflict the majority of the judges and lawyers were killed. As a result, judicial chaos prevailed.[98] Other factual circumstances impeding prosecution and punishment of members of armed opposition groups are threats against the judicial branch and witnesses, a high number of crimes, and the lack of cooperation by victims and witnesses.

The principal purpose of criminal law treaties is to prevent and repress the relevant crime by ensuring its punishment. The Genocide Convention contains an explicit obligation for the territorial state to punish genocide committed by members of armed opposition groups.[99] Similar obligations can be found in a number of specific humanitarian law treaties. The Mines Protocol requires States Parties to prevent and suppress violations, including through penal sanctions, 'by persons or on territory under its jurisdiction or control'.[100] This obligation covers violations by armed opposition groups operating in the state territory. The Ottawa Mines Convention prescribes that states shall take all appropriate legal, administrative and other measures, including penal sanctions, at the national level to prevent and suppress any prohibited activity.[101] The Cultural Property Convention of 1954 obliges the state to prosecute and impose penal or disciplinary sanctions upon persons who commit or order to be committed a breach of this Convention.[102] This obligation also applies to breaches committed by members of armed opposition groups. Finally, the Second Protocol on Cultural Property obliges States Parties to criminalize serious violations of the Protocol under their domestic law and to establish jurisdiction over such violations when committed in their territory.[103] This

---

[97] J. C. O'Brien, 'The International Tribunal for Violations of International Humanitarian Law in the Former Yugoslavia', above, Chapter 3, n. 26, at 648–9.
[98] C. Cissé, 'The End of a Culture of Impunity in Rwanda?' (1998) 1 *YIHL* 161, 175.
[99] Articles I, VI.   [100] Article 14(1) and (2).
[101] Article 9. See S. Maslen, P. Herby, 'Ottawa Treaty', above, n. 74.   [102] Article 28.
[103] Article 15 *juncto* Article 16(1)(a).

obligation also applies to violations by members of armed opposition groups.

In contrast to these specific humanitarian treaties just identified, neither Common Article 3 nor Protocol II obliges the state to investigate, prosecute and punish acts by armed opposition groups committed on their territory in internal armed conflict. Also human rights treaties – the International Covenant and the European and American Conventions – do not explicitly require the state to investigate, prosecute, and punish acts which are prohibited for the state.[104] Notwithstanding these instruments' silence on prosecution and punishment, international bodies have interpreted humanitarian law and human rights treaties as imposing on the state an obligation to bring to trial members of armed opposition groups responsible for violence to life.

International bodies have based this duty to prosecute under human rights treaties on the general obligation to ensure respect for the right to life contained in these treaties.[105] In *Yasa v. Turkey*, the European Court of Human Rights considered the alleged inadequacy of the criminal investigations by Turkey of the armed assault on the applicant, which was, according to the Government, carried out by armed organizations such as the PKK:

The Court recalls that the obligation to protect the right to life under Article 2 of the Convention, read in conjunction with the State's general duty under Article 1 of the Convention to 'secure to everyone within [its] jurisdiction the rights and

---

[104] The International Covenant and American Convention require States Parties to adopt legislation or other measures necessary to give effect to the rights and freedoms recognized in the treaties (Article 2(1) and Article 2, respectively); in addition, these treaties as well as the European Convention require states to ensure that individuals whose rights are violated have an effective remedy before a competent body (International Covenant, Article 2(3); American Convention, Article 25; European Convention, Article 13).

[105] See Human Rights Committee, General Comment 6/16, para. 3 (1982) above, n. 46 (observing that States Parties should take measures to punish deprivation of life by criminal acts); see also Human Rights Committee, General Comment 20/44, para. 8 (1992) above, n. 61; Declaration on the Protection of all Persons from Enforced Disappearance, UN General Assembly Res. 47/133, Article 14 (18 December 1992); Inter-American Court of Human Rights, *Velásquez Rodríguez* case, above, n. 7, para. 166 (holding, in respect of Honduras, that Article 1(1) of the American Convention, requiring states to ensure the rights set forth in the Convention, obliges states to 'investigate and punish any violation of the rights recognized by the Convention'); see generally D. F. Orentlicher, 'Settling Accounts: The Duty to Prosecute Human Rights Violations of a Prior Regime' (1991) 100 *Yale L J* 2537, 2568–82 (discussing the duty to prosecute and punish under the International Covenant, the European Convention and the American Convention) (hereafter, 'The Duty to Prosecute').

freedoms defined in [the] Convention', *requires by implication that there should be some form of effective official investigation when individuals have been killed as a result of the use of force* ... In the instant case, the Government maintained that there was no evidence that State agents had been implicated in the commission of the alleged acts ... In that connection, the Court emphasizes that, contrary to what is asserted by the Government, the obligation is not confined to cases where it has been established that the killing was caused by an agent of the State.[106]

Similarly, the Human Rights Committee observed that Algeria was obliged to ensure that the members of the FIS and GIA and other Islamic groups who commit human rights abuses do not enjoy impunity. The Committee urged Algeria to adopt effective measures 'to ensure that proper investigations are conducted by an independent body to determine who the offenders are and to bring them to justice'.[107] The Inter-American Commission also accepted the obligation of the state to punish violations of the right to life by private groups.[108]

Although neither Common Article 3 nor Protocol II explicitly obliges the state to prosecute and punish violators, there is some evidence that international bodies are gradually accepting such an obligation to be part of international humanitarian law applicable in internal conflicts. With regard to the Chechnyan conflict in the Russian Federation, the Special Rapporteur on Extrajudicial, Summary or Arbitrary Executions expressed his concern about the impunity enjoyed for violations of international humanitarian law, and appealed to the Russian Government to

---

[106] Judgment of 2 September 1998, 88 Reports (1998–VI) at 2411, paras. 98–100 (emphasis added); see also European Court of Human Rights, *Ergi v. Turkey*, above, n. 10, para. 82; European Commission of Human Rights, *Mrs W. v. United Kingdom*, above, n. 79 ('The obligation to protect the right to life is not limited for the High Contracting Parties to the duty to prosecute those who put life in danger but implies positive preventive measures appropriate to the general situation').

[107] Concluding Observations on Algeria 1998, above, n. 12, para. 6; see also Human Rights Committee, CCPR/C/79/Add.56, paras. 4–5 (Concluding Observations on Sri Lanka, 3 October 1995); *Yearbook of the Human Rights Committee* 1983–84, Vol II, 468, para. 339 (Lebanon); see also Y. Dinstein, 'The Right to Life', above, n. 46, p. 119 ('it may be argued that states [parties to the Covenant] must at least exercise due diligence to prevent intentional deprivation of the life of one individual by another, as well as to apprehend murderers and to prosecute them in order to deter future takings of life').

[108] Annual Report of the Inter-American Commission on Human Rights 1980–1, in *Ten Years of Activities 1971–1981*, above, n. 14, 331; see also UN Commission on Human Rights, Res. 1993/71 para. 12 (10 March 1993) (reiterating 'the obligation of all Governments to see to it that all alleged violations of the right to life are properly investigated, including all suspected cases of extrajudicial, arbitrary and summary executions, with a view to bringing to justice those responsible for violations of the right to life, bearing in mind the norms and principles contained in the pertinent international instruments').

ensure that the perpetrators were prosecuted.[109] In addition, the Final Declaration and Programme of Action of the 1993 World Conference on Human Rights reaffirmed that states must prosecute grave violations of international humanitarian law applicable in internal conflicts, such as torture.[110] The reference in Article 1 of the Rome Statute of 1998 to the complementarity of prosecutions by the International Criminal Court with national prosecutions also indicates, by implication, that there is a role to be played by national courts.[111] This provision is reinforced by the Preamble of this Statute affirming that 'the most serious crimes of concern to the international community as a whole must not go unpunished and that their effective prosecution must be ensured by taking measures at the national level'.[112] The 1996 International Law Commission's Draft Code of Crimes against the Peace and Security of Mankind requires states to try or extradite those alleged to have committed violations of Common Article 3 and Article 4 of Protocol II.[113] The Statutes and the case-law of the Yugoslavia and Rwanda Tribunals do not obligate states to prosecute individuals for the crimes recognized therein.[114]

---

[109] 1996 Report of the Special Rapporteur on Extrajudicial, Summary or Arbitrary Executions, above, Chapter 1, n. 139, para. 418.

[110] UN Doc. A/Conf.157/23, reprinted in 32 ILM 166, paras. 56, 60 (1993).

[111] See 1998 Report of the Secretary-General on Fundamental Standards of Humanity, above, Chapter 1, n. 135, para. 6.

[112] See M. H. Arsanjani, 'Rome Statute', above, Chapter 3, n. 13, at 24–5 (discussing the complementarity between national courts and the International Criminal Court). An argument for the state's obligation to prosecute humanitarian law violations committed by armed opposition groups may also be found in the 1949 Geneva Conventions which stipulate that States Parties shall suppress acts contrary to the Conventions other than grave breaches (e.g., Article 146, para. 3, Fourth Geneva Convention), which must be understood as referring to the punishment of such breaches through national legislation. Arguably, this obligation also applies to violations of Common Article 3, see *Commentary 4th Convention*, above, Chapter 1, n. 9, p. 594 (stating that states must 'at least insert in their legislation a general clause providing for the punishment of other [than grave] breaches'); see also Turku Declaration above, Chapter 1, n. 141, Art. 19 (applicable in internal armed conflicts and referring to an obligation of the state to prosecute and punish violations of international humanitarian law. This obligation also applies to violations committed by members of armed opposition groups); see also J. D. Dugard, 'Dealing with Crimes of a Past Regime – Is Amnesty Still an Option?' (The Third Manfred Lachs Memorial Lecture, 13 April 1999) p. 4 (on file with author) (hereafter, 'Amnesty'); but see R. van Elst, 'De Zaak Darco Knezevic: Rechtsmacht over Joegoslavische en Andere Buitenlandse Oorlogsmisdadigers' (1998) 35 *NJB* 1587, 1589 (stating that the state is free in its choice of measures to suppress other than grave breaches).

[113] Above, Chapter 3, n. 8, Article 9.

[114] See T. Meron, 'Internal Atrocities', above, Chapter 3, n. 8, at 555 (pointing out that the activities of these tribunals 'have the beneficial effect of spurring prosecutions

Having demonstrated that states are generally obliged to prosecute acts of armed opposition groups prohibited for the state under human rights and humanitarian law treaties, the question remains: What exactly does a state have to do to be in compliance with this duty? It must first be noted that in order to be able to carry out criminal prosecutions, the state needs an apparatus for the investigatory and prosecution process. Practice shows that the possession of an enforcement apparatus is not, as such, a legal obligation under human rights or international humanitarian law; rather, it is a prerequisite for a state to be able to fulfil its obligations.

In cases where a functioning state justice system is absent, international bodies have stimulated states to set up separate bodies as an alternative for the regular state enforcement mechanisms. Amos Wako, a member of the Human Rights Committee, supported a proposal by El Salvador to set up an independent body for investigating political killings on both sides of the conflict.[115] Similarly, the Special Rapporteur on Extrajudicial, Summary or Arbitrary Executions proposed:

> In the absence of a functioning civilian justice system, or in cases which warrant particular treatment because of their special nature or gravity, Governments may envisage establishing special commissions of inquiry. They must fulfil the same requirements of independence, impartiality and competence as judges in ordinary courts. The results of their investigations should be made public, and their recommendations should be binding for the authorities.[116]

Practice does not provide evidence for the argument that the establishment of such alternative mechanisms amounts to a legal obligation on the part of the state.

Provided that the state has an enforcement apparatus, it must exercise due diligence to act in compliance with its obligation to prosecute.

---

before national courts for serious violations of humanitarian law'); ibid., 570 (arguing in favour of the obligation of the state under international humanitarian law applicable in internal armed conflict to investigate, prosecute and punish violations of these norms: 'As regards the national state of the perpetrators of nongrave breaches, its obligations go further. Given the purposes and objects of the Geneva Conventions and the normative content of their provisions, any state that does not have the necessary laws in place, or is otherwise unwilling to prosecute and punish violators of clauses other than the grave breaches provisions that are significant and have a clear penal character, calls into serious question its good faith compliance with its treaty obligations').

[115] Human Rights Committee, CCPR/C/SR. 716, 29th Sess., para. 33 (8 April 1987).

[116] 1993 Report of the Special Rapporteur on Extrajudicial, Summary or Arbitrary Executions, above, Chapter 2, n. 102, para. 695.

International practice pertaining to the failure to *try* the culprits and to *execute* the sentence rarely contains an express reference to the due diligence rule. Nevertheless, there is some practice showing that the due diligence rule may also be relevant here. The Special Representative for El Salvador observed that during the armed conflict in El Salvador, trials of alleged injurious acts of the FMLN were hampered by fear. He observed that 'no one had been tried and sentenced for political crimes because no judge dared to try anyone, whether from the right wing, the left wing [= FMLN] or the center, since he knew that if he did so he would be murdered'.[117] The Special Representative refrained from suggesting that the failure to try and punish the crimes automatically entailed a violation of an international obligation by El Salvador. Factors, such as the high number of crimes and lack of cooperation by the victims and witnesses may also determine the actual trials and convictions carried out by the state; they may be accepted as mitigating the state's obligation to punish members of armed opposition groups.

At first sight, practice does not seem to make a distinction between the various acts involved in the process of bringing a charge against a member of an armed opposition group for a crime. International bodies often speak in a general way of the duty of the state 'to apprehend and punish' those responsible for harm to civilians. However, a more careful analysis shows a difference between the various aspects of this obligation. It appears that, particularly with regard to the obligation to investigate, the due diligence rule comes into play. The point is that the realization of the obligation to investigate is uncertain and presupposes, besides a government exercising a degree of territorial control, the favourable play of certain risk factors.[118] The realization of trial and punishment of offenders, on the contrary, does not generally depend on uncertain factors.

---

[117] UN Commission on Human Rights, E/CN.4/1502, para. 110 (Final Report on the Situation of Human Rights in El Salvador of J. A. Pastor Ridruejo, 18 January 1982).

[118] 1995 Joint Report of the Special Rapporteur on Question of Torture, and the Special Rapporteur on Extrajudicial, Summary or Arbitrary Executions, above, Chapter 1, n. 8, para. 82 ('Although impunity affects the entire judicial branch, the greatest problems occur during the investigatory phase, which is the responsibility of the *Fiscalía General de la Nación*. Because of the high number of crimes committed in the country, its task is particularly difficult. In many parts of the national territory, the victims themselves or witnesses prefer to remain silent for fear of reprisals or react to the violations by moving to another region, thus making the investigator's task considerably more difficult'); 1985 Final Report of the Special Representative on El Salvador, above Chapter 1, n. 8, para. 177; R. Jennings, A. Watts, *Oppenheim*, above, Chapter 1, n. 59, p. 551.

Accordingly, in *Yasa* v. *Turkey* the European Commission noted that the due diligence rule does not require a state to be successful in the fulfilment of the obligation to investigate and prosecute.[119] Rather the due diligence rule requires that the state *start* an investigation and ensure that the investigation undertaken be *effective*. Factors that play a role in deciding whether an investigation is effective are, *inter alia*, the length of time taken for the investigations viewed against the background of an internal armed conflict. The Court concluded that the investigation carried out by Turkey in this case had not been effective, because it had lasted five years without any progress having been made:

> The Government provided no concrete information on the state of progress of the investigations... which, more than five years after the events, do not appear to have produced any tangible result. Admittedly, the Government said that the investigations were still pending, but they did not provide anything to show that they were actually progressing... In that regard, the last investigative step of which the Court is aware dates back to 21 June 1993, when the expert ballistic report in the investigation into the murder of Hasim Yasa was prepared... whereas the Diyarbakir Public Prosecutor had on 14 April 1993 requested the police to inform him every three months of progress in the investigation... The only explanation given by the Government is that the investigations were taking place in the context of the fight against terrorism and that in such circumstances the police and judicial authorities were constrained to 'proceed with caution and to wait until the results of the various investigations had been cross-checked, thus enabling the perpetrators of earlier crimes and acts of violence to be identified'... The Court is prepared to take into account the fact that the prevailing climate at the time in that region of Turkey, marked by violent action by the PKK and measures taken in reaction thereto by the authorities, may have impeded the search for conclusive evidence in the domestic criminal proceedings. Nonetheless, circumstances of that nature cannot relieve the authorities of their obligations under Article 2 to carry out an investigation, as otherwise that would exacerbate still further the climate of impunity and insecurity in the region and thus create a vicious circle.[120]

Apart from the delay in the investigations, another factor was doubt as to whether a reasonable presumption existed that the actual perpetrators of the offences were members of the PKK. Turkey took the view that, since it believed the attacks in question to be carried out by the PKK or similar terrorist groups, no further investigation on that point was necessary. By requiring the police to maintain their enquiries and report about any progress to the prosecution, Turkey maintained that it had

[119] Application 22495/93, Report of the Commission, above, n. 84, para. 101.
[120] Above, n. 106, paras. 103–4.

satisfied its obligations under the European Convention.[121] The Court rejected this approach. However, it appeared to agree with Turkey that the possibility that the assaults had been committed by the PKK reduced the degree of diligence required from Turkey regarding the effectiveness of the investigations. The Court considered:

> The Court is struck by the fact that the investigatory authorities appear to have excluded from the outset the possibility that State agents might have been implicated in the attacks. Thus, the Public Prosecutor at the Diyarbakir National Security Court considered the incidents in question to have been merely 'a settling of scores between armed organizations'..., whereas the Government considered that all responsibility for the attacks lay with 'terrorists', even though the investigations are not over and no concrete evidence capable of confirming that to be a valid hypothesis has been brought to the attention of the Court... In the instant case, it was therefore incumbent on the authorities to have regard, in their investigations, to the fact that State agents may have been implicated in the attacks... In short, because the investigations carried out in the instant case did not allow of the possibility that given the circumstances of the case the security forces might have been implicated in the attacks... the investigations cannot be considered to have been effective as required by Article 2.[122]

It thus appears that the possibility that the Turkish security forces might have in fact killed his uncle and injured the applicant had not yet been ruled out by the Court, which increased the degree of diligence required from the state in the fulfilment of the obligation to investigate.[123] Using this same reasoning, the Court, in *Kurt v. Turkey*, refused to accept a positive obligation on the part of Turkey to investigate the disappearance of Kurt's son carried out by entities other than the state namely the PKK.[124]

In sum, international practice shows that the state is obliged to prosecute members of armed opposition groups who have injured civilians. This obligation is regulated by the due diligence rule.

Amnesty

The implication of the state's duty to prosecute would be that amnesty for torture and other atrocities by members of armed opposition groups is generally prohibited, as a breach of the duty to prosecute *and* punish.

---

[121] *Ibid.*, para. 105.
[122] *Ibid.*, paras. 105–7. See also *Kaya v. Turkey*, Judgment of 19 February 1998, para. 86.
[123] See also Report of the Commission, above, n. 84, para. 107 (stating that Turkey failed to make any further and more detailed investigation into the attacks on the applicant and his uncle, which amounted to a failure to protect the right to life); see also European Court of Human Rights, *Ergi v. Turkey*, above, n. 10, paras. 83, 85.
[124] *See* above, n. 15, paragraph 9.

It can be used to foreclose prosecutions, and also to cancel sanctions that have already been imposed.[125]

States may choose to grant amnesty to members of armed opposition groups for various reasons. Many amnesties have formed part of transitions to other governments, in which members of the outgoing regime, the armed and security forces, as well as armed opposition groups, are protected from prosecution for abuses committed during internal conflict. Amnesties have also been offered to encourage the surrender of armed opposition groups or their reincorporation in civil society. In the last case, the state may adopt the amnesty law before the internal armed conflict has ended.[126]

International bodies provide evidence for a rule that amnesty for human rights and humanitarian law violations by members of armed opposition groups is in principle forbidden. For example, in *Prosecutor v. Furundžija*, the Yugoslavia Tribunal held that amnesties for torture, including torture by armed opposition groups in violation of Common Article 3, will not receive international legal recognition.[127] Similarly, the Inter-American Commission strongly objected to the impunity that resulted from the Amnesty Law of 20 March 1993 adopted by the Salvadorian Government, which granted a general and absolute amnesty to all persons 'who participated in any way in the commission, prior to January 1, 1992, of political crimes or common crimes linked to political crimes or common crimes in which the number of persons involved is no less than twenty'.[128] The crimes committed by FMLN fell under the amnesty regulation.[129] The Inter-American Commission

---

[125] The term 'amnesty' usually refers to an official law barring criminal prosecutions and is often distinguished from pardons. Pardons generally refer to executive actions mitigating or setting aside punishment for a crime. However, the legal distinction between amnesty and pardon is imprecise; pardons can be used to block prosecutions and amnesties occasionally apply to persons in prison, D.F. Orentlicher, 'The Duty to Prosecute', above, n. 105, at 2543, n. 14; L. Huyse, 'To Punish or to Pardon: A Devil's Choice', n. 2 (paper presented at international conference on 'Reining in Impunity for International Crimes and Serious Violations of Fundamental Human Rights', Siracusa, 16-21 September 1997) p. 2 (on file with author). For present purposes, no principal distinction will be made between the state's duty to investigate, prosecute or punish.

[126] US Delegation Draft (Rev), *State Practice Regarding Amnesties and Pardons* (ICC PrepCom, August 1997) p. 1 (on file with author).

[127] *Furundzjia* case, above, Chapter 3, n. 7, paras. 151-7.

[128] Article 1 of Decree 486, 'General Amnesty Law for the Consolidation of the Peace', reprinted in Inter-American Commission on Human Rights, Report on the Situation of Human Rights in El Salvador, OEA/Ser.L/V/II.85, Doc.28, rev., at 69-70 (1994).

[129] *Ibid.*, 70-1 (stating that this provision applied to 'individuals who, according to the Report of the Truth Commission, participated in acts of violence committed after January 1, 1980').

disapproved of this law, pointing out that El Salvador had 'a legal duty... to use the means at its disposal to carry out a serious investigation of violations committed within its jurisdiction, to identify those responsible, to impose the appropriate punishment'.[130] Support for the conclusion that amnesty for human rights and humanitarian law violations by armed opposition groups are in principle forbidden can also be found in a general comment of the Human Rights Committee, adopted in 1992. The Committee states therein that amnesties covering torture committed by people acting in a private capacity are 'generally incompatible with the duty of States to investigate such acts'.[131]

While this practice suggests that, in principle, immunity is prohibited under international law,[132] there are indications that this prohibition is not absolute. Article 6(5) of Protocol II actually encourages states to give amnesties. It provides: 'At the end of hostilities, the authorities in power shall endeavor to grant the broadest possible amnesty to persons who have participated in the armed conflict, or those deprived of their liberty for reasons related to the armed conflict, whether they are interned or detained.' The idea behind this article is that amnesty laws provide an effective basis for the release of prisoners and return of refugees.[133] The International Committee of the Red Cross has contended that Article 6(5) cannot be interpreted as supporting impunity for violations of international humanitarian law.[134] This interpretation is supported by the agreement concluded in 1998 between the United States and Yugoslavia on Kosovo, which determined that no person would

---

[130] Ibid., 71; see also Inter-American Commission on Human Rights, Third Report on Colombia, above Chapter 1, n. 8, at 158 para. 347.

[131] General Comment 20/44, paras. 2, 15 (1992), above n. 61; see also Declaration on Enforced Disappearances, above, n. 105, Article 18; UN Commission on Human Rights, Res. 1994/39, para. 6 (4 March 1994); 1993 Report of the Special Rapporteur on Extrajudicial, Summary or Arbitrary Executions, above, Chapter 2, n. 102, paras. 285, 691.

[132] Brownlie has asserted that in particular circumstances the granting of amnesty to armed opposition groups constitutes an acceptance of responsibility for their acts on the basis of a ratification of these acts, I. Brownlie, *State Responsibility*, above, n. 50, pp. 176-7.

[133] UN Commission on Human Rights, E/CN.4/Sub.2/1985/16, paras. 16, 18 (Special Rapporteur of the Sub-Commission on Prevention of Discrimination and Protection of Minorities, L. Joinet, Study on Amnesty Laws and their Role in the Safeguard and Promotion of Human Rights, 21 June 1985) (hereafter, Study on Amnesty Laws). See on amnesty, in particular Art. 6 (5), also Chapter 1, Section 2.

[134] See Inter-American Commission on Human Rights, Third Report on Colombia, above, Chapter 1, n. 8 at 157, para. 345 (1999).

be criminally prosecuted for acts related to the conflict in Kosovo, except international crimes.[135]

The United Nations appear to adopt a similar approach. While in the past, some of the amnesties for persons who committed torture and other atrocities have been supported by the United Nations as a means of restoring peace, the organization is currently moving towards a prohibition against amnesties for international crimes. For example, the United Nations signed the peace agreement between the warring sides in Sierra Leone's eight-year civil war, in July 1999, but it entered a reservation to the effect that, for the United Nations, the amnesty granted to the rebels could not cover crimes under international law.[136] Perpetrators of serious violations of Common Article 3 and of some articles of Protocol II are thus not to benefit from amnesties.[137]

It should be noted that, while there is a trend away from amnesty, a new institution has developed which questions prosecution as the only way of dealing with human rights and humanitarian law abuses by armed opposition groups: truth commissions. It goes beyond the purpose of this study to examine these institutions.[138]

The pertinence of territorial control

So far, the obligations that may give rise, under particular circumstances, to the state's accountability for failure to prevent and repress conduct of armed opposition groups acting in its territory, have been identified. Now, the circumstances under which this accountability exists, shall be examined. In particular, I shall argue that the absence of a government or lack of effective control of the government over territory precludes such accountability.

Three factual situations must be distinguished. First, at the low end of the spectrum, there is the situation in which, despite the occurrence of a civil war on the state's territory, the established authorities

---

[135] Rule 10 of the Agreement, *NRC Handelsblad* 6 (Rotterdam, 14 October 1998).

[136] N. Onishi, 'Civil War in Sierra Leone', above, Chapter 1, n. 104; K. Annan, 'Window of African Promise Amid Great Suffering', *International Herald Tribune* (31 July–1 August 1999) p. 8 (hereafter, 'African Promise'). The UN High Commissioner for Human Rights, Mary Robinson, urged the establishment of a Commission of Inquiry in Sierra Leone to investigate and assess human rights violations and abuses, M. Robinson, *Meeting the Challenge of Human Rights*, text available on www.unhchr.ch (visited 27 September 1999).

[137] See L. Joinet, Study on Amnesty Laws, above, n. 133, para. 62.

[138] See on truth commissions and their relationship with amnesty and the duty to prosecute J. D. Dugard, *Amnesty*, above, n. 112, p. 4.

continue to exercise a *degree* of effective control over the *entire* territory and population. This situation presently exists for example in Algeria and Northern Ireland. It existed in Turkey in the beginning of the 1990s. Secondly, in some internal conflicts the established authorities control only *part* of the state territory and population. The armed opposition may control the territory where the government is absent. This situation prevails in Colombia, it occurred in the conflict in El Salvador, and Lebanon. Finally, there are conflicts where the government has ceased to exist, or lacks control over any of its territory. This situation, which may be termed a failed state,[139] exists in Somalia and in Afghanistan. A comparable situation exists when the government lives in exile.

While the previous sections were concerned with the situation where the government has certain control over its entire or part of its territory, this section will focus on the case where the government lacks control over part of or its entire territory or where it has collapsed or lives in exile. A government's ineffectiveness in part or the entire state's territory temporarily, it is submitted, relieves the state from its obligations in the non-controlled areas. The same is true when the government has collapsed or lives in exile.

Before turning to the relevant practice, it should be emphasized that the notion of 'territorial control' must be used with care. In many cases, the notion 'territorial control' is difficult to apply because circumstances in internal conflicts change rapidly.[140] It often happens that territorial control changes hands continuously. Also, territorial control is often not easily definable – it being a matter of degree. While the government's effectiveness in a particular area may be reduced by the activities of armed opposition groups, it may retain a certain degree of influence. Whenever the government exercises a sufficient degree of effectiveness, it is obliged to prevent and repress acts of armed opposition groups to the maximum extent feasible. In all the above situations, the question of accountability of the state will not lie in the stark alternatives of possibility or impossibility, but will rather be a matter of degree. This section is concerned with the extreme case in which the government lacks *any* control whatsoever over part or all of its territory.

---

[139] See generally D. Thürer *et al.*, *Der Wegfall Effektiver Staatsgewalt: 'The Failed State'* (C. F. Müller Verlag, Heidelberg, 1995) (addressing public international law issues arising from the breakdown of effective government) (hereafter, *Failed State*).

[140] C. Greenwood, 'International Humanitarian Law', above, Chapter 1, n. 66, pp. 229–30.

International obligations generally apply to the entire territory of a state.[141] This principle is based on the presumption that the government of the state exercises effective control over its entire territory. As formulated by the UN Commission on Human Rights Working Group on Enforced or Involuntary Disappearances: 'There is no avoiding the fact that Governments have a responsibility for what happens within their borders'.[142]

While territoriality is the predominant principle underlying international obligations, in particular circumstances this principle is replaced by *control* over territory. Thus, in its Advisory Opinion in *Legal Consequences for States of the Continued Presence of South Africa in Namibia*,[143] the International Court of Justice considered that international responsibility for a violation of international obligations in respect of occupied territories was not based upon sovereignty or legitimate title, but on 'physical control'. The Court considered:

> The fact that South Africa no longer has any title to administer the Territory does not release it from its obligations and responsibilities under international law towards other States in respect of the exercise of its powers in relation to this Territory. *Physical control of a territory, and not sovereignty or legitimacy of title is the basis of State liability for acts affecting other States.*[144]

This case concerned the state's control *outside* its territory, but also *inside* its territory factual control over territory and persons may be relevant to the state's international accountability. Indeed, as I will argue hereafter, in internal armed conflicts the effectiveness of the state's control over its

---

[141] Article 29 of the Vienna Convention on the Law of Treaties (1969), reprinted in Brownlie *BDIL* 388 (providing: 'Unless a different intention appears from the treaty or is otherwise established, a treaty is binding upon each party in respect of its entire territory').

[142] UN Commission on Human Rights, E/CN.4/1435, para. 195 (Working Group on Enforced or Involuntary Disappearances, 26 January 1981); compare *Corfu Channel* case (*UK v. Albania*) (Judgment of 9 April 1949) (Merits), 1949 ICJ Rep. 4 ('It is true, as international practice shows, that a State on whose territory or in whose waters an act contrary to international law has occurred may be called upon to give an explanation').

[143] Advisory Opinion of 21 June 1971, 1971 ICJ Rep. 16.

[144] *Ibid.*, para. 118 (emphasis added); similarly, in *Loizidou v. Turkey*, the European Court found that Turkey's acts in Northern Cyprus were 'capable of falling within Turkish "jurisdiction" within the meaning of Article 1 of the Convention', and were, in principle, covered by the European Convention on Human Rights. The Court based its decision on the fact that Turkey exercised effective control in the northern part of Cyprus both through its armed forces and through a subordinate local administration, Judgment of 23 March 1995 (Preliminary Objections), Ser. A 310, para. 62 (1995).

territory is of decisive importance for the evaluation of its accountability under human rights, humanitarian and criminal law treaties relating to acts of armed opposition groups.[145]

Under general international law there are three possible effects of the absence of a government or lack of territorial control of the government on the state's accountability under treaties: (1) temporary impossibility of the operation of treaties; (2) suspension of treaties; and (3) *force majeure* precluding wrongfulness of the state's violation of treaties. These possible effects will be examined in each of three areas: international human rights, humanitarian law and criminal law treaties.

Human rights treaties

Like most treaties, human rights treaties do not expressly allow for taking into account the absence or lack of territorial control of the government when establishing the state's positive obligations. They implicitly assume the existence of a normal situation in which the government exerts a degree of control in its entire territory and over its population. Nevertheless, lack of territorial control or the absence of a government affect the application of human rights treaties and the accountability of the state under these treaties.

Temporary impossibility of the operation of human rights treaties

International practice shows that, when a government is absent or lacks effective control in (part of) its territory, human rights treaties become temporarily inoperative, removing the state's positive obligations under these treaties for the time being.[146]

Accordingly, Opsahl, a member of the Human Rights Committee, made the following observation in 1983 on the operation of the Civil and

---

[145] See K. Doehring, 'Effectiveness', above, Chapter 4, n. 44, at 43; compare also L. Wildhaber, 'Sovereignty and International Law', in R. St. J. Macdonald, D. M. Johnston (eds.), *The Structure and Process of International Law: Essays in Legal Philosophy, Doctrine and Theory* (Martinus Nijhoff, Dordrecht, 1986) pp. 425, 429 (discussing the dichotomy between legal and political sovereignty).

[146] See D. Thürer *et al.*, *Failed State*, above, n. 139, p. 46 (asserting that human rights protection in failed states can hardly be guaranteed because of lack of an administrative infrastructure); ICRC, *Disintegration of State Structures*, above, Chapter 4, n. 12, p. 8 (observing with regard to 'states that are in the process of disintegration' that 'human rights instruments play only a minor role in such situations since their implementation depends largely on the existence of effective state structures').

Political Covenant to Lebanon, where at that time, owing to the civil war, the established authorities exercised only limited territorial control:

> Normally the Committee examined the legal regime applied by a government in full control of the situation. In some cases it considered the human rights situation in a State where the government for one reason or another was not disposed to apply the provisions of the Covenant. But there were also cases in which the government was materially unable to apply the legislative system under examination. Lebanon was an example of that situation, since the government exercised full authority only in the Beirut metropolitan area. *It had to be accepted that in such circumstances the Covenant ceased to be a useful instrument* and the Committee was not an effective organ.[147]

Similarly, in 1989, the UN Commission's Special Rapporteur on Afghanistan considered that Afghanistan's human rights obligations were limited to the part of the territory under control of its established authorities: 'The territorial sovereignty of the Afghan Government is not fully effective since some provinces of Afghanistan are totally or partly in the hands of traditional forces. *The responsibility for the respect of human rights is therefore divided* ... Where the Government has control over the territory, ... the human rights instruments have to be respected.'[148]

The temporary impossibility of the operation of human rights treaties occurs not only when a government lacks control over part of its territory, but also when the government is absent or in exile. For example, in 1994, the UN Commission's Special Rapporteur on Afghanistan observed:

> Although Afghanistan is a party to various international human rights instruments, ... as well as to the Geneva Conventions of 12 August 1949, there is still no administration which could be able to guarantee human rights as enshrined in the above-mentioned instruments. *The adherence of a Government to international human rights instruments has no practical value in such a situation.*[149]

The absence of a government or territorial control does not automatically *terminate* human rights obligations or treaties. In its judgment in the *Case Concerning the Gabcíkovo-Nagymaros Project*, the International Court of Justice recognized that, although the operation of a treaty may

---

[147] CCPR/C/SR.444, 19th Sess., para. 12 (Opsahl, 18 July 1983) (emphasis added); *ibid.*, para. 27.
[148] 1989 Report of the Special Rapporteur on Afghanistan, above, Chapter 4, n. 48, paras. 68–9 (emphasis added).
[149] UN Commission on Human Rights, E/CN.4/1994/53, para. 44 (Final Report on the Situation of Human Rights in Afghanistan by F. Ermacora, 14 February 1994) (emphasis added); see also 1997 Final Report of the Special Rapporteur on Afghanistan, above, Chapter 4, n. 60, para. 21.

be temporarily impossible, this does not necessarily imply that the treaty ceases to exist: 'The treaty may be *ineffective* as long as the condition of necessity continues to exist; it may in fact be *dormant*, but – unless the parties by mutual agreement terminate the treaty – it continues to exist. As soon as the state of necessity ceases to exist, the duty to comply with treaty obligations revives.'[150]

Thus, in the case of the absence of a government or territorial control, the human rights treaties continue to exist until the state parties to the relevant treaty decide otherwise. But the obligations to prevent and repress acts committed by armed opposition groups become temporarily inoperative. As soon as the government has restored its authority over territory or persons, the state must resume its obligations.

It would seem that the effect of the temporary impossibility of the operation of human rights treaties only occurs when the state's further compliance is not possible, owing to forcible or involuntary loss of control of territory as a result of enemy military action. When the state has contributed to the occurrence of loss of territorial control or otherwise to the ineffectiveness of the government, it would seem that its obligations under human rights treaties remain fully valid.[151]

This implies that agreements a state may have concluded with armed opposition groups on the division of human rights responsibilities, do not relieve the former from its obligations under human rights treaties. Accordingly, the Inter-American Commission on Human Rights observed that the San José Agreement on Human Rights, concluded between El Salvador and the armed opposition group, *Frente Farabundo Marti para la Liberacion Nacional* (FMLN) in 1990, assigning equal human rights obligations to both parties,[152] did not affect the obligations of El Salvador under the American Convention on Human Rights.[153]

---

[150] *Hungary v. Slovakia*, 37 ILM 162, 194 (1998) (emphasis added).

[151] Compare Article 5 of Amended Protocol II to the Conventional Weapons Convention ('A party to a conflict is relieved from further compliance with the provisions of sub-paragraphs 2(a) and 2(b) of this Article only if such compliance is not feasible due to forcible loss of control of the area as a result of enemy military action, including situations where direct enemy military action makes it impossible to comply'); Article 31(2) of the ILC Draft Articles on State Responsibility, above, Chapter 4, n. 1 (stating that the state is prevented from invoking *force majeure* or fortuitous event when it has contributed to the occurrence of such a situation); Article 62(2)(b) of the Vienna Convention on the Law of Treaties.

[152] Above, Chapter 1, n. 149. The Agreement stipulated norms which were derived from human rights and humanitarian law treaties to which El Salvador was a party as well as human rights and humanitarian law declarations and principles adopted by the United Nations and the Organization of American States, 6th preambular paragraph.

[153] Inter-American Commission OEA/ser.L/V/II.85, Doc. 28, rev. at 7 (Report on the Situation of Human Rights in El Salvador, 11 February 1994).

An even more pertinent example is that of Colombia. In order to make peace negotiations possible, in November 1998, Colombia decided to clear 40,000 square kilometres of Colombian territory of police and security forces, including the entire judiciary. It transferred its authority in these areas to the FARC, a Colombian armed opposition group.[154] In conformity with the observation of the Inter-American Commission referred to above, it can be said that Colombia remains fully responsible for the protection of the human rights of the civilian population in the transferred areas. The reason is that the Colombian State is not unable to protect, but has chosen to turn over its responsibilities to this armed opposition group. Andrés Pastrana, the President of Colombia, has asserted that if the FARC does not respect human rights in the transferred areas, the Government will reverse the transfer and retake its factual authority there. Furthermore, although the army is gone, he insisted that the Government has more presence there than ever before.[155] If the Government is able to carry out its assertions, Colombia may be in compliance with human rights treaties, the transfer of territory to the FARC raising no serious problems. However, if the state is unable to implement its claims, the conclusion is justified that the unconditional transfer of territory to armed opposition groups, in the way Colombia did, is not permitted under international law.

Finally, it must be noted that the effect of temporary impossibility of the operation of human rights treaties may not occur when, despite the collapse of the central government, *local* authorities continue to function. International obligations of a state rest on all its organs, including lower authorities such as provinces and municipalities.[156] In normal circumstances, violations of international obligations by local authorities are attributed to the state, represented by the government – they are not

---

[154] M. van Royen, 'Guerrilla Tart Geduld Regering Colombia', *NRC Handelsblad* 6 (Rotterdam, 10 November, 1998).

[155] K. DeYoung, 'Colombia's Quagmire Deepens', *International Herald Tribune* (7 July 1999) p. 2; S. Alonso, 'In Noord-Ierland gaat het nog veel trager', *NRC Handelsblad* 6 (Rotterdam, 26 October 1999) (interview with Andrés Pastrana, the President of Colombia).

[156] Article 5 of the 1996 ILC Draft Articles on State Responsibility, above, Chapter 4, n. 1 provides: 'For the purposes of the present articles, conduct of any State organ having that status under internal law of that State shall be considered as an act of the State under international law, provided that organ was acting in that capacity in the case in question'. Article 6 of the Draft Articles provides: 'The conduct of an organ of the State shall be considered as an act of that State under international law, whether that organ belongs to the constituent, legislative, executive, judicial or other power, whether its functions are of an international or an internal character, and whether it holds a superior or a subordinate position in the organization of the State'.

themselves held accountable. However, when the central government is weak or absent, it may be opportune to address directly local authorities, holding them accountable for violations of international law. This was observed by the Special Rapporteur on Afghanistan. He suggested that, in the case of the absence of a government and to avoid a situation where no one bears responsibility for human rights protection, regional administrations must assume responsibility for human rights violations:

> The lack of a central Government poses extreme difficulty and complexity in redressing human rights violations as required by the rules of international law, especially so far as the authorities in Kabul are concerned. It is therefore necessary to stress the importance of accountability at the level of regional administrations, who must assume responsibility for violations of human rights committed in their particular regions.[157]

This idea deserves support. The attribution of accountability to sovereign states, represented by a central government, may in some cases be a convenient way to concentrate and protect internal power. However, in internal conflicts, it may not always be appropriate to address the state as a whole. In such situations, the legal fiction of a state becomes apparent. The disintegration of state structures does not always affect the whole state, but may occur at various levels of intensity and concern different parts of national territory. In such situations, lifting the state's veil may indeed be an appropriate answer in order to safeguard the effectiveness of human rights treaties. It may then become necessary to address, instead of the abstract 'state', agents or some part of its apparatus through whom or which the state acts.[158]

Support for the argument that, when appropriate, state agents or local state entities rather than the state as a whole should be addressed, can be found in two recent cases before the International Court of Justice. In the *Case Concerning the Vienna Convention on Consular Relations*[159] and in its Advisory Opinion on the *Difference Relating to Immunity From Legal Process of a Special Rapporteur of the Commission on Human Rights*,[160] the Court directly addressed a federated entity of the United States and

---

[157] UN Commission on Human Rights, E/CN.4/1996/64, para. 97 (Final Report on Afghanistan by the Special Rapporteur, Choong-Hyun Paik, 27 February 1996).

[158] See e.g., Human Rights Committee, CCPR/C/SR.443, para. 55 (Tomuschat, 14 July 1983) (Lebanon).

[159] *Germany v. United States of America* (Request for the Indication of Provisional Measures, 3 March 1999), 37 ILM 810 (1998).

[160] Advisory Opinion of 29 April 1999, 1999 ICJ Rep. 62.

a Malaysian national court, respectively.[161] The Court considered compliance with the relevant international obligations dependent on the acts of these entities rather than on the central government.

Of course, when regional administrations within the state are held accountable, the conduct of such state bodies must be regarded as an act of that state.[162]

Suspension of treaties

International practice examined above shows that the temporary impossibility of the operation of human rights treaties does not automatically result in the suspension or termination of the treaties. Rather, it gives a state party the right to invoke the impossibility as a ground for suspending the treaty. More particularly, the state may invoke fundamental change of circumstances as a ground for suspension of a human rights treaty, as provided for in Article 62 Vienna Convention on the Law of Treaties.[163] This article provides that a fundamental change of the circumstances prevailing at the time the treaty was concluded, is a ground for termination or suspension.

Unlike international armed conflicts, internal armed conflicts are not the subject of a separate provision in the Vienna Convention.[164] This may suggest that these conflicts are covered by the Conventions' other articles, including Article 62. Support for this argument may be deduced from a recent judgment of the Court of Justice of the European Communities, finding that the effects of the Yugoslav armed conflict, which was partly internal, could be brought under Article 62 of the Vienna Convention.[165] International bodies have not considered Article 62 of the Vienna Convention in relation to the state's obligations under human rights treaties to prevent and repress acts of armed opposition groups. However, because of its potential relevance, this article warrants brief examination.[166]

---

[161] Paras 28 and 67, respectively.
[162] Article 6 of the ILC Draft Articles on State Responsibility, above, Chapter 4, n. 1.
[163] The principle with which this article is concerned is commonly referred to as the doctrine of *rebus sic stantibus*.
[164] The effects of international conflicts on treaties have been regulated in Article 73 of the Vienna Convention.
[165] *A. Racke GmbH & Co. v. Hauptzollamt Mainz*, Case C-162/96 (Judgment of 16 June 1998) [1998-6] ECR, I-3655.
[166] Compare P. Reuter, *Law of Treaties*, above, Chapter 1, n. 131, p. 189 ('there is hardly any theoretical reason why certain treaties should *a priori* escape a possible challenge

It might be contended that Article 62 is not applicable to human rights treaties because these treaties themselves provide rules on this issue.[167] Presumably, in states of emergency, the derogation clauses in human rights treaties apply as a *lex specialis* to the general rules of the Vienna Convention. The question is whether this is also the case when the government has collapsed or is ineffective in (part of) its territory. It may be argued that the human rights derogation clauses were not written for these situations. This argument may reinforce the relevance of the general provisions on suspension of the Vienna Convention, including Article 62, to these situations. However, so far, this question has not been resolved in international practice.

If Article 62 of the Vienna Convention on the Law of Treaties is indeed relevant to human rights treaties, two requirements must be fulfilled in order for a state to successfully invoke 'a fundamental change of circumstances' to suspend a human rights treaty obligation.[168] First, the existence of the circumstances that prevailed at the time of the conclusion of the treaty must have constituted 'an essential basis of the consent of the parties to be bound by the treaty'. Second, the effect of the change of the circumstances must 'radically' 'transform the extent of obligations still to be performed under the treaty'.[169] The state may contend that these requirements are indeed met when it has lost control over (part of) its territory or where the government has collapsed, due to internal armed conflict. With regard to the first requirement, the state may assert that human rights treaties presume the state to be in full control of its territory. When the government has lost its effectiveness or has disappeared from the state territory, it may legitimately claim that the circumstances have changed and that the change is fundamental in the sense that it affects the very facts on which consent to the treaty was based. With regard to the second condition, the state may

due to a change of circumstances'). At the same time, Higgins noted that, in 1963, in practice international tribunals had never released a state from its treaty duties on grounds only of *rebus sic stantibus*. Higgins argues that while the principle is accepted, it is extremely difficult to prove that the criteria are fulfilled in a concrete case, R. Higgins, *The Development of International Law Through the Political Organs of the United Nations* (Oxford University Press, London, 1963), p. 344.

[167] Article 4 of the International Covenant, Article 15 of the European Convention, Article 27 of the American Convention.

[168] If a state claims suspension of a human rights treaty on the basis of the Vienna Convention, it has to follow definite procedures, which are laid down in Articles 65–8 of the Vienna Convention.

[169] Article 62 1(a) and (b), respectively.

reasonably argue that the temporary disappearance of a government or loss of territorial control transforms the positive obligation to protect individuals from other individuals under human rights treaties radically. Indeed, the state then lacks the factual authority to protect individuals.

It should be reiterated that in the absence of international practice, the arguments laid out above remain purely hypothetical.

Force majeure

May a state invoke *force majeure* in order to be exonerated from its accountability when it fails to prevent or repress acts by armed opposition groups contrary to human rights treaties? The irresistibility of the external force distinguishes this from a fundamental change of circumstances. *Force majeure* is defined by Article 31 of the Draft Articles on State Responsibility:

The wrongfulness of an act of a State not in conformity with an international obligation of that State is precluded if the act was due to an irresistible force or to an unforeseen external event beyond its control which made it materially impossible for the State to act in conformity with that obligation or to know that its conduct was not in conformity with that obligation.[170]

Practice of international bodies provides no support for the argument that *force majeure* may limit the state's accountability under human rights treaties. The point is that the due diligence rule, which governs the state's positive obligations under human rights treaties, makes this argument redundant.

A state only violates its due diligence obligation when it fails to prevent or repress acts of armed opposition groups while it is able to do so in view of its material capability and vital military interests. In other words, the due diligence rule precludes a *violation* of human rights treaties if the act or omission concerned 'was due to an irresistible force or to an unforeseen external event beyond its control which made it materially impossible for the State to act in conformity with that obligation or to know that its conduct was not in conformity with that obligation', removing the need for an appeal to *force majeure*.[171]

---

[170] ILC Draft Articles on State Responsibility, above, Chapter 4, n. 1; this article also applies in connection with an obligation 'to act' or to engage in conduct of commission, *ILCYb* 1979, vol. II, 122–33, para. 25.

[171] See I. Brownlie, *State Responsibility*, above, n. 50, pp. 171–2.

Humanitarian law treaties

Since humanitarian law treaties for internal conflicts generally apply to all parties to the conflict, the state and armed opposition groups, the temporary absence of a government or loss of government control over an area do not make the humanitarian law treaties inoperable.[172]

These situations do, however, affect the state's liability for failure to prevent or repress acts of armed opposition groups injuring civilians – by 'transferring' the liability to the armed groups. Article 1 of Protocol II provides that it binds armed opposition groups 'which exercise... control over a part of its [the state's] territory', implying that the government is *not* responsible for observing the Protocol in opposition controlled areas. Also, as mentioned earlier, Article 5 of Amended Protocol II to the Conventional Weapons Convention obliges the state to ensure the exclusion of civilians from certain areas mined by armed opposition groups. But the duty only exists regarding areas that the government actually controls:

2. (a) It is prohibited to use weapons to which this Article applies which are not in compliance with the provisions on self-destruction and self-deactivation in the Technical Annex...
3. A party to a conflict is relieved from further compliance with the provisions of sub-paragraphs 2 (a) and 2 (b) of this Article only if such compliance is not feasible due to forcible loss of control of the area as a result of enemy military action, including situations where direct enemy military action makes it impossible to comply. If that party regains control of the area, it shall resume compliance with the provisions of sub-paragraphs 2 (a) and 2 (b) of this Article.[173]

The state is therefore relieved from compliance when it has forcibly lost control of the area as a result of military action by armed opposition groups. Thus, international humanitarian law treaties provide that the state's obligations thereunder, including the duty to prevent and repress acts of armed opposition groups harming civilians, are limited to the situation where the government still exists and exercises some control over territory. There is no international practice elaborating on this issue.

---

[172] An exception is the Ottawa Convention on Anti-Personnel Mines, which applies only to the state, above, Chapter 1, n. 64. Further, Protocol II does not apply to situations where the established authorities have collapsed, since the Protocol requires government involvement in the conflict (Article 1(1) Protocol II).
[173] Article 5(2) and (3).

International criminal law treaty

The Genocide Convention, like human rights treaties, only applies to the state. The operation of this treaty therefore depends on the existence of a government exercising a minimum of territorial control. If an armed conflict rises to such a level that the government is no longer functioning or lacks effective control in (part of) the state's territory, it would seem that the Genocide Convention becomes inactive in that state or the relevant part of its territory. Thus, here also the general principle of effectiveness appears to apply. International practice provides no evidence for this rule.

6 The quest for accountability

When armed opposition groups involved in internal conflict commit acts injuring civilians, different actors may be held accountable under international law for these acts or for failure to prevent or repress them. This conclusion follows from the practice of international bodies. These actors are: leaders and members of armed opposition groups, armed opposition groups themselves, and the territorial state. The accountability of these three actors is distinct in kind. The question remains how to integrate them.

The accountability of armed opposition groups as such would be the most appropriate answer to the abuses committed by these groups. Grave difficulties, however, centre on this kind of accountability. Accountability of individual leaders and the state, in contrast, are less problematic. Indeed, the accountability of the state is firmly rooted in international law. More recently, the trend of accountability of individuals has entered the body of international law, and has been constantly supported in practice. Similar developments have, however, not taken place with regard to armed opposition groups – their accountability being a grey area in international law.

Group versus individual accountability

In this decade, international law has developed towards criminalization of acts committed by individuals in internal armed conflict, including leaders of armed opposition groups. This development is of great importance. It means that armed opposition groups can be regulated not only through the state and armed opposition groups as an organization, but also through their individual leaders. However, as will be argued hereafter, to the extent that this development replaces the accountability of armed opposition groups as a collectivity it is to be disapproved.

Accountability of armed opposition groups and their individual leaders exist independently of each other and are not interchangeable. These two forms of accountability differ with regard to substantive law, the propositions underlying them, and the measures required. Regarding substantive law, some obligations apply both to armed groups as such and to their leaders. Examples include Common Article 3 and large parts of Protocol II. An overall survey reveals, however, that the substantive obligations are not coextensive. Consider, for example, the Genocide Convention. The prohibition of genocide applies to individual leaders of armed opposition groups; it does not appear to apply to armed opposition groups. Article IX of the Convention refers to the responsibility of a state for genocide; it does not refer to any other entity. On the other hand, some humanitarian law rules are applicable to armed opposition groups but without entailing individual criminal responsibility of the leaders. An example is paragraph (d) of Common Article 3, which prescribes the minimum conditions for a fair trial. This may be because this obligation involves a range of acts or a policy in which many actors participate; it is not suitable for individual criminal responsibility. In this connection, one may question the appropriateness of the inclusion in the Rome Statute of paragraph (d) of Common Article 3.[1] It will be difficult to show individual guilt for violation of the rule on a fair trial.

There is some force in the argument that, in the future, international criminal law will be expanded to cover many other acts. Still, prosecutions by the International Criminal Court will be limited to *serious* violations of international humanitarian law, so that individual accountability before the International Criminal Court will not cover all crimes in internal conflicts.[2]

In addition, the accountability of armed opposition groups and their individual leaders differs regarding the attribution of the act to these actors. Consider, for example, the commission of torture. Leaders of armed opposition groups are accountable when they order subordinates to commit torture. Furthermore, leaders are accountable when they know or have reason to know that subordinates have committed or are

---

[1] Article 8(2)(c)(iv) of the Statute of the International Criminal Court.
[2] See also the Statute of the Special Court for Sierra Leone, art. 1 ('The Special Court shall have the power to prosecute persons most responsible for serious violations of international humanitarian law').

about to commit torture and when they fail to take the necessary and reasonable measures. Groups, on the other hand, can never themselves commit torture, or otherwise contribute physically to an act of torture. Moreover, while the issue of attribution of conduct to armed opposition groups raises serious obstacles, a relationship of subordination is in any case not required. Groups must prevent and repress torture by all their individual members and agencies.

Finally, the measures required to be taken by armed opposition groups and their individual leaders are different. In the case of leaders, such measures may consist of punishment, preventive action, provision of clear orders and training or establishment of a proper reporting system. The measures required from armed opposition groups may go further. In their function as de facto public authorities, they may be obliged to take legislative measures and to prosecute offenders.

While the accountability of armed opposition groups and their individual leaders is therefore not wholly overlapping, there is a tendency in international practice towards criminalization of the behaviour of individual leaders of armed opposition groups and away from the international accountability of the armed groups. The international concern with individual accountability is clearly shown by the establishment of the Yugoslavia and Rwanda Tribunals and the drafting of the Rome Statute. There is no similar concern to establish the international accountability of armed opposition groups. The Rome Statute, for example, contains no provision on the accountability of armed opposition groups.[3] Nor do the Statutes of either the Yugoslavia or Rwanda Tribunals.

One could argue that accountability of leaders of armed opposition groups may imply, in some cases, the accountability of the greater entity itself, when the acts are performed in the furtherance of the group's goals. It should be appreciated, however, that there is some indication that international law is moving in the direction of *dissociating* individual acts from the group context by concentrating *exclusively* on the individual criminal liability. The Yugoslavia Tribunal, for example, has broken off the link between the individual perpetrator and the entity of which he or she is a member by holding that the acts of individual leaders stand on their own and are not necessarily attributable to armed opposition groups in a manner which would implicate group accountability.

---

[3] It does state that no provision in the Statute shall affect the responsibility of *states* under international law, Article 25(4) of the Statute of the International Criminal Court.

Judge Rodrigues has recognized this trend: 'the principle is to prosecute natural persons individually responsible for serious violations of international humanitarian law irrespective of their membership in groups'.[4]

These examples do not prove the existence of a legal principle that leader or member accountability excludes the accountability of the armed opposition group. They do show, however, that while international bodies have given due consideration to accountability of individual leaders of armed opposition groups, they have so far largely ignored the accountability of the groups in favour of the accountability of individual members.

Different reasons account for this tendency. One is that the international community wants to give a strong response to serious crimes. Individuals who commit these crimes are the most obvious targets for legal action. As Lauterpacht wrote: 'there is cogency in the view that unless responsibility is imputed and attached to persons of flesh and blood, it rests with no one'.[5] The group as a collective 'entity' is less visible and it becomes less tangible to apply international rules effectively to them.

Also, states prefer not to recognize the legal existence or international personality of armed opposition groups by attributing acts and omissions to them. They prefer to pass over the group and address the individuals that make up the group. The result is that we are back to the dichotomy of the state and the individual living in the state – subjects that are by now both rather well accepted in international law.

Another reason for the tendency away from international accountability of armed opposition groups is that international bodies lack 'jurisdiction' over the groups.

Some form of legal accountability of armed opposition groups would be an important advance in international law. Three arguments support this proposition. First, leaders are only the executive agents of the organization acting in the international community and which comprises, in some cases, legislative organs, judicial organs, and sometimes even a people. It is only by treating the armed opposition groups as legal

---

[4] *Aleksovski* case, above, Chapter 3, n. 5, Dissenting Opinion of Judge Rodrigues; see also S. Rosenne, 'State Responsibility and International Crimes: Further Reflections on Article 19 of the Draft Articles on State Responsibility', 30 *NYUJ Int'l L. & Pol.* 145, 157 (1997–8) (hereafter, 'State Responsibility and International Crimes').

[5] H. Lauterpacht, *International Law and Human Rights* (Archon Books, USA., reprint 1968) (1950), p. 40.

entities, which are under various international obligations, that the supremacy of international law can be assured. A refusal to recognize the personality of the armed opposition groups is fatal to this.

A second argument is that, in many cases, acts that have been labelled as international crimes are, in reality, acts of a collectivity rather than of isolated wayward individuals. Such crimes are not effectively dealt with by punishing individuals. Crimes against humanity in particular can *only* be committed in the framework of a broad policy of repression.

Finally, while international *law* as applied by international bodies centres on individuals, the international *political order* emerges through a huge variety of actors from multinational companies to indigenous and tribal groups – including armed opposition groups. Armed opposition groups sometimes negotiate with territorial governments and participate in peace conferences organized by the United Nations. The international legal and political orders thus do not operate along parallel lines. When there is no law to implement political decisions, or when political agreements deviate from judgments, resolutions or reports on legal issues, the effectiveness of both international law and international politics in dealing with the problem of armed opposition groups is likely to be low.

In conclusion, to a greater extent than is presently the case, the accountability of the individual leaders of armed opposition groups and of these groups themselves should be integrated and their relation reconsidered.

Group versus state accountability

International practice reveals that the accountability of the territorial state and of armed opposition groups are different in content, as they concern different acts and rest on different propositions. First, while the state is obliged to prevent or repress certain acts of armed opposition groups, armed opposition groups are merely prohibited *themselves* from committing these acts. Further, international bodies have held that the responsibility of the state for acts committed by armed opposition groups is limited to the most serious abuses, threatening the lives of civilians. With regard to other acts of armed opposition groups, such as ill treatment in detention, accountability may only rest with these groups themselves or the members individually. Finally, international bodies consider the prosecution and punishment of abuses by armed opposition groups to be a typical state task.

It follows that state and group accountability exist, at least to some degree, next to each other and are complementary. Evidence from international practice establishes that neither form of accountability provides in itself an adequate answer to the problem of armed opposition groups.

At the same time, there is no doubt that there is a close relationship between these types of accountability – indeed, that they, to some extent, overlap. Both forms of accountability are collective in nature. Both are triggered by acts committed by armed opposition groups. The question arises, therefore, as to the division of accountability between the territorial state and armed opposition groups.

The division of accountability between states and armed groups appears to be determined, *inter alia*, by the effective power of these entities. The state must take the measures within its material ability in the specific circumstances of the case to prevent or repress acts committed by armed opposition groups. Similarly, accountability of armed opposition groups for violations of international norms may vary according to the degree of effective military and political power that they possess, although the UN Commission on Human Rights and the UN Security Council are inclined to hold different kinds of groups, irrespective of their effectiveness, accountable for humanitarian law violations, for the sake of humanity.

Closer analysis of international practice reveals that, in addition to effectiveness and humanity, other factors play a role in international bodies' choice of either form of accountability. International law, to some extent, is biased in favour of established governments and against armed opposition groups. Article 3(1) of Protocol II, for example, provides: 'Nothing in this Protocol shall be invoked for the purpose of affecting the sovereignty of a State or the responsibility of the government, by all legitimate means, to maintain or re-establish law and order in the State or to defend the national unity and territorial integrity of the State'. The provision implies that the territorial state represented by the existing government remains the lawful authority until it is overthrown, and nationals of a state remain subjected to the established government until that moment. The centrality and superiority of the state serves the aim of stability and security in international law. If international bodies should seek to break through the veil of the state and give equal treatment to armed opposition groups, this would amount to the recognition of their belligerent status. It would undermine the perception of the state as a single entity. The clarity in international relations would be affected were injured parties to have to look inside the state to find what entity actually committed the harmful acts concerned.[6]

This heavy focus on the territorial state is no longer appropriate to modern conditions. Rosenne's criticism of the International Law Commission's draft Articles for their one-sided focus on the state underlines this point:

> The more I look at the Draft Articles on State Responsibility, the more I find them inadequate, if not flawed. On the whole, they do not take sufficient account of the consequences of the breakdown of the traditional State system of the nineteenth century, nor of its replacement by a new system which is slowly taking shape before our very eyes. In this new configuration, ... International responsibility can be attributed to entities, which are not deemed states ... It is a system in which the interests of the international community as a whole are to be balanced against the traditional sovereignty of the States. That, I submit, should be the focus of political and academic interest during the coming years, before the final consummation of the codified law of international responsibility.[7]

The international bodies should favour a restrictive interpretation of territorial sovereignty, with stronger emphasis than in times of internal peace on the existence or absence of effective control by the recognized government over a particular area. Notions such as sovereignty, territorial integrity, and stability must be interpreted in accordance with the particularities of internal conflicts. State supremacy is premised on the assumption that the state exercises full authority in its internal legal order, being capable of maintaining law and order. If it fails do so, as in the case of internal armed conflicts, it loses its claim to remain the only legal subject representing the internal legal order on the international level.

One effect of the heavy emphasis on the state system is the practice assigning the task of prosecution and punishment of abuses by armed groups almost exclusively to the state, rather than to the groups themselves. Another example is the limitation of the substantive obligations of armed opposition groups to the duty to respect the most elementary norms of humanity. International bodies have failed to pronounce on measures these groups must take to fulfil their international obligations. Thereby they have done little to make the law applicable to armed opposition groups effective.

---

[6] A. Nollkaemper, 'De dialectiek tussen individuele en collectieve aansprakelijkheid in het Volkenrecht,' Inaugural Lecture, 17 September 1999 (Vossiuspers AUP, Amsterdam, 2000), p. 8.
[7] S. Rosenne, 'State Responsibility and International Crimes', above, n. 4, at 165–6.

A final factor limiting their international accountability is the absence of principles on attribution of violations to armed groups. In the absence of any special rules the idea of applying the general rules used for states should be considered.

In the light of the foregoing observations, the divergence between the practice under human rights treaties and international humanitarian law needs critical review. Under human rights law, the state has a duty not to commit violations and a duty to suppress others from committing them. But no such duties rest on the group. In humanitarian law, there is only a duty not to commit breaches, but this duty extends to both the state and the groups.

The human rights and humanitarian law approaches should be combined. In such a combination international bodies should give priority to the latter. The crucial weakness of the human rights treaties is their exclusive focus on the state as the sole entity bound by the law. Moreover, human rights treaties are not very effective for dealing with internal armed-conflict situations. They tend to treat these as mere emergencies allowing the state to derogate from its human rights obligations in order to defend its internal public order and institutional stability. Humanitarian law, in contrast to human rights law, has been developed to apply specifically in armed conflicts. As the International Court of Justice observed, international humanitarian law applies as a *lex specialis* with regard to human rights law.[8]

Making the necessary extension to humanitarian law will not be easy. The number and variety of armed opposition groups, both in terms of their size and way of operating, will give rise to difficulties. There is some evidence that group accountability will be more readily recognized in cases in which the state's power is weak. As observed by the UN Secretary-General: 'It seems beyond doubt that when an armed group kills civilians, arbitrarily expels people from their homes, or otherwise engages in acts of terror or indiscriminate violence, it raises an issue of potential international concern. This will be especially true in countries where the Government has lost the ability to apprehend and punish those who commit such acts.'[9]

In summary, the state must act against the most serious abuses committed by armed opposition groups to the extent such abuses fall under its control. However, concepts underlying state accountability, such as

---

[8] Advisory Opinion on Nuclear Weapons, above, Chapter 1, n. 34, para. 25.
[9] 1998 Report of the Secretary-General on Minimum Humanitarian Standards, above, Chapter 1, n. 13, para. 64.

state sovereignty, stability, and security should not be dogmatically adhered to at the expense of civilian populations. Not only because, in some cases, armed opposition groups fall entirely outside the state's control, leaving civilians at their mercy, but also because the centrality of the state creates a false dichotomy between the parties to the conflict. It is proposed that international bodies assigning accountability in internal conflict respect the principle of political non-discrimination vis-à-vis civil war parties. While these arguments do not deny that there is a sovereign sphere inside the state which must be protected, they do suggest that this sphere must not be exploited to the point of endangering lives of persons affected by the conflict.

International bodies play a particularly important role in the transformation of the international system relevant to internal conflicts. Their work has become the main focus of international intergovernment. Their practice may contribute to the understanding of internal conflicts not as a matter primarily concerning the territorial state, but as a problem of wider concern.

Conclusion

The provisions of international humanitarian law, international criminal law, and international human rights law are each aimed at different actors. For example, international humanitarian law binds parties to an internal conflict, such as the state and armed opposition groups as a collectivity. International criminal law penalizes particular acts of individuals. In addition, it often obliges the state to prosecute persons for committing these criminalized acts. The provisions of human rights law apply primarily to the state. Each of these three actors – namely armed opposition groups as such, the individual members and leaders of these groups, and the state – may incur international accountability for acts committed by armed opposition groups in internal armed conflicts. Practice of international bodies reveals the following trends as regards the accountability of these actors.

International practice shows that armed opposition groups themselves can be held accountable under international humanitarian law. In order to be held accountable, such groups must at least be organized and engage in military operations. Once armed opposition groups accede to government, the principle of state responsibility applies. At the same time, the international accountability of armed opposition groups is primitive and the prospects for further development are limited. One reason is that there are no supervisory mechanisms set up for the express purpose of monitoring the behaviour of armed opposition groups.

International humanitarian law applicable to armed opposition groups increasingly encompasses humanitarian law originally only applicable to states in international conflicts. One explanation for this practice is that the conventional rules for internal conflicts are too few and too simple to be applied effectively to complex realities of internal conflicts. Furthermore, there is a growing belief among international bodies that human beings are entitled to similar protection in international and internal conflicts. Complete elimination of the distinction between the law for internal and international conflicts is unlikely to happen, however, since this would imply that members of armed opposition groups would be immune from punishment by the national state for participation in the hostilities.

There is little consensus on the question whether armed opposition groups can or should be bound by international human rights law. It is noteworthy that in cases in which international bodies have made an in-depth examination of the question whether human rights norms apply or should apply to armed opposition groups, they have come to the conclusion that they should not. There is some authority for the proposition that human rights instruments do govern armed opposition groups if they exercise governmental functions over portions of the state territory or population.

In addition to armed opposition groups as such, the leaders of these groups can be held responsible under international criminal law for acts committed by their subordinates. Substantive international criminal law has gradually been extended to encompass persons not linked with a state in internal conflicts. The principle of command responsibility applies to both military and civilian leaders. In fact, international practice shows that for the doctrine of command responsibility, distinctions between international and internal armed conflicts and between state actors and non-state actors are irrelevant. This practice fits in with a general tendency in which the formal position of a superior, state or non-state actor, military or civilian, has lost some of its relevance. Instead the emphasis is on the person's actual power over subordinates.

International practice demonstrates that there are clear limits to the state's positive obligation to prevent and repress acts of armed opposition groups with a view to protection of the civilian population living within its territory. Clearly this will have consequences for those under the state's jurisdiction. Civilians falling outside the state's territorial control, or living in a 'failed state' lacking a government, will not enjoy protection by the state under international law. In every other case, the protection the state is able to offer will depend on its factual capabilities.

Bibliography

Abi-Saab, G., 'Non-International Armed Conflicts' in *International Dimensions of Humanitarian Law* (UNESCO, Martinus Nijhoff, Dordrecht, 1988), pp. 217–39.
Abi-Saab, R., *Droit humanitaire et conflits internes* (Institut Henry Dunant, Geneva, 1986).
  'Humanitarian Law and Internal Conflicts: the Evolution of Legal Concern', in A. J. M. Delissen and G. J. Tanja (eds.), *Humanitarian Law of Armed Conflict – Challenges Ahead* (Martinus Nijhoff, The Hague, 1991), pp. 209–23.
Acuña, T. F., *The United Nations Mission in El Salvador – A Humanitarian Law Perspective* (Kluwer Law International, The Hague, 1995).
Akehurst, M., 'State Responsibility for the Wrongful Acts of Rebels – An Aspect of the Southern Rhodesian Problem' (1968–9) 43 *BYIL* 49–70.
  A Modern Introduction to International Law (HarperCollins, 6th edn., Chatham, 1987).
Aldrich, G. H., 'The Law Applicable in Non-International Armed Conflicts: Problems and Prospects' (speech delivered at symposium 'Law and Conflicts in Our Times – The Meaning of International Humanitarian Law in Internal Armed Conflicts', The Hague, 13 November 1997) (unpublished).
  'New Life for the Laws of War' (1981) 75 *AJIL* 764–83.
Alkema, E. A., 'The Enigmatic No-Pretext Clause: Article 60 of the European Convention on Human Rights' in J. Klabbers and R. Lefeber (eds.), *Essays on the Law of Treaties* (Kluwer Law International, 1998).
Alston, P. (ed.), *The United Nations and Human Rights – A Critical Appraisal* (Clarendon Press, Oxford, 1992).
America's Watch Committee, *Violations of the Laws of War by Both Sides in Nicaragua 1981–1985* (New York, March 1985).
  Violations of Fair Trial Guarantees by the FMLN's Ad Hoc Courts, May 1990, p. 512.
Amnesty International, *Political Violence in Colombia – Myth and Reality*, AI Index: AMR 23/01/94 (New York, 1994).
  Algeria – Civilian Population Caught in a Spiral of Violence, AI Index: MDE 28/23/97 (New York, 1997).

Amnesty International Report 1999 (Amnesty International Publications, London, 1999).

Arsanjani, M. H., 'The Rome Statute of the International Criminal Court' (1999) 93 *AJIL* 22–43.

Bailey, S. D., *The UN Security Council and Human Rights* (St. Martin's Press, New York, 1994).

Balencie, J-M. and A. de la Grange, *Mondes Rebelles* (Editions Michalon, Paris, 1996).

Bantekas, I., 'The Contemporary Law of Superior Responsibility' (1999) 93 *AJIL* 573–95.

Baxter, R., 'Jus in Bello Interno: the Present and Future Law' in J. Moore (ed.), *Law and Civil War in the Modern World* (Johns Hopkins University Press, Baltimore, 1974), pp. 518–36.

Best, G., *War & Law Since 1945* (Clarendon Press, Oxford, reprint 1996).

Bing Bing Jia, 'The Doctrine of Command Responsibility in International Law – with Emphasis on Liability for Failure to Punish' (1998) XLV *NILR* 325–47.

Blomeyer-Bartenstein, H., 'Due Diligence' (1992) 1 *EPIL* 1110–15.

Bond, J. E., 'Application of the Law of War to Internal Conflicts' (1973) 3 *Ga. J. Int'l & Comp. L.* 345–84.

Bothe, M., 'Relief Actions' (1982) 4 *EPIL* 173–8.

'The Role of National Law in the Implementation of International Humanitarian Law' in C. Swinarski (ed.), *Studies and Essays on International Humanitarian Law and Red Cross Principles in Honour of Jean Pictet* (International Committee of the Red Cross, Martinus Nijhoff, Dordrecht, 1984), pp. 301–12.

Bothe, M. et al., *New Rules for Victims of Armed Conflicts* (Martinus Nijhoff, The Hague, 1982).

Bourloyannis, C., 'The Security Council of the United Nations and the Implementation of International Humanitarian Law' (1992) 20 *Denv. J. Int'l L. & Pol'y* 335–55.

Boven, T. C. van, 'Reliance on Norms of Humanitarian Law by United Nations' Organs' in A. J. M. Delissen and G. J. Tanja (eds.), *Humanitarian Law of Armed Conflict – Challenges Ahead* (Martinus Nijhoff, The Hague, 1991), pp. 495–513.

Briggs, H. W., *The International Law Commission* (Cornell University Press, Ithaca, New York, 1965).

Brownlie, I., 'International Law and the Activities of Armed Bands' (1958) 7 *ICLQ* 712–35.

System of the Law of Nations – State Responsibility (Clarendon Press, Oxford, reprint 1986) (1983), vol. I.

The Rule of Law in International Affairs (Kluwer Law International, The Hague, 1998).

Principles of Public International Law (Clarendon Press, Oxford, 5th edn., 1998).

Buergenthal, T. and D. Shelton, *Protecting Human Rights in the Americas – Cases and Materials* (N. P. Engel, Kehl, 4th edn., 1995).
Cassese, A., *International Law in a Divided World* (Clarendon Press, Oxford, 1986).
  'On the Current Trends Towards Criminal Prosecution and Punishment of Breaches of International Humanitarian Law' (1998) 9 *EJIL* 1–17.
  'The Statute of the International Criminal Court: Some Preliminary Reflections' (1999) 10 *EJIL* 144–71.
Cerna, C. M., 'Human Rights in Armed Conflict: Implementation of International Humanitarian Law Norms by Regional Intergovernmental Human Rights Bodies' in F. Kalshoven and Y. Sandoz (eds.), *Implementation of International Humanitarian Law* (Martinus Nijhoff, Dordrecht, 1989), pp. 31–67.
Christenson, G. A., 'Attributing Acts of Omission to the State' (1991) 12 *Mich. J. Int'l L.* 312–70.
Cissé, C., 'The End of a Culture of Impunity in Rwanda?' (1998) 1 *YIHL* 161–88.
Clapham, A., *Human Rights in the Private Sphere* (Clarendon Press, Oxford, reprint 1998) (1996).
  'The Question of Jurisdiction under International Criminal Law over Legal Persons: Lessons from the Rome Conference on an International Criminal Court', in M. T. Kamminga, S. Zia Zarifi (eds.), *Liability of Multinational Corporations Under International Law* (Kluwer Law International, 2000) (in print).
Conforti, B., *The Law and Practice of the United Nations* (Kluwer Law International, The Hague, 1996).
Davidson, S., *The Inter-American Human Rights System* (Dartmouth, Aldershot, 1997).
Denaud, P., *Algérie: Le FIS, sa direction parle...* (Editions L'Harmattan, Paris, 1997).
Denaud, P. and V. Pras, *Kosovo: naissance d'une lutte armée, UCK* (Editions L'Harmattan, Paris, 1999).
Dennis, M. J., 'The Fifty-Fourth Session of the UN Commission on Human Rights' (1999) 93 *AJIL* 246–52.
Dijk, P. van, '"Positive Obligations" Implied in the European Convention on Human Rights: Are the States Still Masters of the Convention?' in M. Castermans and F. van Hoof (eds.), *The Role of the Nation State in the 21st Century* (Kluwer Law International, The Netherlands, 1998), pp. 17–33.
Dinstein, Y., 'The Right to Life, Physical Integrity, and Liberty' in L. Henkin (ed.), *The International Bill of Rights* (1981), pp. 114–37.
Dixon, R., 'Prosecuting the Leaders: the Application of the Doctrine of Superior Responsibility before the United Nations International Criminal Tribunals for the Former Yugoslavia and Rwanda' in A. L. W. Vogelaar *et al.*, 'The Commander's Responsibility in Difficult Circumstances' *NL Arms Netherlands Annual Review of Military Studies 1998* (Gianotten BV, Tilburg, 1998), pp. 109–29.

Doehring, K., 'Effectiveness' (1995) 2 *EPIL* 43–8.
Draper, G. I. A. D., 'Human Rights and the Law of Armed Conflicts: General Principles of Implementation', *Résumé des cours: Cinquième session d'enseignement* (International Institute of Human Rights at Strasbourg, 1–26 July 1974), reprinted in M. A. Meyer and H. McCoubrey (eds.), *Reflections on Law and Armed Conflicts* (Kluwer Law International, The Hague, 1998), pp. 141–4.
  'The Relationship Between the Human Regime and the Law of Armed Conflict (1971) 1 *Israel YBHR* 191–207, reprinted in M. A. Meyer and H. McCoubrey (eds.), *Reflections on Law and Armed Conflicts* (Kluwer Law International, The Hague, 1998), pp. 125–40.
  'Wars of National Liberation and War Criminality', in M. A. Meyer and H. McCoubrey (eds.), *Restraints on War: Studies in the Limitation of Armed Conflict* (Oxford University Press, Oxford, 1979), reprinted in *Reflections on Law and Armed Conflicts* (Kluwer Law International, The Hague, 1998), pp. 180–93.
  'Humanitarian Law and Human Rights' (1979) *Acta Juridica*, 199–206, reprinted in M. A. Meyer and H. McCoubrey (eds.), *Reflections on Law and Armed Conflicts* (Kluwer Law International, The Hague, 1998), pp. 145–50.
Dugard, J. D., 'Dealing with Crimes of a Past Regime – Is Amnesty Still an Option?' (The Third Manfred Lachs Memorial Lecture, 13 April 1999) (to be published).
  The Role of Lawyers before International Courts (Paper presented at conference 'Independent Defence Before the International Criminal Court' organized by the International Criminal Defence Attorney Association, The Hague, 1–2 November 1999) (unpublished).
Eide, A., 'The New Humanitarian Law in Non-International Armed Conflict', in A. Cassese (ed.), *The New Humanitarian Law of Armed Conflict* (Editoriale Scientifica S.r.l., Napoli, 1979), pp. 277–309.
Eide, A. et al., 'Combating Lawlessness in Gray Zone Conflicts Through Minimum Humanitarian Standards' (1995) 89 *AJIL* 215–23.
Elst, R. van, 'De Zaak Darco Knezevic: Rechtsmacht over Joegoslavische en Andere Buitenlandse Oorlogsmisdadigers' (1998) 35 *NJB* 1587–93.
Falk, R. A., 'Introduction', in R. A. Falk (ed.), *The International Law of Civil War* (John Hopkins Press, Baltimore, 1971), pp. 11–16.
Fawcett, J. E. S., *The Application of the European Convention on Human Rights* (Clarendon Press, Oxford, 2nd edn., 1987).
Fischer, H., 'The International Criminal Court: a Critical Review of the Results of the Rome Conference' (paper delivered at Symposium in Honour of Judge Antonio Cassese at the Occasion of the Award of an Honorary Doctorate by Erasmus University Rotterdam, Rotterdam, 5 November 1998) (unpublished).

Fitzpatrick, J., *Human Rights in Crisis* (University for Pennsylvania Press, Philadelphia, 1994).
Forsythe, D. P., 'Legal Management of Internal War: the 1977 Protocol on Non-International Armed Conflicts' (1978) 72 *AJIL* 272–95.
Frowein, J. A., *Das De Facto-Regime im Völkerrecht* (Carl Heymanns Verlag KG, Köln, 1968).
  The Legal Aspects of International Terrorism (Martinus Nijhoff, Dordrecht, 1988).
Genugten, W. J. M. van, and L. Zegveld, 'The Military Commander, UN Operations and Human Rights' in A. L. W. Vogelaar *et al.*, 'The Commander's Responsibility in Difficult Circumstances' *NL Arms Netherlands Annual Review of Military Studies 1998* (Gianotten BV, Tilburg, 1998), pp. 57–71.
Goldman, R. K., 'International Humanitarian Law and the Armed Conflicts in El Salvador and Nicaragua' (1987) 2 *Am. U. J. Int'l L. & Pol'y* 539–78.
  'Codification of International Rules on Internally Displaced Persons' (1998) 324 *IRRC* 463–6.
Goodwin-Gill, G. S., *The Refugee in International Law* (Clarendon Press, Oxford, second edn., 1996).
Goose, S. D., 'The Ottawa Process and the 1997 Mine Ban Treaty' (1998) 1 *YIHL* 269–91.
Green, L. C., *Essays on the Modern Law of War* (Transnational Publishers, Inc., Dobbs Ferry, 1985).
  The Contemporary Law of Armed Conflict (Manchester University Press, Manchester, 1993).
  'War Crimes, Crimes against Humanity, and Command Responsibility' Spring (1997) *NWR* 26–68.
Greenwood, C., International Humanitarian Law, in F. Kalshoven (ed.), *The Centennial of the First International Peace Conference* (Kluwer Law International, Netherlands, 2000), pp. 161–259.
Hampson, F. J., 'Human Rights Law and International Humanitarian Law: Two Coins or Two Sides of the Same Coin?' (1992) 91/1 *Bulletin of Human Rights* 46–54.
Harris, D. J. *et al.*, *Law of The European Convention on Human Rights* (Butterworths, London, 1995).
Herby, P., 'Third Session of the Review Conference of States Parties to the 1980 United Nations Convention on Certain Conventional Weapons (CCW)' (1996) 312 *IRRC* 361–8.
Higgins, R., *The Development of International Law Through the Political Organs of the United Nations* (Oxford University Press, London, 1963).
  'International Law and Civil Conflict', in E. Luard (ed.), *The International Regulation of Civil Wars* (Thames and Hudson Ltd, London, 1972), pp. 169–86.
  Problems and Process: International Law and How We Use It (Clarendon Press, Oxford, 1994).

'The Role of Domestic Courts in the Enforcement of International Human Rights: the United Kingdom', in B. Conforti, F. Franciani (eds.), *Human Rights in Domestic Courts* (1997), pp. 37–58.

Hoof, G. J. H. van, and K. de Vey Mestdagh, 'Mechanisms of International Supervision', in P. van Dijk (ed.), *Supervisory Mechanisms in International Economic Organisations* (Kluwer, Deventer, 1984), pp. 1–45.

Human Rights Watch, 'Violations of the Rules of War by the Insurgent Forces', in *Federal Republic of Yugoslavia: Humanitarian Law Violations in Kosovo*, vol. x, No 9 (D).

Huyse, L., 'To Punish or to Pardon: A Devil's Choice' (paper presented at international conference 'Reining in Impunity for International Crimes and Serious Violations of Fundamenta Human Rights', Siracusa, 16–21 September 1997) (unpublished).

Hyde, C. C., II *International Law Chiefly as Interpreted and Applied by the United States* (Little Brown and Company, Boston, 1947).

International Committee of the Red Cross, *Annual Report 1994* (International Committee of the Red Cross, Geneva, 1995).

Armed Conflicts Linked to the Disintegration of State Structures (Preparatory Document for the First Periodical Meeting on International Humanitarian Law, Geneva, 19–23 January 1998).

International Institute of Humanitarian Law, 'Règles du droit international humanitaire relatives à la conduite des hostilités dans les conflits armés non internationaux' (XIVth mtg, San Remo, 14 September 1989), reprinted in (1990) 785 IRRC 415–42.

International Law Association, *Report of the Sixty-Eighth Conference* (Report of the Committee on Accountability of International Organisations, London, 1998), pp. 584–615.

Report of the Sixty-Eighth Conference (Report of the Committee on Human Rights Law and Practice on 'The Exercise of Universal Jurisdiction in Respect of Gross Human Rights Offences' (London, 1998)), pp. 563–83.

Jasica, R., Internationales Humanitäres Recht und Menschenrechte' (1994) 1 HV 4-7.

Jean, F. and J-C. Rufin (eds.), *Économie des guerres civiles* (Hachette, Paris, 1996).

Jennings, R. and A. Watts, *Oppenheim's International Law* (Longman, London, 9th edn., 1996).

Kalshoven, F., *De Positie van de Niet-Bezette Burgerbevolking in een Gewapend Conflict, in het Bijzonder met het Oog op de Massaal Werkende Strijdmiddelen (NBC-Wapens)* (Mededelingen van de Nederlandse Vereniging voor Internationaal Recht No 61, Kluwer, Deventer, February 1970).

Belligerent Reprisals (A. W. Sijthoff, Leiden, 1971).

'Reaffirmation and Development of International Humanitarian Law Applicable in Armed Conflicts: the Diplomatic Conference Geneva 1974–1977' (1977) 8 NYIL 107–35.

Constraints on the Waging of War (International Committee of the Red Cross, Geneva, 2nd edn., 1991).
  and L. Zegveld *Constraints on the Waging of War* (International Committee of the Red Cross, Geneva, 3rd edn., 2001).
  'Development of Customary Law of Armed Conflict' (Asser Colloquium, 27 November 1998) (unpublished).
  'The Undertaking to Respect and Ensure Respect in All Circumstances: From Tiny Seed to Ripening Fruit' in (1999) 2 *YIHL* 3–61.
  'State Sovereignty vs. International Concern in Some Recent Cases of the Inter-American Court of Human Rights' in *Liber Amicorum Pieter Kooijmans*, (to be published).
Keijzer, N., 'Introductory Observations' to: *War Crimes Law and the Statute of Rome: Some Afterthoughts?* (Report of the International Society for Military Law and the Law of War, 1999).
Klip, A. and G. Sluiter (eds.), *Annotated Leading Cases of International Criminal Tribunals: the International Criminal Tribunal for the Former Yugoslavia 1993–1998* (Intersentia, Antwerp, 1999).
Kooijmans, P. H., 'The Security Council and Non-State Entities as Parties to Conflicts' in K. Wellens (ed.), *International Law: Theory and Practice* (Kluwer Law International, The Netherlands, 1998), pp. 333–46.
Laffin, J., 'The World in Conflict 1990' (1990) 4 *War Annual*.
Lauterpacht, H., *Recognition in International Law* (Cambridge University Press, Cambridge, 1947).
  International Law and Human Rights (Stevens and Sons, Ltd., reprint 1968) (1950).
  Development of International Law by the International Court of Justice (Cambridge University Press, Cambridge, reprint 1996) (1958).
LeBlanc, L., *The United States and the Genocide Convention* (Duke University Press, Durham, 1991).
Levrat, N., 'Les conséquences de l'engagement pris par les Hautes Parties Contractantes de "faire respecter" les conventions humanitaires', in F. Kalshoven and Y. Sandoz (eds.), *Implementation of International Humanitarian Law* (Martinus Nijhoff, Dordrecht, 1989), pp. 263–96.
Mahoney, P. and F. Sundberg, 'The European Convention on Human Rights: A Case Study of the International Law Response to Violence' in K. H. Mahoney and P. Mahoney (eds.), *Human Rights in the Twenty-First Century* (Martinus Nijhoff, The Hague, 1993), pp. 361–76.
Malanczuk, P., *Akehurst's Modern Introduction to International Law* (Routledge, London, 7th edn., 1997).
Maslen, S., P. Herby, 'An International Ban on Anti-Personnel Mines – History and Negotiation of the "Ottawa Treaty"' (1998) 325 *IRRC* 693–713.
Matas, D., 'Armed Opposition Groups' (1995) 24 *MLJ* 621–34.

McCoubrey, H. and N. D. White, *International Organizations and Civil Wars* (Dartmouth, Brookfield, 1995).
McDonald, A., 'The Year in Review' (1998) 1 *YIHL* 113-60.
Meron, T., 'On the Inadequate Reach of Humanitarian and Human Rights Law and the Need for a New Instrument' (1983) 77 *AJIL* 589-605.
  Human Rights in Internal Strife: their International Protection (Grotius Publications Limited, Cambridge, 1987).
  'The Geneva Conventions as Customary Law' (1987) 81 *AJIL* 348-70.
  Human Rights and Humanitarian Norms as Customary Law (Clarendon Press, Oxford, 1989).
  'International Criminalization of Internal Atrocities' (1995) 89 *AJIL* 554-77.
  'The Continuing Role of Custom in the Formation of International Humanitarian Law' (1996) 90 *AJIL* 238-9.
  'Crimes under the Jurisdiction of the International Criminal Court', in H. A. M. von Hebel *et al.* (eds.), *Reflections on the International Criminal Court* (T. M. C. Asser Press, The Hague, 1999), pp. 47-55.
  'Is International Law Moving Towards Criminalization?' (1998) 9 *EJIL* 18-31.
Morris, V. and M. P. Scharf, *The International Criminal Tribunal for Rwanda* (Transnational Publishers, Inc. New York, 1998).
Nollkaemper, A., 'De Dialectiek tussen Individuele en Collectieve Aansprakelijkheid in het Volkenrecht', Inaugural Lecture, 17 September 1999 (Vossiuspers AUP, Amsterdam, 2000).
Norwegian Institute of Human Rights, *Making the Reporting Procedure under the International Covenant on Civil and Political Rights More Effective* (No. 8, Oslo, 1991).
Nowak, M., *UN Covenant on Civil and Political Rights – Commentary* (N. P. Engel, Kehl, 1993).
Obradovic, K., 'Que faire face aux violations du droit humanitaire? – quelques réflexions sur le rôle possible du CICR' in C. Swinarski (ed.), *Studies and Essays on International Humanitarian Law and Red Cross Principles in Honour of Jean Pictet* (International Committee of the Red Cross, Martinus Nijhoff, Dordrecht, 1984), pp. 483-94.
O'Brien, J. C., 'The International Tribunal for Violations of International Humanitarian Law in the Former Yugoslavia' (1993) 87 *AJIL* 639-59.
Oraá, J., *Human Rights in States of Emergency in International Law* (Clarendon Press, Oxford, 1992).
Orentlicher, D. F., 'Settling Accounts: the Duty to Prosecute Human Rights Violations of a Prior Regime' (1991) 100 *Yale L. J.* 2537-615.
Parks, W., 'Command Responsibility for War Crimes' (1973) 62 *Mil. L. Rev.* 1-104.
Partsch, K. J., 'Individual Penal Responsibility Provided by the Additional Protocols to the Geneva Conventions' (Second Round Table on Current Problems of International Humanitarian Law, San Remo, 3-6 September 1975).

Paust, J., 'Superior Orders and Command Responsibility' in M. C. Bassiouni (ed.), *International Criminal Law* (Transnational Publishers, Inc., New York, 1986), vol. III, pp. 73–88.

Paust, J. et al., *International Criminal Law – Cases and Materials* (Carolina Academic Press, Durham, 1996).

Petrasek, D., 'Moving Forward on the Development of Minimum Humanitarian Standards' (1998) 92 *AJIL* 557–63.

Pictet, J. S. (ed.), *Commentary IV Geneva Convention Relative to the Protection of Civilian Persons in Time of War* (International Committee of the Red Cross, Geneva, reprint 1994) (1958).

PIOOM 'Interdisciplinary Research Program on Causes of Human Rights Violations' *World Conflict and Human Rights Map* (Leiden University, The Netherlands, 1998).

Pisillo-Mazzeschi, R., 'The Due Diligence Rule and the Nature of International Responsibility of States' (1992) 35 *GYIL* 9–51.

  'Forms of International Responsibility for Environmental Harm', in F. Francioni and T. Scovazzi (eds.), *International Responsibility for Environmental Harm* (Graham & Trotman, London, 1991), pp. 15–35.

Plattner, D., 'La portée juridique des déclarations de respect du droit international humanitaire qui émanent de mouvements en lutte dans un conflit armé' (1984-5) XVIII *RBDI* 298–320.

  'The Penal Repression of Violations of International Humanitarian Law Applicable in Non-International Armed Conflicts' (1990) 30 *IRRC* 409–20.

Ramcharan, B. G. (ed.), *The Right to Life in International Law* (Martinus Nijhoff, Dordrecht, 1985).

Ratner, S. R. and J. S. Abrams, *Accountability for Human Rights Atrocities in International Law* (Clarendon Press, Oxford, 1997).

Reidy, A. and F. J. Hampson and K. Boyle, 'Gross Violations of Human Rights: Invoking the European Convention on Human Rights in the Case of Turkey' (1997) 15/2 *NQHR* 161–73.

Reuter, P., *Introduction to the Law of Treaties* (Kegan Paul International, London, 1995).

Rodley, N. S., 'Can Armed Opposition Groups Violate Human Rights Standards?' in K. H. Mahoney and P. Mahoney (eds.), *Human Rights in the Twenty-First Century* (Martinus Nijhoff, The Hague, 1993), pp. 297–318.

Röling, B. V. A., 'Aspects of the Criminal Responsibility for Violations of the Laws of War', in A Cassese (ed.), *The New Humanitarian Law of Armed Conflict* (Editoriale Scientifica S.r.l., Napoli, 1979), pp. 199–231.

Rosenne, S., 'State Responsibility and International Crimes: Further Reflections on Article 19 of the Draft Articles on State Responsibility' (1997–8) 30 *NYUJ Int'l L. & Pol.* 145–66.

Sandoz, Y. et al. (eds.), *Commentary on the Additional Protocols of 8 June 1977 to the Geneva Conventions of 12 August 1949* (Martinus Nijhoff, Geneva, 1987).

Sassòli, M., 'Mise en oeuvre du droit international humanitaire et du droit international des droits de l'homme: une comparaison' in (1987) XLIII *Ann. SDI* 24–61.

Schwarzenberger, G., *International Law as Applied by International Courts and Tribunals – the Law of Armed Conflict* (Stevens and Sons, London, 1968), vol. II.

Shelton, D., 'State Responsibility for Covert and Indirect Forms of Violence', in K. E. Mahoney and P. Mahoney (eds.), *Human Rights in the Twenty-First Century* (Martinus Nijhoff, The Hague, 1993), pp. 265–76.

Shraga, D. and R. Zacklin, 'The International Criminal Tribunal for the Former Yugoslavia' (1994) 5 *EJIL* 360–80.

Silvanie, H., 'Responsibility of States for Acts of Insurgent Governments' (1939) 33 *AJIL* 78–103.

Simma, B. (ed.), *The Charter of the United Nations – A Commentary* (Oxford University Press, Oxford, 1995).

Simma, B. and A. L. Paulus, 'The Responsibility of Individuals for Human Rights Abuses in Internal Conflicts: a Positivist View' (1999) 93 *AJIL* 310–13.

Takemoto, M., 'The 1977 Additional Protocols and the Law of Treaties', in *Studies and Essays on International Humanitarian Law and Red Cross Principles in Honour of Jean Pictet*, C. Swinarski (ed.) (International Committee of the Red Cross, Martinus Nijhoff, Dordrecht, 1984), pp. 249–60.

Taylor, T., *The Anatomy of the Nuremberg Trials* (Bloomsbury, London, 1993).

Thürer, D. et al., *Der Wegfall Effektiver Staatsgewalt: 'The Failed State'* (C. F. Müller Verlag, Heidelberg, 1995).

Tomuschat, C., 'What is a "Breach" of the European Convention on Human Rights?' in R. Lawson and M. de Blois (eds.), *The Dynamics of the Protection of Human Rights in Europe* (Kluwer Academic Publishers, Dordrecht, 1994), pp. 315–35.

United Nations, *The United Nations and Cambodia 1991–1995* (2 UN Blue Book Series, United Nations, New York, 1995).

The United Nations and El Salvador 1990–1995, 4 UN Blue Book Series, United Nations, New York, 1995).

Vasak, K., 'Human Rights: As a Legal Reality' in K. Vasak (ed.), *The International Dimensions of Human Rights* (Greenwood Press, Westport, 1982), pp. 3–10.

Weil, P., 'Le droit international en quête de son identité' (1992) 237-VI *Recueil des Cours* 222.

Wildhaber, L., 'Sovereignty and International Law', in R. St J. Macdonald and D. M. Johnston (eds.), *The Structure and Process of International Law: Essays in Legal Philosophy, Doctrine and Theory* (Martinus Nijhoff, Dordrecht, 1986), pp. 425–52.

Wilhelm, R.-J., 'Problèmes relatifs à la protection humaine par le droit international dans les conflits armés ne présentant pas un caractère international' (1972) 137-III *Recueil des Cours* 311–417.

Zegveld, L., The Inter-American Commission on Human Rights and International Humanitarian Law: a Comment on the *Tablada* Case' (1998) 324 *IRRC* 505–11.

'Responsibility of Leaders of Armed Opposition Groups under the Rome Statute', in *War Crimes and the Statute of Rome: Some Afterthoughts* (Report of the International Society for Military Law and the Law of War, 1999).

Zegveld, L. and F. Kalshoven, *Constraints on the Waging of War* (International Committee of the Red Cross, Geneva, 3rd edn., 2001).

Zegveld, L. and H. van Sambeek, 'Law and Conflicts in Our Times – the Meaning of International Humanitarian Law in Internal Armed Conflicts' (1998) 1 *HV* 70–1.

Index

accountability
  attribution *see* attribution of acts
  evidence of accountability, 134–52
  governments *see* state accountability
  groups and individuals compared, 220–4
  groups and states compared, 224–8
  groups as such, 133–63
  leadership *see* leadership accountability
  levels of accountability, 3, 97
  problem defined, 3
  successful groups, 155–7
  terminology, 5
additional Protocols
  national liberation movement, 17–18
  Protocol I *see* Protocol I (1977)
  Protocol II *see* Protocol II (1977)
Afghanistan
  attribution of acts, 154, 156
  de facto control, 154
  detention/internment, 29, 65, 66, 67
  executions, 64, 67
  Geneva Conventions (1949), 22, 29
  government collapse, 2, 150, 208
  human rights, 48, 150, 211, 214
  humanitarian relief, 88
  internal armed conflict, 4
  International Committee of the Red Cross (ICRC), 88
  local authorities, 214
  prisoners, 29, 90
  Protocol II (1977), 22
  Taliban, 64, 150, 154, 156
  territorial control, 211
  UN Commission on Human Rights, 64, 65, 66, 88, 90, 150, 154, 211, 214

  UN Security Council, 48, 150
  White House Executive Order (1999), 154
Algeria
  Armed Islamic Group (GIA), 169
  Human Rights Committee, 168–9, 189, 199
  internal armed conflict, 4, 208
  Islamic Salvation Army (FIS), 169
  territorial control, 208
American Convention on Human Rights (1969)
  Commission *see* Inter-American Commission
  El Salvador, 50, 212
  Honduras, 167
  human rights concept, 40–1
  international humanitarian law, 160
  prosecution, 198
  right to life, 47, 184
  state accountability, 166
  state parties, 39, 41
amnesties
  Congo, 37
  El Salvador, 205–6
  governmental transition, 205
  Human Rights Committee, 206
  internal armed conflict, 37, 164, 188, 197
  International Committee of the Red Cross (ICRC), 206
  international criminal law, 37
  Kosovo, 207–8
  Protocol II (1977), 37, 206
  Sierra Leone, 37, 207
  state accountability, 164, 188, 197, 204–7
  torture, 204, 205, 206
  UN Commission on Human Rights, 37

UN Secretary-General, 37
United Nations, 207
Amnesty International (AI)
  internal armed conflict, 23
  surveys, 2
Ando, Nisuke, 172
Angola
  humanitarian relief, 88
  Protocol II (1977), 146
  UN Security Council, 77, 88
  UNITA, 77
Argentina
  armed forces, 10, 60-1, 137-8
  executions, 60, 61
  Tablada case, 10, 60-1, 137, 160
armed forces
  Argentina, 10, 60-1, 137-8
  individual criminals, 105
  internal disturbances, 137-8
  requisite care, 168
armed opposition groups
  accountability *see* accountability
  attribution of acts, 134, 152-5, 222, 227
  command and control *see* Leadership
  compliance, capability, 35
  fighting each other, 1, 4, 164
  Geneva Conventions (1949), adherence, 14-15
  guerrillas, 35, 62, 134
  independent entities, 15
  individuals compared, 16
  insurgents *see* insurgents
  legal restraints, 9-58
  legal status *see* legal personality
  legislation, 70-4, 187, 188, 222
  membership, 105, 153
  multilateral treaties, 26-8
  objectives, 1
  obligations *see* obligations
  organizational structure, 1, 35, 133-4, 138-40, 154-5
  splinter entities, 135
  state accountability, 164-219
  successful groups, 155-7
  terminology, 3-4, 134
  uniforms, 75
attribution of acts
  Afghanistan, 154, 156
  armed opposition groups, 134, 152-5, 222, 227
  Colombia, 155

Congo, 156
Inter-American Commission, 153, 155
International Law Commission, 153, 154, 155, 156, 157
torture, 222
UN Commission on Human Rights, 153, 225
UN Observer Mission in El Salvador (ONUSAL), 152-3
UN Security Council, 153, 225
Yugoslavia, 156
autonomy, objectives, 1

belligerent status
  Common Article 3, 36
  customary humanitarian law, 2
  Geneva Conventions (1949), 2
  prisoners *see* prisoners of war
Bond, J. E., 36
booby-traps, Protocol II on mines and booby-traps (1996), 26, 27, 85-6, 146, 147, 184, 188
Bosnia-Herzegovina, 112-13, 116-17, 149

Cambodia, 4
Chechnya
  internal armed conflict, 4
  international humanitarian law, 199-200
  killings, 175
child recruitment, 21, 63, 103
civilian protection
  civilian immunity, 75, 76
  civilian objects, 79-82
  civilians defined, 75
  Common Article 3, 82-4, 189
  densely populated areas, 79
  direct/indirect participation in hostilities, 75, 76, 84
  distinction principle, 76-7
  dual-use facilities, 81
  essential protection, 52
  forced movement, 21
  from other individuals, 167-8, 171, 172, 173
  general protection, 76-84
  humane treatment, 61, 82-3
  indiscriminate attacks, 77, 78
  insurrections, 176, 181, 183
  Inter-American Commission, 75-6, 79, 80-1

244   INDEX

civilian protection (*cont.*)
  international armed conflict, 33
  international bodies, 77
  International Criminal Tribunal for the Former Yugoslavia, 76, 77, 80
  International Criminal Tribunal for Rwanda, 75
  landmines *see* landmines
  obligations, 3, 75–92
  precautions *see* precautionary measures
  prevention *see* preventative measures
  Protocol I (1977), 75, 77, 78–9, 80, 82, 84
  Protocol II (1977), 75–80, 83–7, 89, 91–2, 189
  reprisals, 59, 75, 89–92
  self-defence, 196
  starvation, 21, 59, 75, 86–9
  state accountability, 165
  UN General Assembly Resolutions, 76–7, 80
  UN Observer Mission in El Salvador (ONUSAL), 78, 82
  UN Security Council, 77
civilian victims
  fundamental rights, 3
  government collapse, 2
  state accountability, 164
collective punishment, 91
Colombia
  Army of National Liberation (ELN), 81, 84, 169
  CONVIVIR, 196
  disappearances, 171–2
  executions, 84, 192
  Forces of Colombia (FARC), 84, 169, 213
  guerrilla movements, 62
  hostages, 84, 90
  human rights, 21, 41, 46, 47, 52, 54, 192, 213
  Human Rights Committee, 171–2
  Inter-American Commission
    attribution of acts, 155
    civilian objects, 80–1
    civilian protection, 80–1, 84
    customary law, 21
    death threats, 195
    detention/internment, 65, 84
    foreseeability of harm, 192
    international humanitarian law, 41, 54, 61, 155
    Protocol II (1977), 21, 61, 75, 80, 145
  right to life, 47, 90
  state accountability, 169–70, 213
  Third Report (1999), 11–12, 21, 41, 52, 54, 61, 75, 84, 85, 155
  internal armed conflict, 4, 61, 62
  International Covenant on Civil and Political Rights (1966), 171–2
  kidnapping, 47, 62
  killings, 62
  landmines, 85
  National Committee of Victims of the Guerrilla War, 195
  self-defence, 196
  territorial control, 208, 213
  UN Commission on Human Rights, 46
command and control *see* leadership
Common Article 3
  applicability
    binding effect, 20, 42
    determination, 13
    express declaration, 14
    geographic, 61
    international bodies, 12, 13, 35
    questioned by states, 53
    temporal, 61–2
    threshold, 35, 53, 147
  belligerent status, 36
  civilian protection, 82–4, 189
  conflict internationalized, 18
  customary humanitarian law, 20, 24, 25, 31, 32
  detention/internment, 65–7, 84
  El Salvador, 25, 50
  essential protection, 52
  evidence of accountability, 134–48, 151
  executions, 68–9
  fair trial, 221
  fundamental guarantees, 62
  grave breaches, 103
  hostages, 62
  humane treatment, 59–62, 65–9, 82–3
  ICJ decisions, 10, 19, 174
  insurgents, 135
  Inter-American Commission, 61, 135, 137, 138, 145–6
  internal armed conflict, 18, 33–4, 135, 138, 143
  International Committee of the Red Cross (ICRC), 137–8, 140
  International Criminal Court, 101, 141–2, 221

International Criminal Tribunal for the Former Yugoslavia, 102, 135, 136, 144
International Criminal Tribunal for Rwanda, 19, 135, 136
leadership accountability, 99–100, 221
legal restraints, 2, 9–26
legislation, 187
Nicaragua, 10, 19, 24, 174
obligations, 15, 16, 92
precautionary measures, 189
prosecution, 21, 67–9, 198
provisions, 9–10
reprisals, 89, 92
special agreements/declarations, 17, 18, 25, 28–30, 50, 148
state accountability, 173–7
territorial control, 135, 136, 146
torture, 205
UN Commission on Human Rights, 11, 135, 138
UN Security Council, 11, 135, 138–41
violations, 103, 105, 112, 142, 157, 184, 205, 207
violence to life and person, 62, 82, 199, 200
war crimes, 103
Congo
amnesties, 37
attribution of acts, 156
Protocol II (1977), 146
Convention on the Prevention and the Punishment of the Crime of Genocide (1948), 44, 108–9, 178, 185, 189, 197, 221
Convention Relating to the Status of Refugees (1951), 180
Conventional Weapons Convention (1980), Protocol II on mines and booby-traps (1996), 26, 27, 85–6, 146, 147, 184, 187, 188, 218
counter-insurgency, 39
Court of Justice of the European Communities, 215
crimes
against humanity *see* crimes against humanity
amnesties *see* amnesties
common criminality, 37
criminal organizations, 55, 56, 58
Draft Code of Crimes Against the Peace and Security of Mankind, 175, 200
genocide *see* genocide

individuals *see* individual criminals
killings *see* killings
penalties, 184
Protocol II (1977), 102, 103, 184
rape, 107, 142
torture *see* torture
war *see* war crimes
see also international criminal law
crimes against humanity
acts of policy, 107, 108, 224
criminal responsibility, 44, 106–8
International Criminal Court, 108
International Criminal Tribunal for the Former Yugoslavia, 107, 108
International Criminal Tribunal for Rwanda, 107, 108
International Military Tribunal (Nuremberg), 107, 108
leadership accountability, 107
organizational membership, 105
Sierra Leone, 108
UN Secretary-General, 44
war crimes compared, 105, 107
see also genocide
criminal responsibility
crimes against humanity, 44, 106–8
genocide, 108–10
individual criminals, 44, 97, 98–100, 102, 105, 108–10, 112, 223
International Criminal Court, 98, 101, 113–14, 130, 221
International Criminal Tribunal for Rwanda, 98, 105, 112
ordering crimes, 111–14, 123, 221
war crimes, 97, 98–100, 102, 105
see also leadership accountability
cultural property
civilian objects, 81–2
Inter-American Commission, 21
International Criminal Tribunal for the Former Yugoslavia, 27–8, 81–2
legal restraints, 21, 27–8, 33
precautionary measures, 188–9
prosecution, 197–8
Cultural Property Convention (1954)
destruction/damage, 81, 93
evidence of accountability, 146, 147, 148
international humanitarian law, 27–8, 146, 147, 148, 197–8
Second Protocol, 27, 28, 146, 188, 189, 197–8
special agreements, 148

customary humanitarian law
  applicability criteria, 2
  applicability of norms, 18–25
  belligerent status, 2
  Common Article 3, 20, 24, 25, 31, 32
  consent, 2
  evidence of accountability, 147
  Inter-American Commission, 30, 32
  internal armed conflict, 30–3, 53
  international bodies, 22, 24
  International Criminal Tribunal for the Former Yugoslavia, 20–1, 22–5, 26, 30–2, 76
  military manuals, 23
  obligations, 26
  Protocol II (1977), 20–2, 25
  territorial control, 2
  UN Commission on Human Rights, 30, 32–3
  undeveloped, 4
  see also international humanitarian law
customary international law
  International Criminal Tribunal for Rwanda, 21–2
  UN General Assembly Resolutions, 23, 31, 32, 76
  UN Security Council, 23, 31–2

de facto authorities
  Afghanistan, 154
  Common Article 3, 135
  Draft Articles on State Responsibility, 155
  insurgents, 135
  international human rights law, 150, 230
  international humanitarian law, 16
  leadership accountability, 122, 123–4
  legal status, 15
  legislation, 222
  organizational structure, 1, 118, 155
  stable presence, 54
  territorial control, 1, 15, 16, 54, 135, 150, 152, 154
  torture, 179
detention/internment
  Afghanistan, 29, 65, 66, 67
  Colombia, 65, 84
  Common Article 3, 65–7, 84
  fair trial, 66
  Geneva Convention IV (1949), 65–6, 67
  human rights, 66
  humane treatment, 60, 65–7, 83
  Inter-American Commission, 65
  International Committee of the Red Cross (ICRC), 67
  state accountability, 181, 224
  UN Commission on Human Rights, 65, 66–7
  UN Security Council, 67
  see also Prisoners
dictatorships, rebellion, 58
disappearances
  Colombia, 171–2
  Human Rights Committee, 171–2
  Turkey, 170, 171
  UN Commission on Human Rights, 209
displaced persons, Guiding Principles on Internal Displacement (1998), 49, 52, 150–1
Draft Articles on State Responsibility
  attribution of acts, 153, 154
  critique, 226
  de facto authorities, 155
  force majeure, 217
  insurrections, 176, 181
  obligations of result/conduct, 166
  successful groups, 156, 157
Draft Code of Crimes Against the Peace and Security of Mankind, 175, 200
due diligence
  availability of means, 191, 192
  command responsibility, 111
  foreseeability of harm, 191, 192, 194
  international armed conflict, 82
  prosecution, 202, 203
  state accountability, 182, 191–2, 202, 203

El Salvador
  American Convention on Human Rights (1969), 50, 212
  amnesties, 205–6
  children, 63
  Common Article 3, 25, 50
  enforcement apparatus, 201
  FMLN *see* Frente Farabundo Martí para la Liberación Nacional
  freedom of movement, 186–7
  human rights, 11, 21, 32–3, 49–51, 63–4
  Human Rights Committee, 201
  humanitarian relief, 88–9
  indiscriminate attacks, 78

Inter-American Commission, 205-6
internal armed conflict, 4, 26, 32
International Covenant on Civil and
    Political Rights (1966), 50
ONUSAL *see* UN Observer Mission in
    El Salvador
prosecution, 70-4
Protocol I (1977), 32, 33
Protocol II (1977), 11, 25, 33, 50, 63,
    70-2, 78, 145, 146
San José Agreement on Human Rights
    (1990), 16-17, 49-51, 186, 212
special agreements, 16-17, 25-6, 49-51,
    186-7, 212
territorial control, 208
UN Commission on Human Rights, 11,
    32-3, 63-4, 88-9, 145
violence to life and person, 63-4
European Commission on Human Rights
    prosecution, 203
    right to life, 185, 191, 193, 195
European Convention on Human Rights
    (1950)
    applicability, 39
    'ensure respect', 173
    freedom of assembly, 167
    prosecution, 198
    right to life, 168, 170, 184, 185, 191,
        198-9
    rights secured/ensured, 166, 168
European Court of Human Rights
    Çakici case, 171
    criminal investigation, 203-4
    Ergi case, 168, 170-1, 190, 192-3, 194
    international humanitarian law, 161
    Kilic case, 193
    Kurt case, 171, 204
    Platform 'Ärzte für das Leben' case, 167
    positive obligations, 167, 168, 170, 191
    protection from other individuals, 167,
        190
    state accountability, 161, 167, 168, 170,
        171, 172, 190, 203-4
    Turkey, 168, 170-1, 190, 192-4, 198-9,
        203-4
    Yasa case, 193, 198-9, 203-4
European Court of Justice (ECJ), 215
Executions
    Afghanistan, 64, 67
    Argentina, 60, 61
    Colombia, 84, 192

Common Article 3, 68-9
UN Commission on Human Rights, 48,
    64, 69, 175, 192
see also killings
expulsions, Convention against Torture
    (1984), 179
extradition, 175

fair trial, 66, 103, 221
force majeure, 217
forum, prosecution, 134, 157-63
Frente Farabundo Martí para la Liberación
    Nacional (FMLN)
    amnesties, 205
    attribution of acts, 151-2
    children, 63
    indiscriminate attacks, 78
    legislation, 70-4, 187
    ONUSAL, 16-17, 63, 70-4, 78, 145,
        152-3, 186-7
    prosecution, 202
    special agreements, 16-17, 25-6, 49-51,
        186-7, 212
    see also El Salvador

Geneva Convention III (1949)
    internal armed conflict, 36
    judicial guarantees, 69
    military courts, 69
    rights of appeal, 71
    special agreements, 29
Geneva Convention IV (1949)
    detention/internment, 65-6, 67
    fair trial, 65-6, 103
    occupying powers, 71
    rights of appeal, 71
Geneva Conventions (1949)
    accessor states, 14-15
    Afghanistan, 22, 29
    armed opposition groups, adherence,
        14-15
    belligerent status, 2
    Common Article 1, 92-3, 173, 174
    Common Article 2, 174
    Common Article 3 *see* Common Article 3
    'ensure respect' obligation, 173, 174, 175
    grave breaches, 103, 111
    High Contracting Parties, 14
    International Criminal Tribunal for the
        Former Yugoslavia, 25
    leadership accountability, 120

Geneva Conventions (1949) (*cont.*)
  legal restraints, 9–26
  national liberation movements, 17–18, 35
  obligations, 92–3
  ordering crimes, 111
  prosecution, 67
  ratification, 15, 24
  state accountability, 173, 174
  war crimes, 103
genocide
  criminal responsibility, 108–10
  definition, 108
  Genocide Convention (1948), 44, 108–9, 178, 185, 189, 197, 221
  International Court of Justice (ICJ), 178
  International Criminal Court, 109
  International Criminal Tribunal for the Former Yugoslavia, 109
  International Criminal Tribunal for Rwanda, 109
  International Military Tribunal (Nuremberg), 108
  leadership accountability, 109, 221
  legislation, 185
  outside armed conflict, 105
  prosecution, 197
  state accountability, 178, 185, 189, 197, 219, 221
  territorial control, 219
  UN Secretary-General, 109
  Yugoslavia, 178
Georgia, UN Security Council, 31
government
  accountability *see* state accountability
  amnesties, 205
  de facto see de facto authorities
  established authorities, 166
  in exile, 208, 211
  human rights obligations, 53–4, 148–9, 166–7
  laws, 70–1
  occupying powers, 71
  states distinguished, 165
  territory *see* territorial control
government collapse
  Afghanistan, 2, 150, 208
  anarchic conflict, 139, 140, 144
  civilian victims, 2
  failed states, 208, 230
  leadership accountability, 119
  Liberia, 140, 144
  local authorities, 213–15
  political power, 1
  Somalia, 2, 139, 140, 141, 208
  UN Secretary-General, 227
Greenwood, Christopher, 161
Guerrillas
  Colombia, 62
  organization, 35
  terminology, 134
Guiding Principles on Internal Displacement (1998), 49, 52, 150–1

Hague Conventions (1907), war crimes, 103
high intensity conflicts, 2
Honduras, 167, 171
hostages, 62, 84, 90
human rights
  Afghanistan, 48, 150, 211, 214
  Algeria, 168–9, 189, 199
  America *see* Inter-American Commission
  American Convention *see* American Convention on Human Rights (1969)
  Colombia, 21, 41, 46, 47, 52, 54, 192, 213
  concept, 46
  detention/internment, 66
  El Salvador, 11, 21, 32–3, 49–51, 63–4
  freedom of assembly, 167
  freedom of movement, 186–7
  government/governed, 53–4
  international law *see* international human rights law
  life *see* right to life
  national liberation movements, 46
  reconceptualization, 51–5
  Sri Lanka, 48
  terrorism, 42, 46, 48, 191, 195
  UN Commission *see* UN Commission on Human Rights
  violations denounced, 39, 48, 64
Human Rights Committee
  Algeria, 168–9, 189, 199
  amnesties, 206
  Colombia, 171–2
  disappearances, 171–2
  El Salvador, 201
  international humanitarian law, 161
  Lebanon, 195, 210–11
  precautionary measures, 189–90
  Sri Lanka, 196
  state accountability, 161, 168–9, 171–2, 179, 185, 189

INDEX 249

torture, 179, 185, 206
see also International Covenant on Civil and Political Rights (1966)
Human Rights Watch, 2, 23
humane treatment
  civilian protection, 61, 82–3
  Common Article 3, 59–62, 65–9, 82–3
  detention/internment, 60, 65–7, 83
  fundamental guarantees, 62–4
  hors de combat, 60, 66
  hostages, 62
  humiliating and degrading treatment, 62
  international bodies, 60
  non-combatants, 60–1, 66, 82
  non-derogable guarantees, 61
  prisoners, 59–74
  prosecution, 21, 60, 67–74
  protected persons, 60–1
  Protocol II (1977), 59–67, 69–73
  violence to life and person, 62, 63–4, 82
humanitarian relief
  Afghanistan, 88
  Angola, 88
  consent, 86, 87
  El Salvador, 88–9
  International Committee of the Red Cross (ICRC), 87, 88
  Protocol II (1977), 86, 87
  Somalia, 86, 88, 113
  UN Commission on Human Rights, 88
  UN General Assembly Resolutions, 87–8
  UN Security Council, 88, 113

immunities
  civilian immunity, 75, 76
  prisoners of war, 36
  prosecution, 36, 38, 188, 198, 206
  see also amnesties
independent observers, International Committee of the Red Cross (ICRC), 22
indiscriminate attacks, 77, 78
individual criminals
  armed forces, 105
  criminal responsibility, 44, 97, 98–100, 102, 105, 108–10, 112, 223
  levels of accountability, 3, 97
  organizational membership, 55, 56, 58, 105
  tribunals, 20

individual obligations
  armed opposition groups compared, 16
  international criminal law, 16, 44
  international human rights law, 43–4, 52
  leaders *see* leadership accountability
insurgents
  Common Article 3, 135
  counter-insurgency, 39
  terminology, 134
  territorial control, 135
insurrections, 137, 176, 181, 183
Inter-American Commission
  attribution of acts, 153, 155
  civilian/military objects, 80–1
  civilian protection, 75–6, 79, 80–1
  Colombia *see* Colombia
  Common Article 3, 61, 135, 137–8, 145–6
  cultural property, 21
  customary humanitarian law, 30, 32
  detention/internment, 65
  El Salvador, 205–6
  fundamental guarantees, 62
  grave-breaches regime, 104
  human rights concept, 40–1
  individual petitions, 158
  internal armed conflict, 13, 61, 135, 137
  internal disturbances, 137–8
  international human rights law, 39, 40–1, 42, 43, 47, 52
  international humanitarian law, 41, 52, 65, 155, 158–62
  mandates, 158–62
  member states, observations, 159, 160
  precautionary measures, 79, 81
  protected persons, 60–1
  Protocol I (1977), 75, 80
  Protocol II (1977), 21, 61, 75, 80, 145–6
  Regulations, 159
  reporting procedure, 158, 159
  reprisals, 90
  right to life, 47, 90, 180
  Tablada case, 10, 60–1, 137, 160
  terrorism, 159
  Velásquez Rodríguez case, 167
  see also American Convention on Human Rights (1969)
Inter-American Court of Human Rights
  individual petitions, 159
  international humanitarian law, 160–1

internal armed conflict
　amnesties, 37, 164, 188, 197
　Amnesty International (AI), 23
　civilian participation, 75-6
　Common Article 3, 18, 33-4, 135, 138, 143
　conflict internationalized, 18
　criminal activity, 36-7
　cultural property, 27-8, 81-2
　customary humanitarian law, 30-3, 53
　direct/indirect participation, 75, 76, 84
　duration of conflict, 138
　examples, 4
　grave-breaches regime, 103-5
　Human Rights Watch, 23
　humanitarian norms, 34
　immunity from prosecution, 36, 38, 188
　independent observers, 22
　Inter-American Commission, 13, 61, 135, 137
　internal disturbances, 136-8, 143, 147
　international bodies, 33-4, 35, 230
　international conflict compared, 33-8, 77-8, 123, 124, 127
　International Criminal Court, 141, 142
　International Criminal Tribunal for the Former Yugoslavia, 19, 20, 22-3, 34, 35-6, 107, 112, 123, 124, 127, 135, 137
　International Criminal Tribunal for Rwanda, 19, 20, 107, 112, 135, 137
　international human rights law, 52-3, 168
　international humanitarian law, 20, 52, 53, 62
　mass media, 23
　military necessity, 82
　misinformation, 23
　party to conflict, 135, 137, 138, 139, 140, 151-2
　prevalence, 1-2
　prisoners of war, 36, 38
　protection of civilians see civilian protection
　Protocol I (1977), 32, 33-4, 78-9
　Protocol II (1977), 18, 34, 143-4
　territorial scope, 136
　war crimes, 57-8, 99
　see also human rights
international armed conflict
　acts of omission, 114
　civilian protection, 33
　due diligence/non discrimination, 82
　grave-breach regime, 111
　inter-ethnic conflict, 35
　internal conflict compared, 33-8, 77-8, 123, 124
　leadership accountability, 111, 112, 114, 123, 124, 128
　ordering crimes, 112
international bodies
　applicable norms, 12, 13, 35
　attribution of acts, 134
　civilian protection, 77
　Common Article 3, 12, 13, 35
　customary humanitarian law, 22, 24
　humane treatment, 60
　internal armed conflict, 33-4, 35, 230
　international human rights law, 39, 52, 54
　international law, 4
　obligations recognized, 16, 17
　opinio iuris, 22, 24
　Protocol II (1977), 12, 13, 53, 77
　right to life, 180-1
　starvation, 87
　state accountability, 164, 165, 228
International Committee of the Red Cross (ICRC)
　Afghanistan, 88
　amnesties, 206
　Common Article 3, 137-8, 140
　confidential discussions, 162
　detention/internment, 67
　human rights, 46
　humanitarian relief, 87, 88
　independent observers, 22
　leadership accountability, 115
　national justice system, 73
　special agreements, 29
International Court of Justice (ICJ)
　Advisory Opinion on Nuclear Weapons, 19, 85, 227
　binding declarations, 13
　Common Article 3, 10, 19, 174
　evidence of general practice, 26
　Gabcíkovo-Nagymaros Project, 211-12
　genocide, 178
　international bodies, 4
　international humanitarian law, 227
　Namibia, 209
　Nicaragua, 10, 19, 174

state agents/local entities, 214-15
territorial control, 209, 211-12
International Covenant on Civil and
    Political Rights (1966)
  Bosnia-Herzegovina, 149
  Colombia, 171-2
  Committee see Human Rights Committee
  El Salvador, 50
  individual obligations, 43-4
  international humanitarian law, 161
  Lebanon, 210-11
  legislation, 187
  obligations, 44
  prosecution, 198
  Protocol II (1977), 64, 70
  right to life, 183-4
  state accountability, 166, 173
  state parties, 38-9
  torture, 179, 185
  violence to life and person, 64, 198
International Covenant on Economic,
    Social and Political Rights (1966), 43,
    44
International Criminal Court
  binding declarations, 13
  Common Article 3, 101, 141-2, 221
  crimes against humanity, 108
  criminal responsibility, 98, 101, 113-14,
    130, 221
  draft Statute, 55, 56, 57
  fair trial, 221
  genocide, 109
  internal armed conflict, 141, 142
  juridical persons, 57
  leadership accountability, 111, 113-14,
    117, 119-20, 124, 127-8, 130-2, 222
  legal persons, 56-7
  national courts, 200
  natural persons, 56, 58
  nullum crimen sine lege rule, 101
  Protocol II (1977), 101, 142
  Rome Conference (1988), 56, 57
  serious violations, 221
  substantive law, 101
  territorial control, 142, 143
  war crimes, 102, 142
international criminal law
  amnesties, 37
  civilian victims, 2
  crimes against humanity see crimes
    against humanity

  criminal organizations, 55-8
  genocide see genocide
  individual obligations, 16, 44
  individual responsibility see individual
    criminals
  international crimes, 37, 207, 224
  jurisdiction, 103
  legal restraints, 55-8
  levels of accountability, 3, 97
  multilateral treaties, 178-80
  non-state actors, 46
  prosecution, 197
  state accountability, 178-80
  war crimes see war crimes
International Criminal Tribunal for
    Rwanda
  Akayesu case, 11, 19, 21
  binding declarations, 13
  civilian protection, 75
  Common Article 3, 19, 135, 136
  crimes against humanity, 107, 108
  criminal responsibility, 98, 105, 112
  customary international law, 21-2, 22-4
  evidence of accountability, 135, 136,
    137, 138, 141, 144
  genocide, 109
  internal armed conflict, 19, 20, 107, 112,
    123, 135, 137
  Kayishema case, 105, 110, 121, 122, 124
  leadership accountability, 100, 110-12,
    115-19, 121, 123-5, 128-32, 222
  Protocol I (1977), 75
  Protocol II (1977), 11, 16, 21-2, 61, 144-5
  war crimes, 105-6
International Criminal Tribunal for the
    Former Yugoslavia
  Aleksovski case, 98, 106, 116-17, 119,
    120-1, 123, 126, 127, 129, 132
  binding declarations, 13
  Celebici case, 24, 110, 122, 125, 127, 129
  civilian protection, 76, 77, 80
  Common Article 3, 102, 135, 136, 144
  crimes against humanity, 107, 108
  criminal responsibility, 98-9, 102, 106,
    112
  cultural property, 27-8, 81
  customary humanitarian law, 20-1,
    22-5, 26, 30-2, 76
  emerging states, 35
  evidence of accountability, 135-6, 138,
    141, 144

International Criminal Tribunal (cont.)
    Furundžija case, 100, 112, 205
    Geneva Conventions (1949), 25
    genocide, 109
    grave-breaches regime, 103
    internal armed conflict, 19, 20, 22–3, 34, 35–6, 107, 112, 123, 124, 127, 135, 137
    Kordić case, 21
    leadership accountability, 100, 102, 106, 111–12, 115–19, 121–32, 222
    Martić case, 90, 91
    Nikolić case, 107
    protected persons, 60
    Protocol II (1977), 20–1, 25, 61–2, 102, 144
    reprisals, 90–1
    Rome Statute (1998), 101
    special agreements, 29–30
    Tadić case (Interlocutory Appeal), 19, 20, 26, 27–8, 29, 77, 81, 102, 135
    Tadić case (merits), 60, 107, 112, 123
    torture, 110, 113, 179, 205
    UN General Assembly Resolutions, 23, 31, 32, 76
international human rights law see human rights
international human rights law
    applicability, 47–9, 52, 148–9
    change of circumstances, 215–17
    civilian victims, 2
    de facto authorities, 150, 230
    effective authority, 149
    evidence of accountability, 148–51
    force majeure, 217
    government obligations, 53–4, 148–9, 166–7
    individual obligations, 43–4, 52
    Inter-American Commission, 39, 40–1, 42, 43, 47, 52
    internal armed conflict, 52–3, 168
    international bodies, 39, 52, 54
    legal restraints, 38–55
    legislation, 185–6
    local authorities, 213–15
    multilateral treaties, 38–49, 148–51, 166–73, 185–6, 210–17
    obligations of conduct, 166, 167, 171
    obligations of result, 166, 167
    prosecution, 198–200
    reconceptualization, 51–5
    rights secured/ensured, 166, 173
    special agreements, 49–51, 212
    state accountability, 166–173, 183–4, 185–6, 227
    supervision, 51, 52
    temporary impossibility, 210–15
    territorial control, 150, 210–17
    Turku Declaration (1990), 48–9, 52, 54–5
    UN Commission on Human Rights, 39–40, 41–3, 46, 47–8, 54–5
    UN Secretary-General, 40, 42–6
    UN Security Council, 47, 48
international humanitarian law
    applicability, 13, 20, 149
    civilian victims, 2
    Colombia, 41, 54, 61, 155
    Cultural Property Convention (1954), 27–8, 81, 146, 147, 148, 197–8
    distinguishing features, 23
    evidence of accountability, 146–8
    grave breaches, 103–5
    Inter-American Commission, 41, 52, 65, 155, 158–62
    internal armed conflict, 20, 52, 53, 62
    International Court of Justice (ICJ), 227
    interpretation, 12
    legal restraints, 26–38
    minimum legal standard, 13, 64
    multilateral treaties, 26–8
    obligations, 15, 16
    prosecution, 197–8
    state accountability, 173–8, 227
    territorial control, 218
    third party monitoring, 14
    UN Security Council, 32, 138–40, 225
    violations, 73, 74, 155, 157, 175, 200, 221
    violence to life and person, 62, 63–4, 82, 180, 198, 199
    see also customary humanitarian law
international law
    command responsibility, 98, 111, 230
    customary see customary international law
    enforcement, 133
    international bodies, 4
International Law Commission
    attribution of acts, 153, 154, 155, 156, 157
    Draft Code of Crimes against the Peace and Security of Mankind, 175, 200
    leadership accountability, 100
    state accountability, 153, 154, 155, 156, 157, 166, 176, 181

see also Draft Articles on State Responsibility
International Military Tribunal (Nuremberg)
 crimes against humanity, 107, 108
 criminal organizations, 55, 56, 58
 genocide, 108
 leadership accountability, 98
 Nuremberg Charter, 55, 56
International Military Tribunal (Tokyo), 98

Jennings, Sir Robert, 24
judiciary
 independence, 72
 judicial guarantees, 68, 69
 killings, 197

Kabila, Laurent, 37, 156
Kalshoven, F., 23, 91
kidnapping, 47, 62
killings
 Chechnya, 175
 Colombia, 62
 criminal law, 185–6
 execution *see* executions
 judiciary, 197
 legislation, 185–6
 Rwanda, 197
 Sierra Leone, 104
 Sri Lanka, 196
 Sudan, 68, 175
 violence to life and person, 62, 63–4, 82, 180, 198–200
 war crimes, 103, 104
Kosovo, 4, 207–8

landmines
 Colombia, 85
 legislation, 184–5, 187
 Ottawa Convention on Anti-Personnel Mines (1997), 184, 188, 197
 precautionary measures, 188–9
 prohibition, 27, 33, 59, 75, 85–6, 146, 147, 197
 prosecution, 197
 Protocol II (1977), 85
 Protocol II on mines and booby-traps (1996), 26, 27, 85–6, 146, 147, 184, 187, 188, 218
 territorial control, 218

UN Observer Mission in El Salvador (ONUSAL), 86
Lauterpacht, H., 223
leadership
 effectiveness, 1
 norms enforced, 68, 97
leadership accountability
 ability to prevent/punish, 128–31
 acts of subordinates, 97, 109–10, 221–2, 230
 civilian leaders, 117–21, 123, 230
 command responsibility
  crimes against humanity, 106–7
  due diligence, 111
  genocide, 109–10, 221
  group leaders, 111–21
  international law, 98, 111, 230
  omission, 111, 114–17
  principles, 115, 230
  Protocol I (1977), 114–15, 120
  state accountability, 165
 Common Article 3, 99–100, 221
 control and authority, 121–4, 155
 criteria, group leaders, 121–31
 de jure/de facto control, 122, 123–4
 direct responsibility, 111
 government collapse, 119
 group accountability compared, 221–4
 'had reason to know', 125–6
 international armed conflict, 111, 112, 114, 123, 124, 128
 International Committee of the Red Cross (ICRC), 115
 International Criminal Court, 111, 113–14, 117, 119–20, 124, 127–8, 130–2, 222
 International Criminal Tribunal for the Former Yugoslavia, 100, 102, 106, 111–12, 115–18, 121–32, 222
 International Criminal Tribunal for Rwanda, 100, 110–12, 115–19, 121, 123–5, 128–32, 222
 International Law Commission, 100
 knowledge, 124–8
 levels of accountability, 3, 97
 'necessary and reasonable measures', 129
 ordering crimes, 111–14, 123, 221
 prosecution, 131–2
 Protocol I (1977), 114–15, 120, 124–5, 128–9

254   INDEX

leadership accountability (cont.)
   Protocol II (1977), 99–100, 221
   Sierra Leone, 98, 108, 111, 114, 117, 120, 124, 127, 130-2
   superior–subordinate relationship, 115–16, 118–19, 121–4, 128–31
   torture, 107, 113, 221-2
   UN Security Council, 113
   violations condoned, 97
   war crimes, 99–106
Lebanon
   Human Rights Committee, 195, 210-11
   internal armed conflict, 4
   International Covenant on Civil and Political Rights (1966), 210-11
   territorial control, 208, 210-11
legal personality
   accountability, 152
   groups unrecognized, 18, 141, 163, 223-4
   International Criminal Court, 56–8
   juridical person, 57
   national legal status, 56-7
   natural persons, 56, 58
   states, 165
legislation
   armed opposition groups, 70–4, 187, 188, 222
   Common Article 3, 187
   de facto authorities, 222
   discretion, 188
   genocide, 185
   inadequacy, 188
   International Covenant on Civil and Political Rights (1966), 187
   international human rights law, 185-6
   killings, 185-6
   landmines, 184-5, 187
   Protocol II (1977), 187
   state accountability, 183–8
   territorial scope, 186–7
Liberia, 140, 144
life
   human rights *see* Right to life
   violence to life and person, 62, 63-4, 82, 180
   see also executions; killings
local authorities, 213–15

mass media, 23
Meron, T., 49

military manuals, customary humanitarian law, 23
military necessity
   internal armed conflict, 82
   state accountability, 165, 183, 191
multilateral treaties,
   'ensure respect' obligation, 173, 174, 175, 176-7
   international criminal law, 178–80
   international human rights law, 38–49, 148–51, 166–73, 185–6, 210–17
   international humanitarian law, 26–8
   origin of obligations, 15, 16
   Vienna Convention (1969), 30, 215–16

Namibia, 209
national liberation movements
   Additional Protocols, 17–18
   Geneva Conventions (1949), 17–18, 35
   human rights, 46
   Protocol I (1977), 18, 35
   territorial control, 35
Nicaragua
   Common Article 3, 10, 19, 24, 174
   Contras, 10, 19, 174
   ICJ decisions, 10, 19, 174
   internal armed conflict, 4, 174
Northern Ireland
   internal armed conflict, 4
   Irish Republican Army (IRA), 118
   Sinn Fein, 118
   terrorism, 191, 195

obligations
   Common Article 3, 15, 16, 92
   customary humanitarian law, 26
   Geneva Conventions (1949), 92–3
   human rights, government obligations, 53–4, 148–9, 166–7
   humane treatment *see* humane treatment
   individual *see* individual obligations
   international humanitarian law, 15, 16
   leaders *see* leadership accountability
   origin
      inter-state treaties, 14–18
      multilateral treaties, 15, 16
   protection of civilians *see* civilian protection
   Protocol II (1977), 15, 16, 92, 93
   ratification, 15, 16, 17

recognized by international bodies, 16, 17
special agreements, 17, 25, 28–30, 51
states *see* state accountability
substantive, 59–74
towards prisoners *see* prisoners
underdevelopment of law, 92–3
ONUSAL *see* UN Observer Mission in El Salvador
Organization of American States, 40, 160

Pastrana, Andrés, 213
Peru, 46
Philippines, 46
places of worship, 21
Plattner, D., 68
precautionary measures
  Common Article 3, 189
  cultural property, 188–9
  Human Rights Committee, 189–90
  Inter-American Commission, 79, 81
  landmines, 188–9
  leadership accountability, 128–31
  Protocol II (1977), 76, 77, 189
  state accountability, 182, 183
  UN General Assembly Resolutions, 77
  see also civilian protection
prisoners
  Afghanistan, 29, 90
  humane treatment, 59–74
  prosecution, 60, 66
  reprisals, 90–1
  see also detention/internment
prisoners of war
  equivalent treatment, 38
  Geneva Convention III (1949), 29
  immunity from punishment, 36
  internal armed conflict, 36, 38
prosecution
  advocates, 69–70
  amnesties *see* amnesties
  Common Article 3, 21, 67–9, 198
  criminal investigation, 198–9, 203–4
  cultural property, 197–8
  due diligence, 202, 203
  enforcement apparatus, 201–4
  fair trial, 66, 103, 221
  forum, 134, 157–63
  Geneva Conventions (1949), 67
  genocide, 197
  humane treatment, 21, 60, 67–74

immunities, 36, 38, 188, 197, 206
impartiality, 72, 73
international criminal law, 197
international human rights law, 198–200
international humanitarian law, 197–8
judicial guarantees, 68, 69
judicial independence, 72
judicial structure, 197
landmines, 197
leadership accountability, 131–2
military courts, 69
Protocol II (1977), 21, 67, 69–73, 198
regularly constituted courts, 68, 69
rights of appeal, 71, 72
state accountability, 196–204
treason, 197
UN Observer Mission in El Salvador (ONUSAL), 70–4
Protocol I (1977)
  analogical application, 77, 78
  civilian protection, 75, 77, 78–9, 80, 82, 84
  command responsibility, 114–15, 120
  El Salvador, 32, 33
  Inter-American Commission, 75, 80
  internal armed conflict, 32, 33–4, 78–9
  International Criminal Tribunal for Rwanda, 75
  leadership accountability, 114–15, 120, 124–5, 128–9
  national liberation movements, 18, 35
  special agreements/declarations, 18, 29
  UN Observer Mission in El Salvador (ONUSAL), 78–9
  war crimes, 102
Protocol II (1977)
  accessor states, 14, 15
  Afghanistan, 22
  amnesties, 37, 206
  Angola, 146
  applicability
    binding effect, 42
    determination, 13
    express declaration, 14
    geographical, 61
    international bodies, 12, 13, 53
    temporal, 61–2
    threshold, 53, 143, 144, 145
  child recruitment, 63
  civilian protection, 75–80, 83–7, 89, 91–2, 189

Protocol II (1977) (*cont.*)
  Colombia, 21, 61, 75, 80, 145, 146
  conflict internationalized, 18
  Congo, 146
  crimes, 102, 103, 184
  customary humanitarian law, 20-2, 25
  detention/internment, 65-7
  El Salvador, 11, 25, 33, 50, 63, 70-2, 78, 145, 146
  essential protection, 52
  evidence of accountability, 134, 136, 142-8
  fundamental guarantees, 62-4
  grave breaches, 103
  High Contracting Parties, 14
  humane treatment, 59-67, 69-73
  humanitarian relief, 86, 87
  Inter-American Commission, 21, 61, 75, 80, 145-6
  internal armed conflict, 18, 34, 143-4
  International Covenant on Civil and Political Rights (1966), 64, 70
  International Criminal Court, 101, 142
  International Criminal Tribunal for the Former Yugoslavia, 20-1, 25, 61-2, 102, 144
  International Criminal Tribunal for Rwanda, 11, 16, 21-2, 61, 144-5
  judicial guarantees, 69
  landmines, 85
  leadership accountability, 99-100, 221
  legal restraints, 9-26
  legislation, 187
  obligations, 15, 16, 92, 93
  precautionary measures, 76, 77, 189
  prosecution, 21, 67, 69-73, 198
  ratification, 15, 20, 22
  reprisals, 89, 91, 92
  right to life, 64
  Sierra Leone, 146
  sovereignty, 225
  special agreements/declarations, 17, 18, 29, 51
  Sri Lanka, 146
  starvation, 87
  state accountability, 173-7
  Sudan, 145, 146
  territorial control, 142, 143, 146, 218
  UN Commission on Human Rights, 22, 145
  UN Observer Mission in El Salvador (ONUSAL), 78, 145
  UN Secretary-General, 143-4
  violations, 103, 105, 112, 157, 184, 207
  war crimes, 102, 103
punishment
  ability to prevent/punish offenders, 128-31
  collective punishment, 91
  immunity from punishment, 36
  UN Declaration (1975), 149

rape, 107, 142
ratification
  Geneva Conventions (1949), 15, 24
  obligations, 15, 16, 17
  Protocol II (1977), 15, 20, 22
rebels, 134
refugees, 180
relief *see* humanitarian relief
reprisals
  collective punishment, 91
  Common Article 3, 89, 92
  definition, 89
  Inter-American Commission, 90
  International Criminal Tribunal for the Former Yugoslavia, 90
  prisoners, 90
  prohibition, 59, 75, 89-92
  Protocol II (1977), 89, 91, 92
  quasi-reprisals, 91
  right of reprisal, 89-90
  UN General Assembly Resolutions, 90, 91
right to life
  American Convention on Human Rights (1969), 47, 184
  European Commission on Human Rights, 185, 191, 193, 195
  European Convention on Human Rights (1950), 168, 170, 184, 185, 191, 198-9
  Inter-American Commission, 47, 90, 180
  international bodies, 180-1
  International Covenant on Civil and Political Rights (1966), 183-4
  Protocol II (1977), 64
  state accountability, 175, 180-1, 183-5, 191, 193, 195
  UN Commission on Human Rights, 48, 175
Rome Statute (1998) *see* International Criminal Court
Rosenne, S., 226
Russian Federation, Chechnya, 4, 175, 199-200

INDEX 257

Rwanda
  criminal proceedings *see* International Criminal Tribunal for Rwanda
  FAR, 144
  internal armed conflict, 4
  judicial structure, 197
  killings, 197
  Rwandan Patriotic Front (RPF), 16, 144–5

secession, objectives, 1
Sierra Leone
  grave breaches, 104–5
  killings, 104
  Protocol II (1977), 146
  Revolutionary United Front (RUF), 98, 108, 130
  Special Court, 37, 98, 101, 105, 108
    amnesties, 37, 207
    Common Article 3, 101
    crimes against humanity, 108
    leadership accountability, 98, 108, 111, 114, 117, 120, 124, 127, 130–2
    Protocol II (1977), 101
  torture, 104
  UN Commission on Human Rights, 104
Somalia
  anarchic conflict, 139, 140
  government collapse, 2, 139, 140, 141, 208
  humanitarian relief, 86, 88, 113
  internal armed conflict, 4
  starvation, 86
  UN Commission on Human Rights, 150
  UN Secretary-General, 139, 144
  UN Security Council, 88, 113, 138–41
South Africa, Namibia, 209
sovereignty
  effective control distinguished, 209
  legal personality, 18, 141, 163
  Protocol II (1977), 225
  territorial control, 18, 141, 152, 225, 226
special agreements
  accountability, 148
  Common Article 3, 17, 18, 25, 28–30, 50, 148
  Cultural Property Convention (1954), 148
  El Salvador, 16–17, 25–6, 49–51, 186–7, 212
  Geneva Convention on the Treatment of Prisoners of War (1949), 29

  International Committee of the Red Cross (ICRC), 29
  International Criminal Tribunal for the Former Yugoslavia, 29–30
  international human rights law, 49–51, 212
  obligations, 17, 25, 28–30, 51
  Protocol I (1977), 29
  Protocol II (1977), 17, 18, 29, 51
  UN Observer Mission in El Salvador (ONUSAL), 16–17, 50, 51, 186–7
  unquestionably binding, 29, 30
Sri Lanka
  human rights, 48
  Human Rights Committee, 196
  internal armed conflict, 4
  killings, 196
  Liberation Tigers of Tamil Eelam (LTTE), 48, 196
  Protocol II (1977), 146
  self-defence, 196
starvation
  international bodies, 87
  prohibition, 21, 59, 75, 86–9
  Protocol II (1977), 87
  Somalia, 86
state accountability
  American Convention on Human Rights (1969), 166
  amnesties, 164, 188, 197, 204–7
  applicable law, 166–80
  armed opposition groups, 164–219
  civilian protection, 165
  civilian victims, 164
  coalitions, 156–7
  command responsibility, 165
  Common Article 3, 173–7
  detention/internment, 181, 224
  Draft Articles *see* Draft Articles on State Responsibility
  due diligence, 182, 191–2, 202, 203
  enforcement, 3
  'ensure respect' obligation, 173, 174, 175, 176–7
  Geneva Conventions (1949), 173, 174
  genocide, 178, 185, 189, 197, 219, 221
  groups fighting each other, 164
  international bodies, 164, 165, 228
  International Covenant on Civil and Political Rights (1966), 166, 173
  international criminal law, 178–80

state accountability (*cont.*)
  international human rights law, 166–173, 183–4, 185–6, 227
  international humanitarian law, 173–8, 227
  legislation, 183–8
  margin of appreciation, 195
  military necessity, 165, 183, 191
  obligation to take action, 180–207
  obligations of result/conduct, 166–7
  positive obligations, 167–72, 176, 178, 182, 191
  preventative measures, 182, 183
  prosecution, 196–204
  Protocol II (1977), 173–7
  right to life, 175, 180–1, 183–5, 191, 193, 195
  rights secured/ensured, 166, 173
  successful groups, 155–7
  supreme authority, 163, 164, 182, 225, 226
  territorial control, 165, 182–3, 207–19, 225–6
  terrorism, 191, 192
  torture, 178–80, 192
states
  American Convention on Human Rights (1969), 39, 41
  Common Article 3, 53
  failure *see* government collapse
  Geneva Conventions (1949), 14–15
  government distinguished, 165
  International Covenant on Civil and Political Rights (1966), 38–9
  legal capacity, warface, 89
  legal personality, 165
  Protocol II (1977), 14, 15
  reprisals, 89
  sovereignty *see* sovereignty
subversive groups, 134
Sudan
  Ganyiel incident, 68
  internal armed conflict, 4
  killings, 68, 175
  Protocol II (1977), 145, 146
  Sudan Independence Army (SSIA), 68
  Sudan People's Liberation Army (SPLA), 68, 145
  UN Commission on Human Rights, 68, 145

Tajikistan, UN Security Council, 67
territorial control
  Afghanistan, 211
  Colombia, 208, 213
  Common Article 3, 135, 136, 146
  customary humanitarian law, 2
  de facto authority, 1, 15, 16, 54, 135, 150, 152, 154
  defence of integrity, 183
  effective control, 207–8, 209
  failed states, 208
  genocide, 219
  insurgents, 135
  International Criminal Court, 142, 143
  international human rights law, 150, 210–17
  international humanitarian law, 218
  landmines, 218
  Lebanon, 208, 210–11
  national liberation movements, 35
  partial control, 208
  pertinence, 207–19
  physical control, 209
  Protocol II (1977), 142, 143, 146, 218
  rapid change, 208
  sovereignty, 18, 141, 152, 225, 226
  state accountability, 165, 182–3, 207–19, 225–6
  temporary ineffectiveness, 208, 212
terrorism
  human rights, 42, 46, 48, 191, 195
  Inter-American Commission, 159
  Northern Ireland, 191, 195
  state accountability, 191, 192
torture
  amnesties, 204, 205, 206
  attribution of acts, 222
  Committee against Torture, 178–9
  Common Article 3, 205
  Convention against Torture (1984), 178–80
  de facto authorities, 179
  definition, 178
  expulsions, 179
  Human Rights Committee, 179, 185, 206
  International Covenant on Civil and Political Rights (1966), 179, 185
  International Criminal Tribunal for the Former Yugoslavia, 110, 113, 179, 205
  leadership accountability, 107, 113, 221–2

public officials/official capacity, 178, 179
Sierra Leone, 104
state accountability, 178–80, 192
UN Commission on Human Rights, 179
UN Declaration (1975), 149
war crimes, 100, 103, 104
treason, prosecution, 197
Turkey
 criminal investigation, 198–9, 203–4
 disappearances, 170, 171
 European Court of Human Rights, 168, 170–1, 190, 192–4, 198–9, 203–4
 internal armed conflict, 4, 208
 state accountability, 168, 170–1, 192–4, 208
 territorial control, 208
 Workers' Party of Kurdistan (PKK), 168, 170, 171, 190, 192, 203–4
Turku Declaration on Minimum Humanitarian Standards (1990), 48–9, 52, 54–5

UN Charter, internal armed conflict, 2
UN Commission on Human Rights
 Afghanistan, 64, 65, 66, 88, 90, 150, 154, 211, 214
 amnesties, 37
 attribution of acts, 153, 225
 Colombia, 46
 Common Article 3, 11, 135, 138
 Congo, 37
 customary humanitarian law, 30, 32–3
 detention/internment, 65, 66–7
 disappearances, 209
 El Salvador, 11, 63–4, 88–9, 145
 executions, 48, 64, 69, 175, 192
 fundamental guarantees, 62
 humanitarian relief, 88
 international human rights law, 39–40, 41–3, 44, 47–8, 54–5
 mandates, 158
 non-binding declarations, 13
 Peru, 46
 Philippines, 46
 Protocol II (1977), 22, 145
 right to life, 48, 175
 Sierra Leone, 104
 Somalia, 150
 Sub-Commission on Prevention of Discrimination and Protection of Minorities, 49
 Sudan, 68, 145
 torture, 179
UN General Assembly Resolutions
 civilian protection, 76–7, 80
 customary international law, 23, 31, 32, 76
 Declaration on torture and punishment (1975), 149
 humanitarian relief, 87–8
 International Criminal Tribunal for the Former Yugoslavia, 23, 31, 32, 76
 judicial independence, 72
 precautionary measures, 77
 reprisals, 90, 91
 UN Observer Mission in El Salvador (ONUSAL), 78
UN Observer Mission in El Salvador (ONUSAL)
 attribution of acts, 152–3
 children, 63
 civilian protection, 78, 82
 fundamental guarantees, 62
 landmines, 86
 prosecution, 70–4
 Protocol I (1977), 78–9
 Protocol II (1977), 78, 145
 special agreements, 16–17, 50, 51, 186–7
 UN General Assembly Resolutions, 78
 see also El Salvador
UN Secretary-General
 amnesties, 37
 children, 63
 crimes against humanity, 44
 genocide, 109
 government collapse, 227
 grave-breaches regime, 103
 international crimes, 37
 international human rights law, 40, 42–6
 Protocol II (1977), 143–4
 Somalia, 139, 144
UN Security Council
 Afghanistan, 48, 150
 Angola, 77, 88
 attribution of acts, 153, 225
 binding decisions, 13
 Chapter VII, 13
 civilian protection, 77
 Common Article 3, 11, 135, 138–41
 customary international law, 23, 31–2
 detention/internment, 67

UN Security Council (*cont.*)
  Georgia, 31
  humanitarian relief, 88, 113
  international human rights law, 47, 48
  international humanitarian law, 32, 138–40, 225
  international peace and security, 144
  leadership accountability, 113
  mandates, 158
  Somalia, 88, 113, 138–41
  Tajikistan, 67
United Nations
  amnesties, 207
  peace conferences, 224
United States Military Commission, *Yamashita* case, 98
Usama bin Laden, 154

Vienna Convention on the Law Treaties (1969), 30, 215–16
violations
  Common Article 3, 103, 105, 112, 142, 157, 184, 205, 207
  condoned by leadership, 97
  human rights, 39, 48, 64
  international humanitarian law, 73, 74, 155, 157, 175, 200, 221
  Protocol II (1977), 103, 105, 112, 157, 184, 207
  serious violations, 103, 105, 112, 142, 207, 221
  see also crimes; war crimes
violence
  Common Article 3, 62, 82, 199, 200
  El Salvador, 63–4
  International Covenant on Civil and Political Rights (1966), 64
  international humanitarian law, 62, 63–4, 82, 180, 198, 199
  sexual violence, 142

Wako, Amos, 201
war crimes
  Common Article 3, 103
  crimes against humanity compared, 105, 107
  criminal responsibility, 97, 98–100, 102, 105
  Geneva Conventions (1949), 103
  grave-breaches regime, 103–5
  Hague Conventions (1907), 103
  internal armed conflict, 57–8, 99
  International Criminal Court, 102, 142
  International Criminal Tribunal for Rwanda, 105–6
  jurisdiction, 103
  killings, 103, 104
  leadership accountability, 99–106
  Protocol I (1977), 102
  Protocol II (1977), 102, 103
  sexual violence, 142
  torture, 100, 103, 104
  see also crimes; violations
World Conference on Human Rights (1993), 200

Youmans claim, 155
Yugoslavia
  attribution of acts, 156
  Bosnia-Herzegovina, 112–13, 116–17, 149
  criminal proceedings *see* International Criminal Tribunal for the Former Yugoslavia
  Croatian Defence Council (HVO), 112
  genocide, 178
  internal armed conflict, 4
  Jokers, 112
  Kosovo, 4, 207–8
  Republika Sryska, 112

CAMBRIDGE STUDIES IN INTERNATIONAL AND COMPARATIVE LAW

Books in the series

Principles of the institutional law of international organisations
C. F. Amerasinghe

Fragmentation and the international relations of micro-states
Jorri Duursma

The Polar regions and the development of international law
Donald R. Rothwell

Sovereignty over natural resources
Nico Schrijver

Ethics and authority in international law
Alfred P. Rubin

Religious liberty and international law in Europe
Malcolm D. Evans

Unjust enrichment
Hanoch Dagan

Trade and the environment
Damien Geradin

The changing international law of high seas fisheries
Francisco Orrego Vicuña

International organizations before national courts
August Reinisch

The right to property in commonwealth constitutions
Tom Allen

Trusts
A comparative study
Maurizio Lupoi

On civil procedure
J. A. Jolowicz

Good faith in European contract law
Reinhard Zimmerman and Simon Whittaker

Money Laundering
Guy Stessens

International Law in Antiquity
David J. Bederman

The Enforceability of Promises in European Contract Law
James Gordley

International Commercial Arbitration and African States
Amazu A. Asouzu

The Law of Internal Armed Conflict
Lindsay Moir

Diversity and Self-Determination in International Law
Karen Knop

Remedies against International Organisations
Basic Issues
Karel Wellens

International Human Rights and Humanitarian Law
René Provost

Sharing Transboundary Resources:
International Law and Optimal Resources Use
Eyal Benvenisti

Accountability of Armed Opposition Groups in International Law
Liesbeth Zegveld

9 780521 811309